Public Relations Metrics

GW01066354

The core question for every public relations researcher is how public relations works: what it does in, to and for organizations, publics, or in the public arena. The answer to this question varies according to the methodologies the researcher uses. To address this circumstance, and to contribute toward establishing a solid research foundation, *Public Relations Metrics* goes beyond the "how to" of public relations research methods to think formally about research itself.

Chapters in this volume explore the issue of metrics in public relations from a theoretical angle—taking into account epistemology and conceptualization—and consider questions of definitions and measurement tools. Examples of actual research projects demonstrate a variety of metrics in implementation.

Responding to the basic truth that increasing knowledge requires study anchored in solid research programs, this volume makes a major step toward promoting relevant, timely, and well-considered research. It is certain to change how public relations research is conducted in the coming years, and as such it is required reading for scholars, researchers, and practitioners working in the public relations arena.

Betteke van Ruler, Ph.D., is Professor of Communication and Organization in the Amsterdam School of Communication Research at the University of Amsterdam in the Netherlands. Her research focuses on the practice of communication management and the relationship between organizations and the press.

Ana Tkalac Verčič, Ph.D., is Assistant Professor of Marketing and Marketing Communications at the Graduate School of Business and Economics in Zagreb, Croatia. Her major research interests are focused on attitude and attitude change in public relations. She is a former Fulbright scholar and a recipient of various other grants and scholarships.

Dejan Verčič, Ph.D., FCIPR, is a partner at Pristop Agency and Professor of Public Relations and Communication Management at the University of Ljubljana, Slovenia. Among his clients are governments, domestic and international corporations, and associations. He organizes the Lake Bled International Public Relations Research Symposia, held annually.

LEA'S COMMUNICATION SERIES
JENNINGS BRYANT/JAMES E. GRUNIG:
GENERAL EDITORS

Public Relations Metrics

Research and Evaluation

**Edited by
Betteke van Ruler, Ana Tkalac Verčič,
and Dejan Verčič**

NEW YORK AND LONDON

First published 2008
by Routledge
270 Madison Ave, New York, NY 10016

Simultaneously published in the UK
by Routledge
2 Park Square, Milton Park, Abingdon, Oxon OX14 4RN

Routledge is an imprint of the Taylor & Francis Group, an informa business

© 2008 Taylor & Francis

Typeset in Times New Roman by
Florence Production Ltd, Stoodleigh, Devon
Printed and bound in the United States of America on acid-free paper by
Edward Brothers, Inc.

All rights reserved. No part of this book may be reprinted or reproduced
or utilized in any form or by any electronic, mechanical, or other means,
now known or hereafter invented, including photocopying and recording,
or in any information storage or retrieval system, without permission in
writing from the publishers.

Trademark Notice: Product or corporate names may be trademarks
or registered trademarks, and are used only for identification and
explanation without intent to infringe.

Library of Congress Cataloging in Publication Data
Public relations metrics: research and evaluation / [edited] by Betteke
van Ruler, Ana Tkalac Verčič, and Dejan Verčič.
     p. cm.—(LEA's communication series. Public relations subseries)
  1. Public relations—Evaluation. 2. Public relations—Research.
  I. Ruler, Betteke van, 1948– II. Verčič, Ana Tkalac.
  III. Verčič, Dejan.
  HM1221.P785 2007
  659.2072—dc22   2007022952

ISBN 10: 0–8058–6272–2 (hbk)
ISBN 10: 0–8058–6273–0 (pbk)
ISBN 10: 1–4106–1679–7 (ebk)

ISBN 13: 978–0–8058–6272–0 (hbk)
ISBN 13: 978–0–8058–6273–7 (pbk)
ISBN 13: 978–1–4106–1679–1 (ebk)

Contents

Preface

Public relations as a scientific discipline needs to recognize significant realities, predict consequences of various behavioral opportunities, and guide action. This book is meant to contribute to the formation of these skills. Since its starting-point in the 1970s, when most discourse on the topic was found in a few textbooks, professional trade publications, and the emerging journal *Public Relations Review*, the discipline has grown steadily. The breadth and depth of analysis has increased, and the work is slowly becoming less derivative and more original in its theory building. But many scholars lament that the research being done is often too applied or just research for the sake of research. And virtually all available books on research and evaluation are introductory books that lack more in-depth discussions of the questions "what?" and "why?" J. E. Grunig (in this book) argues that this circumstance might be caused by a lack of conceptualization. We suggest that there is also a lack of epistemological and methodological foundations, which would provide the calculus for conceptualization, and a lack of diversity in this respect as well. The development of these foundations and appropriate measurement tools are an important goal of the scholarly community. To discuss these foundations, together with its offspring in measurement tools and research projects, the 12th International Public Relations Research Symposium, BledCom 2005, was devoted to gathering scholarly questions, reviews, and state-of-the-art knowledge regarding these issues. The presentations at BledCom 2005 inspired the production of this book. Some of its chapters had their origins at this conference, and, as BledCom 2005 also revealed questions that were not covered by the papers presented, we invited scholars to contribute chapters to respond to those questions.

Thus, this book addresses *thinking* about public relations, rather than the process of conducting research. It discusses the issue of metrics in public relations from a theoretical angle—its epistemology and conceptualization— as well as exploring questions of definitions and measurement tools, and it provides examples of research projects. It is a book for those scholars who are interested in a deeper consideration of public relations research—the "what?" and "why?"—and for those who contribute to the conceptualization of research in their future work.

Contributors

Barbara Baerns, Ph.D., Professor of Media and Communication Science, from 1989 to 2004 Professor of Theory and Practice of Journalism and Public Relations at the Free University of Berlin, where she established the specialist course of study "Public Relations," and the integrated postgraduate course of study "European Master's Degree in Public Relations (Communication Management)." From 1982 to 1989 she was Professor of Journalism and Communication at the Ruhr University of Bochum after writing her post-doctoral Habilitation and receiving her Venia legendi there in 1982. Prior to this she worked as a political editor as well as in public relations. She gained her Ph.D. in 1967. She has published on the limits of the public media processing viable information, on problems of differentiating advertising from program contents, and on the evaluation of public relations.

Mafalda Eiró-Gomes, Ph.D., is Adjunct Professor of Public Relations and Communication Theory at Lisbon's Superior School of Mass Communication and Media Arts. She holds a License in Public Relations and an M.Sc. and a Ph.D. in Communication Sciences from the New University of Lisbon. She is a Researcher in Philosophy of Language and Pragmatics at the Philosophy of Language Institute, New University of Lisbon, and has published work both in the fields of Pragmatics and Public Relations. She is voluntary PR Consultant for Portuguese Non-Governmental Organizations such as Instituto Marquês de Vale Flor, Médicos do Mundo (Medicins du Monde Portugal) and CAIS. In 2007, she became Scientific Coordinator of the first Portuguese Master program in Strategic Public Relations Management at Lisbon's Superior School of Mass Communication and Arts, and Scientific Coordinator of the first degree in Public Relations and Executive Secretariat available in all Portuguese-speaking Africa at the University of Cape Verde.

Nigel de Bussy is Senior Lecturer in Public Relations at Curtin Business School, Perth, Western Australia. He holds a Ph.D. from Curtin University of Technology and an M.A. from the University of Oxford. Before becoming a full-time academic, Dr. de Bussy gained more than a decade's experience in public relations consultancy in the UK and Australia. He is a past State

President of the Public Relations Institute of Australia. His work has appeared in the *Journal of Communication Management*, the *Journal of Marketing Communications*, and the *International Journal of Advertising*. Dr. de Bussy has a particular interest in stakeholder theory and its implications for public relations scholarship and practice.

João Duarte, M.Sc., is Professor of Publics Relations at Lisbon's Superior School of Mass Communication and Media Arts, Lisbon's Polytechnic Institute. He is simultaneously engaged in PR practice and has worked as an in-house PR professional in the public sector as well as in private companies. He is currently serving as Executive Officer of the Global Alliance for Public Relations and Communication Management, the umbrella organization for PR professional associations worldwide. He holds a License in Public Relations and an M.Sc. in Communication Sciences from the New University of Lisbon. He is a doctoral student focusing his research on the concept of "publics" in Public Relations. He is the founding President of the Portuguese Public Relations and Communication Students Association.

Anne Gregory FRSA, FCIPR, is Professor of Public Relations at Leeds Metropolitan University, which has the largest Public Relations Department in Europe. She is Director of the Centre for Public Relations Studies and the UK's only full-time professor in the subject. Her research is in strategic communication, public relations ethics, and practitioner capabilities. Anne comes from a practitioner background, having worked both in-house and in consultancy in senior positions, most recently with Weber Shandwick, before becoming an academic. She is still heavily involved in practice, particularly in the public sector, and her current clients include the UK Government Cabinet Office and the Department of Health. Anne was President of the UK Chartered Institute of Public Relations in 2004 and led it to chartered status. She has written *Planning and Managing Public Relations Campaigns*, edited *Public Relations in Practice*, and authored numerous book chapters and papers in academic and practitioner publications. She is Fellow of the Royal Society of Arts and Pro-Vice-Chancellor of Leeds Metropolitan University.

James E. Grunig is a Professor Emeritus of Public Relations in the Department of Communication at the University of Maryland College Park. He is the co-author of *Excellent Public Relations and Effective Organizations: A Study of Communication Management in Three Countries*, *Managing Public Relations*, *Public Relations Techniques*, and *Manager's Guide to Excellence in Public Relations and Communication Management*. He is editor of *Excellence in Public Relations and Communication Management*. *Excellent Public Relations and Effective Organizations* received the 2002 PRIDE award of the Public Relations Division of the National Communication Association as the best book in public relations in the previous two years. In addition to his books, Grunig has written 225 other publications such as book chapters, journal articles, reports, and papers. He has won six major awards in public relations: The Pathfinder Award for excellence in public relations research of the Institute for Public Relations Research and Education; the Outstanding Educator Award of the Public Relations Society of America (PRSA); the Jackson, Jackson and Wagner Award for behavioral science research of the PRSA Foundation; the Alexander Hamilton Medal for Lifetime Contributions to Professional Public Relations of the Institute for Public Relations; the Lloyd Dennis Award for Distinguished Leadership in Public Affairs (with L. A. Grunig) from the Public Affairs and Government Section of PRSA; and the Dr. Hamid Notghi Prize for Career Achievement in Public Relations from the Kargozar Public Relations Institute, Tehran, Iran. He also won the most prestigious lifetime award of the Association for Education in Journalism and Mass Communication (AEJMC), the Paul J. Deutschmann Award for Excellence in Research.

Larissa A. Grunig, Professor Emerita, recently retired from the faculty of the University of Maryland, College Park, where she had taught public relations and communication research since 1978. She has received the Pathfinder Award for excellence in research, sponsored by the Institute for Public Relations; the Jackson, Jackson, and Wagner Behavioral Science Prize; and the Outstanding Educator Award of the Public Relations Society of America. She was co-founder and co-editor of the *Journal of Public Relations Research* and has written more than 200 articles, book chapters, monographs, reviews, and conference papers on public relations, activism, science writing, feminist theory, communication theory, and research. She was a member of an international grant team, sponsored by the IABC Research Foundation, investigating excellence in public relations and communication management. The newest *Excellence* book won the 2002 PRIDE award sponsored by the Public Relations Division of the National Communication Association. She co-authored the first book about women in public relations. Dr. Grunig serves as a consultant in public relations.

Chun-ju Flora Hung, Ph.D., is Assistant Professor in the Department of Communication Studies, Hong Kong Baptist University. Her research interests are relationship management, strategic management, crisis communication, reputation management, conflict resolution, and intercultural communication. Her recent research and publications include: Exploring types of organization-public relationships and their implications for relationship management in public relations (for *Journal of Public Relations Research*, 2005), and Glocalization: Public relations in China (*Public Relations in Asia*, edited by K. Sriramesh). She won the faculty top paper in the Public Relations Division in the 2004 International Communication Association conference. In 2001, she won the award of Ketchum 2001 Walter Lindenmann Scholarship from the Institute for Public Relations.

Julia Jahansoozi is a Principal Lecturer and leads the Division of Applied Communication within the Lancashire Business School, University of

Central Lancashire. She has an M.Sc. in Public Relations from the University of Stirling, where she is completing her Ph.D. Her previous educational background was in psychology, political science, and publishing studies. She has worked in the private, public, and non-profit sectors in Canada and the UK. Julia's research interest is in organization—public relationships and areas relating to CSR. She has published and co-authored papers, articles, and book chapters.

Alenka Jelen, M.Sc., is a Public Relations Adviser and Teaching Assistant at the University of Ljubljana. She has rich experience in media practice, as she has worked as a radio journalist, news director, overseas correspondent, television host, and advertising copywriter. She holds an M.Sc. in International Applied Communication from the University of Central Lancashire and is currently a Ph.D. student at the University of Ljubljana. In 2005, she received EUPRERA's (The European Public Relations Education and Research Association) Jos Willems Award for best B.A. dissertation, "International Comparison of Communication Study Programmes in the Field of Communication Studies."

Jan Kleinnijenhuis is Professor of Communication Science at the Vrije Universiteit Amsterdam. His publications deal with news selection and news effects. Most of them are based on a combination of content analysis and opinion survey research and appear in journals such as the *Journal of Communication* and *Harvard International Journal of Press and Politics*. Together with Paul Pennings and Hans Keman, he wrote *Doing Research in Political Science* (Sage, 1999, 2006).

Wim van der Noort is Senior Research Consultant and Coordinator at the Public Information and Communication Office of the Ministry of General Affairs in the Netherlands. The department carries out a broad range of communication research for different ministries and other governmental organizations. For many years, he has been involved in media research and audience measurement. He is chairman of the Technical Committee of NOM, the Joint Industry Committee of publishers, agencies and advertisers that commissions the National Readership Survey in the Netherlands. He presented a number of papers at the Worldwide Readership Research Symposia and other conferences.

Frank E. Ovaitt Jr. is President and CEO of the Institute for Public Relations, an independent foundation dedicated to the science beneath the art of public relations and located at the University of Florida. He has served as Managing Director of Crossover International Inc., a communications management firm that he founded in 1995. Previously Ovaitt was Vice President—Corporate Affairs for MCI, International PR Vice President for AT&T, and Editorial Services Director for the Monsanto Company. He also has served as Chief Marketing Officer for Enamics, Inc., a business technology management company in Stamford, Connecticut. He is a member of the Arthur W. Page Society, accredited by the Public Relations Society of America, and former Co-Chair of the International Public Relations Association's Campaign for Media Transparency. Frank holds a Bachelor of Journalism degree from the University of Missouri and an M.B.A. from New York University.

Professor Ronél Rensburg is Head of the Department of Marketing and Communication Management at the University of Pretoria (since 2000). She is Chairperson of the School of Management Sciences in the Faculty of Economic and Management Sciences. She is currently also the President of the Southern Africa Institute for Management Scientists (SAIMS), and board member of the International Federation of Management Scientists (IFSAM). She is also a board member of the Ron Brown Institute (RBI) for the enhancement of business incubation in Africa. Prof. Rensburg is also a member of PRISA (Public Relations Institute of Southern Africa), a member of the ICA (International Communication Association) and a company director of the PRISA Education and Training Centre. She serves on the editorial boards of five international academic journals in the fields of marketing, communication, and management sciences. Ronél Rensburg holds the degrees B.A. (Communication), Honours (Communication), Masters in Communication, and a Doctorate in Communication Science. She has published books and articles (nationally and internationally) on corporate communication, speech communication, political communication, and corporate social investment and public relations. Her current area of research is the role of reputation management and stakeholder engagement in corporate governance. She has a specific interest in serving the SADC-region of Africa where communication theory, research, and practice are concerned. Ronél Rensburg is very involved in the New Partnership for Africa's Development (NEPAD). She writes presentations and speeches for prominent business leaders and South African politicians on a continual basis.

Tanya le Roux, M.Com. Communication Management, is a lecturer in the School of Communication Studies at the North-West University, Potchefstroom, South Africa, where she is Subject Co-ordinator for the field of Corporate Communication Management. She previously worked as communication practitioner and manager in the banking sector in the UK and South Africa. She also does consulting work in South Africa, focusing on stakeholder relationship management. Her research interests are focused on corporate communication management in South Africa and specifically the constraints experienced by practitioners to contribute to the communication management function, proving its strategic worth to the organization. She has presented papers at leading international conferences, as well as national conferences, and currently focuses on completing her Ph.D.

Manfred Rühl, Dr. habil., Dr. rer. pol., Diploma in Economics, is Chair and Professor Emeritus of Communications, University of Bamberg. After graduating from University of Erlangen-Nürnberg, he was invited to be

Scholar-in-Residence, The Annenberg School of Communications, University of Pennsylvania (1969–1970); later on he was Visiting Professor at the Universities of Mainz and Zürich. As Professor of Communications at University of Hohenheim (Stuttgart), he organized Germany's first Graduate Programme for Journalism and Public Relations (since 1976). He served as President of the Deutsche Gesellschaft für Publizistik- und Kommunikationswissenschaft (1980–1982), and as Member-at-Large, Board of Directors, International Communications Association (1977–1980). His fields of study are General Communication Theory, Theory of Communication Policy, Science of Science, Journalism, and Public Relations. A recent book is entitled *Publicizing. A Sensemaking History of Public Communication* (in German); the title of a forthcoming book reads *Communication Cultures and World Society* (in German).

Betteke van Ruler, Ph.D., is Professor of Communication Science within the Amsterdam School of Communication Research. She is doing research on the practice of communication management and the relationship between organizations and the press, and is currently Chair of the ICA PR Division and President of The European Public Relations Education and Research Association, EUPRERA. She holds the Bob Heath Award for best top paper of the PR Division of the International Communication Association (2004), re professionalism in public relations. Recent books are *Public Relations and Communication Management in Europe* (co-editor Dejan Verčič) and *Communication Management in Communication Scientific Perspective* (in Dutch).

Claire Spencer, FCIPR, has had a twenty-year career in communications, spanning advertising (Dorlands, Euro RSCG) and public relations, with a focus on research for planning and measurement. Claire applied her skills to a PR environment first at her own consultancy, Handel Communications, and latterly at Manning Selvage & Lee where she was Planning Director for four years and developed a proprietary tool—i to i tracker®—to measure communications effectiveness. Following a sabbatical year, when Claire sailed around the world with her family, she set up i to i research as a Publicis Groupe company, specializing in research for communication planning and evaluation. In 2005, i to i research worked with the London 2012 Olympic Bid team on research to understand how advertising, PR, and word of mouth were influencing public support.

Ana Tkalac Verčič, Ph.D., is an Assistant Professor of Marketing and Marketing Communications at the Graduate school of Business and Economics, in Zagreb. She holds an M.Sc. in Psychology from the University of Zagreb and a Ph.D. in Public Relations from the same University. She is a former Fulbright scholar and a recipient of various other grants and scholarships. She is a member of the management board of the Croatian Public Relations Society. Her major research interests are focused on attitude and attitude change in public relations. She has published and co-authored numerous papers in the area of public relations and marketing communications, and she regularly participates in leading international conferences.

Dejan Verčič, Ph.D., FCIPR, is a partner at Pristop Agency and Professor of Public Relations and Communication Management at the University of Ljubljana. Among his clients are governments, domestic and international corporations, and associations. He holds a Ph.D. from the London School of Economics. In 2000 he received a special award from the Public Relations Society of Slovenia. In 2001 he was presented with the Alan Campbell-Johnson Medal for special achievements in the field of international public relations by the Institute of Public Relations (UK). Since 1994 he has organized the annual Lake Bled International Public Relations Research Symposia. His most recent publications are books *The Global Handbook of Public Relations* (co-editor K. Sriramesh) and *Public Relations and Communication Management in Europe* (co-editor Betteke van Ruler).

Jon White, Ph.D., FCIPR, is a consultant specializing in management and organization development, public relations and public affairs management, whose clients have included multinational companies, consultancies, and government organizations. He holds a Ph.D. from the London School of Economics, where he has taught Corporate Communications. He is also a visiting fellow at Henley Management College, a university level management development center in the UK, and is visiting professor at the University of Birmingham, University of Central Lancashire and University of Lugano. He is a co-organizer of the Bled International Public Relations Research Symposia. He has written several books on public relations management and a number of reports and articles on aspects of the practice, most recently drafting the UK Chartered Institute of Public Relations policy statement on measurement and evaluation in 2005.

Iris Wong Kit-ying, M.A. Her research interests mainly focus on crisis communication and management, relationship management and reputation management. She has conducted a study on the correlation between crisis response strategies and organization–stakeholder relationship. She is currently working for the Hong Kong Committee for UNICEF in exploring and launching various fundraising and advocacy activities via different channels. She has built up and maintained a strong relationship with donors, sponsors, and the media. Thus, in her area of study, relationship management is one of her greatest interests.

Ansgar Zerfass, Ph.D., is Professor of Communication Management at the University of Leipzig. Prior to this, he worked in management positions at various companies and institutions for more than ten years. He holds a university degree and doctorate in business administration and a postdoctoral lecture qualification (Habilitation) in Communication Science. He has received several awards both for his academic work and his communication campaigns, among them the Ludwig-Schunk-Award for economic science, the German Public Relations Award, and the German Multimedia Award. Recently, he was elected "PR Head of the year 2005" by the German Public Relations Association (DPRG). Ansgar Zerfass is author and editor of seventeen books and numerous articles on corporate communication and interactive communication, most recently the *Handbook of Corporate Communication* (in German).

Acknowledgments

We would like to thank the many colleagues who made this project possible, not only as contributors, but also as participants in the BledCom conferences, where we have spent much of our time discussing the basics of public relations in a globalized world. The contributors are not only colleagues, but they are also friends. We would like to thank them all for their patience, and some for their willingness to rewrite their drafts once and then again, in order to make this the best book possible. We also want to express our appreciation to Linda Bathgate, Editor at Lawrence Erlbaum Associates, Publishers (now Routledge), for her support, and to the Erlbaum staff for their help with the production. Last, but not least, we would like to thank the reviewers of the first draft of the book for their extremely detailed comments and constructive criticism.

Amsterdam, Ljubljana, Summer 2007
Betteke van Ruler, Ana Tkalac Verčič, Dejan Verčič

1 Public Relations Metrics

Measurement and Evaluation— An Overview

Betteke van Ruler, Ana Tkalac Verčič, and Dejan Verčič

1. Introduction

As Botan and Taylor (2004: 645) state, public relations is both a professional practice and an academic field. In both communities research is done but this is not necessarily the same kind of research. A recent dissertation on the use of research in public relations practice in Ireland (McCoy, 2006) confirmed what has been known from many other studies in other countries as well: a common measurement tool for doing research in public relations practice is the "eyes and ears" method—talking to an unsystematic selection of members of the public or the media, reading some reports and drawing conclusions on the basis of these reports, or listening to solicited or unsolicited feedback from superiors or members of a public without systematically planning the research or analyzing the results. This is what Pavlik (1987: 91) called "seat-of-the-pants" research; Broom and Dozier (1990) have called it "informal research" and Rühl (in this book) terms it "laymen's research." The use of these kinds of laymen's research might be due to the immaturity of the profession and its rapid growth, but it is detrimental to its prestige and its status, in practice as well as in the scholarly community.

Already in 1987, Pavlik concluded that half of all the systematic research on public relations was applied research, dealing with various communication techniques and program areas of public relations, and that most of the other research was introspective, touching many areas including education, ethics, roles, etc. Evaluation research gets increased attention, he foresaw in 1987, but "there is no answer to the broad question: What can public relations contribute to overall organizational effectiveness?" and he suggested focusing on relationships (p. 122). Some years before, in 1984, Ferguson, too, promoted relationships as the unit of analysis and a focus on theorizing (see Botan & Taylor, 2004: 648). Almost twenty years later Heath (2001: 3) concluded that the concept of relationships has become widely discussed and studied and is seen as a key concept in public relations (see also J. Grunig, 1992; Ledingham & Bruning, 2000).

Botan and Hazleton (2006) stated that public relations research has matured. Yet, in a critical response to public relations theory building so far, Cheney and Christensen (2001) speculated about "a Western managerial and rationalist bias in public relations research" (p. 182).

Apart from the discipline's youth, the problems with research and evaluation in public relations might also be caused by a lack of conceptualization, according to J. E. Grunig (in this book). We would suggest that there is not only a lack of conceptualization but probably also a lack of epistemological and methodological foundations, which provide the calculus for conceptualization, and surely a lack of diversity in this respect. The developments of these foundations and of appropriate measurement tools are to be seen as an important goal of the scholarly community.

2. The Territory of Public Relations Research

Just like Pavlik in 1987, Botan and Hazleton (1989) concluded that public relations theory was in an underdeveloped condition at the time. Vasquez and Taylor (2000), Sallot, Lyon, Acosta-Alzuru, and Jones (2003), and Botan and Taylor (2004) could be much more positive. Their overviews of research done until the millennium change prove that the field is expanding. Vasquez and Taylor (2000) reported seven areas of public relations research: two-way symmetrical communication; roles; issues management; negotiation; publics in the public relations process; international public relations; and public relations and communications technology. They repeat Pasadeos, Reufro, and Hanily (1999) in their conclusion that "it would help the field greatly if some young scholars were to break with the current mold and undertake more audience-centered research" (p. 48) and followed Pasadeos *et al.* in their call for topical diversity of scholarship and, consequently, a need for more diversity in methods (Vasquez & Taylor, 2000: 334). Botan and Taylor (2004) concluded that the most striking trend in public relations has been the movement from a functionalist perspective to a co-creational one, focusing on publics as co-creators of meaning and emphasizing the building of relationships with all publics. They, too, lamented that there is hardly any diversity.

Botan and Hazleton (2006: 7–8) developed an interesting hypothesis of the one-dimensionality of topical diversity in public relations research so far by using Kuhn's concept of anomaly (1970). An anomaly is an unexpected fact or a research finding that a paradigm in its original form did not anticipate. If the paradigm can be adjusted to incorporate the anomaly, normal science may continue. Failure to adequately incorporate anomalies can result in a crisis, e.g., a widely spread recognition of the failures of a paradigm. Botan and Hazleton (p. 9) claim that public relations scholars have not (yet) identified major anomalies that existing models fail to address. We agree with them that it makes no sense to develop alternatives just to replace former paradigms. Instead, the development of additional and different theories of public relations needs to be encouraged, as well as the engagement of all scholars in frequent and public debates over the merits and weakness of all theories of public relations.

We are grateful that we are able to contribute to this by providing challenging ideas on epistemological and conceptual topics in public relations research as well as insights into developments in Europe and Africa in this book.

3. The Basics of Research

The journal overviews and readers on the development of public relations theory are focused on the area of research topics and the concepts in use, not on the research measurement techniques. The first book on how to conduct public relations research was *Public Relations Research* of Brody and Stone (1989). This book was not meant for scholars but for students and practitioners, and was, consequently, very elementary. The second one came out only one year later—Broom and Dozier's *Using Research in Public Relations: Applications to Program Management* (1990)—which focused on the same audience and was a reader friendly research book: "friendly to students and practitioners who fear of numbers, have math anxiety or say they have little aptitude for research" (p. xiii).

The scholarly community kept silent in this respect until 2002, when Don Stacks published his *Primer of Public Relations Research* (2002). He laments (p. v) that the idea for writing this book came up over a decade ago, but that no publisher was willing to take a chance on public relations research. His statement, "My treatment is based on the belief that public relations practitioners need to understand the research process—not that they will conduct research daily (some will), but they will have to make important and informed decisions about hiring research firms, evaluating their proposals and end products, as well as helping to determine how that research benefits the 'bottom line'" (p. vi), shows that this book is, again, an introductory book. He refers to the many research methods books that are available in sociology, psychology, business and communication to the reader who wants a more in-depth understanding of the relationship between theory, method, and analytical tool, e.g., to methodology. We would suggest that a mature field of research has its own advanced books in this respect and we see a need for the development of books that go further than just elementary research methods.

The purpose of research is to build theories to solve the problems researchers face in working in a domain (Littlejohn, 1995). The core question for every public relations researcher is how public relations works, what it does in, to and for organizations, publics, or in the public arena, e.g., society at large. The answer to this question depends on the methodologies the researcher uses. Behind this term stands the "personal biography of the researcher: he or she approaches the world with a set of ideas, a framework (theory, ontology) that specifies a set of questions (epistemology, analysis)" (Denzin & Lincoln, 2000: 18–19). Whether predefined by *Weltanschauung* or constructed in its peer group (cf. Sallot *et al.*, 2003: 30), our understanding of phenomena is built on certain underlying philosophical assumptions (Foreman-Wernet, 2002: 6). These philosophical assumptions and the subsequent chosen methodology, including a set of theories, conceptualization, operationalization and appropriate methods, form the researcher's calculus for doing research. A mature discipline provides as many calculi as can be invented. So, functionalistic oriented calculi should have a place under the public relations research sun, as well as constructivistic ones in its natural or most radical forms.

4. A Public Relations Research Grid

Public relations is where management and communication meet. As a human activity it includes everything we know about human behavior; as an organizational activity it encompasses everything we know about organizational behavior; and as a social activity it subsumes everything we know about social and societal behavior. When observing public relations and reflecting on it, we can use all the knowledge available in modern academe and in practical use. From such a point of view, we know in principle everything there is to know about public relations research and evaluation. However, in practice, we still have a long way to go.

Biology, chemistry, and physics do not make up medical science, much less a physician. In the same way, psychology, sociology, communication, and political science do not make up public relations science, much less a competent practitioner and even less so a competent public relations organization. Research on, for, and in public relations is needed if it is ever to become an equal partner at the top board table and an equal member of academia. As Botan and Hazleton (2006) showed in the introductory chapter of their second book on public relations theory—entitled, aptly, *Public Relations Theory*—positions in public relations have increased substantially in both business practice and academic teaching since their first *Public Relations Theory* book (Botan & Hazleton, 1989); but, again, we are not there yet.

Fifteen years ago, J. Grunig and colleagues made an overview of research findings while building his "excellence theory" (J. Grunig, 1992). We believe that our book contributes to this body of growing knowledge.

Public relations research territory is wide open. To navigate through it, in Chapter 5 of this book, J. Grunig proposes to distinguish between research in, on, and for public relations, and to observe it on four levels: the program level, the functional level, the organizational level, and the societal level. We suggest that two more levels of analysis may be useful: the project level and the individual level. Merging J. Grunig's proposal with our ideas, we organized and visualized types of research in, on, and for public relations in a public relations research grid (see Table 1.1). This grid supports our earlier observation that "a feasible concept of public relations needs more indicators than relationships alone to reflect the plural nature of its service to organizations and its publics" (van Ruler & Verčič, 2005: 240).

Table 1.1 Public relations research grid

Level/purpose	On	For	In
Society	(1) SOC-O	(7) SOC-F	(13) SOC-I
Organization	(2) ORG-O	(8) ORG-F	(14) ORG-I
Function	(3) FUN-O	(9) FUN-F	(15) FUN-I
Program	(4) PROG-O	(10) PROG-F	(16) PROG-I
Project	(5) PROJ-O	(11) PROJ-F	(17) PROJ-I
Individual	(6) IND-O	(12) IND-F	(18) IND-I

Let us first explain the grid's structure and then its eighteen constitutive cells. We can research public relations on at least six different levels moving from less to more complex: individual, project, program, function, organization, and society as a whole. These levels of reality and analysis can overlap, but they present different ontological, epistemological, and methodological questions. We should be able to differentiate between them and see them separately before we integrate them into a holistic picture. On each of these levels we can research what we can learn about public relations in order to understand what it is, where it comes from, and what it does (the "On" column). For each of these levels we can develop research to produce knowledge for use in public relations (the "For" column), and we can observe research done in public relations practice (the "In" column). Six levels of research by three types of purpose (on the role and consequences of public relations, for the development of public relations technology, and in the execution of public relations practice) give us eighteen different research situations. We can assume that public relations research is not equally distributed across these cells—we have not yet investigated that. We now turn to a detailed description of each cell.

(1) SOC-O

Research on public relations on a *societal level* studies what public relations means to contemporary society and for the future(s). (From a present point of view, the future exists as a multitude of possibilities, which is why we talk about future in the plural.) A textbook explanation at this level of conceptualization is positive: "The practice serves society by mediating conflict and by building the consensual relationships needed to maintain social order. Its social function —its mission—is accomplished when it replaces ignorance, coercion, and intransigence with knowledge, compromise, and adjustment" (Cutlip, Center, & Broom, 2000: 25). Monographs studying public relations at this level of analysis are critical and see public relations as corrupt for political democracy and economic freedoms. Mayhew's (1997) study on the new public and Olasky's (1987) work on corporate public relations are two examples of this type of research.

(2) ORG-O

Research on public relations on an *organizational level* studies what public relations contributes to contemporary organizations and their competences. On an organizational level we need research on what public relations means— as a concept, as a study area, and as a practice—to contemporary organizations, irrespective of whether they consciously attend to them or not. The excellence-study triology is a very good example of this type of research (J. Grunig, 1992; Dozier, L. Grunig, & J. Grunig, 1995; L. Grunig, J. Grunig, & Dozier, 2002). Many studies have been made on organizations–environment relationships in other disciplines; here, we just mention economic ecology (Hannan & Freeman, 1993).

(3) FUN-O

Research on public relations on a *functional level* examines what public relations is, how it differs from other related disciplines (like marketing and human resources), specialization, and institutionalization. Public relations as a specialized function of management makes sense only if it is necessary. Public relations is about "maximizing, optimizing, or satisfying the process of meaning creation using informational, persuasive, relational, and discursive interventions to solve managerial problems by co-producing societal (public) legitimations" (van Ruler & Verčič, 2005: 266) and "[w]hat distinguishes communication managers from other managers when they sit down at the table is that they contribute special concern for broader societal issues and approaches to problems" (ibid.: 264). Cutlip's (1994) history, Avenarius and Armbrecht's (1992) questioning of the status of public relations, and Banks's (1995) conceptualization of multicultural public relations are examples of this type of research. Maloney's *Rethinking Public Relations* (2000) deserves special mention. As long as the problem remains with naming the discipline ("corporate communication," "communication management," "reputation management," "public affairs," etc.), more work will be needed to clarify the muddy waters.

(4) PROG-O

Research on public relations on a *program level* is interested in what public relations does to relations between focal organizations and different stakeholders such as employees, customers, civil service officials, politicians, media, communities, and activists. Numerous studies on media relations are an example of such research efforts (Jeffers, 1977; Pincus, Rimmer, Rayfield, & Cropp, 1993; Cameron, Lynne, & Curtin, 1997; Bollinger, 1999; Curtin, 1999; DeLorme & Fedler, 2003; Shin & Cameron, 2003). Here we have to note that except for journalists and editors, no other group was researched systematically—at least not in the public relations literature. However, again a lot of work has been done in other disciplines, and employees, for instance, have been researched extensively in organizational communication studies.

(5) PROJ-O

Research on public relations on a *project level* should investigate what public relations projects are and how they are different from other types of project. There are quite a few books of the "how to" type, but we are not aware of any research in this field.

(6) IND-O

Research on public relations on an *individual level* studies what individuals do with and in public relations, and what public relations does with individuals. Research into the roles of public relations practitioners (Dozier, 1992) is an example of a well-developed line of research in this area.

(7) SOC-F

Research for public relations on a *societal level* should enable societies for productive use of public relations. Ławniczak's (2001) *Transition Public Relations—An Instrument for Public Systematic Transformation in Central and Eastern Europe* is a good example.

(8) ORG-F

Research for public relations on an *organizational level* should enable organizations, especially their top management, to use public relations. *The Excellence Study* trilogy (J. Grunig, 1992; Dozier *et al.*, 1995; L. Grunig *et al.*, 2002) is both on and for public relations at the organizational level.

(9) FUN-F

Research for public relations on a *functional level* seeks to help the PR practice professionalize and institutionalize itself. The excellence project is an example of this type of research, too (J. Grunig, 1992; Dozier *et al.*, 1995; L. Grunig *et al.*, 2002).

(10) PROG-F

Research for public relations on a *program level* aims at enabling organizations to improve their competence for public relations program management in their relations with stakeholders. Extensive work is now in progress to increase competences for international public relations programs (Sriramesh & Verčič, 2003).

(11) PROJ-F

Research for public relations on a *project level* hopes to lead to improving the public relations practitioner's competences for project management. Allen's (1980) work on Program Evaluation Review Technique (PERT) as a tool for planning, scheduling, and controlling is an example, as is Nager and Allen's (1984) work on public relations management by objectives.

(12) IND-F

Research for public relations on an *individual level* should arm public relations practitioners to do their jobs better and more easily. Public relations techniques have been published (e.g., Bivins, 1999), but there are no studies directed at actually helping public relations practitioners—the rare exception is the excellence project.

(13) SOC-I

Research in public relations on a *societal level* tells us about how societies as a whole employ public relations. Here we have Kunczik's (1997) *Images of Nations and International Public Relations*, but not much more.

(14) ORG-I

Research in public relations on an *organizational level* tells us about how organizations use public relations. The primary mode of research in this area is the case study (see Moss and DeSanto, 2002, for good examples).

(15) FUN-I

Research in public relations on a *functional level* informs us on public relations as it operates. This type of research has been reported in some case studies, but explicit treatments, as in Spencer and Jahansoozi's Chapter 10, in this volume, are rare.

(16) PROG-I

Research in public relations on a *program level* deals with what organizations are researching in their public relations programs. Fombrun and Rindova's (2000) report on reputation management at Royal Dutch/Shell and its use of research is an example.

(17) PROJ-I

Research in public relations on a *project level* tells us what organizations are researching in their public relations projects. Verčič and Pek-Drapal (2002) have produced such a report.

(18) IND-I

Research in public relations on an *individual level* tells us about individuals researching in public relations. We are not aware of such a study.

We assume that this public relations research grid can help us to find the gaps in our body of knowledge and to focus on topical and methodological diversity.

5. The Content of this Volume

As we have discussed, the problems with research and evaluation in public relations might be caused by a lack of theoretical, methodological, and philosophical foundations. In order to discuss these foundations, together with its offspring in measurement tools and research projects, the 12th International Public Relations Research Symposium, BledCom 2005, was devoted to gathering scholarly questions, reviews, and state-of-the-art knowledge regarding this subject. BledCom 2005 inspired the production of this book. Some of its chapters were presented at this conference, and, as BledCom 2005 also revealed questions that were not covered by papers presented, we invited some scholars to contribute a chapter.

This book is about how to consider public relations research rather than on how to carry out research. It discusses the issue of metrics in public relations from a theoretical angle—its epistemology and conceptualization—as well as questions of definitions and measurement tools, and it gives some examples of research projects.

Laymen, professionals, and scholars think and talk differently about public relations because they reflect differently on public relations, using different epistemic and methodical lenses. That is why, in the first part of this book, "Fundamentals of Public Relations Research," Manfred Rühl introduces three types of public relations theory. When talking about public relations, non-experts use common sense, assessing it with trial-and-error measurements. They evaluate with their own eyes and ears, and believe that they do not need any theoretical knowledge. According to Rühl, professional perspectives require a scientific body of knowledge that preconditions public relations know-how and provides working theories for professional approaches to public relations. A third type of public relations theory is the one proposed by scholars. Scholarly public relations concepts are based on theories of knowledge ("know why" theories); empirical, historical, and/or phenomenological methods are used to formulate these theories. In this context, Rühl mentions Botan and Taylor (2004), who prefer to view public relations as a sub-field of communication with its own research and methods.

With tested and retested knowledge, public relations scholarship conflicts with uncontrolled opinions. Rühl claims that, as long as public relations research is not going beyond empirical piecemeal research, it has no systemic conception to help it to be identified as a discipline. Therefore, in Chapter 2, he raises questions such as: "Do the suggested system/environment theory, communication system theory, and societal system theory provide adequate basis for scholarly public relations when differentiated from action, behavioral, and media systems?"; "Is scholarly public relations research prepared to interrelate problems of producing and receiving public relations in specific relations to publics, freedom of communication, public moods, and public opinions?"; and, finally, "In what respect is scholarly public relations a social science?"

In Chapter 3, Alenka Jelen starts with the provocative observation that public relations as a scientific discipline appears to have a somewhat inferior status compared to other well-established disciplines within the social sciences. So, it is a social science but a rather weak one. She draws a picture of the nature of current public relations research in terms of the scientific public relations agenda so far and the ways this agenda is being implemented. Her study shows that most public relations research still focuses on the public relations profession, and, moreover, that it is almost exclusively devoted to the ways of conceptualizing and facilitating (excellent) communication management anchored in North American practice and academe. She describes a shortage of research on, discussion of, and reflection on the methodological advantages and shortcomings of research published in the field. Most research is descriptive in nature and dominated by the quantitative tradition, lacking reflection on conceptualization and appropriateness. Her conclusion is that public relations researchers should expand their topical and methodological horizons so that "they would discover the forest in all its richness and complexity, rather than seeing just the trees." Jelen claims that topical and methodological diversity could offer an opportunity to establish a more coherent body of knowledge and perhaps lead to a unifying theory, the absence of which leaves the public relations discipline in an uncertain state, renders it irrelevant within the academic community, and reduces its respect and credibility in the eyes of other disciplines.

Would considering public relations as a social science be beneficial for its research? And, if so, how? In Chapter 4, Jan Kleinnijenhuis uses the well-known PRSA (Public Relations Society of America) definition of public relations as "helping an organization and its publics to adapt to each other," which provides a rationale for the claim that public relations can be seen as a social science. This definition delineates which types of theory and which types of empirical evidence are relevant when considering public relations. For example, Kleinnijenhuis notes that theories and insights dealing with relationships between an organization and its publics are potentially useful. This fits a network perspective, which is quite popular in social sciences these days. He shows that the network approach is worthwhile for the study of public relations since network models take relationships between objects as their dependent variables. Starting from a historical sketch of the development of the network approach in social sciences, the chapter addresses its relevance and limitations for the field of public relations. Kleinnijenhuis repeats the six theoretical approaches that were defined by Janet Bridges (2004) and concludes that the network approach is useful for the accentuation and the further development of the insights gained from these six theoretical approaches. He also claims that this approach is helpful for practice because these insights appear to address the problems that public relations professionals encounter in their profession.

Grunig picks up the glove that Rühl threw into the ring in Chapter 2 regarding the basic fundaments of public relations theory and methodology, concentrating, in Chapter 5, on the issue of conceptualization of research questions in theory-building as well as in management-decision oriented research. Public relations practitioners today recognize the need to include measurement in their practice. However, most measurement programs fail to answer the questions and solve the problems they were developed to answer. For Grunig, the greatest problem in public relations is not the lack of measurement but the lack of conceptualization. Measurements are just tools that researchers use to test their ideas. Public relations programs result from ideas developed by practitioners, just as research hypotheses result from ideas of academic scholars. As Grunig points out, measurement in itself has little value unless it is preceded by well-constructed conceptualization. He therefore concentrates on the development of a conceptual framework that can be used to guide research in the daily practice of public relations, on the profession of public relations, and for the development of the practice of public relations (in, on, and for public relations). He brings us back to basics, describing the components of conceptualization in the conceptual process of turning theoretical concepts into theoretical propositions, and operational concepts into hypotheses, which he sees as fundamental in all kinds of research projects. Having elaborated on this, Grunig concentrates on quantitative methods to do formative and summative research at different levels of public relations. First, he discusses the program level, which is aimed at the development and evaluation of public relations activities. Second, he describes the organizational level, focusing on the development and evaluation of the relationships between the organization and its publics in order to develop public relations programs. Third, he looks at the functional level, concentrating on formative and summative evaluations of how public relations is organized and what it does. Research on the functional level is most of all "benchmarking" research of critical success factors and best practices. Fourth, he elaborates on the societal level, focusing on the cumulative impact of what public relations does at the program, functional, and organizational levels.

L. A. Grunig furthers the discussion by stating that we should measure what we consider essential. To show what she sees as essential, L. A. Grunig introduces metaphor to explain and inspire scholars and practitioners to conduct the kind of inquiry that truly has value. As she explains in Chapter 6, much of that research is qualitative in nature. The best metaphor for what public relations is or should be and do is the "thinking heart" of the organization. Inspired by a Dutch Jewish woman, Etty Hillesum, who died in Auschwitz in 1943, L. A. Grunig uses this metaphor to explain that the value of public relations is most of all to subjugate self-interest in order to connect with and serve others. In the context of an organization, this means that public relations is or should be focused on social responsibility, based in both thinking and feeling. To do this, public relations needs to translate interest in "the other" into a spectrum of research methodologies that allow building knowledge about both the other and ourselves, so that the "heart" can become active, engaging in such activities as communicating. Qualitative research is oriented at a phenomenon's quality rather than at its quantity, focusing on the "how" and "why" rather than "how many" or "to what extent" questions. Suitable methodologies for this "thinking-heart" are consequently mostly qualitative. The key tenets of qualitative research, she explains, include that research and the people who create it are connected, that establishing rapport matters, that less may be more, that reciprocity matters, that people are diverse, that research is not neutral, that ethical issues abound, that reflexivity is a hallmark, and that field studies can be holistic.

The second part of the book, "Public Relations Methods, Cases, and Specific Topics," aims to make the first part more concrete. In its opening chapter, Ansgar Zerfass constructs a corporate communications scorecard (CCS). Several companies experiment with scorecards in communication management, but so far this type of measurement lacks any theoretical framework. Starting with the Harvard Business School balanced scorecard and evaluating existing communication management scorecards, Zerfass proposes a framework for managing and evaluating corporate communications on both strategic and operational planning as well as evaluation. He claims that the CCS shows how to link established methods of PR measuring to overall business objectives, highlighting the ways in which communication contributes to a company's profitability.

In Chapter 8, Barbara Baerns paints a sobering picture of the sophistication of winning German public relations campaigns between 1970 and 2001. She concludes that the *Goldene Brücke* ("Golden Bridge") prize applications have become increasingly extravagant, and that the instruments and media that were used in the public relations projects followed developments in information and communication technology. However, the increasingly elaborate media equipment does not provide a sufficient precondition for successful communication management in terms of problem solving and efficacy, and she finds hardly any improvement on that point.

In Chapter 9, Wim van der Noort shows that it is possible to improve the management of communication campaigns. As head of the research department of the Dutch Public Information and Communication Office, he oversees the evaluation of all Dutch governmental mass-media campaigns in order to get a long-term picture of its efficiency and effectiveness. On the basis of over 120 cases, a software tool has been developed to provide campaign managers with guidelines on the budget they need for achieving their campaign objectives, the communication effects that they can expect from the campaign, and how best to allocate budgets to the various media types.

Chapter 10, by Claire Spencer and Julia Jahansoozi, shows a more detailed picture of how research has been used for formative evaluation of the campaign to get the Olympic Games to London in 2012. The research concentrated on one part of the campaign, namely, the need to portray "an enthusiastic country" where Britons, and particularly Londoners, were seen to be supportive of the Games being held in their country.

Iris Wong and Chun-ju Flora Hung, in Chapter 11, give an example of the measurement of organization–public relationship during the SARS crisis in Hong Kong. They explore how an organization's crisis response affects the relationships with the public. They conclude that it is very hard to find direct causal relations, especially because of the sensitivity of the issue.

In Chapter 12, Mafalda Eiró-Gomes and João Duarte promote the use of case studies for evaluating public relations programs in formative ways. By describing how evaluation is used in a campaign to launch the first mortgage product for non-EU citizens in Portugal, they show that the case study is a cheap but good tool because of its learning potential; they do this by giving an "insider's picture." For the authors, the case study is valuable as a tool to complement traditional evaluations by PR practitioners, especially to be applied to extraordinary campaigns which break the normal standards. In addition, they claim, a case study might be a good aid for a benchmark approach to the professional practice.

In Chapters 13 and 14 our attention is directed to Africa, where public relations is taking root but has its own, very specific, problems. First, Ronél Rensburg gives an overview of what is going on in research and evaluation in Africa. To evaluate public relations, researchers need to be aware of the complexities of conducting social science research on the African continent. Rensburg explores the standing of social science research, summarizes what has already been achieved in public relations, and what the research topics for African public relations researchers will be in the next few years. Rensburg also reflects on the possibilities of novel public relations metrics for Africa and promotes the future investigation of different and synthesized research programs and philosophies in public relations for the continent. In Chapter 14, Tanya le Roux turns to the difficulties of doing research with questionnaires in a country where most people are illiterate and where written language has a totally different meaning than in the West. This means that measurement scales need to be adapted to their particular context of use. She does that for the organizational communication satisfaction and employer–employee relationship scales as developed by Francis and Woodcock, the original International Communication Association (ICA) audit scale, and the relationship statements on integrity and dependability of Grunig and Hon. She shows us the worries about reliability and validity when adapting scales and provides the measurement of this adaptation.

In Chapter 15 we turn to a subject which is often mentioned but, until now, hardly ever dealt with scientifically in public relations: stakeholder thinking. Despite their obvious parallels, stakeholder and public relations literature have developed in relative isolation from each other. Nigel de Bussy leads us through the stakeholder literature and examines the vexed issue of who (or what) is a stakeholder and the even more sensitive question of the construct of legitimacy within stakeholder thinking.

In Chapters 16 and 17, two initiatives on research and evaluation from the practitioners' point of view are introduced. Frank E. Ovaitt Jr. describes what the U.S. Institute for Public Relations and the Commission on Measurement and Evaluation do, and Anne Gregory and Jon White acquaint us with the Chartered Institute of Public Relations work on research and evaluation.

6. The Public Relations Research Grid

To demonstrate how our public relations research grid functions, chapters from this book have been included in it (see Table 1.2). Not surprisingly, the cell at the intersection of "Function" and "On" is the most popular. We believe that the majority of work in public relations research can be located there.

What we do not have in our book are chapters on an individual level; furthermore, only one chapter discusses research in public relations. How symptomatic this is for the global research practice has yet to be determined.

We believe that not only is public relations becoming increasingly important in contemporary life, but it is essential for an enlightened future. The chapters in this volume and our overview presented in the public relations research grid show that although a lot of work has been done in empirical studies on public relations, many questions remain unanswered and study is needed in greater depth.

One single project, *Excellence in Public Relations and Communication Management* (J. Grunig, 1992; Dozier *et al.*, 1995; L. Grunig *et al.*, 2002), has done more than many other studies to increase our understanding of what public relations is, what it does, what it could be, and what it could do. This is an important lesson because it demonstrates what we lack in public relations research—namely, more large-scale and thorough studies that investigate substantial parts of reality and, in the process, produce new knowledge. If we want to know more, we will have to study more, and to do this we need to develop solid research programs instead of small, ad hoc, projects.

Table 1.2 Chapters in this book located on the public relations research grid

Level/purpose	On	For	In
Society	Rensburg	le Roux	
Organization	de Bussy	Zerfass	
Function	Rühl, Jelen, Kleinnijenhuis, J. Grunig, L. Grunig, Baerns, Ovaitt, Gregory & White		
Program	van der Noort	Wong & Hung	
Project	Eiró-Gomes & Duarte		Spencer & Jahansoozi
Individual			

Public relations needs to start cultivating its own research. The notion of "cultivation" is taken from J. Grunig (2006) and Hung (2007), who use it to prescribe what companies should do in their relationship with publics—public relations should be concerned with the cultivation of the relationships between organizations and their publics. At the same time, it is essential that the whole public relations community should start cultivating its own research base in order to establish firm ground for future growth and development. Academics and practitioners are equally responsible for investing more in research and for the dissemination and critical exchange of their findings.

7. Our View Forward

Public relations as a scientific discipline needs to recognize significant realities, predict consequences of various behavioral opportunities, and guide action: "Recognition, prediction, and action are the first three tests of real progress in science" (Deutsch, 1986: 10). We believe, therefore, that empirical research in public relations is needed, and public relations research needs to grow its knowledge base. There is a physical reality out there that we want to manipulate, and "[p]hysical reality, however, means that a large number of different and mutually independent operations will give consistent results. In that sense, *reality* is a quantitative concept" (ibid.: 5) In other words, public relations practice is a quantitative concept and we need to conceptualize, operationalize, measure, and evaluate it as such.

Public relations research needs to be relevant, practical, useful, credible, understandable, and timely (Morris, Fitz-Gibbon, & Freeman, 1987). We are not so sure that the current research practice can live up to this, but they are reasonable requirements and should be pursued. The public relations research community must reconnect with the world of public relations practice and ask itself which research questions are relevant, which questions are practical, which are useful, which are credible, which are understandable, and which are timely. To these questions we need to produce constructive answers. We believe that the research grid that we presented here (see Tables 1.1 and 1.2) offers an organization tool that locates every question on a mental map, enabling us to start with knowledge management in public relations—in other words, with the generation of knowledge, its codification, and its transfer (Ruggles, 1997). This needs to be done not as an ethnocentric, but as a truly global endeavor (Verčič, van Ruler, Bütschi, & Flodin, 2001; L. Grunig *et al.*, 2002; Sriramesh and Verčič, 2003; van Ruler, Verčič, Bütschi, & Flodin, 2004; van Ruler & Verčič, 2005).

References

Allen, T. H. (1980). PERT: A technique for public relations management. *Public Relations Review*, 6, 38–49.

Avenarius, H., & Armbrecht, W. (Eds.) (1992). *Ist Public Relations Eine Wissenschaft? Eine Einführung*. Opladen, Germany: Westdeutscher Verlag.

Banks, S. P. (1995). *Multicultural public relations: A social-interpretive approach.* Thousand Oaks, CA: Sage.

Bivins, T. H. (1999). *Public relations writing: The essentials of style and format* (4th ed.). Lincolnwood, IL: NTC.

Bollinger, L. (1999). *Exploring the relationship between the media relations writer and the press: An analysis of the perceptions, goals and climate of communication.* Unpublished doctoral dissertation. University of South Carolina.

Botan, C., & Hazleton, V. (Eds.) (1989). *Public relations theory.* Hillsdale, NJ: Lawrence Erlbaum Associates.

Botan, C., & Hazleton, V. (2006). Public relations in a new age. In C. H. Botan & V. Hazleton (Eds.), *Public relations theory II* (pp. 1–18). Mahwah, NJ: Lawrence Erlbaum Associates.

Botan, C., & Hazleton, V. (Eds.) (2006). *Public relations theory II.* Mahwah, NJ: Lawrence Erlbaum Associates.

Botan, C. H., & Taylor, M. (2004). Public relations: State of the field. *Journal of Communication, 54,* 645–661.

Bridges, J. A. (2004). Corporate issues campaigns: Six theoretical approaches. *Communication Theory, 14*(1), 31–77.

Brody, E. W., & Stone, G. C. (1989). *Public relations research.* New York: Praeger.

Broom, G. M., & Dozier, D. M. (1990). *Using research in public relations: Applications to program management.* Englewood Cliffs, NJ: Prentice-Hall.

Cameron, G., Lynne, S., & Curtin, P. A. (1997). Public relations and the production of news: A critical review and theoretical framework. *Communication yearbook 20* (pp. 111–155). Thousand Oaks, CA: Sage.

Curtin, P. A. (1999). Re-evaluating public relations information subsidies: Market-driven journalism and agenda-building theory and practice. *Journal of Public Relations Research, 11*(1), 53–90.

Cutlip, S. M. (1994). *The unseen power: Public relations, a history.* Hillsdale, NJ: Lawrence Erlbaum Associates.

Cutlip, S. M., Center, A. H., & Broom, G. M. (2000). *Effective public relations* (8th ed.). Upper Saddle River, NJ: Prentice Hall.

DeLorme, D. E., & Fedler, F. (2003). Journalists' hostility toward public relations: An historical analysis. *Public Relations Review, 29*(2), 99–124.

Denzin, N. K., & Lincoln, Y. S. (2000). Introduction. The discipline and practice of qualitative research. In D. K. Denzin & Y. S. Lincoln (Eds.), *Handbook of qualitative research* (2nd ed., pp. 1–29). Thousand Oaks, CA: Sage.

Deutsch, K. W. (1986). What do we mean by advances in the social sciences? In K. W. Deutsch, A. S. Markovits, & Platt, J. (Eds.), *Advances in the social sciences, 1900–1980: What, who, where, how?* (pp. 1–12). Lanham, MD: University Press of America.

Dozier, D. M. (1992). Organizational roles of practitioners. In J. Grunig (Ed.), *Excellence in public relations and communication management* (pp. 327–357). Hillsdale, NJ: Lawrence Erlbaum Associates.

Dozier, D. M., with Grunig, L. A., & Grunig, J. E. (1995). *Manager's guide to excellence in public relations and communication management.* Hillsdale, NJ: Lawrence Erlbaum Associates.

Ferguson, M. A. (1984). *Building theory in public relations: Interorganizational relationships as a public relations paradigm.* Paper presented to the Public Relations Division, Association for Education in Journalism and Mass Communication Annual Convention, Gainesville, FL. Cited by Sallot *et al.* (2003).

Fombrun, C. J., & Rindova, V. P. (2000). The road to transparency: Reputation management at Royal Dutch/Shell. In M. Schultz, M. J. Hatch, & M. H. Larsen (Eds.), *The expressive organization: Linking identity, reputation, and the corporate brand* (pp. 77–96). Oxford, England: Oxford University Press.

Foreman-Wernet, L. (2002). Rethinking communication: Introducing the sense-making methodology. In B. Dervin & L. Foreman-Wernet, with E. Lauterbach (Eds.), *Sense-making methodology reader, selected writings of Brenda Dervin* (pp. 3–16). Cresskill, NJ: Hampton Press.

Grunig, J. E. (Ed.) (1992). *Excellence in public relations and communication management.* Hillsdale, NJ: Lawrence Erlbaum Associates.

Grunig, J. E. (2006). Furnishing the edifice: Ongoing research on public relations as a strategic management function. *Journal of Public Relations Research, 18*(2), 151–176.

Grunig, L. A., Grunig, J. E., & Dozier, D. M. (2002). *Excellent public relations and effective organizations: A study of communication management in three countries.* Mahwah, NJ: Lawrence Erlbaum Associates.

Hannan, M., & Freeman, J. (1993). *Organizational ecology.* Cambridge, MA: Harvard University Press.

Heath, R. L. (2001). Shifting foundations. Public relations as relationship building. In R. L. Heath (Ed.), *Handbook of public relations* (pp. 1–9). Thousand Oaks, CA: Sage.

Hung, C. J. F. (2007). Toward the theory of relationship management in public relations: How to cultivate quality relationships. In E. L. Toth (Ed.), *The future of excellence in public relations and communication management: Challenges for the next generation* (pp. 443–476). Mahwah, NJ: Lawrence Erlbaum Associates.

Jeffers, D. W. (1977). Performance expectations as a measure of relative status of news and public relations people. *Journalism Quarterly, 61*(1), 27–34.

Kuhn, T. S. (1970). *The structure of scientific revolutions.* Chicago: University of Chicago Press.

Kunczik, M. (1997). *Images of nations and international public relations.* Mahwah, NJ: Lawrence Erlbaum Associates.

Ławniczak, R. (2001). Transition public relations—an instrument for systematic transformation in Central and Eastern Europe. In R. Ławniczak (Ed.), *Public relations contribution to transition in Central and Eastern Europe* (pp. 7–18). Poznan, Poland: Poznańska drukarnia Naukowa.

Ledingham, J. A., & Bruning, S. D. (Eds.) (2000). *Public relations as relationship management. A relationship approach to the study and practice of public relations.* Mahwah, NJ: Lawrence Erlbaum.

McCoy, M. (2006). *Public relations evaluation.* Belfast: University of Ulster (unpublished dissertation).

Maloney, K. (2000). *Rethinking public relations: The spin and the substance.* London, New York: Routledge.

Mayhew, L. H. (1997). *The new public: Professional communication and the means of social influence.* Cambridge, England: Cambridge University Press.

Morris, L. L., Fitz-Gibbon, C. T., & Freeman, M. E. (1987). *How to communicate evaluation findings.* Newbury Park, CA: Sage.

Moss, D., & DeSanto, B. (Eds.) (2002). *Public relations cases: International perspectives.* London, New York: Routledge.

Nager, N. R., & Allen, T. H. (1984). *Public relations management by objectives.* New York, London: Longman.

Olasky, M. N. (1987). *Corporate public relations: A new historical perspective.* Hillsdale, NJ: Lawrence Erlbaum Associates.

Pasadeos, Y., Reufro, R., & Hanily, M. (1999). Influential authors and works of public relations scholarly literature: A network of recent research. *Journal of Public Relations Research, 11*, 29–52.

Pavlik, J. V. (1987). *Public relations: What research tells us.* Newbury Park, CA: Sage.

Pincus, J. D., Rimmer, T., Rayfield, R. E., & Cropp, F. (1993). Newspaper editor's perceptions of public relations: How business, news and sports editors differ. *Journal of Public Relations Research, 5*(1), 27–45.

Ruggles III, R. L. (1997). Tools for knowledge management: An introduction. In R. L. Ruggles III (Ed.), *Knowledge management tools* (pp. 1–8). Boston: Butterworth-Heinemann.

Sallot, L. M., Lyon, L. J., Acosta-Alzuru, C., & Jones, K. O. (2003). From aardvark to zebra: A new millennium analysis of theory development in public relations academic journals. *Journal of Public Relations Research, 15*(1), 27–90.

Shin, J.-H., & Cameron, T. G. (2003). Informal relations: A look at personal influence in media relations. *Journal of Communication Management, 7*(3), 239–253.

Sriramesh, K., & Verčič, D. (2003). *The global public relations handbook: Theory, research, and practice.* Mahwah, NJ: Lawrence Erlbaum Associates.

Stacks, D. W. (2002). *Primer of public relations research.* New York, London: The Guilford Press.

van Ruler, B., & Verčič, D. (2004). *Public relations and communication management in Europe: A nation-by-nation introduction to public relations theory and practice.* Berlin, New York: Mouton de Gruyter.

van Ruler, B., & Verčič, D. (2005). Reflective communication management: Future ways for public relations research. In P. J. Kalbfleisch (Ed.), *Communication yearbook, 29* (pp. 239–273). Mahwah, NJ: Lawrence Erlbaum Associates.

van Ruler, B., Verčič, D., Bütschi, G., & Flodin, B. (2004). A first look for parameters of public relations in Europe. *Journal of Public Relations Research, 16*, 35–63.

Vasquez, G.M., & Taylor, M. (2000). Public relations: An emerging social science enters the new millennium. In W.B. Gudykunst (Ed.), *Communication yearbook 24* (pp. 319–342). Thousand Oaks, CA: Sage.

Verčič, D., & Pek-Drapal, D. (2002). Raising environmental awareness in Slovenia: A public communication campaign. In D. Moss & B. DeSanto (Eds.), *Public relations cases: International perspectives* (pp. 167–179). London, New York: Routledge.

Verčič, D., van Ruler, B., Bütschi, G., & Flodin, B. (2001). On the definition of public relations: A European view. *Public Relations Review, 27*, 373–387.

Part I

Fundamentals of Public Relations Research

2 Public Relations Methodology

Should We Bother (If It Exists)?

Manfred Rühl

1. Some Historical Remarks on Epistemology and Methodology

A public relations theory would not be researchable without the premises and preconditions of epistemic and methodic theories. Reflecting on world society's public relations, embedding all possible public relations subsystems, this chapter views methodological and epistemological public relations problems from the perspective of a system/environment theory—complementary to a functional analysis—both based on a human communication theory (Ronneberger & Rühl, 1992; Holmström, 1996). I do not believe in a universal public relations perspective. Instead, public relations is thought of as one of world society's everyday public communication systems, with a special function, to distinguish it from journalism, advertisement, and propaganda, epistemically reconstructed with the help of system/environment theory, and methodically controlled with the method of functional equivalence (Luhmann, 1995, Chapter 1). We start off sketching public relations lay perspectives and professional perspectives, before emphasizing scholarly perspectives.

Our point of departure reflects three general observations on the historical background of epistemology and methodology. (1) Theorizing in (natural) sciences, humanities, and social sciences means reviewing preserved theories, conceived through epistemological theories and monitored by methodological theories. (2) In the past fifty years, a virtual reconstruction from philosophical to scientific epistemology and methodology proceeded hesitantly in communications (Anderson, 1996). (3) Before the nineteenth century, there was no public interest in science and the people doing it. The scholar, as a privileged subject of cognition, discovering new things, was taken for granted. Increasingly, however, the scholar was neglected in favor of the researcher. In the twentieth century, researchers and scholars in their solitary life were ousted by scientific or scholarly communities, operating, co-operating, coordinating, and competing cross-disciplinarily more and more. Scholarly knowledge was no longer considered fixed knowledge; it evolved from previous knowledge, through *perspectives by incongruity*, leaving previous knowledge *for mop-up work* (Burke, 1965; Bachelard, 1938; Kuhn, 1962).

In the 1930s a *science of science* was introduced (Ossowska & Ossowski, 1936), specified as the *social function of science* (Bernal, 1939), when structural–functionalism founded a *sociology of science*, relating science structures to favorable or unfavorable effects and their impact on society (Merton, 1957a; 1957b). Post World War II, the evolution of cybernetics— first-order cybernetics (Ashby, 1956) and second-order cybernetics (von Foerster, 1987)—offered more opportunities for abstract theoretical reflections on steering and controlling a discipline. What is of interest is not the factual work in laboratories or libraries, but the theories produced by scholarly communities, published as texts in books, journals, or on the Internet, forming libraries and archives as social memories of scholarship, to be re-activated and reproduced by their readers (Rühl, forthcoming).

2. Three Types of Public Relations Theory

The term "theory" is insufficient indication for the work on theories, although philosophers and scholars have been theorizing for thousands of years. According to a long-standing tradition, a scholarly theory is defined as a set of propositions, the least general of which must be verifiable. If successfully tested, a theory is said to permit the explanation and prediction of observable events under given conditions. At least since Immanuel Kant (1724–1804), the philosophy of science has enabled scholarship to reflect on epistemological and methodological premises and preconditions, and to compare disciplinary theory problems cross-disciplinarily. When systems theory problemizes public relations as a whole to contrast it to society's complexity (Ronneberger & Rühl, 1992), this is done specifically to transform environmental disorganization into a system's organized complexity. Laymen, practitioners, and scholars think and talk differently about public relations because they reflect on public relations using different epistemic and methodic tools. The patterns of these three types of theory are set out in Table 2.1.

2.1. Lay Perspectives

In public relations, when we speak of laymen we do not mean a class of unordained subjects; rather, we refer to social roles of societal systems (families, households, schools, regions, economies, traffic, politics, health) of a functional differentiated society (Luhmann, 1997). Public relations laymen—in their capacity of parent, citizen, consumer, road user, voter, patient, etc.—utter opinions on public relations. Public relations laymen have had some experience with public relations, and, rightly or wrongly, they assess public relations. Even when acting in public relations, for many laymen, public relations is a waste of money; it is "often understood only as a technical area—or as a cash cow" (Botan & Taylor, 2004: 646). Arguing about public relations, non-experts prefer to operate with common-sense theory, a rationality not to be controlled by philosophy of science. Common-sense utterances on public relations imply

Table 2.1 Pattern of theories taking part in reconstructing "normal" public relations
theory

	Terminology	*Epistemology*	*Methodology*
Non-expert/lay public relations	Inexpert concepts	Common-sense theories	Trial-and-error theories
Expert/ professional public relations	Expert concepts	Know-how theories	Working theories
Scholarly public relations	Scholarly concepts	Theories of knowledge	Theories of experience (empirics, historics, functionalism, dialectics, phenomenology, etc.)

normal theories as sets of ideas about the subject in question. Most people
have an elaborate set of associations about public relations, evaluating it as
something good, not so good, or as something bad. Many downgrade public
relations for one reason or another, considering it to be immoral.

Laymen describe and argue about public relations using metaphors, examples,
and anecdotes, drawing on first-hand experiences, personal feelings, sympathy,
antipathy, and the like. Epistemologically, non-experts draw fundamentally on
"what-is?" questions, assuming that there is a "real public relations"—the
essence of public relations, to be thought of platonically as an ideal form into
which fit all the past, present, and future public relations realities of this world.
Typical "what-is?" questions are: "What is public relations?"; "What does it
mean?"; "What is it good for?"; and "What is its place in everyday life?" As
to the reliability of public relations, non-experts tend to agree with Horatio:
"So have I heard, and do in part believe it" (*Hamlet*, I, 1). When laymen dislike
journalists, they compare them with public relations people, and tend to see
journalism as "endangered." Non-experts are prone to locate their subjective
perspectives in a cryptic hierarchy, placing journalism on top and public
relations at the bottom. Journalists are the good guys; public relations people
are the bad guys.

Laymen assess public relations with trial-and-error measurements. They
evaluate public relations directly—"with my own eyes and ears"—they believe
that they can form ideas about public relations unprejudiced and without any
relevant theoretical knowledge, perceived with intact senses only, before any
abstract concepts and without any theory. Non-experts prefer emotions, using
unclear moral standards. In an era of globalized print and electronic texts,
laymen confuse public relations with advertising, journalism, and propaganda.
They opinionize and opinionate public relations by norms, out of control of a
comparable rationality, so their opinions on public relations are quite irrational.

2.2. Professional Perspectives

Today, public relations practitioners usually work as professionals. In contrast with public relations as a craft, the process of professionalization starts with an academic education in a college or at a university. Public relations' body of scientific knowledge preconditions public relations *know-how*, achieved with how-to-do instruments during socialization in organizations such as corporations, agencies, associations, councils, hospitals, armies, churches, and museums. Practitioners strive for an appropriate income while setting the scene for a career in public relations and related fields. Public relations' *normative* structures are acquired and advanced in academic institutions. Like laws, they are given formal norms and are controlled by jurisprudence, whereas ethical codes, standards, principles, trust, confidence, conventions, and tact are given informal norms, cultivated by professional organizations (Avenarius, 1998), in part specific structures of work organizations. Everyday public relations is organizational public relations decision-making, structured and stabilized by roles, norms, and values, with an impact on power, authority, autonomy, leadership, and the presentation of self (Goffman, 1959; Ronneberger & Rühl, 1992: 226–248; Kohring, 2004; Rühl, 1986, 1994, 2005). Nevertheless, justifying public relations action and thought, practitioners like to quote from the biographies of the "Grand Old Men of public relations," assuming that they can utter lasting truths about public relations practices. When experts give advice to other experts, such as "act properly and talk about it" (Zedtwitz-Arnim, 1981), they show a special consciousness as public relations do-gooders.

When public relations is practiced in relation to organizational systems, individualistic public relations methodology is in a crisis of explanation. Take the abbreviation *profi* in German, meaning an individual's contemplation of ego. Almost a century ago, social scientists such as Georg Simmel, Max Weber, Emile Durkheim, Talcott Parsons, Sidney, and Beatrice Webb inquired into work, occupations, vocations, and professions. They defined *professions* as vocations/occupations prolonged and specialized through intellectual education and training, qualifying for particular services with much commitment (Rühl, 1972). Since the 1950s, social science research shifted its focus from static professions to dynamic *professionalization* (Ronneberger & Rühl, 1992: 163–183; Rühl, 1980: 100–115). Practitioner's usage of *profi* has nothing to do with this research tradition of profession and professionalization.

2.3. Scholarly Perspectives

Reviewing North American public relations research of the last two decades, Carl Botan and Maureen Taylor find "public relations is becoming much more theoretic than in its early days as an academic field," suffering, however, from two inherent flaws. First, all content of content-analysis studies "enters into the process as equal contributions with differentiations made based only on frequency rather than on any qualitative assessments." Second, "they cannot escape the question all content analyses must face, namely, how representative is the content of the chosen outlets?" (Botan & Taylor, 2004: 650). The authors maintain the traditional theory–research dichotomy, which raises two questions: Are (empirical) public relations theory and research really opposites? And, Is research in public relations not always theory-based, and if so, what kinds of theory are relevant for public relations research, which—unlike research in logics or cybernetics—is always empirical communication research?

Public Relations Theory (Botan & Hazleton, 1989) is probably the first systematic overview of public relations as a scholarly field of research. It starts from the pluralism of established social science theories, grouping 19 papers on public relations into meta-theory, theory, and applied theory. *Ist Public Relations eine Wissenschaft?* (Is Public Relations a Science?) by Avenarius and Armbrecht (1992) brought together public relations scholars from America and from German-speaking countries to review and discuss theoretical and meta-theoretical positions and backgrounds. *Theorie der Public Relations* (A Theory of Public Relations) by Ronneberger and Rühl (1992) restructures public relations as a communication reality in society. Converging with a variety of social science disciplines, and with a key theoretical triad (system/environment theory, communication theory, and society theory), the authors view scholarly public relations as a systemic unity in difference to societal, market, and organizational references.

Many public relations researchers assume a kind of system unity, without seriously trying to design it epistemologically. The scholarly public relations community teaches and does research with the aid of *structural* units (concepts) and *operative* units (methods, models, metaphors). As far as I can see, there are no macro-theoretical concepts of public relations to deal with problems like public relations globalization. When public relations operates as a self-organizing (or "autopoietic") persuasion system, observing and reconstructing models—at organizational micro-level, market-form meso-level, and societal macro-level—it can be distinguished (but not separated) from society, especially from other systems of public communication such as advertisement, journalism, or propaganda. Society's viewpoint differentiating public relations as a functional system can be described as *enforcing and fostering public interest and public trust* (Ronneberger & Rühl, 1992; Rühl, 2005). To achieve and keep stability and self-control for public relations achievements and tasks, the public relations system is self-structuring and restructuring organizations, markets, and households, social role sets, positions in organizations, a variety of norms, values, and decision-making programs. In relation to public relations and the scientific system, scholarly public relations can be viewed as the intersection of both. As a persuasion system—that is, a special kind of public communication system, as a system unity in contrast to the world societal environment—scholarly public relations can be restructured and reproduced at three interrelated levels: the fact, the temporal, and the social dimensions. These levels are discussed in sections 3.1–3.3 below.

3. Dimensions of Communication Systems

Strictly speaking, the complexity of communication systems cannot be observed directly. Attempts to reconstruct communication systems do engage in processes of reducing communication as emerging reality, transforming an unorganized outside into an organized inside. A self-referential theory of communication systems cannot help but perform the very operations it describes "autologically," as communication back to communication, with special consequences for the structure of complexity and evolution (Luhmann, 1992). Communication arises as a synthesis of its essential components: information, sense-making, theme, utterance, understanding, always in search for connectivity [*Anschlussfähigkeit*]. Communication systems relate to society's complexity as a cultural communication horizon. Without interrelations with preserved communication cultures, human communication could not find orientation and would not take place, not on earth, not to speak of communication with extraterrestrials.

Do you remember Pioneer 10, NASA's first space probe to find its way out of our solar system? On board was a metal plaque with pictures of earthlings and depictions of mathematical and biological systems, just in case Pioneer met an extraterrestrial civilization. NASA saw a chance for communication, and actually expected extraterrestrials to be as literate as earthlings with a high-school education, able to read mathematical and biological symbol systems, which revealed the origin of Pioneer 10. Instead, Pioneer 10 has been out of NASA's control since 2003, flying through the universe without any purpose and without hope for any kind of communication.

3.1. The Fact Dimension

The *fact dimension* of human communication systems refers to "*all objects of meaningful intentions*" (in psychic memories) and "*themes of meaningful communication*" (in social memories) (Luhmann, 1995: 76). As to factual elements: *sense-making* stands for "the known," "the meaningful"; *information* refers to "a surprising newness"; *themes* "limit" alternative communications; and *utterances* (*messages*) stimulate further communication.

From the fifteenth century, printed texts have gained a central position in human communication, without silencing mankind. Before the invention of the printing press there were just handwritten books. Printed books, newspapers, and journals became objects of marketing, as *commodities* for commercial markets, and as readable *works* for markets of literacy. In any case, communication is based on recalling memorized communication. Social memories are kept in books, files, computers, archives, libraries, and museums, to be activated by psychic memories, to accomplish understanding through communication. Collecting the components of human communication in symbolizing modes (words, gestures, pictures, music), spoken and written languages are pivotal for human communication. It is "a marvel of language" to use the Negative (Burke, 1965), and human languages have a built-in self-reference, enabling to communicate about communication (Luhmann, 1992).

Whenever human communication succeeds, sense-making informations are limited by pre-selected themes ("stick to the subject"), and when communication is (more or less) well understood, themes may prompt future communication. In order to read the world better, languages developed metaphors, concepts, images, patterns, attitudes, paradigms, and other communication "simplifiers." Nevertheless, there is no perfect human communication, and therefore, mankind is usually dissatisfied with what is said, heard, or read, usually promising to do better next time (Ronneberger & Rühl, 1992, Chapter 5).

3.2. The Temporal Dimension

In the *temporal dimension* of public relations systems, there is no unique beginning, no big bang, and there is no foreseeable end to public relations. But there is "social" time, measured differently than "natural" time as used by physicists or cosmologists. Ideas, pictures, images, biases, and prejudices are conceptually and theoretically dependent on socio-historic time. When there are attempts to assess public relations in its temporal dimension with data of bibliometric studies to demonstrate both strengths and limitations, it remains unclear how this can be done, perceiving time to be measured "objectively."

"The *temporal dimension* is constituted by the fact that the difference between before and after, which can be immediately experienced in all events, is referred to specific horizons, namely, is extended into the past and the future." In our days, time becomes more and more independent from immediate experiences, "ordered only according to the when and not to the who/what/where/how of experience and action. Time becomes neutral with reference to presence and absence" (Luhmann, 1995: 78–79). Public relations systems are interrelated with different pasts, with different social impacts and different psychic effects. At least, unilateral models assuming a universal public relations are unable to grasp what circular (or spiral) models come closer to: building theories of public relations as re-entering into preserved public relations theories, in order to reconstruct them, to be more helpful, at least for some time.

3.3. The Social Dimension

It is not social action and social behavior but communication that is mankind's most sophisticated achievement: people express themselves and inform meaningfully, in past, present and future. An individual such as Robinson Crusoe is able to scratch himself whenever he has an itch (behavior), and he can plan and build a boat (action). Communication, however, becomes real only in the social system formed by Robinson and Friday, with aspects of English communication cultures of the early eighteenth century, introduced to Friday. "The *social dimension* concerns what one at any time accepts as like oneself, as an 'alter ego', and it articulates the relevance of this assumption for every experience of the world and fixing of meaning" (Luhmann, 1995: 80).

In modern world society, three types of communication systems can be re-constructed: (1) *simple systems*, such as conversations, phone calls, and small talk; (2) *organized social systems*, such as agencies, corporations, associations, supermarkets, political parties, hospitals, newsrooms, and casinos; and (3) *societal systems*, such as politics, economy, religion, science, and education. All these communication systems have a history and they have problems to solve. Though the three types of social systems—simple, organized, and societal— are connected when they compete, co-ordinate, and co-operate, they cannot be reduced to one another. In the social dimension, public relations systems can be identified from the outside as one of *everyday public-persuasion systems* (Ronneberger & Rühl, 1992) and be viewed from the inside as "both a professional practice and a sub-field of communication with its own research and theory base" (Botan & Taylor, 2004: 645).

As a functionally differentiated system of persuasion, public relations incurs social costs: production, distribution, and reception of public relations have to be paid for out of scarce resources. There is *valid money* and *otherwise useful time*, but there are also *public attention, professional work, sense-making information, enforceable themes, stabilizing laws, ethical principles, public trust* and *private confidence*. These public relations resources are in short supply, they are divisible, and payment can be achieved (and obstructed) on many social markets (economic markets included). Social time can be paid for with valid money, but most public relations resources cannot be paid for by money.

4. Public Relations Epistemology

As used by social scientists and philosophers, methodology and epistemology are often indistinguishable. Broadly speaking, the most basic scholarly questions can be raised concerning the pursuit of hypothetical truth. With tested and retested knowledge, public relations scholarship is in stark conflict with un-controlled opinions. For opinions, Gaston Bachelard (1938) used the term *epistemological obstacles*. Choosing opinions as bases for scholarly truth tempts to operate with an inadequate apparatus of cognition and leads to inadequate ways of producing empirical knowledge. As an empirical discipline, scholarly public relations questions have to be tested against scholarly produced data. Whether this can be done adequately with data from survey research or content analysis—that is, with positivistic–behavioral based research techniques—is a matter of debate. Epistemologically, there is no doubt that public relations is one of world society's modern public communication systems: "thus the concept of system refers to something that is in reality a system and thereby incurs the responsibility of testing its statement against reality" (Luhmann, 1995: 12). Epistemological theories reflect the status of "normal" (Kuhn, 1962) public relations theories, questioning in the first place the communication cultural forms of their utterances. Social sciences encompass several disciplines—such as sociology, economics, ethnology, social psychology, and communications—with differing concepts, theorems, models and other structures. Some of them carry familiar titles, even though they may mean something different.

Classical epistemology presupposes single researchers or individual scholars as unique knowing subjects to find out (by introspection) how others act in relation with reality. By traditional epistemological rules, analyzing, modeling, measuring, writing, reading, comparing, and interpreting, the activities of scholars have to be open to tests and scrutiny by competent members of the scholarly community. Many of these traditional epistemological rules are questionable from a modern perspective; however, a discussion is not yet in sight.

By way of illustration, let us have a closer look at an epistemological obstacle in public relations research. In the social sciences, the concept *subject* is based on *epistemological individualism*. As a concept, the subject seems to be a practical one for action and behavior theories, but is impractical for communication–systems research (Rühl, 1997). In the 1960s and 1970s there were two dominant tendencies in the social sciences on both sides of the Atlantic. One focused on special languages of sociology and social psychology to master the essential insights and procedure of social behavior or social action (very seldom of communication), contributing to the knowledge of "the social." The other tendency emphasized scientific research techniques, epistemologically based on critical rationalism, especially on the texts of Karl R. Popper (1959) and Imre Lakatos (1970). For single disciplinary usage, Popper and Lakatos selected examples from natural sciences, not from social sciences.

In contrast, a rather original empirical communication-and-society approach was offered by Harold D. Lasswell (1948) in a classic essay. Lasswell identified three societal functions of communication: (1) surveillance of the environment; (2) correlation of the different parts of society in response to environment; and (3) transmission of the social heritage from one generation to the next. Related groups of specialists carrying out these functions were identified (Lasswell & Kaplan, 1950). Doing *empirical propaganda research*, especially content analysis since the mid-1920s (Lasswell, 1925, 1927), and defining a differentiated societal *public relations function* shortly before the USA entered World War II (Lasswell, 1941: 71–79), this pioneering work with its epistemology of persuasive communication processes has been branded in textbooks as the infamous technical "Lasswell formula."

For decades, the "Lasswell formula" and the "Shannon model"—a one-way engineering source–message–channel–receiver model (Shannon & Weaver, 1949)—have dominated communication textbooks. Shannon's S-M-C-R model of a signal transportation theory was helpful for questions such as "Which kind of channel can bring through the maximum amount of signals?" and "How many signals transmitted will be destroyed by noise under way from transmitter to receiver?" This model can give audio-visual aid for stimulating persuasion effects, but Shannon's usage of the concepts "communication" and

"information" is misleading in communications because of its asemantic motivation: "The semantic aspects of communication are irrelevant to the engineering problem" (Shannon & Weaver, 1949: 28). Signals cannot be transformed
into sense-making information.

During the 1960s and the 1970s, *The Process of Communication* (Berlo,
1960), based on the S-M-C-R model, was the main textbook in North American
university courses in communication studies (Rogers, 1994: 416). *Communication* (Ruesch & Bateson, 1951), based on a semantic, societal, and cultural
epistemology, was less influential. Public relations, entitled *publicity*, was
referred to in a textbook on mass communication (Schramm, 1960). But *Public
Relations Theory* (Botan & Hazleton, 1989) was the first systematic summery
of public relations research tendencies, differentiating types of theory, applied
in combination for solutions of public relations problems.

As to communication systems in public relations theory building, many
misunderstandings remain. Central is an amalgamation of theories of action,
interaction, behavior, media, language, and pictures, usually combined with
teleological, structuralist, Marxist, phenomenological, or historical methods.
When the epistemological differences between these amalgamations are left
unspecified, the different statements seem to mean the same.

As long as public relations research is not going beyond empirical piecemeal
research, it has no systemic conception to help it identify a disciplinary unit.
Public relations scholars doing survey research and content analysis in order
to test specific hypotheses by relating data, cannot verify their concepts. There
are no explanations why the compared experiences qualify as public relations
theories. In view of society's complexity of public relations systems, besides
micro-analytical procedures, meso- and macro-analytical research strategies
refer to something that is in reality a system. Thus the concept of system/
environment gets the responsibility of testing its statements against reality.
Renouncing a system/environment theory with universal public relations
validity raises the question whether the critics are ready to suggest an alternative.
Astonishingly, the unconditional ways in which a "practical" public relations
research uses fashionable terminology, slogans, catchphrases, and jargon—
together with the concept of subject—pretends that they were researchable
concepts.

Scholarly public relations challenges preserved public relations theories in
terms of perspective by incongruity (Burke, 1935). Modern physicists and
cosmologists still dream of a final theory (Hawking, 1988; Weinberg, 1992).
Scholarly public relations cannot afford such dreams when it studies society's
complex public relations systems to solve intricate public relations problems.
"We employ the concept of world as a concept for the *unity of the difference
between system and environment* and use it as an ultimate concept, one free
of further differences" (Luhmann, 1992: 208). If *innovations* are put on the
agenda of public relations researchers, this means planning, designing,
measuring, and evaluating in order to formulate new kinds of questions on
new kinds of public relations problems, in a circular communication process.

Working with scholarly knowledge, pulling together concepts, models, and theories of public relations from psychic and social memories, this is updating scholarly knowledge by retention, selection, variation, and reconstruction.

5. On Methodology of Communications

When sciences and humanities became professions with self-selected tasks to formulate problems hypothetically, they worked on them with methods, solving problems by measuring. A pertinent technique for measuring public relations is not in sight. At textbook level, *methods* are described as instructions or strategic maxims for systematically planned research procedures, aiming for certain goals, tasks, and a certain kind of knowledge. In this understanding, methods are adequate instruments for planned operations to achieve scholarly knowledge.

In the nineteenth century, *measurement* was the method of natural sciences, especially in physics and chemistry as exact sciences. They developed a language of precision, oriented at logics and mathematics, rendering their results in formulas. Measurement in this understanding is a method of checking the results on the basis of exact procedures. However, each method presupposes a theory, with methodological theories adding up to a *methodology*. In this way, methods are the products of methodological research, generalizing the conditions for correct problemizing in various disciplines. But each disciplinary scholarship formulates its own research questions, testing and controlling with their own methods and techniques, self-criticizing its own knowledge.

Scholarly public relations was never a colony for the governance of methodology. Although operating with an amalgamation of basic theories, there is community pressure to answer almost all communication questions with survey research or content analysis. Abraham Kaplan gave to his ironic *Law of the Instrument* the following explanation:

> Give a small boy a hammer, and he will find that everything he encounters needs pounding. It comes as no particular surprise to discover that a scientist formulates problems in a way which requires for their solution just those techniques in which he himself is especially skilled.
>
> (Kaplan, 1964: 28)

Dominating communication models are reduced to a few variables, representing a kind of minimum requirement for human communication. What is missing is the semantic dimension, the sense-making of information. Without paying attention to making sense, communication metaphors, patterns, examples, images, and other types of simplifying communication remain unclear, when it is said that communication has "content" while the semantics of its factual, temporal, and social dimensions are not discussed.

Before testing communication problems through data collection, we should advocate more transparency of the concepts and theories that we use. It is proposed that scholarly public relations texts should be tested, breaking-up terminological, epistemological, and methodological structures, differenti-ating researchable from non-researchable ones before using them for data aggregation.

Yet, many questions are left open. How do we differentiate between public relations, advertisement, propaganda, and journalism? Do the suggested system/ environment theory, communication system theory, and societal system theory provide adequate groundwork for scholarly public relations, when differentiated from action systems, behavioral systems, or media systems? Is scholarly public relations research prepared to interrelate problems of producing and receiving public relations in specific relations to publics, freedom of communication, public moods, or public opinions? In what respect is scholarly public relations a social science?

At the turn to the twentieth century in Europe and North America, scholars such as Emile Durkheim, Albert Schäffle, Charles H. Cooley, Max Weber, Georg Simmel, George Herbert Mead, Robert Ezra Park, and Karl Bücher formed a social science community, founding what became communications as a scholarly discipline. At the same time, a growing epistemological and methodo-logical discontent can be observed. Causality as basic category, operating with the means/ends schema, was considered insufficient for the new challenges of world's growing complexity (Sachsse, 1987). In the twentieth century, system rationality, cybernetics, and communications enforced *discursive knowledge*, mirroring certain aspects of reality, and discussing *relational knowledge* with *functional thinking* (Cassirer, 2003). When *second-order cybernetics* (von Foerster, 1982) and *Autopoiesis* (Maturana, 1981) developed as a theory to account for self-replicating operations, they used their own output as input. Niklas Luhmann (1995) adapted autopoiesis to the "social" to model the realms of various forms of human communication in society. He describes social systems such that it meets the conditions of autopoietic closure, proposing to think of social systems as *communication systems*, co-operating with the external mode of *consciousness* of psychic systems and the mode of *life* of organic systems. Life and consciousness are indispensable for communication, but they cannot be transformed into communication.

With communication as the most sophisticated human ability to express one-self, communication is an emergent reality, a unique state of affairs. To signify communication *in prudentia* there are strict limitations on the correct use of this potential for actualizing what is not an actual fact. Luhmann (1995: 46) elaborates on communication qualifications with the help of a fable:

> The hedgehog and his mate, in their fake race with the hare, showing up in alternation at the turning points instead of actually running, possess, as a social system, *prudentia* in comparison with the hare: they can communicate quickly in a very selective way, while the hare can merely run quickly.

Communication, not action, deserves scholarly public relations attention, not as an act, but as communication connectivity.

6. Conclusion

Nowadays, when dealing with methodological theory, almost automatically the question arises, "Of what use is it in practice?" The questions connected are leading to problems of operations in scholarly public relations, traditionally called *objectivity, facts or fiction, subject's pure reasoning*, and the like. The question of public relations' usefulness is not a scholarly question. As pointed out, it is world society's public relations system that is in need of an epistemological and methodological discussion for teaching and research, something that only scholars are qualified for and willing to do.

References

Anderson, James A. (1996). *Communication theory: Epistemological foundations*. New York, London: Guilford.

Ashby, W. Ross (1956). *An introduction to cybernetics*. New York: Wiley & Sons.

Avenarius, Horst (1998). *Die ethischen Normen der Public Relations: Kodizes, Richtlinien, freiwillige Selbstkontrolle (Ethical norms of public relations: Codes, guidelines, voluntary self-control)*. Neuwied, Kriftel: Luchterhand.

Avenarius, Horst, & Armbrecht, Wolfgang (Eds.) (1992). *Ist Public Relations eine Wissenschaft? Eine Einführung (Is public relations a science? An introduction)*. Opladen: Westdeutscher Verlag.

Bachelard, Gaston (1938). *La formation de l'esprit scientifique. Contribution à une psychoanalyse de la connaissance objective (The formation of the scholarly mind. Contribution to a psychoanalysis of objective cognition)*. Paris: Vrin.

Berlo, David K. (1960). *Process of communication. An introduction to theory and practice*. New York, Chicago: Holt, Rinehart & Winston.

Bernal, John Desmond (1939). *The social function of science*. London: Routledge.

Botan, Carl H., & Hazleton, Vincent (Eds.) (1989). *Public relations theory*. Hillsdale, NJ, Hove and London: Erlbaum.

Botan, Carl H., & Taylor, Maureen (2004). Public relations: State of the field. *Journal of Communication, 54*, 645–661.

Burke, Kenneth (1965). *Permanence and change. An anatomy of purpose*. With an introduction by Hugh Dalziel Duncan (2nd ed.). Indianapolis, New York: Bobbs-Merill.

Burke, Kenneth (1966). A dramatistic view of the origins of language and postscripts on the negative. In Kenneth Burke (Ed.), *Language as symbolic action. Essays on life, literature, and method* (pp. 419–436). Berkeley, Los Angeles: California University Press.

Cassirer, Ernst (2003). *Substance and function: And Einstein's Theory of Relativity*. Translation by William Curtis Swabey and Marie Collins Swabey. Mineola, NY: Dover Publications.

Foerster, Heinz von (1987). *Observing systems* (2nd ed.). Salinas: Intersystems.

Goffman, Erving (1959). *The presentation of self in everyday life*. Garden City, NY: Doubleday.

Hawking, Stephen W. (1988). *A brief history of time: From the Big Bang to Black Holes*. New York: Bantam.

Holmström, Susanne (1996). *An intersubjective and social system's public relations paradigm. Public relations interpreted from systems theory (Niklas Luhmann) in opposition to the critical tradition (Jürgen Habermas)*. Dissertation, University of Roskilde, Denmark.

Kaplan, Abraham (1964). *The conduct of inquiry. Methodology for behavioral science*. Scranton, PA: Chandler.

Kohring, Matthias (2004). *Vertrauen in Journalismus. Theorie und Empirie* (*Trust in journalism. Theory and empirical knowledge*). Konstanz: UVK.

Kuhn, Thomas S. (1962). *The structure of scientific revolutions*. Chicago, London: Chicago University Press.

Lakatos, Imre (1970). Falsification and the methodology of scientific research. In Imre Lakatos & Alan Musgrave (Eds.), *Criticism and the growth of knowledge* (pp. 91–196). Cambridge, England: Cambridge University Press.

Lasswell, Harold D. (1925). Prussian schoolbooks and international amity. *Journal of Social Forces*, 3, 718–722.

Lasswell, Harold D. (1927). *Propaganda technique in the World War*. London, New York: Kegan Paul, Trench, Trubner. Ph.D. dissertation, University of Chicago, 1926.

Lasswell, Harold D. (1941). *Democracy through public opinion*. Menasha, WI: Banta.

Lasswell, Harold D. (1948). The structure and function of communication in society. In Lyman Bryson (Ed.), *The communication of ideas: A series of addresses* (pp. 37–51). New York: Cooper Square.

Lasswell, Harold D., & Kaplan, Abraham (1950). *Power and aociety. A framework for political inquiry*. New Haven, CT, London: Yale University Press.

Luhmann, Niklas (1992). Autopoiesis. What is communication? *Communication Theory*, 2, 251–259.

Luhmann, Niklas (1995). *Social systems*. Translated by John Bednarz, Jr., with Dirk Baecker. Foreword by Eva M. Knodt. Stanford: California University Press.

Luhmann, Niklas (1997). *Die Gesellschaft der Gesellschaft* (*Society of society*) (2 vols.). Frankfurt am Main: Suhrkamp.

Maturana, Humberto R. (1981). Autopoiesis. In Milan Zeleny (Ed.), *Autopoiesis. A theory of living organization* (pp. 21–33). New York, Oxford, England: Oxford University Press.

Merton, Robert K. (1957a). *Social theory and social structure* (1938) (2nd reviewed ed.). Glencoe: Free Press.

Merton, Robert K. (1957b). Science and the social order (1942). In *Social theory and social structure* (pp. 537–549) (2nd reviewed ed.). Glencoe: Free Press.

Ossowska, Maria, & Ossowski, Stanislaw (1936/1966). The science of science. *Organon 1936*, 1, 1–12.

Popper, Karl R. (1959). *The logic of scientific discovery*. London: Hutchinson.

Rogers, Everett M. (1994). *A history of communication study. A biographical approach*. New York: Free Press; Oxford, England, Singapore, Sidney: Maxwell Macmillan.

Ronneberger, Franz, & Rühl, Manfred (1992). *Theorie der Public Relations: Ein Entwurf* (*A theory of public relations: A design*). Opladen: Westdeutscher Verlag.

Ruesch, Jurgen and Bateson, Gregory (1951). *Communication. The social matrix of psychiatry*. New York: Norton.

Rühl, Manfred (1972). *Zur Professionalisierung von Berufskommunikatoren* (*On professionalizing communicators*) (= Forschungsbericht 28 des DFG-Sonderforschungsbereichs 22 "Sozialisations- und Kommunikationsforschung" (Research Report No. 28, DFG funded Collaborative Research Center 22 "Socialisation and Communication Research"), Universität Erlangen-Nürnberg, Sozialwissenschaftliches Forschungszentrum.

Rühl, Manfred (1980). *Journalismus und Gesellschaft. Bestandsaufnahme und Theorieentwurf (Journalism and society. Stocktaking and theoretical design)*. Mainz: v. Hase und Koehler.

Rühl, Manfred (1986). Das Selbstbild der Architekten. Eine Untersuchung von Image-Faktoren im Prozeß des Image-Wandels (The image of the architects. A study on image factors in the process of the image change). In Mitarbeit von Kurt R. Hesse & Klaus Zeller, *Analysen und synthesen* (Vol. 1). Bamberg: Forschungsstelle für Kommunikationspolitik.

Rühl, Manfred (1994). Europäische Public Relations. Rationalität, Normativität und Faktizität (European public relations: Rationality, normativity and factuality). In Wolfgang Armbrecht & Ulf Zabel (Eds.), *Normative Aspekte der Public Relations. Grundlagen und Perspektiven. Eine Einführung (Normative aspects of public relations. Bases and perspectives. An introduction)* (pp. 171–194). Opladen: Westdeutscher Verlag.

Rühl, Manfred (1997). Braucht die kommunikationswissenschaftliche Publizistikforschung das un-praktische Subjekt? (Does communications' research need the impractical subject?). In Heinz Bonfadelli & Jürg Rathgeb (Eds.), *Publizistikwissenschaftliche Basistheorien und ihre Praxistauglichkeit (Public communications' basic theories and their suitability in practice)* (= Diskussionspunkt 33) (pp. 25–40). Zürich: Seminar für Publizistikwissenschaft.

Rühl, Manfred (2005). Vertrauen-kommunikationswissenschaftlich beobachtet (Observing trust from a communications perspective). In Beatrice Dernbach & Michael Meyer (Eds.), *Vertrauen und Glaubwürdigkeit. Interdisziplinäre Perspektiven (Trust and credibility. Interdisciplinary perspectives)* (pp. 121–134). Wiesbaden: VS Verlag für Sozialwissenschaften.

Rühl, Manfred (forthcoming) *Kommunikationskultur und Weltgesellschaft (Communication cultures and world society)*. Wiesbaden: VS Verlag für Sozialwissenschaften.

Sachsse, Hans (1987). *Kausalität–Gesetzlichkeit–Wahrscheinlichkeit: Die Geschichte von Grundkategorien zur Auseinandersetzung des Menschen mit der Welt (Causality, conformity to (natural) law, probability: The story of basic categories for the discussion of Man with the World)* (2nd ed.). Darmstadt: Wissenschaftliche Buchgesellschaft.

Schramm, Wilbur (Hrsg.) (1960). *Mass communications*. Urbana: University of Illinois Press.

Shannon, Claude E. and Weaver, Warren (1949). *The mathematical theory of vommunication*. Urbana, Chicago, London: University of Illinois Press.

Weinberg, Steven (1992). *Dreams of a final theory*. New York: Pantheon Books.

Zedtwitz-Arnim, Graf Georg Volkmar (1981). *Tu Gutes und rede darüber. Public Relations für die Wirtschaft (Act properly and talk about it. Public relations for the economy)*. München: Heyne.

3 The Nature of Scholarly Endeavors in Public Relations

Alenka Jelen

1. Introduction

Public relations as a scientific discipline appears to have a somewhat inferior status compared to other well-established disciplines in the social sciences arena. One possible explanation is that public relations has only recently become a distinct scholarly discipline with growing research and a body literature of its own (Sallot, Lyon, Acosta-Alzuru, & Jones, 2003; Synnott & McKie, 1997). In the 1980s, public relations was considered a professional field that could base its theoretical assumptions on research developed in and for other social sciences, including sociology, psychology, and anthropology, as well as more recent disciplines such as communication and media studies, journalism, political science, and management (Dozier & Lauzen, 2000; L'Etang & Pieczka, 1996). Thus, scientific research and theory development dealing primarily and specifically with public relations phenomena were not widely believed to be worthy of scholarly investigation (Pavlik, 1987), but public relations practice quickly professionalized and the first public relations academic journals were established as well as the first comprehensive study on public relations profession—Grunig's *Excellence* study. This clearly indicated that public relations was becoming an applied social science, with an increasing demand for satisfactory theory development (Sallot *et al.*, 2003).

The demands for theory, as well as other problems such as the discipline's legitimacy and credibility, blurred definitions, boundaries and purpose, and questions of appropriate methodology and epistemology are common for every scientific discipline at the earliest stages of its development (L'Etang, 1996). A great deal of public relations scientific debate has dealt with defining and redefining the field, setting the boundaries, and searching for its purpose (Pasadeos & Renfro, 1992; Verčič, van Ruler, Buetschi, & Flodin, 2001), whereas the critical examinations of scholarly endeavors in terms of methodology and epistemology, though the subject of sparkling and extensive debate in other respected disciplines, surface only occasionally in public relations (Cutler, 2004; L'Etang & Pieczka, 1996). Closer examination of the public relations literature showed that only two significant empirical studies have dealt explicitly with the nature of public relations theory and research development within the past five years; Sallot *et al.*'s (2003) content analysis of academic articles investigating the status of theory building by public relations scholars and Cutler's (2004) analysis of the methodological advantages and shortcomings of case studies. Both studies confirm Pasadeos and Renfro's (1992) assumption that empirical studies that examine whether there is enough appropriate scientific research to warrant the respectable and credible social science status for public relations are needed—yet absent—in the field. The authors also propose that such empirical studies may stimulate the public relations scientific field and encourage it to develop greater topical and methodological diversity.

Using Pasadeos and Renfro's as well as Cutler's and Sallot *et al.*'s recommendations, in this chapter we give a general picture of the nature of current public relations research in terms of the scientific public relations agenda and the ways this agenda is being studied scientifically. But first, in section 2, we introduce some underlying assumptions and define key terms in order to clarify the discussion. Next, the literature on scientific features of public relations is reviewed, particularly with respect to the scope of the topical agenda and the scientific tools used to explore it. Methodology briefly introduces the pragmatic grounded theory approach used in the study underpinning this chapter; it is followed by a presentation of empirical results and their link to the theoretical aspects dealt with in section 5. The most significant findings of the study are summarized in the conclusion; briefly, they suggest that public relations researchers should expand their topical and methodological horizons so that they would discover the forest in all its richness and complexity, rather than seeing just the trees.

2. Explicating Assumptions and Defining Concepts

2.1. Basic Assumptions

Our basic assumption here is that public relations is not just a professional field but also an applied social science. We also assume that scientific public relations needs a theory to advise practice, to advance academia, and to survive as an independent discipline (Pavlik, 1987; van Ruler, Verčič, Buetschi, & Flodin, 2004). To develop theories, public relations needs a paradigm focus, otherwise "there may be such activity we call 'research in public relations' but there will not be much theory development" (Ferguson, 1984: 7). We believe that the focus of public relations research is studying phenomena associated with various aspects of building and maintaining mutually beneficial "public" relationships between organizations or social institutions and their publics (L. Grunig, J. Grunig, & Dozier, 2002; Ferguson, 1984; Heath, 2001; Ledingham, 2003; Pavlik, 1987; Sallot *et al.*, 2003; van Ruler *et al.*, 2004). While studying these phenomena, public relations needs to adopt the practices of scientific research, mainly because the theory and the body of knowledge need to be empirically supported by research and involve generalizations taken from empirical evidence (Ledingham, 2003; Pavlik, 1987; Sallot *et al.*, 2003). Following from these assumptions, theory building and scientific research represent the basic elements of the public relations scientific discipline. For this reason, they are defined, classified, and explained in a way that is understood throughout the chapter below.

2.2. Defining Theory and Scientific Research in Public Relations

"Theory" can be understood in several ways; it is beyond the scope of this chapter to do more than briefly explain how "theory" as a concept is usually understood in the public relations academic community. In their study, Sallot *et al.* (2003) state that theory in public relations has typically been thought to "comprise a body of scientific generalizations describing functional relationships among empirically measured or inferred variables" (p. 29). Theory in public relations as such should not be understood merely as an explanation of public relations phenomena, but rather as a system of thought based on research findings that describe, explain, and promote understanding, prediction, and control of phenomena (Ferguson, 1984; Littlejohn & Foss, 2005). It is these elements that separate theory from a model—models illustrate the "interrelationships among the parts of the modelled process" (Ledingham, 2003). It is also important to distinguish between working theories underpinned by "know-how knowledge" items, concerned with specific concepts limited in generalizability, and scientific theories with more abstract, "know-why knowledge" items that can be applied to various contexts and situations (van Ruler *et al.*, 2004). In addition, public relations needs not only working and scientific theories, but also a general or leading theory that "unifies a discipline, providing an umbrella framework for exploring issues within that discipline" (Ledingham, 2003: 192). A leading theory—currently absent in the field—would be of great importance, not merely because it would represent the foundation of the discipline and its credibility, but also because it would have a heuristic function that focuses the research agenda and guides further studies to systematically fill the gaps in the body of knowledge (Littlejohn & Foss, 2005; Moss, Macmanus, & Verčič, 2003). The public relations body of knowledge, on the other hand, is defined as an outline that identifies and codifies the existing body of public relations' technical and scientific literature to enable its fuller use and affirmation; it also serves as a strong basis for theory building (Littlejohn & Foss, 2005; McElreath & Blamphin, 1994; McKie, 2001; Verčič, 2000).

If theory and knowledge are not to be merely anecdotal and limited in generalizability, they need to base their assumptions on data obtained by scientific research, which should, as "an empirical study involving systematic collection and interpretation of data with the basic purpose to increase understanding" (Pavlik, 1987: 16), lie at the heart of any scientific discipline. Pavlik suggested that there are three ideal types of research in public relations: basic, applied, and introspective. More recently, Karlberg (1996) divided research into two categories; practitioner research, which resembles Pavlik's applied research, and scientific research, which is similar to Pavlik's notion of basic research. Pavlik's introspective research—which looks at the profession and the discipline itself by investigating the public relations profession, education, history, the scholarly research, and other elements that underpin the public relations field—can fall in each of the two categories, but usually finds itself in the scientific domain. Here we adopt Karlberg's distinction, as it seems that more recently public relations has evolved into two sometimes overlapping, sometimes conflicting branches: the applied branch, with well-established applied research, and the theory-based branch, underlined by a strong scientific research tradition (see also Ledingham & Bruning, 2000; Sallot *et al.*, 2003). Applied research is designed to solve specific practical strategic and planning problems and is explicitly wed to the self-interests of its sponsoring clients. In contrast, scientific research is, at least in principle, publicly sponsored and assumed to serve the broadest public interest. Being concerned with under-standing concepts, phenomena, and the practice of public relations, scientific research is devoted to theory building, contributing to the body of knowledge. In our discussion we also make use of Karlberg's definitions of instrumental and critical scientific research:

> Instrumental research refers to pragmatic research conducted under the premise that theories are instruments that function as guides to practice, with their validity determined by the efficacy of those practices. Instru-mental public relations research, therefore, is concerned with the micro-level questions and techniques; the "how-to" of public relations. In contrast, critical research is concerned with theorising, or critiquing, the broader social, political, and economic implications of public relations practices. It is concerned with the macro-level effects of public relations in contem-porary society.
>
> (Karlberg, 1996: 264)

In this way, instrumental research represents the groundwork for working theories, whereas critical research has the potential to develop scientific theories. We now turn to the examination of the literature on scientific public relations.

3. Review of the Literature on the Nature of Scientific Public Relations

While some quite introspective empirical studies were conducted in the 1990s on the nature of public relations scientific discipline (McElreath & Blamphin, 1994: Morton & Lin, 1995; Pasadeos & Renfro, 1992; Pasadeos, Renfro, & Hanily, 1999; Synnot & McKie, 1997), there have hardly been any empirical studies explicitly dealing with recent research in the discipline, except for those mentioned earlier, namely, Sallot *et al.*'s (2003) and Cutler's (2004) studies. Apart from this low number of relevant studies, all the works listed here tend to focus on North American public relations scholarship, which makes it some-what difficult to draw consistent assumptions regarding research in public relations from the existing literature. However, there are some studies that indirectly address the discipline's development and critically evaluate research (Dozier & Lauzen, 2000; Holtzhausen, 2000, 2002; Karlberg, 1996; L'Etang & Pieczka, 1996; van Ruler *et al.*, 2004).

Many of the authors mentioned here agree that PR scholars have recently made tremendous progress in establishing a more academic and research-oriented approach to public relations, though the discipline still appears to suffer from low respect and credibility in the eyes of other disciplines. Perhaps the clearest illustration of this is made in Morton and Lin's (1995) content and citation analyses of academic articles, in which they conclude that public relations is "a discipline that is little cited by other disciplines." Pasadeos *et al.* (1999) attribute this low citation index to the discipline's youth; Ledingham (2003) believes the lack of respect is due to the absence of a leading public relations theory that would be rooted in solid empirical basis. Van Ruler *et al.* (2004) suggest that this basis currently looks like jelly, being "impressive on the face of it, but lacking substance" (p. 56) mostly due to a lack of (good) research and a properly defined research agenda. To improve that, public relations scholars need to expand their relatively insular topical and methodological horizons (Dozier & Lauzen, 2000; Karlberg, 1996; McElreath & Blamphin, 1994; Pasadeos *et al.*, 1999).

3.1. Insular Topical Agenda in Public Relations

In a bibliometric study of the public relations scholarly literature, Pasadeos *et al.* (1999) note, "unlike other disciplines, public relations is typified by concentration of topics" (p. 29). Similarly, van Ruler *et al.* (2004), Spicer (2000), and Holtzhausen (2000) note that, given the variety of intellectual perspectives in public relations (managerial perspective, relational perspective, psychological perspective, etc.), the topics studied greatly repeat themselves in public relations literature, reproducing rather than producing knowledge. The literature is to a large extent concerned with describing and debating the public relations practice, accumulating a large body of "know-how" knowledge and working theories (Dozier & Lauzen, 2000; Holtzhausen, 2002; Pasadeos & Renfro, 1992; Pasadeos *et al.*, 1999; Sallot *et al.*, 2003; Synnott & McKie, 1997), whereas researchers devoted far less energy to exploring "the wider social implications of public relations activity" and "understanding its role in contemporary society" (Karlberg, 1996: 264). Even though the professional orientation of scholarly work is common and beneficial for young academic disciplines that strive to prove their legitimacy and importance, L'Etang and Pieczka (1996) suggest that the practice's interference with the academic research agenda is a potential threat to academic freedom and might result in the loss of academic credibility. In addition, Dozier and Lauzen (2000) argue that "these linkages to the profession tend to foster a certain intellectual myopia, a systemic near-sightedness regarding alternative perspectives" (p. 7), mostly because a "public relations practitioner is inadequately trained and ill situated to prescribe the scholarly agenda in the intellectual domain of public relations" (p. 20). Consequently, "public relations as a mature intellectual domain requires a conscious uncoupling of the intellectual agenda from the day-to-day thoughts, actions, and preoccupations of practitioners" (p. 4). Nevertheless, it appears that research remains focused on the public relations profession and is, moreover, almost exclusively devoted to the ways of conceptualizing and facilitating (excellent) communication management anchored in North American practice and academia (Holtzhausen, 2002; Verčič *et al.*, 2001).

3.2. Scholarly Preoccupation with Management Function and the Excellence *Study*

Even a cursory examination of public relations' scholarly journals shows the considerable fascination with producing more sophisticated knowledge to understand strategic managing of public relations within organizations (Holtzhausen, 2002; Karlberg, 1996; McElreath & Blamphin, 1994; Sallot *et al.*, 2003). The preoccupation with public relations as strategic communication management with measurable outcomes is understandable. Management topics appear to be of a high value for other disciplines. Management studies are cited significantly more often by non-public relations scholars than studies dealing with other aspects of public relations (Morton & Lin, 1995), which indicates that "jumping on the management bandwagon was clearly a political move to achieve higher status and credibility, rather than an intellectual decision" (L'Etang, 2004: 219). In terms of more pragmatic reasons, Dozier and Lauzen (2000) argue that the financial and symbolic power of the industry "influences the research questions that public relations scholars ask, the theories they build, the methods they use, and ultimately, the interests they serve" (p. 6). This great symbolic and financial dependence on practice results in public relations scholars acting as if they must only address the problems of public relations profession within organizational settings (McKie, 2001).

The nature of the public relations profession and its contributions to the goals of the organization was also the focus of the fifteen-year *Excellence* study, the most comprehensive study ever undertaken of the communication profession, from 1985 (L. Grunig *et al.*, 2002). For various reasons the study still has a prominent position in the field. First of all, by concentrating on public relations as a management function the *Excellence* study has possibly made the biggest contribution in establishing public relations as a serious field of study (Holtzhausen, 2002). Second, it introduced a longitudinal research-based approach to studying public relations phenomena by applying scientific methods developed in other social sciences. In addition, on the basis of solid empirical groundwork, it developed credible theories on, or, some would argue, models of (Dozier & Lauzen, 2000; Karlberg, 1996; Ledingham, 2003) public relations roles, two-way communication, symmetrical communication, gender and communication, integration of communication activities, and internal communications (L. Grunig *et al.*, 2002). As a result, dealing with, expanding, and testing the excellence concepts within increasingly diverse settings has greatly reshaped the research agenda and focused scholarly endeavors all over the world on selected issues, data, and explanations, but probably to the exclusion of others (Dozier & Lauzen, 2000; Holtzhausen, 2002). In other words, the study that had made the discipline worthy of scholarly endeavors started representing an obstacle to unrestrained scientific development in the field (Karlberg, 1996). On the one hand, the fixation of the topical agenda on one standard model that would apply to various situations has a great tendency to lead to a static scientific field (Littlejohn & Foss, 2005); on the other hand, by concentrating on the United States practice, the *Excellence* study discourages the examination of the public relations profession elsewhere and, to some extent, hinders geographical diversity in the field.

3.3. Dominance of North American Scholarship

North American scholarship has until recently had an agenda-setting effect on public relations research all over the world (Moss *et al.*, 2003; Verčič, 2000), not only because of the *Excellence* study, but also because the intellectual and practical aspects of public relations in general started developing and expanding rapidly in the United States. At the end of the twentieth century, the major textbooks and the two most prominent public relations journals—*Public Relations Review* and *Journal of Public Relations Research*, which seldom publish non-American scholarship—originated in the United States (L'Etang & Pieczka, 1996; van Ruler *et al.*, 2004). In addition, the PRSA (Public Relations Society of America) body of knowledge, initially published in 1988 with updates in the early 1990s, commands a prominent position in the field, yet contains little, if any, references to work conducted outside the United States. A European public relations body of knowledge, mandated by EUPRERA (European Public Relations Education and Research Association), though gaining in importance, lacks solid structure and coherence. This prevents it from receiving due recognition (Moss *et al.*, 2003; van Ruler *et al.*, 2004). Besides, it represents just one of the many alternative bodies of knowledge needed to counter-balance North American scholarship. Consequently, the majority of public relations research continues to be based largely on models and theoretical frameworks developed for and in the United States (Moss *et al.*, 2003), including the large proportion of the theoretical framework outlined in this chapter. As emphasized by Verčič *et al.* (2001), "as long as U.S. practice and U.S. theory are the sole sources of conceptual work in the field, public relations will be short of global inclusiveness and the validity it needs to become a true academic discipline and profession" (p. 377). Combined with the professional orientation and narrow definition of public relations as (excellent) organizational communication management, this prevalence of North American perspectives causes topical insularity that prevents public relations from progressing toward a coherent and solid body of knowledge.

4. Scientific Public Relations Research

If there has not been much work on epistemological and agenda-building issues in the recent literature, there has been even less research, discussion, or reflection on the methodological advantages and shortcomings of research published in the field. Cutler (2004) observes, "a survey of indexes for the two main journals, *Public Relations Review* and *Journal of Public Relations Research*, found no articles that specifically addressed methodological issues in public relations research" (p. 366). This critical examination of methodological trends would be of great importance, mainly because a large volume of respectable published research is assumed to warrant a respectable and credible stature of scientific discipline (Cutler, 2004; L'Etang & Piezcka, 1996; Pasadeos & Renfro, 1992). Public relations research appears to be lacking in both volume and respectability since philosophical discussions tend to dominate the field and the "bulk of research is applied descriptive research with limited generalisability" (McElreath & Blamphin, 1994: 70). Of the three goals—to describe areas of interest, to explain cause–effect relationships, and to predict future situations and conditions (Pavlik, 1987)—scientific public relations research has paid most of its attention to the first one. This is a bit problematic, since descriptive studies tend to simplify and summarize observed phenomena and can be used only marginally as a solid ground for theory development.

4.1. Quantitative vs. Qualitative Research Traditions

In addition to being descriptive, public relations research is dominated by a short-term quantitative tradition (Cutler, 2004; McElreath & Blamphin, 1994; McKie, 2001; Morton & Lin, 1995; Rühl, 2005). The prominence of such a tradition is understandable because of the discipline's practical orientation—which demands "immediate" results—and greater respect for "old scientific" quantitative research approaches in the academic community (McKie, 2001; Pavlik, 1987). Morton and Lin (1995) observe that public relations academic articles using quantitative research are cited significantly more often than those using qualitative approaches. Holtzhausen (2002) further suggests that because public relations researchers and theorists are desperate to prove that public relations is a discipline to be taken seriously, they focus much of their research on quantitative analyses. The recent insight, well established in psychological and management literature, that not everything that counts can be counted and not everything that can be counted, counts, seems to go unnoticed in public relations. McElreath and Blamphin and McKie observe that, with few exceptions, public relations scholars have yet to come to grips with the shift in research paradigms from the tradition of logical positivism and value-free, neutral scientific observations to the new ideas of phenomenological deconstructionism and deliberately value-added participant observations (see also Holtzhausen, 2000). This is to say that the humanistic and yet unpredictable public relations field needs to move toward more interpretative approaches, or even more to the cross-validation of findings through triangulation of methods. Such a methodological shift would help to answer "why" as well as "what" questions and demonstrate a higher validity and reliability of research findings.

4.2. Methodological Insularity and Related Concerns

The prevalence of the quantitative tradition is also apparent at the level of methods used to study public relations phenomena. Pavlik (1987) and Rühl (2005) suggest that some public relations scholars tend to give the impression that all research questions require survey or content analysis. In contrast, Cutler (2004) observes that case studies are used in up to a third of the published articles in the public relations literature and, thus, have a prominent position in the field. This commitment to a particular methodology denies public relations the opportunity to explore its boundaries and "develop analyses which can allow it to both draw on, and make contributions to, the vast area of human endeavors studied by the social sciences" (Hazelton & Botan, 1989: 14). Additional concerns are the applicability of the case-study method in public relations as case studies tend to be understood as anecdotal narratives, usually ending as moral rather than methodologically rigorous analyses requiring triangulation and an explanation of the methodologies implemented (Cutler, 2004; L. Grunig *et al.*, 2002; L'Etang & Piczka, 1996).

The scholarly misunderstandings and sketchiness of social scientific methods seem to go beyond the case-study method. Cutler (2004) observes, "understanding and application of appropriate methodology is a major issue for public relations researchers" (p. 372). Researchers frequently fall short of rigorously evaluating their research practices, considering their methods with care, trying to avoid methodological failures or using suitable tools of inquiry well established in other social sciences. An additional consideration is the non-transparency of the methods and methodological procedures used; most of the published research fails to "properly describe the data gathering method, thereby rendering it impossible to build on, or replicate the research" (Cutler, 2004: 373), which is of special importance in qualitative research. The non-transparent, sketchy, as well as insular application of methods "reduces the field's conceptual resources, and reinforces low academic and intellectual status" (McKie, 2001: 75). In other words, it seems that through greater understanding of methodological issues and the appropriate, transparent application of multiple methods, public relations research can obtain more extensive and more solid empirical ground needed for credible theory development (Holtzhausen, 2000).

4.3. Limited Amount of Resources in the Field

Topical and methodological diversity in scientific public relations are, to some extent at least, hindered by a problem that, with few exceptions, is overlooked in the literature, namely, the lack of resources in scientific public relations.

L'Etang and Pieczka (1996) quite critically question whether public relations scholars have sufficient financial support to tackle doctoral and postdoctoral research since very few universities are actually carrying out research into public relations (see also Pavlik, 1987; van Ruler *et al.,* 2004); they also note that in this respect "it seems little thought is given to academic development and the future of the discipline" (p. 6). Cutler (2004) also briefly touches on the subject by stating "a greater amount of resources could yield far greater results than is evident at present" (p. 371). Since the funding for scientific research largely comes from the industry, more advanced collaboration between academia and the profession is vital for public relations science to prosper and develop (Dozier & Lauzen, 2000; Koper, 2005). Higher investments would probably attract more researchers and postgraduate students to the field and increase the amount of critical, not merely instrumental, research, which in turn would probably lead to the expansion of topical and methodological horizons. With an improved and expanded scientific empirical database, public relations might facilitate the growth of scientific theories in the body of knowledge and perhaps obtain greater respect and credibility in the social sciences arena. Moreover, following the logic of a "magic circle," greater respect might result in greater investment into the discipline coming from the industry as well as from society.

4.4. Implications of (Insular) Research

Campbell, Daft, and Hulin identify two informal epistemologies in social science:

> One could describe the process of knowledge accumulation as if a large number of researchers were throwing mud at a wall. The mud that sticks to the wall is knowledge and should be retained. That which falls off is indeed mud and should be discarded. This theory of knowledge accumulation suggests that the more individuals there are throwing different kinds of mud, the more likely it is that some of them will throw something that sticks. A contrasting approach suggests that knowledge accumulates by means of individuals carefully mapping out areas likely to yield information: prospecting through rubble and dirt to find the ore-bearing rock.
>
> (as cited in Ferguson, 1984: 5)

Drawing on the assumptions stated above, it appears that public relations researchers are still throwing mud at the wall. With a gradually increasing amount of—mostly descriptive—research that lacks a degree of careful and systematic considerations of the topical agenda and applied methodology, public relations has managed to answer questions with "mud that stuck to the wall" concerning excellent public relations practice, its role in the organizational settings and has filled many gaps in the North American-biased body of knowledge. The field as such appears to have a pretty good idea about the many "trees" (the nature and characteristics of profession and its place within organizational setting), but falls short in seeing the multitude and complexity of the "forest" (understanding the sociological premises of public relations, its role and implications for the society at large). To see and understand the "forest," more research is needed that would employ the full array of methodologies when studying public relations phenomena within and outside the "resource-rich" organizational arena (Dozier & Lauzen, 2000; L'Etang & Pieczka, 1996; Rühl, 2005). Even though Morton and Lin (1995) suggest that quantitative research and articles on managerial topics should suffice for public relations to warrant an applied social science status, other authors (almost urgently) call for the expansion of topical and methodological horizons (Holtzhausen, 2002; Pasadeos & Renfro, 1992; Pasadeos *et al.*, 1999; Sallot *et al.*, 2003). It appears that topical and methodological diversity offer an opportunity to establish a more coherent body of knowledge and perhaps a unifying theory, the absence of which currently brings the public relations discipline to a greater level of uncertainty, renders it irrelevant within the academic community, and lessens its respect and credibility in the eyes of other disciplines.

4.5. Empirical Analysis of Scholarly Endeavors

The research on which this chapter is based was steered by the general research question "What is the nature of recent public relations scholarly endeavors in contributing to the body of knowledge?" Given the lack of introspective studies dealing with public relations academia, the scarcity of research examining public relations scholarship, and the limitations in drawing hypotheses for the study from material written for other purposes, a pragmatic explorative approach was deemed the most appropriate. Within this approach, primary research employed in-depth semi-structured interviews with twelve public relations scholars conducted at the 12th International Public Relations Symposium BledCom 2005 and at British universities. The scholars were deliberately selected according to their reputed acquaintance with the nature of the public relations discipline and their symbolic representation of different geographical areas. Besides serving as a principal means of gathering in-depth information on scholarly experience and perceptions of the recent scientific work, the interviews were designed to be essentially heuristic and served as an exploratory device to identify significant trends, which in turn were further investigated in a content analysis of academic articles published in *Journal of Communication Management, Journal of Public Relations Research*, and *Public Relations Review* since 2001. These three journals are assumed to be representative of the focus of (English) public relations scholarship. A cursory content analysis of thirty (ten from each journal) randomly selected articles identified relevant referential units, and counted their occurrence in articles. However, it is worth noting that the data obtained needs to be carefully considered due to the biased nature of the interviews and small-scale content-analysis research. If the interview and/or circumstances had been different and if the plethora of scientific public relations literature had been taken into account, the nature of research in the field might prove to be a bit different than this chapter suggests. Nevertheless, the research findings represented below largely support the assumptions and conclusions made in the existing public relations literature.

5. Findings of the Study and Discussions

Most of the participants acknowledged that, in the social sciences arena, public relations is not highly respected and that its credibility is not particularly great. The most commonly given reasons for this state of affairs were in fact positioned outside public relations academia proper—namely, in the discipline's youth; in the lack of understanding what public relations is about in other scientific domains; and in the nature of the public relations profession. None of the respondents directly addressed the nature of research when asked why public relations is lacking respect and credibility in the academic community. The rationale behind this can be found in one respondent's statement that "the scientific nature of the discipline is not something that I lose sleep over," which prompted other respondents to elaborate that scholars have spent a lot of time demonstrating that public relations can be accepted as an academic discipline and for that reason they have not been very critical of what they accepted as good research. The lack of critical examination of the field resulted in scholarly unawareness of epistemological and methodological shortcomings and, consequently, in an insufficient scholarly effort devoted to the expansion of the topical and methodological horizons. This is also demonstrated in the findings presented below.

5.1. Current Topical Agenda in Public Relations

A majority of respondents supported the assumption of Pasadeos *et al.* (1999) that public relations is typified by a concentration of topics resulting in repetitive literature and a repetitive topical agenda at public relations conferences. As one respondent emphasized, there is "quite a bit in terms of reproduction of knowledge which is needed and important, but it is also important for us to go to the production level." The literature review suggests that this topical concentration emerged due to its practical orientation, in particular its fixation on management and the excellence concepts; the dominance of North American scholarship only strengthened the trend. According to the findings of the study underlying this chapter, these assumptions need to be slightly modified.

5.2. Practical Orientation of the Scholarly Agenda

According to the interview results, the scientific public relations agenda is almost exclusively steered by practitioners. Some of the respondents acknowledged that mere responsiveness to the practical needs leads public relations to provide and supply knowledge for particular practical settings. Settings which are so diverse that "they perhaps delay the establishment of a coherent theory and a solid body of knowledge," as one respondent commented. In this manner, the definition of what belongs to the body of knowledge should be at least to some extent uncoupled from the day-to-day practices as already suggested by Dozier and Lauzen (2000). The majority of the respondents, however, rather agreed with Morton and Lin's (1995) suggestion that public relations should be responsive to problems in practice, as the fundament of every scientific discipline is to help advance the profession. One respondent elaborated:

> Public relations is a professional field, like architecture, like journalism, and we in academia have an obligation, ideally, to work toward solving problems that face the practitioner community. It does not mean that our research is then not theoretical, but I think that we have to keep in mind the needs of the practitioners.

The strong professional orientation of research was also demonstrated in the content analysis of academic articles included in the research sample. In these articles, words referring to practical or applied public relations are portrayed four times as often as expressions of academic public relations (see Table 3.1). Correlation analysis showed hardly any connection between practical/ applied and academic expressions, showing that practical orientation, though dominating the field, lacks an academic approach to studying public relations phenomena.

Within this practical orientation, some areas appear to get more scholarly attention than necessary. According to respondents' opinions, a great amount of effort was invested in, among others, describing and understanding the nature of the public relations profession within and outside organizational settings, particularly public relations roles, organizational communication and campaign implementation, (North American) women in public relations, and media relations. The debate in these areas was important as they were key problems in the practice, but public relations probably needs comparative studies in these areas only occasionally. An examination of the titles and abstracts of the articles included in the sample clearly indicated that published scholarly work appears to be gradually overcoming the preoccupation with roles and models, as none of the articles dealt with these topics exclusively. Fewer articles have been published on gender discrepancies and the feminization of the field, the public relations profession, and the excellence/symmetry concepts. At the same time, new topical areas emerge including political public relations and public affairs, new communication technologies, the role of emotions in public relations, and fundraising. Nevertheless, as already concluded by Pasadeos *et al.* (1999) and Sallot *et al.* (2003), the public relations topical agenda remains responsive only to the public relations practice and, as demonstrated below, continues its strong fixation on public relations as a management function.

Table 3.1 Expressions of practical/applied and academic public relations in *Journal of Communication Management, Journal of Public Relations Research,* and *Public Relations Review*

Category	Referential unit	Frequency	Percentage
Practical/applied	Manage	593	26
public relations	Practice	553	25
	Profession	316	14
	Employ	256	11
	Applied	75	4
N^a		1,793	80
Academic public	Theory	285	13
relations	Education	78	3
	University	50	2
	Science	24	1
	Academia	17	1
N^b		454	20

Notes: Total word count score = 2,247.

a Number of times practical/applied public relations expressions occur in the selected articles.
b Number of times academic public relations expressions occur in the selected articles.

5.3. Management Function and the Excellence Study

The examination of the articles included in the sample showed that almost a third (eight out of thirty) were dealing with "Management and corporate public relations." In addition, the frequency of the word "Manage" was higher than any other expression identified in the analysis (see Table 3.1), perhaps indicating that the public relations literature is evolving mainly around managerial concepts. This was most clearly illustrated by a respondent's statement that the conceptualization of public relations as a strategic management function lies in the essence of the public relations paradigm and represents a central focus of the *Excellence* study, which established a basis for the coherent body of knowledge. Consequently, the *Excellence* study is perceived as strongly influencing the topical agenda in the field, yet the content analysis portrayed a considerably different picture.

With only one article in the sample explicitly dealing with the excellence/symmetrical communication and the lowest word-count score of all expression categories identified in the research, the fixation on excellence concepts appears to be much weaker than expected. Among the excellence phrases, the word "Grunig" accounted for more than half of the expressions, whereas "excellence" was seldom mentioned (see Table 3.2). It is important to note that "Grunig" can also appear as a reference to any of the published works by J. E. Grunig or L. A. Grunig. Since there was a significant statistical association between "Grunig" and the other two excellence concepts identified in the analysis, the study included the expression "Grunig" in the word count of the expressions of excellence, but, nevertheless, carefully considered implications of its occurrence. A correlation analysis further demonstrated a positive association between expressions of academic public relations and expressions of excellence, indicating that academically oriented debates, and perhaps theory-building too, still tend to evolve around the *Excellence* study and the Grunigs' work.

On these figures alone it is hard to decide whether the assumption about scholarly preoccupation with the excellence concepts should be rejected because of the small sample of academic articles and the relatively narrow definition of "excellence" expressions that were included in the word count. Respondents often suggested that the excellence concepts and models have an agenda-setting influence on research perhaps to the exclusion of other, equally valid topics in public relations research, implying that at present the *Excellence* study tends to represent a barrier to the unrestrained development of other theories in the field. This led to the question whether public relations should perhaps adopt a non-excellence or even a non-managerial approach to the discipline. One respondent indicated that, in this case, public relations might lose its focus or even disappear. Some other respondents agreed with him, but at the same time emphasized that scholars need to broaden the management perspective in terms of impacts and the role that public relations plays in society. Another respondent, however, explicitly stated that public relations need to break free of the narrow definition as organizational communication management, mainly because a management perspectives exclude the study of important public relations phenomena outside the management box, as also indicated by Heath (2001) and Holtzhausen (2000). In addition, this management box tends to be anchored in Western experience.

5.4. Dominance of Western Scholarship

According to the interview results, it is no longer true that North American scholarship and practice exert an agenda-setting effect on research elsewhere. Scholarly endeavors in the field started gaining geographical diversity with the development of the European body of knowledge, which attempts to challenge

Table 3.2 Expressions of *Excellence* in *Journal of Communication Management*, *Journal of Public Relations Research*, and *Public Relations Review*

Expression	Frequency	Percentage
Grunig	167	61
Symmetry	81	30
Excellence	24	9

Note: Total word count = 272.

the North American perspective. Nevertheless, the European body of knowledge with a Western orientation does not differ greatly from the North American paradigm, indicating that the discipline still falls short in geographical diversity. One respondent provided an example:

> If you look at the public relations literature that deals with rhetorical perspectives of public relations, it only talks about the rhetoric of Greek philosophers as if rhetorical philosophies had not developed in other parts of the world. There are lots of rhetorical principles in Confucianism and many such principles have been developed by Chinese, Indian, and Egyptians philosophers, but they are seldom considered.

Another obstacle to the geographical diversity of public relations scholarship that proved to be absent in the review of the literature, but was raised by respondents who originate from and work in non-English speaking countries, appears to be the global academic ignorance of research or bodies of knowledge developed and published in languages other than English. Perhaps we could conclude from this that the fixation on Western—or, rather, North American— principles and practice merely exists in English literature. That would explain why the content analysis, which focused on academic journals published in English, with two of the journals (*Public Relations Review* and *Journal of Public Relations Research*) based in the United States, confirmed the assumption that the North American concepts dominate in public relations literature.

In examined articles, expressions referring to the United States were far more frequent than geographical expressions referring to Europe, whereas words referring to Asia hardly occurred (see Table 3.3). In addition, there is a statistically significant correlation between "American/United States/USA" and "Asia," which might indicate that articles dealing with Asian concepts tend to compare themselves with or lean on public relations developed in the United States. It is important to consider that "International"/"Global" are used relatively frequently, but, given the small number of words referring to "Asia," this might indicate that when using the words "International" or "Global," scholars refer to public relations as understood in Western societies. However, one needs to be careful while drawing such conclusions, as the selected journals are by no means representative of public relations research. Furthermore, expressions of geographical area do not necessarily relate to the public relations field. Hence, the interview results that suggest that the public relations focus is shifting from heavy reliance on phenomena, models, and scientific tradition developed in the United States to Europe might have a bit more weight. Despite this slight geographical dispersion, the statement "as long as U.S. practice and U.S. theory are the sole sources of conceptual work in the field, public relations will be short of global inclusiveness and the validity it needs to become a true academic discipline and profession" (Verčič *et al.*, 2001: 377), cannot yet be discarded; we need only replace "U.S." with "Western." For this reason, scientific public relations should make every effort for greater geographical diversity.

Table 3.3 Expressions of geographical areas in *Journal of Communication Management*, *Journal of Public Relations Research*, and *Public Relations Review*

Expression	Frequency per journal			Frequency	Percentage
	JCM	JPRR	RR		
United States, America, USA	15	76	231	322	54
International/global	65	99	34	198	34
Europe	17	4	44	65	11
Asia	1	4	3	8	1

Note: Total word count = 593.

5.5. Trends in Current Public Relations Research

A lack of critical examination of scientific research in the field results in the absence of systematic and coherent research parameters against which scientific public relations research could or should be evaluated. McElreath and Blamphin (1994) suggest, "the value and efficiency of quantitative and qualitative research are similar in their emphasis on internal and external reliability and validity" (p. 74). That these standards may be defined too narrowly is evinced by one respondent's statement that "elegant and well-executed basic research addresses a real question of interest, employs appropriate methodology, and comes up with the findings of theoretical and practical relevance." Indeed, when providing the parameters for evaluation of research, respondents emphasized various aspects. Some focused on the research outcome as they stated that research can be evaluated on the basis of its ability to evolve relevant working and scientific theories that build upon themselves and eventually contribute to the development of a coherent theoretical structure. Other respondents focused on the process rather than the outcome, and provided criteria that can be divided into external and internal parameters. External parameters encompass research circumstances such as the scholars conducting research, their methodological competency, and an institution funding and supporting research undertaken. Internal research parameters, on the other hand, encompass scientific methodo-logical criteria such as validity, reliability, technical correctness, as well as scholarly comprehensiveness and transparency in applying particular methods. These internal parameters represent a focal point of the findings and discussion on scientific public relations research, to which we now turn.

5.6. Amount and Type of Research

McElreath and Blamphin (1994) observe that the body of published public relations knowledge comprises more discussion articles than research papers. Despite the assumption that the amount of public relations research has increased in the years following their study, the content analysis confirmed their observation. More than half of the academic articles included in the sample (seventeen out of thirty) did not use a primary research approach. Research is not merely deficient in quantity, but also in quality. One respondent explained:

> There is much pressure on young scholars to produce a lot of knowledge as they are trying to get promoted within the universities, so that leads people to do a lot of research quickly and not reflectively enough . . . A lot of researchers currently seem to just "jump around," do one thing in one area and move to another one, meaning there is not a lot of research that builds on itself.

A majority of respondents went on to emphasize that the research tended to be largely instrumental or "at the edge of applied" in nature. As noted in the literature review, the trouble with instrumental research, though valuable for the practice, is that it is focused on specific rather than general concepts and therefore fails to provide a solid ground for unifying scientific theory development. This is not to say that research done so far needs to be discarded—it was of great importance—but it appears that public relations became mature enough to adopt a critical research approach that would employ a wider range of scientific research practices and methods than is evident at present.

5.7. Methods

The literature review suggests that the public relations discipline is dominated by quantitative research (McElreath & Blamphin, 1994; McKie, 2001; Rühl, 2005), yet the respondents indicated that the prevalence of quantitative research appears to be one of the epistemological obstacles hindering public relations. At the same time—as a respondent observed—in the current positivist scientific society dominated by quantitative assessment procedures, it is difficult for a discipline not to do quantitative research. Another respondent noted that psychology found itself in a similar situation:

> Psychology felt that because it is a serious science, [research] it conducted had to be quantitative. Then it realized how much it lost by ignoring the qualitative side. There should be recognition that both methodological traditions are valid and reliable and that they complement rather than nullify each other.

The content analysis of the articles demonstrated that this recognition is beginning to emerge in public relations academic journals. Pragmatic research approaches or triangulation were used in five out of thirteen research articles in the sample (in most cases triangulating surveys and interviews), followed by the sole survey method (four articles), experiment (one article), content analysis (one article), ethnography (one article), and, surprisingly, case study (one article). This result disproves Cutler's (2004) assumption that case studies are used in up to a third of published research papers, but the disagreement may be due to the small sample of articles included in our study and/or the fact that Cutler's study considered only articles published in *Public Relations Review*. However, this finding could also indicate that the case-study method is giving way to triangulation, whereas surveys seem to be keeping a prominent position in the field.

According to these findings, the public relations field is not characterized by methodological diversity. Respondents unanimously recommended that public relations should start implementing scientific methods well developed in more advanced social sciences, including sociology, psychology, and anthropology. Many of them—in particular ethnography, participant observation, experimental research, and the relatively recently established action research and social network analysis—have a great promise to contribute to a greater in-depth understanding of complex public relations phenomena and, consequently, to provide a more solid empirical ground for theory development. In this way, the majority of public relations scholars, despite moving toward pragmatic approaches, appear to be, as already observed by McElreath and Blamphin (1994) and McKie (2001), rather slow in shifting to more interpretative research paradigms well established in other social sciences.

The occurrence of this methodological shift is at least to some extent hindered by limited scholarly understanding of scientific methods and research procedures. The problem starts with the research process: instead of first thinking about formulating and defining a real research problem, and then selecting a method that would satisfactorily solve it, scholars tend to work the other way around. One respondent emphasized:

> Abraham Kaplan, who wrote in the 1960s on the enquiry in behavioural science, said: "Give a little boy a hammer and you will be surprised what hammering means in this world." In a similar way, for many scholars a research method is just an instrument that they master to do research instead of a carefully chosen tool that could solve a research problem best.

Apart from the limited understanding of the research process, there appears to be a general lack of understanding of quantitative and qualitative research methodologies, and great confusion about the different standards of the two, especially when considering validity, reliability, and sampling strategies. In addition, respondents stressed that applied research methods are not always transparently described. More detailed examination of methodological sections in research articles confirmed this assumption. Research papers were quite transparent when explaining sampling procedures, data gathering, and analysis, but rather weak in describing the rationale for applied methodology and its limitations. In general, articles using qualitative inquiries were somewhat less transparent than those employing quantitative methods and, thus, as noted by Cutler (2004), make it impossible to build on or replicate the research. This scholarly non-transparency, sketchiness, and insularity might result in questionable research conclusions that have a potential to undermine discipline's credibility and respect.

5.8. The Nature of Current Research

Looking at the nature of current research with Campbell *et al.*'s mud-throwing metaphor in mind, we must conclude that empirical data support the suggestion that public relations scholars, although not in as large numbers as the metaphor suggests, instead of accumulating knowledge by digging through dirt to find the solid rock, throw mud at the wall using the mud that was already on the wall. In other words, researchers seem to give little thought to the critical evaluation of scientific work and devote little effort to expanding topical and methodological horizons, which is not beneficial for public relations science. Perhaps the most important consequence of this topical insularity manifests itself in research dealing with the same topics, resulting in reproduction rather than production of knowledge.

Public relations scholars seem to be reproducing knowledge of the public relations (excellent management) practice, which appears to be more beneficial for academia than for the industry. Moreover, it reduces the importance and pervasive influence of public relations phenomena outside the domain of the "resource-rich" organizational arena. In addition, as in many other sciences, (re)production of knowledge continues to concentrate on the Western hemisphere, curtailing geographical and multicultural diversity. Besides being topically insular, scholarly works involve little evidence derived from empirical data, which indicates that there is not enough research in the field. Furthermore, the scope of applied methods is still quite narrow with quantitative research methods, surveys in particular, dominating the published body of knowledge. Some respondents argued that public relations research needs to move away from this "old fashioned" positivistic nature of inquiry to a more interpretative and critical tradition—as suggested by Holtzhausen (2002)—whereas others emphasized that public relations needs to take positivistic approaches seriously and that the "ease with which positivism is criticized in the public relations community actually shows the absence of a scientific spirit if the discipline," as one respondent said.

In summary, the results demonstrated that the scholarly endeavors reflect topical and methodological insularity, which prevents public relations from seeing the complexity of the "forest." By seeing and understanding many "trees" instead, the published body of knowledge currently represents "a metaphor to show that public relations has some scientific basis for practice," as one respondent said, rather than a solid groundwork for theory development. As already suggested in the literature review, to improve that, public relations scholars should devote more time to consider epistemological and methodological issues. This is not as simple as it appears, since researchers are not "paid for thinking about scientific nature of public relations, but rather to produce results," as one respondent said, which points to one of the greatest obstacles facing public relations scientific development: the lack of resources. We'll turn to this in the next section.

5.9. Lack of Resources in Scientific Public Relations

Interviews elicited that the main reason for the field's insularity is not the lack of scholarly interest to engage in the scientific advancement of public relations, but rather the limited available resources. The majority of the respondents stressed that academia and professional bodies are not taking any real interest in (critical) scientific public relations research. Needless to say, unconditional no-questions-asked funding does not exist in public relations, according to one respondent. This lack of interest and resources is most clearly reflected in underinvested, short-term oriented, published scholarship based on limited samples and aiming at instant results relevant for the industry. Consequently, many interesting questions remain unanswered, many prospective methods are unused, and much scientific work is uncritically evaluated; all this is exacerbated by the lack of investment that would attract more researchers to the field. The consequences of that were most clearly illustrated by one respondent's answer when queried about her major criticism of the discipline:

> I do not know that I even want to respond, because whatever I say would be critical of the people who do research in these areas and we are a very small community of scholars, in which relationships are really important. So, I do not want to appear in your article as being critical of people, whose research, I think, went down that wrong path. The community is too small.

The expansion of the scholarly community as well as scholarly horizons requires that a greater amount of resources is invested in scientific public relations. As one respondent stated, there are already some positive developments emerging:

> With the recognition of public relations' importance more funds are invested in the discipline. There are more doctoral students who are trained within academic communities as public relations researchers, which is extremely important because that is the only way the field can get enough fundamental research on the basis of which real knowledge is produced in any science.

According to the logic of the "magic circle," all these developments should provide for a more coherent, solid, and holistic body of knowledge, which should prove relevant to other disciplines and society, improve the image of public relations as an academic discipline, and, thus, further encourage investment.

6. Conclusion

On the whole, the findings of the study on which this chapter is based support studies dealing with the nature of public relations as a scientific discipline. The field is topically insular; research almost exclusively deals with the public relations practice, showing little interest in discussing the position of public relations within social science. When compared to other studies, the findings demonstrate that there has been a gradual movement away from the topical fixation on the excellence concepts and North American intellectual tradition, but the topical agenda remains anchored in management aspects and Western experience, resulting more in the reproduction than in the production of knowledge. This fascination with public relations practice is also reflected in the insufficient volume of scientific research, which appears to be mostly instrumental and of limited methodologically. These methods are not always appropriately and transparently applied, possibly due to the limited scholarly understanding of methodological issues. There is a lingering assumption that public relations is to be taken more seriously if it uses positivistic research approaches and methods, unjustifiably ignoring interpretative tools of inquiry. Consequently, surveys remain a popular tool, though public relations research appears to be moving slowly toward triangulated or pragmatic, but not necessarily phenomenological, approaches. In short, the findings of the study show that the public relations field appears to be familiar with many "trees," but needs to expand its topical and methodological horizons to start seeking an understanding of the complexity of the "forest." This expansion is also hindered by the lack of resources and researchers in the field; however, this expansion is necessary if public relations is to develop a leading theory and gain greater respect and credibility in the eyes of other academic disciplines.

This chapter is an initial attempt to portray the nature of recent research in public relations, a subject that hardly surfaces in the literature. Existing studies deal with either topical agendas or methodological issues separately, but we explored both in comparable settings, though at the expense of a more in-depth investigation of either. First, future studies are therefore recommended to test or verify these assumptions through more detailed and extensive examinations of the public relations published body of knowledge and the nature of academia. Second, future studies might also examine broader epistemological and methodological considerations, circumstances surrounding the public relations discipline, and influences of public relations research within and outside its domain. Thus, the chapter primarily serves as an explorative device for future studies that would critically examine scholarly endeavors, portray a more holistic picture of scientific features of public relations, and perhaps compare them with those in other social scientific disciplines.

Acknowledgments

I would like to express my gratitude to the public relations scholars who provided invaluable support, guidance and encouragement while conducting the research underpinning this chapter. Many thanks to Guenther Bentele, Anne Gregory, James Grunig, Larissa Grunig, Julia Jahansoozi, Eric Koper, Jacquie L'Etang, Manfred Rühl, Betteke van Ruler, Krishnamurthy Shriramesh, Dejan Verčič, and Jon White.

References

Cutler, A. (2004). Methodical failure: The use of case study method by public relations researchers. *Public Relations Review, 30*(3), 365–375.

Dozier, D. M., & Lauzen, M. M. (2000). Liberating the intellectual domain from the practice: Public relations, activism, and the role of the scholar. *Journal of Public Relations Research, 12*(1), 3–22.

Ferguson, M. A. (1984, August). *Building theory in public relations: Inter-organizational relationships as a public relations paradigm.* Invited paper presented to the Public Relations Division, Association for Education in Journalism and Mass Communication Annual Convention, Gainesville, FL.

Grunig, L. A., Grunig, J. E., & Dozier, D. M. (2002). *Excellent public relations and effective organizations: A study of communication management in three countries.* Mahwah, NJ: Lawrence Erlbaum Associates.

Hazelton, V., Jr., & Botan, C. H. (1989). The role of theory in public relations. In C. H. Botan & V. Hazelton, Jr. (Eds.), *Public relations theory* (pp. 3–15). Hillsdale, NJ: Lawrence Erlbaum Associates.

Heath, R. L. (2001). Public relations as relationship building. In R. L. Heath (Ed.), *Handbook of public relations* (pp. 1–9). Thousand Oaks, CA, London, New Delhi: Sage.

Holtzhausen, D. R. (2000). Postmodern values in public relations. *Journal of Public Relations Research, 12*(1), 93–114.

Holtzhausen, D. R. (2002). Towards a postmodern research agenda for public relations. *Public Relations Review, 28*(3), 251–264.

Karlberg, M. (1996). Remembering the public in public relations research: From theoretical to operational symmetry. *Journal of Public Relations Research, 8*(4), 263–278.

Koper, E. (2005). IPR's charter status signals a fresh start, but collaboration with academia is vital. *PR Week*, March 4, 23.

Ledingham, J. A. (2003). Explicating relationship management as a general theory of public relations. *Journal of Public Relations Research, 15*(2), 181–198.

Ledingham, J. A., & Bruning, S. D. (2000). A longitudinal study of organization–public relationship dimensions: Defining the role of communication in the practice of relationship management. In J. A. Ledingham & S. D. Bruning (Eds.), *Public relations as relationship management* (pp. 55–69). Mahwah, NJ, London: Lawrence Erlbaum Associates.

L'Etang, J. (1996). Public relations as diplomacy. In J. L'Etang & M. Pieczka (Eds.), *Critical perspectives in public relations* (pp. 14–34). London: International Thompson Business Press.

L'Etang, J. (2004). *Public relations in Britain: A history of professional practice in the 20th century.* Mahwah, NJ: Lawrence Erlbaum Associates.

L'Etang, J., & Pieczka, M. (1996). Public relations education. In J. L'Etang & M. Pieczka (Eds.), *Critical perspectives in public relations* (pp. 1–13). London: International Thompson Business Press.

Littlejohn, S. W., & Foss, K. A. (2005). *Theories of human communication* (8th ed.). Belmont, CA: Thomson Wadsworth.

McElreath, M. P., & Blamphin, J. (1994). Partial answers to priority research questions— and gaps—found in the public relations society of America's body of knowledge. *Journal of Public Relations Research, 6*(2), 69–103.

McKie, D. (2001). Updating public relations: "New science," research paradigms and uneven developments. In R. L. Heath (Ed.), *Handbook of public relations* (pp. 75–91). Thousand Oaks, CA, London, New Delhi: Sage.

Morton, L. P., & Lin, L. Y. (1995). Content and citation analyses of *Public Relations Review*. *Public Relations Review, 21*(4), 337–349.

Moss, D., Macmanus, T., & Verčič, D. (Eds.) (2003). *Perspectives on public relations research*. London, New York: Routledge.

Pasadeos, Y., & Renfro, B. R. (1992). A bibliometric analysis of public relations research. *Journal of Public Relations Research, 4*(3), 167–187.

Pasadeos Y., Renfro, B. R., & Hanily, M. L. (1999). Influential authors and works of the public relations scholarly literature: A network of recent research. *Journal of Public Relations Research, 11*(1), 29–52.

Pavlik, J. V. (1987). *Public relations: What research tells us*. Newbury Park, CA, London, New Delhi: Sage.

Rühl, M. (2005). *Public relations methodology: Is there, and if, should we bother? Public relations metrics: Evaluation and measurement*. Paper presented at the 12th International Public Relations Symposium BledCom 2005, Lake Bled, Slovenia.

Sallot, L. M., Lyon, L. J., Acosta-Alzuru, C., & Jones, K. O. (2003). From aardvark to zebra: A new millennium analysis of theory development in public relations academic journals. *Journal of Public Relations Research, 15*(1), 27–90.

Spicer, C. H. (2000). Public relations in a democratic society: Value and values. *Journal of Public Relations Research, 12*(1), 115–130.

Synnott, G., & McKie, D. (1997). International issues in PR: Researching research and prioritizing priorities. *Journal of Public Relations Research, 9*(4), 259–282.

van Ruler, B., Verčič, D., Buetschi, G., & Flodin, B. (2004). A first look for parameters of public relations in Europe. *Journal of Public Relations Research, 16*(1), 35–63.

Verčič, D. (2000). The European public relations body of knowledge. *Journal of Communication Management, 4*(4), 341–354.

Verčič, D., van Ruler, B., Buetschi, G., & Flodin, B. (2001). On the definition of public relations: A European view. *Public Relations Review, 27*(4), 373–387.

4 Empirical Research in Contemporary Social Sciences Relevant to Public Relations

Toward a Network Approach

Jan Kleinnijenhuis

1. Introduction

The definition of public relations by the Public Relations Society of America (PRSA) as "Public relations helps an organization and its publics adapt mutually to each other" is an interesting one, although it may not provide much insight into what PR practitioners actually do to accomplish their task (van Ruler, 2000). The definition appears to legitimize PR through an association with the socially desirable goal of mutual adaptation, which is typical of a *professional perspective* in Rühl's terminology (this volume). However, the definition enables also a *scholarly perspective* on public relations in the terminology of Rühl. The PRSA definition delineates which types of theory and which types of empirical evidence are relevant for reflecting on public relations. The focus on mutual adaptation stipulates that theories and empirical insights dealing with relationships between, on the one hand, an organization and its managers, and on the other, its stakeholders or "publics," are potentially useful. "The key dependent variable is relationships," according to J. E. Grunig (in this volume). Since relationships between social entities such as organizations and their stakeholders are central to network theory, the definition serves as a prelude to a network perspective to the study *on* public relations (as contrasted with research *in* public relations, or research that is directly useful *for* public relations, cf. J. Grunig in this volume). Other definitions of public relations, such as "the communicative expression of competing organizations and groups in pluralist states" (Moloney, 2005) locate public relations also as a communication activity in a network of organizations and groups, but the focus is on competition rather than adaptation.

In this chapter a number of theoretical approaches and empirical findings regarding public relations will be discussed that fit in with such a network perspective on public relations. The chapter starts with an overview of the rise of the network paradigm in the social sciences. Two recent overviews of theoretical approaches to corporate campaigns, and communication in general, will serve to elaborate on the network perspective as the theoretical point of departure of the study of public relations: a seminal book by Peter R. Monge and Noshir Contractor on network theories of communication (Monge & Contractor, 2003), and an article by Janet A. Bridges (2004) in which she delineates six theoretical approaches for thinking about corporate campaigns.

With regard to empirical findings, this chapter is deliberately eclectic. No attempt will be made to perform a meta-analysis of the PR literature, nor even to summarize the vast body of research that is referred to in the theoretical literature. The aim of the empirical findings presented here is simply to elucidate basic insights that can be gained by taking a network perspective.

2. The Rise of the Network Perspective in the Social Sciences

The sociologist Manuel Castells was probably the first to profoundly analyze the transition toward the network society of our information age. According to Castells, the network society is increasingly constructed around *flows*—from those of capital and organizational interaction to those of sound bites and symbols—rather than around the *stocks* that were necessary to maintain a single community—livestock, food, buildings, military protection (Castells, 1996). The information and communication technology (ICT) revolution of the 1980s and 1990s has placed on a radically higher plane the infrastructural organization of flows to enable personal and organizational interactions and communicative exchanges. Within a few decades, our globe was rewired and furnished with satellites to meet the demands of the new means of interaction and telecommunication such as the telefax, satellite television, the Internet, and the Blackberry.

Scholarly interest in networks—in patterns of entities and relations between them—has increased spectacularly during the last decades. In a wide variety of scientific disciplines, graphs and networks became pivotal to the core paradigm. Networks of information exchange have gained a central place in computer science (e.g., text and hypertext, ftp, and http). In epidemiology, network patterns of diffusion and contagion attracted attention (e.g., AIDS, SARS). Evolutionary biologists, starting from early predator–prey models came to relate the evolutionary success of species to the strategies used by their specimens in evolving dynamic networks (Maynard Smith, 1983).

Maynard Smith's (1920–2004) link between the theory of games and the theory of dynamic networks inspired social scientists to think of interactions as repeated games. The most important insight from computer simulations was that selfish, egoistic actors would behave cooperatively rather than destructively toward each other when the time horizon of possible revenge in the future for one's current destructive moves—also labeled as "the shadow of the future"—was distant enough (Axelrod, 1984). Furthermore, complex strategies were shown to be less successful than simple ones, such as Tit for Tat (Axelrod, 1984), or Pavlov in the case of noisy games (Nowak & Sigmund, 1993).

The experimental social-psychology literature on social dilemmas adds to these insights that even in a one-shot dilemma, respondents cooperate more often than could be expected (Kerr & Kaufman-Gilliland, 1994; Utz, Ouwerkerk, & van Langen, 2004; van Langen, Ouwerkerk, & Tazelaar, 2002). Apparently, respondents tend to react as if the time horizon of possible revenge for a destructive move is very long, which suggests that the fear for future revenge in the case of disloyal behavior is hard-wired in the human brain.

Networks gained attention also due to the work on power structures and interlocking directorates (Knoke, 1990) and due to the analysis of daily political events that shape world politics (Azar, 1993 (1982); Schrodt, 2001). These findings highlighted how nations—and other complex organizations—shaped events not only to influence each other bilaterally, but also to influence others through multilateral negotiations and multilateral coalition building.

Sociological research pointed toward weak ties and structural holes as the structural features of networks (Burt, 1992; Granovetter, 1973). Strong ties within groups are important when it comes to attitudinal change and ultimate decision making, but weak ties with outer groups are more important for obtaining knowledge that would not be available otherwise (Weenig & Midden, 1991).

Networks also arose as a central concept in cognitive psychology to model the cognitive maps that underlie reaction times to draw inferences (e.g., Collins & Quillian, 1969). Due to the pioneering work of Robert Axelrod (1976), these cognitive maps attracted attention in other social sciences as well (Young, 2001). Kathleen Carley (1986) was probably the first to urge for an integration of social network approaches with cognitive network approaches.

In summary, the network approach in the social sciences resulted in new insights into mutual adaptation, which is defined as the primary goal of public relations. Cooperation and mutual adaptation are more common than was to be expected according to the rational models of economic behavior that prevailed until the 1980s, not only when the *shadow of the future* is long. Apparently, organizations maintain a variety of relations with each other and with their stakeholders, whereas even weak ties can be shown to result in significant advantages. The network participants can be shown to develop elaborated cognitive maps of their network.

From a pragmatic point of view, these results are too abstract, however. The research findings do not give any details regarding the precise contributions of the public relations profession to establish mutual adaptation, nor of the precise contribution of other activities at the interfaces between organizations and publics, such as diplomacy, public affairs, or sales management.

3. The Rise of the Network Perspective in Communication Science

In the relatively new study of communication science, network approaches were mostly borrowed from neighboring disciplines. Recently, however, the network approach has started to gain a central position in the discipline, especially due to the seminal work of Peter Monge and Noshir Contractor (2001, 2003). Monge and Contractor provide an outline of an overarching "multi-theoretical multi-level network approach" (MTML) that would fit the needs of the discipline. Figure 4.1 gives the basic idea.

Figure 4.1 includes a number of dependencies. It should be noted that the figure presented by Monge and Contractor is not a model of the relationships between four variables, but a model of the relationships between four *classes* of variables. Whereas *attributes* of actors, especially those of individuals, are the focal dependent variables in ordinary social science theories (e.g., their knowledge, attitudes, behaviors), from a network perspective, the *relations* between them must also be explained.

The communicative characteristics of the relations between each pair of nodes in the *focal network* (either actors, issues (e.g., concepts, circumstances, variables), values and norms—in short, "meaning objects") are expected to depend on:

a. endogenous communicative characteristics of the focal type of the connections between other pairs of nodes in the same focal network, e.g., whether one's communication partner was recommended by a friend (the balance principle; Heider, 1946);
b. other (exogenous) characteristics of the connections between pairs of nodes in the focal network; e.g., whether consulting one's current communication partner was compulsory by law;
c. exogenous attributes of a particular node in the network, e.g., power, wealth, and communication facilities of actors;
d. endogenous focal attributes of actors. Engaging in relationships depends on attributes of actors, e.g., on their perceptions of transaction and communication costs.

Note that a, b, c, and d above correspond with arrows a, b, c, and d in Figure 4.1 below.

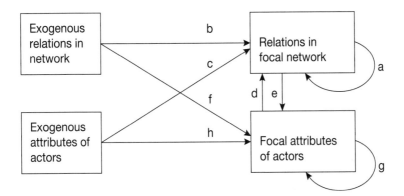

Figure 4.1 The Monge–Contractor MTML model (adapted from Monge & Contractor, 2003: 70).

The focal attributes of actors (e.g., communication facilities, power resources, reputations of actors) are expected to depend not only on other attributes of actors (type *g* and type *h* relationships) as in the traditional social sciences approach, but also on network relations (types *e* and *f*):

e.   Type *e* relationships are predominant in the theory of social action. According to the theory on the social capital of actors, the focal attributes of actors depend on the "social capital" they are able to marshal from their relationships. The theory of structural holes is a special case of the theory on social capital (Monge & Contractor, 2003: 156–157).

f.   Type *f* relationships connect attributes of actors with exogenous network characteristics, for example one's reputation with one's formal position in a hierarchy.

Monge and Contractor show that their model integrates a number of classic social science theories that had, until then, been studied only in isolation, such as theories of rational self-interest and collective action, theories of contagion, theories of cognitive consistency, exchange and dependency theories, and theories about social support and (co)evolutionary theories.

Cognitive consistency theories may serve as an example of the integration of theories in a network perspective. In balance theory, according to Heider (1946), each edge of a triadic relation is expected to depend on the other two edges, thus amounting to "endogenous" relationships (type *a*). Balance theory predicts that—among other things—organizations exert pressure on other organizations to conform to the organizations one cooperates with, and also that organizations will try to punish those who consistently cooperate with competitors. Many authors have supplemented balance theory with other explanations. Newcomb (1953), for example, asked whether exogenous characteristics of relationships (e.g., having many contacts) would make a difference when respondents disagreed about an issue (type *b* explanation). Others asked whether exogenous personality characteristics (type *c* influences, such as influences from dogmatism or self-monitoring) made a difference when it comes to the reduction of imbalance. From a network perspective, consistency theories can be generalized from theories about triangular relationships toward theories about quadrilateral and manifold relationships (Kleinnijenhuis, de Ridder, & Rietberg, 1997; van Cuilenburg, Kleinnijenhuis, & de Ridder, 1986).

Many other theories from the field of communication science permit an even more simple translation. Agenda-setting theory (McCombs & Shaw, 1972), which maintains that the media agenda sets the issue priorities of the general public, for example, is a very simple theory of *contagion*. Issue ownership theory (Meijer, 2004; Meijer & Kleinnijenhuis, 2006) can be conceived as contagion that is conditional on former issue reputations.

3.1. Simplifications and Curtailments of the Monge–Contractor Model

Although in theory the variety of patterns of "other relations" on which a specific relation may depend is unlimited, only five types seem to appear in communication science theories, namely:

- measures of outdegree (e.g., the number of connections of an actor as a measure to explain the likelihood of a connection of that actor with one specific other actor);
- measures of indegree (e.g., the number of positive relationships toward an actor—thus, the support for an actor—as a measure to explain the likelihood that an actor will engage in a positive relationship with a specific other actor);
- measures of indirect paths (e.g., transitivity in balance theory: whether the sign of an indirect path between two meaning objects (obtained by multiplying the signs of the constituent links) corresponds with the sign of the direct link;
- measures of in-betweenness (e.g., structural holes theory: whether indirect relationships between each pair of two other actors would change when a specific actor were to stop acting/communicating);
- measures of reciprocity (e.g., diagnostics about the behavior of others toward ego that underlie strategies in iterative games, such as Tit for Tat, TF2T, or Pavlov; remarkably, these diagnostics are usually based on bilateral relations, rather than on multilateral relations in the full network and/or on actor attributes).

Although the theoretical variety of focal attributes of actors on the basis of which they decide to cooperate with others is endless, their variety in actual communication theories is also limited.

One striking simplification of the general Monge–Contractor model is a dynamic model in which characteristics of the focal network at time t, as well as focal attributes of actors, depend on characteristics of the focal network and on focal actor attributes at an earlier point in time. If "instantaneous influence" is out of the question—for example, when the time span between measurements is short compared to the duration of changes—then the dynamic model reduces to a series of autoregressive regression models, with features of the relations in the focal network and focal attributes at time t as the dependent variables.

The parameters of the regression equations can be estimated provided that data are available with respect to relevant aspects of the focal relations between actors in the network for subsequent time intervals (e.g., days, weeks, quarters). A choice for researchers is how the regression parameters should be estimated:

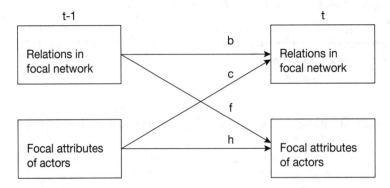

Figure 4.2 A dynamic Monge–Contractor MTML model without instantaneous
          influence.

- separately for each specific dyad or each specific actor;
- for all dyads/actors (often labeled as the Pooled Time Series Cross Sectional approach, e.g., Pennings, Keman, & Kleinnijenhuis, 2006: 174–179);
- for all dyads/actors, but starting from a random effects model (often labeled as a "multilevel" model in the social sciences (Gelman & Hill, 2007; Snijders & Bosker, 1999) or as a "mixed" model in psychology) with the assumption that parameters for specific dyads and specific actors will be distributed normally (Skrondal & Rabe-Hesketh, 2004).

3.2. Limitations of the Current Network Approach

Although an overarching network approach is worthwhile from a theoretical perspective, research results are often disappointing when compared to the wealth of qualitative knowledge.

Oversimplified Relationships Between Actors

The data to test network theories were often too limited. Often the question simply was whether or not a relationship between a pair of actors existed, which was measured only once or only a few times. Needless to say, this is far too simple from the point of view of any social science theory. From the point of view of most social sciences, at least three aspects of relationships should be incorporated (van Cuilenburg *et al.*, 1986):

- the *frequency* of an interaction within a given time-span;
- the average degree of *positiveness/negativity* of an interaction within a given time-span (e.g., cooperation–conflict, success–failure, good–evil, pro–con);
- the *ambiguity* (within variance) of positiveness/negativity of interactions within a given time-span, as well as the *inconsistency*, also labeled as *divergence* (between variance), of these interactions.

Depending on the problem area, further aspects to consider could be the formal versus informal nature of relationships, their statutory regulation, their symbolic versus real nature, and their public versus secret nature. Depending on the problem area, it may be worthwhile to extend the network between actors with the issues they deal with as additional nodes and, consequently, with the issue positions they oppose or support as additional relations. Furthermore, the assumption that relationships are static through time could be relaxed.

Static Behavior Based on Static Cognitive Maps

Most empirical research relied on extremely simple assumptions about the behavior of actors. Goal-directedness and utility considerations were usually reduced to heuristic rules that actors would follow. Learning and evolution were usually neglected. Axelrod (1984) argued that learning algorithms will fail in iterative games because their behavior tends to become complicated, which will usually result in punishments by simple rule-based strategies like Tit for Tat and, ultimately, to an escalation of conflicts. It should be noted that Axelrod studied only binary bilateral games without any noise. In the case of continuous multilateral games[1] with noise, learning may help. Two types of learning received most attention in the literature.

Reinforcement learning means that the behavior toward others is chosen on the basis of a utility function whose parameters have been re-estimated in light of the most recent evidence. Reinforcement assumes an actor in an ivory tower who reacts to the personal utility of the outcomes from a black box consisting of an environment inhabited by other actors.

Evolutionary learning, on the other hand, means that behavior is based on social rules by definition, but that the rules may change in an evolutionary process. As a matter of conceptual confusion, rules are often denoted as strategies in the literature on games and evolution, although goal-directedness in its common-sense meaning is absent. Evolutionary *modeling* (van den Bergh, 2004) has only recently started to attract attention in communication science (Monge & Contractor, 2003). Selection by *phenotype* means that actors mimic successful strategies of other actors. Selection by *genotype* means that actors recombine elements of their own successful strategies as well as that of others.[2] Research results indicate that evolutionary learning outperforms reinforcement learning when the past gives only ambiguous predictions of the future (in a "non-Markovian" world; cf. de Croon, van Dartel, & Postma, 2005).

Although the notion is widespread that each actor's behavior is based on his or her own cognitive network, researchers only recently published on, for example, knowledge sharing, updating one's cognitive map on the basis of cognitive maps of other participants, or on concealing strategic information (de Vries, van den Hooff, & de Ridder, 2006).

A Lack of Data

The most severe limitation for network models is that the data to estimate the parameters are lacking. In the literature, time and again binary data are presented on relationships between eighteen monks from Sampson's well-known study of monks in a monastery (Sampson, 1968). Only a small minority of social scientists use large-scale longitudinal network data, for example, with regard to the development of hyperlinks between web sites on the World Wide Web. This lack of data is remarkable given the possibilities to obtain content analysis data both with respect to relationships between actors and with respect to the cognitive maps of separate actors (de Ridder & Kleinnijenhuis, 2001; Young, 2001).

4. Bridging the Gap Between Network Theory and Public Relations

In summary, Monge and Contractor's seminal book applies successfully the network framework to the study of the dynamics of communication within and between organizations, but the approach still fails to give a more precise clue to the contributions of public relations professionals to maintaining cooperation and mutual adaptation. Janet Bridges (2004) sketched six concentric theoretical approaches to issues management that are useful for bridging the gap between theories and the practice of issues management, or even public relations practices in general. Here, we will elucidate each of her six concentric approaches by highlighting empirical findings about issues management and public relations from a network perspective.

4.1. Systems Theory

Many public relations scholars consider systems theory as the foundation for public relations (J. Grunig, 1992; see also Rühl, this volume). The specifications of systems theory used by public relations scholars nicely fit in with the network perspective. Systems theory decomposes the organization into integrated, interdependent parts such as the management board, employers and the public relations department, and the organizational environment into a variety of possible stakeholders, who may affect the organization in some way. Systems theory focuses on the *relations* that the organization establishes with the environment. These relations are designed to serve the *goal* of the organization to remain strong.

Systems theory is closely related to first- and second-order cybernetics (Heylighen & Joslyn, 2001). Organizations attempt to realize their goals by striving for control over their environment. This means that the *variability* of possible outcomes—as measured by *entropy*—is reduced, either by anticipating ("feedforward") possible disturbing, destructive or cooperative actions from other actors, or by reacting to actual disturbances and actual cooperation ("feedback"). Negative feedforward and negative feedback refer to suppression of what is expected to happen, and what actually happened, respectively;

positive feedforward and positive feedback denote enhancing what is expected to happen, and to what happened, respectively. Reduction of imbalance (Heider, 1946), which comes down to reducing the variability of the signs of direct and indirect relationships between two actors in a network, is an example of entropy reduction. The conservative bias in systems theory is that in the final count, organizations will always strive for a reduction of variance—toward *homeostasis*—by suppressing major disturbances from the outer world. Thus, organizations provide negative responses to all kinds of developments and all kinds of initiatives by other actors that could possibly lead them further away from their ultimate goals. However, in order to enable such a negative response, they may provide positive feedback to many subordinated developments and initiatives (e.g., spending time and money to talk with environmental pressure groups (positive feedback), in order to prevent these groups organizing a consumer boycott (negative feedforward)).

Second-order system theory asks the "constructivist" question of how actors in a first-order system manage to arrive at a cognitive map—a model—of themselves and of their own interaction with their environment that is useful for the actors in pursuing their own goals most efficiently (Heylighen & Joslyn, 2001). The answer is that organizations build their cognitive map by monitoring their environment for possible changes, changes in the cognitive maps of stakeholders included. Second-order system theory adds cognitive engineering to the action repertoire that organizations have at their disposal to reduce the variability of possible outcomes in order to achieve their goals. When cognitive engineering is taken into account, organizations may consider attempts to disseminate the organization's cognitive map, as well as public relations attempts to strive for a cognitive map that is shared with stakeholders.

Whereas first-order system theory gives public relations professionals a theoretical underpinning for homeostasis and mutual adaptation, second-order system theory gives them a justification for monitoring the organizational environment for possible "disturbances" that would endanger achieving the ultimate goals of an organization. Disturbances (e.g., a decrease in consumer trust) should be encountered with negative feedforward or negative feedback at the level of the ultimate organizational goals (e.g., cost reduction), perhaps by means of positive feedforward and positive feedback at the level of subordinate goals (e.g., higher PR costs).

Although cognitive maps that do not take into account important environmental parameters are of little use, in many circumstances simple cognitive maps may still do a better job than complex ones. In order to react to a sudden attack an elaborated cognitive map resulting in a complex model of one's antagonists may be less valuable then a simple decision heuristic such as Tit for Tat (Axelrod, 1984). Systems theory acknowledges the possibility that denying or dampening signals from the organizational environment may be worthwhile because it minimizes transaction costs. Thus, second-order systems theory does not, by definition, entail that organizations should always learn more about their environment, or about their public relations attempts to deal with it—cf. J. Grunig, this volume. Second-order systems theory leaves open the possibility that a cognitive map resulting from denying or dampening signals may suggest more effective ways to achieve one's goals than a complex map with excessive knowledge obtained by monitoring the environment in detail.

Sharing cognitive maps with stakeholders will reduce disturbances from the environment only when the goals, or important subordinate goals, of the organization coincide with those of its stakeholders. It makes no sense, for example, for successful managers who act upon the maxim of value for shareholders to strive for a mutual understanding with employees about the large revenues for shareholders. Thus, second-order systems theory does not lend unequivocal support to the public relations precept that public relations professionals should always strive for mutual awareness, mutual understanding and agreement— cf. J. Grunig, this volume.

4.2. Powerful Stakeholder Theory

The early work of Lippmann (1922) and Schattschneider (1960) on public opinion and pluralistic democracy suggested that the answer to the question of whether actors—and even *division lines* between actors—would manifest themselves in the public debate depended on the nature of the most salient issues on the media agenda. Issues on the media agenda set the public agenda (McCombs & Shaw, 1972). Consequently, issues on the media agenda have an effect on the preferences of actors for specific coalitions between them. Issues affect which actors will build a coalition, and who will fail to do so. If employment is the most important issue, then agreement between employers and employees is likely. Promotion of the attention for wages will decrease the likelihood of this coalition, but may increase the likelihood of agreement between shareholders and management. Elimination of the issue of wages or of the environmental issue from the media agenda may result in the absence of employee unions or of environmental pressure groups, respectively, as serious actors in the public debate. Thus, the concepts of division lines between actors is closely related to whether actors and issues appear to be partitioned into coalitions (Doreian, Batagelj, & Ferligoj, 2005).

Division lines between actors often do not change when a single issue is added, however. Old division lines between organizations tend to absorb new issues. Schattschneider (1960) showed that old division lines between actors, for example along the left–right axis, tend to be re-activated when new issues come to the fore. Corporate attention for issues is not completely dependent on the societal agenda or the media agenda, but primarily on the perceived power of the stakeholders that promote an issue. Organizations reckon primarily with the interests that must be served first in order to survive.

Stakeholder theory has many ramifications for public relations. Established division lines between actors should not be overlooked, nor issues of powerful stakeholders. But some room remains to promote issues that enable agreement within a new coalition of actors, or even the emergence of new division lines between actors.

Positioning new issues is a major theme in the literature on marketing and corporate strategy, albeit under a variety of confusing headings. The development of the market for computers is a well-known case (Lynch, 1997). Until the 1970s, IBM was confidently the market leader in large "computers" in special air-conditioned rooms in buildings of large companies that reliably undertook tasks never before operated by machinery, such as accounting, invoicing, and payroll. In the late 1970s, a number of small companies such as Apple, Sinclair, and Commodore launched "personal" computers, which, though they could not handle large-scale computational tasks such as business accounting at the time, could be placed on everyone's desktop. The issue now became whether a computer was *personal* in the sense of being on your own desktop as a toy for your own games, your own texts, and your own hobbies. It took IBM years to acknowledge that this niche market had a future. IBM nevertheless made a remarkable comeback in the early 1980s with their introduction of the IBM *Personal* Computer, which soon became the standard for office automation in the 1980s as the successor of the typewriter. Since IBM was a late entrant to the PC market, it could not use its own proprietary standards. IBM acquired the semiconductor chips from Intel and the operating software from Microsoft and had to accept that Intel and Microsoft would remain independent, thus enabling them to improve and to sell their own products on their own. Since the issue was still one of whether a computer was personal, improvements in the Microsoft operating system software (Windows) were far more important for the PC market than the IBM label on the box. New competitors that also used Intel chips and the Microsoft operating system, such as Dell, Hewlett Packard, and many Asian manufacturers, could therefore initiate competition on price with IBM. The label "Intel inside" easily beat the IBM label for being the hallmark of solidity. Since the issue was still whether a personal computer would be useful for you personally, new coalitions of companies and new division lines between them could emerge, which brought IBM almost to bankruptcy in the early 1990s.

The 2002 landslide election victory of the assassinated newcomer to the political scene in the Netherlands, Pim Fortuyn, may serve as another example of the creation of new dividing lines between actors by promoting a new issue (Kleinnijenhuis, Oegema, de Ridder, van Hoof, & Vliegenthart, 2003). In the aftermath of 9/11, the vested coalition parties PvdA (Social Democrats), VVD (Conservative Liberals), and D66 (neo liberals) were very much aware of the danger that the eloquent newcomer Pim Fortuyn could win many voters by addressing the issue of immigrants in relation to societal problems such as unemployment, crime, Islam, and terror. They decided to ignore him by emphasizing serious differences of opinion between the vested parties themselves along the traditional dividing line between leftist and rightist parties with respect to crime-fighting and to social welfare provisions as a means to inspire people to get a job. However, this polarization along the left–right division line had as a drawback that months before the elections, public opinion polls showed that the coalition parties were marked down on their own issues by the voters. The left-wing parties had convinced the voters that the right-wing Minister Korthals accepted that passengers from the Netherlands Antilles who had ingested cocaine entered the Netherlands freely. The right-wing parties had convinced the voters that the left-wing parties would make no effort to encourage the enormous number of social security recipients in the Netherlands —many of whom had been declared "disabled"—to strive for an appropriate job. In the meantime, the eloquent Pim Fortuyn was still getting television attention. He continued to do better in the polls, although he was ignored by the major parties, which of course made the vested parties nervous. In a news-paper interview three months before the elections, Pim Fortuyn provoked the consensual political opinion further with his statements that the Dutch constitu-tion should be rewritten so as to allow for discrimination, and that no Islamite would be allowed to enter the Netherlands if he were to become the prime minister. That same day, on the evening TV news, the vested parties unanim-ously declared that Pim Fortuyn should be ignored in the political debate because his statements went too far, because he was a right-wing extremist, and because he was apparently not aware of what had happened to Anne Frank. However, by declaring unanimously on the news that Pim Fortuyn was wrong to consider immigrants a serious issue was equivalent to putting the immigrant problem on the public agenda. A content analysis of newspaper and television news reveals that from that moment, the media replaced the dividing line between leftist and rightist parties with that between Pim Fortuyn and the vested coalition parties, which resulted in a dramatic loss for the coalition parties and an unprecedented election victory, out of the blue, for Pim Fortuyn's party and for the CDA, who were the only other party to address the immigrants issue, albeit in softer tones ("the multicultural society is not something to strive for").

Thus, starting from a network perspective, powerful stakeholder theory looks at how issues management contributes to the dividing lines between actors that are conducive for achieving organizational goals.

4.3. Legitimacy Gap Theory

As a third theoretical approach, Bridges discusses legitimacy and expectancy gaps, based among others on the work of Heath (1997). A legitimacy gap exists when an organization is evaluated negatively, usually because of a discrepancy between perceptions of organizational behavior or between organizational per-formance, and society's expectations.

Whether a legitimacy gap will be perceived depends mainly on an organiza-tion's reputation with respect to the *issues* in the public debate. The first question, therefore, is how issues affect the legitimacy gap. *Issue ownership* (Budge & Farlie, 1983; Petrocik, 1996; Petrocik , Benoit, & Hansen, 2003), a concept from political science, may be the clue to understanding why an emphasis in the media on a specific issue may result in a legitimacy gap. Ownership of an issue means that an organization has such a strong reputation with regard to an issue, that observers (voters, consumers, journalists, stakeholders) will think that all competing organizations fall short of meeting performance standards. To put it differently, competitors of an issue owner will often face a legitimacy gap. Issue ownership can be measured with questions such as "which of the following <organizations> do you think is most capable of solving problems with respect to <issue>?," or "for which of the following <issues> do you think <organization> offers the best solution?" Accruing issue ownership often takes several years of excellent performance and excellent public relations, but it may nevertheless be lost almost overnight, for example when an organization gets caught up in negative issues (e.g., Enron losing its reputation as a goldmine for shareholders due to the publicity on fraud). Issue ownership theory originally dealt with political parties. It comprises two parts, one part dealing with the issues that organizations are expected to emphasize, the other, with the effects of a media emphasis on owned issues (Abbe, Goodliffe, Herrnson, & Patterson, 2003). Regarding the first part, research results show that parties throughout the years indeed stress their own issues more frequently than their competitors, but the tendency that all parties will discuss all the dominant issues at a given point in time is a stronger one (Sigelman & Buell, 2004). This is consistent with the empirical findings regarding stakeholder theory that organizations usually pay attention to the issues raised by their most powerful stakeholders. With regard to the second part, issue ownership theory predicts that a party will attract voters when issues are emphasized on which a party has already a solid vested reputation. Media attention for issues owned by an organization increases the likelihood that a person will vote for that party. Issue ownership appears to play a role in corporate communication also. Media attention for business issues sets the public agenda for these issues, and media consumers who come to associate an organization with an "owned" issue will evaluate that organization more positively (Meijer & Kleinnijenhuis, 2006).

Second, a legitimacy gap could be the result of rising expectations. Typically, expectations will continue to rise after a period of growth, although real world progress might have come to an end, which gives rise to growing dissatisfaction over essentially the same business performance as the previous year. Stagnant growth and, in general, relative deprivation, has been identified in the social science literature as one of the causes of social riots and even revolutions (Gurr, 1970). Expectations will rise also when a company becomes the market leader. Compared to minor companies, the top companies are expected not only to achieve their economic goals and to obey the law, but also to assume higher levels of social responsibility, such as environmental care, distributive justice, sponsoring, and philanthropy. Expectations will be lowered gradually when the available evidence over a long period of time shows that not a single organization was able to meet high expectations. Expectations may be lowered actively by public relations professionals using inoculation techniques (Pfau, 1995), for example by inconspicuously spreading negative rumors about the countries of export—which would not immediately incite shareholders to sell their shares because the danger is too far away—a few months before the CEO's press conference about receding quarterly figures—which, it is hoped, will still not incite the "inoculated" shareholders to sell their shares because the bad news had been anticipated.

Third, a legitimacy gap could be the result of emerging perceptions of poor organizational performance. Publicity and rumors about poor performance, either at VIP-parties, in the professional media, in the general media, or in special-interest Internet discussion groups, are usually at the heart of these perceptions. A poor performance will provoke indignation when the news entails that peers—e.g., competitors in the same branch of industry—performed better. Relational content analysis of the news (Kleinnijenhuis *et al.*, 1997) is a research technique to assess the perceived performance of companies with respect to the relevant issues. As an example, Table 4.1 presents such content analysis data from a study covering three years (July 1997 to July 2000) by Meijer (2004), who investigated whether selected companies fell short of performance standards and if they did, established the source of under-performance: the media themselves, or quoted and paraphrased sources such as company spokesmen ("internal"), their industry, the government, or the trade unions. Meijer selected two companies from a number of industrial branches to assess also whether a company fell short relative to another company from the same branch: +1 indicates a brilliant performance, 0, a neutral performance, and –1, an extremely disappointing one. Here, we will not focus on the development over time (see, e.g., Shin, Cheng, Jin, & Cameron, 2005).

The data from Table 4.1 suggest that legitimacy gaps are sometimes shared by all actors who express their view in the news. The Dutch railway company NS (*Nederlandse Spoorwegen*, "Dutch rail"), for example, is criticized by all actors. Trains in the Netherlands were late and not a single actor was satisfied with the precise nature of the privatization of the railways. But this is the exception rather than the rule. The legitimacy gap of most companies is due to the criticisms of specific other actors. Shell and British Petroleum, for example, still get support from the industry although many other actors criticize the oil companies. And in another example, although Albert Heijn (a big super-market chain) is criticized by almost every actor, the company is still supported by the trade unions. Table 4.1 shows also that half of the companies do not speak with one voice in the media, with the notable exception of two banks, British Petroleum, and Schiphol Airport. Firms that do not speak with one voice expose themselves to outside criticism. Finally, Table 4.1 shows that usually one of the two competitors in an industrial sector faces a higher legit-imacy gap than the other. For a variety of reasons, Albert Heijn (high prices and dubious labeling of products), ABN AMRO (no successes in mergers and take-overs), Shell (trying to be the best of the class, despite the Brent Spar affair), and NS (delays, disputed privatization) faced a higher legitimacy gap than their direct competitors Super de Boer, RABO, British Petroleum, and Schiphol Airport, respectively. Thus, the network perspective offers insights into the precise nature of legitimacy gaps.

Table 4.1 Legitimacy gaps of eight companies from four industrial branches according to voices in the press (ranging from −1 = criticisms only to +1 support only)

		Media		Internal		Industry		Government		Countries		Experts, NGO		Empl. union		Other actors	
		Row %	Gap	Row %	Gap	Row %	Gap	Row %	Gap	Row %	Gap	Row %	Gap	Row %	Gap	Row %	Gap
Retail	Albert Heijn	15	−0.48	4	−0.17	56	−0.22	2	−0.15	2	1.00	4	−1.00	5	0.10	11	−0.69
	Super de Boer		—		—	100	0.75		—		—		—		—		—
Banks	ABN AMRO	28	−0.30	12	0.44	37	−0.09	6	−0.11	2	−0.40	8	−0.42	3	0.56	3	−0.47
	Rabobank	19	−0.14	17	0.45	43	0.62	3	0.69	0	1.00	4	−0.19	2	0.23	11	−0.23
Oil	Shell	10	−0.29	25	−0.40	27	0.44	5	−0.61	19	−0.05	12	−0.33	2	−0.63	0	1.00
	BP	3	−1.00	25	0.04	51	0.92	5	1.00	2	−1.00	14	−0.71		—		—
Traffic	NS	8	−0.54	8	−0.68	20	0.27	29	−0.29	1	0.22	4	−0.80	25	−0.21	4	−0.34
	Schiphol	10	−0.39	4	0.32	26	0.03	34	−0.20	4	0.09	16	−0.35	3	−0.55	4	−0.01

Source: Meijer, 2004: 100.

4.4. Issue Life-Cycle Theory

In their overview of the state of the art in public relations, Botan and Taylor (2004) consider issue life-cycle theory, which discusses the origins, the development, and the decay of issues over time, as one of the most important theories in public relations. It is often assumed that issues have a "natural history" of rising, declining, and remaining in a final equilibrium stage where change in interest is minimal. A new issue is often raised by a discontented group, but other actors will take over the issue only if the perception exists that the problem can be solved (Downs, 1972). If an issue gets enough media attention, it will raise public concern (McCombs, Pablo Llamas, Lopez-Escobar, & Rey, 1997; McCombs & Shaw, 1972). Political actors, too, will usually prioritize the issue, albeit sometimes with symbolic politics rather than with a new policy (Edelman, 1985). Labeling, or "framing," is important to expand an issue. Overarching labels such as "the war on terror" (Bush, Jr.) do not only suggest a new us–them *division line* between actors (see section 4.2), but also open up windows of opportunity for new *issue entrepreneurs*, such as businesses for smart search engines, spyware and decryption software to detect extremists and terrorists, but also for developers of firewalls and encryption software to protect viable information. When many actors become involved with an issue, they will want to engage in public relation efforts to secure advantageous legislation.

News-selection research suggests that issues do not follow an autonomous "natural" history, but, rather, that their development depends stochastically on the precise action–reaction spirals between the media and a variety of elite actors, such as firms with a material interest in an issue, investors, political actors, trade unions (Kleinnijenhuis, 2001). Whenever an issue is so important that journalists acknowledge that it deserves attention, they will usually pay attention to the statements of the primary source who brought the issue to the fore. The primary source is the actor with the most successful efforts in raising news about an issue—with high-profile actions, press contacts, press releases, leaking "confidential" information, and so on. By definition, actors with a high material interest who want to keep the press out of their business seldom serve as the primary sources for the press. Journalists are usually well aware of the reputation of their sources. Typically, they cite and paraphrase their sources accurately with respect to their "owned issues"—in other words, relative to the areas in which they are highly regarded. The next turn in the action–reaction spiral is governed by the golden rule of a free press that it will listen to both sides. Usually, the combination of a primary source and an issue gives journalists a hint about whom to ask to give a comment. Table 4.2 lists a few likely quadruples of a primary source, owned issues, responding secondary actors, and expected media focus.

Table 4.2 shows, for example, that news about successes and failures of various competitors in an industrial branch is to be expected when investors—such as bankers, shareholders, and stock market analysts—are the primary source of the news, because these actors usually emphasize financial performance

Table 4.2 Primary sources, owned issues, secondary actors and expected media focus (adapted from Kleinnijenhuis, 2001)

Primary source	Owned issues primary source (journalists will give the lead to primary source)	Secondary actors who will be asked by journalists to respond	Expected focus of the media on:
Management of the firm, CEO	"Core business" of the firm; profit margins; shareholder value; strategy; innovation; mergers and take-overs; new products	Stock market analysts; competitors; perhaps labor unions, consumers and pressure groups (in the case of issues bearing on social responsibility)	• Sound bites CEO (especially on TV) • Issue news regarding mergers and innovations • News on support and criticism from stock market analysts, competitors, or perhaps labor unions, political parties, or pressure groups
Employees, labor unions	Terms of employment: wages, wholesale dismissals, benefit programs, fringe perquisites, strikes	Management; job market (competing firms, suppliers, customers); court (labor law); governments (social policy)	• News on support and criticism
Investors (bankers, analysts, shareholders)	Financial performance: profits, growth, share prices, investment risks, (deceptions in) accounting, corporate governance	Other investors; management; CEO	• News on issues of business performance • Horse race news, comparative news on successes and failures based on shareholder value
Consumers, consumer unions	Consumer satisfaction with products (price, performance, simplicity of use, compatibility, user risks, service, fashionableness); casualties, damage due to product use	Management; political parties, government; court (in the case of damage claims)	• Lifestyle news • News on ethical issues (e.g. in the case of genetic engineering of products) • News on support and criticism
Pressure groups (e.g. environment, human rights, anti-globalism)	External effects of business on the environment, human rights (e.g. child labor in third world countries), coopera-tion with authoritarian regimes, bribery)	Management; political parties, govern-ment (in the case of broad societal issues or abuse of business power)	• News on societal issues and on corporate responsibility • News on support and criticism
Politicians, parties	"Own issues" of their party	Other parties; government	• News on societal issues
Government, ministers, president, prime minister	Macro-economic policy and economic growth; law enforcement (e.g. tax evasion) and law abuse (e.g. corruption and fraud)	Political parties; court (in the case of prosecution of offenders); CEOs (in the case of serious disputes on the macro-economic policy)	• News on social and economic issues • News on support and criticism

compared to the financial performance of competitors; this will prompt journalists to look for comments from competitors. The analysts and spokesmen from the different companies with whom the journalists talked are not deemed newsworthy enough to be portrayed visually, for example in television news. On the basis of their information about the relative performance of competitors, journalists are prompted to tell their own story about successes and failures and about winners and losers. This type of news is unlikely, however, when the primary source of the news is the CEO of a large company announcing a major take-over. In this case, it is likely that the newsworthy CEO will be seen on television news. On the basis of the comments gathered by journalists from stock-market analysts, competitors, and perhaps from trade unions and special-interest pressure groups, some supportive or critical notes with respect to the take-over will also enter the news.

If all secondary actors who are asked to give their comments revert immediately back to their own issues, and if other media do not jump on the issue of the primary source, then the issue will soon abate or even become extinct. The news turmoil accelerates, however, when a secondary actor is provoked to launch a public defense or a public attack. In the case of attack and defense news, the division lines between the actors gain importance, with many actors responding on the basis of coalition preferences, rather than on the basis of their precise preferences with respect to the issue that was brought forward by the primary source, or on the basis of the frame that was used by the primary actor. The nature of the news will also change. More attention will be paid to conflicts and to the successes and failures of the adversaries. Many issues neither become extinct, nor accelerate after a news shock, but return to their equilibrium; this equilibrium may be cyclic. The quarterly figures of the major companies quoted on the stock exchange market, for example, give rise, each quarter, to a predictable pattern of responses from financial experts and the trade unions.

To put it differently, Table 4.2 does not represent universally applicable knowledge with respect to action–reaction spirals according to the news. What is needed is not an improved version of a still static Table 4.2, or a new version of the "natural history" of issues, but applied research *in* or *for* public relations —referring to the terminology of J. Grunig, this volume—to assess the nature of the dynamic networks that evolve around a company's issues.

4.5. Rhetorical Analysis

Rhetorical analysis, the fifth theoretical approach to corporate issues campaigns discussed by Bridges (2004), dates back to the early Greeks, but it was rediscovered in the past fifty years, due to the work of, among others, Stephen Toulmin (1958). Rhetorical analysis focuses on the argumentative structure of the texts that actors produce to constitute their relationships with each other. Rhetorical analysis brings in the—partly convergent and partly divergent— *cognitive networks of the actors themselves*, whereas the four theoretical approaches discussed earlier dealt with one network of relations between actors and issues.

Rhetorical analysis is understood in the social sciences and humanities as a matter of quoting propositions almost literally (van Eemeren, Grootendorst and Snoeck Henckemans, 2002), but from a network perspective one should *rewrite propositions as relations between meaning objects*, such as actors, issues (means and ends of policies included), ideals or values, and perceived realities (Carley, 1986; van Cuilenburg *et al.*, 1986). Rewriting the propositions extracted from statements, speeches, debates, policy proposals, press releases, or from news items about them, results in a network representation of argumentative texts for each of the observed actors. A network representation of the available argumentative texts results in a *cognitive network* (or "cognitive map") for each of the observed actors. Taken together, these cognitive networks give detailed information about shared meanings and shared interpretations. Shared interpretations arise from acknowledging the same actors, issues, and values, and from acknowledging the same relations between them. Recognizing different actors or different issues—e.g., different policy considerations, or different policy options—indicates differences in awareness and knowledge. Different values, different perceived realities, and different perceived relations between meaning objects reveal differences of opinion. An analysis of differences in awareness and differences of opinion in combination with an analysis of shared meanings and interpretations is the soil for a sensible transfer of information as well as for the design of attractive appeals and convincing arguments, both in negotiations and in public debates. Such an analysis explores the room for mutual adaptation. An analysis of cognitive networks may also reveal how arguments develop in the course of events, which in turn may result in a completely different climate of opinion within a few years. The revival of neo-classicism as the successor of Keynesianism in the economic outlook of the press of the early 1980s may serve as an example (Kleinnijenhuis *et al.*, 1997).

Rewriting propositions extracted from argumentative texts as elementary statements about relations between actors, issues, ideals, and perceived realities is precisely what is aimed at by a network content analysis of texts (de Ridder & Kleinnijenhuis, 2001; Kleinnijenhuis *et al.*, 1997; Popping, 2000; van Cuilenburg *et al.*, 1986), also called "cognitive mapping" (Axelrod, 1976; Carley, 1986; Young, 2001). As an example, Plato's classical syllogism is rewritten in the first row of Table 4.3 as a triangular network of Socrates, human beings, and mortality.

In a network representation, an argument reduces to an indirect path between two objects that is in balance with the direct link. If complete association is represented as +1, and complete dissociation as –1, then the sign of an indirect path can be obtained by multiplying the signs of its constitutive links. An indirect path is an argument for a direct link whenever their signs correspond to each other. As a further example, Table 4.3 lists the argument of why the EU should forbid Microsoft to integrate the Media Player into its operating system. The argument consists of two links, namely that the EU forbids setting

Table 4.3 Toward a network representation of propositions in argumentation

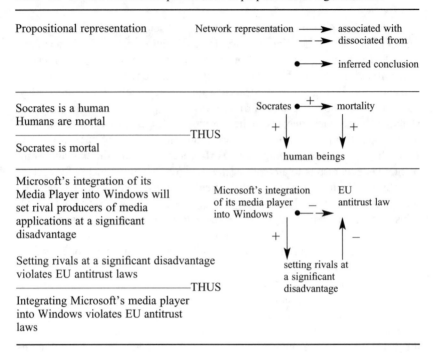

rivals at a disadvantage, whereas integrating the Media Player in Windows is a case of putting rivals at a disadvantage. Of course, many different arguments—many different indirect paths of varying lengths—may be proposed in order to support a given claim.

   Although actors can agree or disagree about almost everything, three major types of dispute are often distinguished: disputes about facts (including causal relations, true intentions of actors, and so on), disputes about values (including goals and goal hierarchies), and pragmatic disputes about the best means to achieve one or more goals (Schellens, 1985):

Dispute about facts	Do EU laws really forbid setting rivals at a disadvantage?
Dispute about values	Is forbidding setting rivals at a disadvantage justifiable?
Pragmatic dispute	Will a ban on the integration of Media Player with Microsoft Windows be of much help for Microsoft's rivals, such as RealPlayer?

To account for argumentation about facts, one should include not only actors and issues in the reconstruction of an actor's cognitive network, but also reality as perceived by that actor. To account for disputes about values, one should include an actor's ideals, values, and norms in the cognitive network. To account for pragmatic disputes, the means and the goals that are discussed should be included in the reconstruction of an actor's cognitive network. In summary, the cognitive networks of actors center around actors, issues (at the level of goals, but also at the level of means), around what is *ideal* (values and norms) and about what is the case in *reality*.

4.6. Social-Exchange Theory

Social-exchange theory considers relations between actors as the result of negotiations, adaptation, and exchange between selfish actors who attempt to make the most of their material or informational resources. The win–win approach that may result from negotiation of mutual benefits (J. Grunig, 1992) directly ties public relations to social-exchange theory (Bridges, 2004: 67).

The available research evidence suggests that most inter- and intra-organizational relations are created and maintained on the basis of exchange mechanisms. If exchanges are no longer rewarding, or as new or competitive others offer better bargains in the exchange, links begin to dissolve (e.g., Monge & Contractor, 2003: 209–222). Social-exchange theory introduces *game theory* into the network approach. Selfish actors would not meet their commitments once other actors have delivered on promise. Since other actors can be expected to be selfish, not a single actor would even deliver on promise except when trust is vested that the "shadow of the future" is long enough to enable revenge of the violation of contract duties (Axelrod, 1984). Trust is essentially committing to an exchange before you know how the other will reciprocate (Monge & Contractor, 2003: 213). Trust beyond what is observable—which is often based on faith in laws promising that ultimately the Sovereign will punish a breach of confidence—is seen as the basis for social, political, and economic exchange (Fukuyama, 1996). Negative news about others diminishes trust (Cappella & Jamieson, 1997), which may result in a creeping sleeper effect on future decisions to cooperate with others, although behavioral intentions toward others may remain unaltered in the short run (Kleinnijenhuis, van Hoof, & Oegema, 2006).

From a communication point of view, the interesting question is how mutual adaptation and exchange can be achieved when actors have an interest not to deliver once others have delivered. Usually, this state of affairs is modeled as a social dilemma, in the form of a generalization of the classical prisoner's dilemma. What does the obvious answer that trust should be fostered really mean when actors face a social dilemma? The simple answer is that convincing arguments should be given as to why the state of affairs is not a prisoner's dilemma. Convincing arguments could be given that the state of affairs really resembles a lose–lose chicken game, in which any actor's non-delivery will result in a catastrophe for every actor, regardless of whether the other actor delivers. One could also provide convincing arguments that the state of affairs really resembles a win–win assurance game, in which mutual cooperation is much more worthwhile for each of the actors than not delivering once others have delivered. The awkward complication is that isolated arguments about the state of affairs will often not convince actors. Instead of isolated arguments, a discourse coalition is required, which is shaped by actors who know that it is in their best interests to shape a common belief that the state of affairs is not a social dilemma, but a lose–lose game, or a win–win game, or even both a lose–lose and a win–win game. A discourse coalition is shaped by actors who believe that it is in their best interest to believe that they are all in the same boat on a stormy ocean (lose–lose) with land on the far horizon (win–win). In a study of discourse coalitions with respect to environmental protection, Hajer (1995) gives examples of the rise and decline of discourse coalitions. The environmental hype of the early 1970s shaped an environmental discourse coalition based on lose–lose chicken-game perceptions that were based, among others, on the Club of Rome report on the limits of growth. This discourse coalition disintegrated because of its lack of positive incentives for polluting businesses. "Small is beautiful" was not enticing enough. In the late 1980s, a new environmental discourse coalition emerged based on win–win assurance game perceptions which, in turn, were based, among others, on reports of the OECD (Organization for Economic Cooperation and Development) and other international organizations on industrial growth due to investments in sustainable production lines. It is easily observed that the latter discourse coalition disintegrated because in the late 1990s the highest growth rates were not achieved in old industrial branches who had turned to sustainable growth, but in the ICT branch. The message from most definitions of public relations is that PR efforts should shape and bolster strategic discourse coalitions that enable exchange and mutual adaptation despite incentives not to cooperate and not to deliver.

5. Summary and Discussion

In public relations, "the key dependent variable is relations" (J. Grunig, this volume). Therefore, this chapter is aimed at an adoption of the network approach for public relations, since network models take relations between objects as their dependent variables. Starting from a historical sketch of the development of the network approach in the social sciences—especially in the communication discipline—the chapter addresses the relevance and the limitations of the network approach for the field of public relations.

The network perspective was applied in the remainder of the chapter to discuss how the six theoretical approaches to public relations that were delineated by Janet Bridges (2004) could be elaborated further to arrive at valuable insights *on* public relations—more than *in* or *for* public relations (cf. J. Grunig this volume). A number of examples were given to elucidate the contributions from the network perspective. Standard network approaches suffer from several limitations, however, such as an oversimplified view on the nature of relations between actors, a static view on the cognitive maps of actors, and a lack of data.

This chapter attempts to show that the network approach is nevertheless worthwhile for the study on public relations. In the age of the web electronic media and business archives, large-scale content analysis studies that start from a network approach (de Ridder & Kleinnijenhuis, 2001; Popping, 2000; Roberts, 1997; Young, 2001) come within the reach of public relations scholars so as to obtain the relational data that are required to test theories, in and for public relations. New approaches to network analysis may also overcome the other limitations.

The network perspective is useful for the accentuation and the further development of insights that can be gained from six theoretical approaches that were delineated by Janet Bridges (2004). The network approach appears to have a great potential for research *in* and *for* public relations professionals (cf. J. Grunig, this volume) also, because these insights appear to regard the problems that public relations professionals encounter in their profession. Starting from *systems theory*, the network perspective adds details to answers to the questions of whether monitoring an organization's environment is always worthwhile, and whether mutual awareness is always desirable. A network perspective on *stakeholder theory* asks of issues management how it contributes to division lines between actors that are conducive for achieving organizational goals. A network perspective on *legitimacy gap theory* results in attention for issue ownership, for the usage of inoculation techniques and for support, and criticism for organizations according to the media. A network perspective on *issue life-cycle theory* asks for a much more dynamic analysis of the issue-specific interactions between primary sources, owned issues, and secondary actors, and for attention to the limitations of framing efforts. *Rhetorical analysis* brings in the cognitive networks of each separate actor, whereas the four previous approaches dealt with the network of actors and issues as observed by one actor. Network theory requires that the propositions that are simply quoted in most treatises on argumentation be rewritten as statements about the relations between actors, issues, ideals (values and norms), and perceived realities. The network perspective offers the key to acknowledge shared meanings and interpretations, differences in awareness, and differences of opinion that public relations professionals could use to develop worthwhile information and convincing arguments. Finally, *social-exchange theory* introduces the theory of games. From a network perspective, the question becomes one of how communication efforts may contribute to the emergence of lose–lose or win–win discourse coalitions that overcome the inclinations of actors not to cooperate and not to deliver.

Notes

1   It should be noted that Axelrod was one one of the first social scientists to treat bilateral games between two actors in the context of a wider network, but he considered only strategies based on information about the history of the bilateral game—as did unfortunately the overwhelming majority of the researchers who

followed Axelrod's track—thereby neglecting strategies that are based on information about the complete network, e.g., CAESAR, divide-and-conquer.

2   A website with FAQs on evolutionary computing is /www.cs.bham.ac.uk/Mirrors/ ftp.de.uu.net/EC/clife/www/.

References

Abbe, O. G., Goodliffe, J., Herrnson, P. S., & Patterson, K. D. (2003). Agenda setting in congressional elections: The impact of issues and campaigns on voting behavior. *Political Research Quarterly, 56*(4), 419–430.

Axelrod, R. A. (1976). *Structure of decision.* Princeton, NJ: Princeton University Press.

Axelrod, R. A. (1984). *The evolution of cooperation.* New York: Basic Books.

Azar, E. E. (1993 [1982]). *Conflict and Peace Data Bank (COPDAB), 1948–1978* (computer file). College Park: University of Maryland.

Botan, C. H., & Taylor, M. (2004). Public relations: State of the field. *Journal of Communication, 54*(4), 645–661.

Bridges, J. A. (2004). Corporate issues campaigns: Six theoretical approaches. *Communication Theory, 14*(1), 31–77.

Budge, I., & Farlie, D. J. (1983). *Explaining and predicting elections: Issues effects and party strategies in twenty-three democracies.* London: George, Allen & Urwin.

Burt, R. S. (1992). *Structural holes: The social structure of competition.* Cambridge, MA: Harvard University Press.

Cappella, J. N., & Jamieson, K. H. (1997). *Spiral of cynicism: The press and the public good.* New York, Oxford, England: Oxford University Press.

Carley, K. M. (1986). An approach for relating social structure to cognitive structure. *Journal of Mathematical Sociology, 12*(2), 137–189.

Castells, M. (1996). *The rise of the network society.* Oxford, England, Malden, MA: Blackwell.

Collins, A., & Quillian, M. R. (1969). Retrieval time from semantic memory. *Journal of Verbal Learning and Verbal Behavior, 8,* 240–247.

de Croon, G. d., van Dartel, M. F., & Postma, E. O. (2005). Evolutionary learning outperforms reinforcement learning on non-Markovian tasks. Universiteit Maastricht, obtained from fg.decroon@unimaas.nl.

de Ridder, J. A., & Kleinnijenhuis, J. (2001). Media monitoring using CETA: The stock-exchange launches of KPN and WOL. In M. West (Ed.), *Applications of computer content analysis* (pp. 165–184). Westport, CT, London: Ablex.

de Vries, R., van den Hooff, B., & de Ridder, J. A. (2006). Explaining knowledge sharing: The role of team communication styles, job satisfaction and performance beliefs. *Communication Research, 33*(2), 1–21.

Doreian, P., Batagelj, V., & Ferligoj, A. (2005). *Generalized blockmodeling.* Cambridge, England: Cambridge University Press.

Downs, A. (1972). Up and down with ecology: The "issue-attention cycle." *The Public Interest, 28,* 38–50.

Edelman, M. (1985). *The symbolic uses of politics* (2nd ed.). Urbana: University of Illinois Press.

Fukuyama, F. (1996). *Trust: The social virtues and the creation of prosperity.* New York: Free Press.

Gelman, A., & Hill, J. (2007) *Data analysis using regression and multilevel/hierarchical models.* Cambridge, England: Cambridge University Press.

Granovetter, M. (1973). The strength of weak ties. *American Journal of Sociology*, *81*(6), 1287–1303.

Grunig, J. E. (1992). *Excellence in public relations and communication management.* Hillsdale, NJ: Erlbaum.

Gurr, T. R. (1970). *Why men rebel.* Princeton, NJ: Princeton University Press.

Hajer, M. (1995). *The politics of environmental discourse: Ecological modernization and the policy process.* Oxford, England, New York: Clarendon Press.

Heath, R. L. (1997). *Strategic issues management: Organizations and public policy challenges.* Thousand Oaks, CA: Sage.

Heider, F. (1946). Attitudes and cognitive organization. *Journal of Psychology*, *21*, 107–112.

Heylighen, F., & Joslyn, C. (2001). Cybernetics and second-order cybernetics. In R. A. Meyers (Ed.), *Encyclopaedia of physical science and technology.* New York: Academic Press.

Kerr, N. L., & Kaufman-Gilliland, C. M. (1994). Communication, commitment, and cooperation in social dilemmas. *Journal of Personality and Social Psychology*, *66*(3), 513–529.

Kleinnijenhuis, J. (2001). Organisatiereputatie en publiciteit. In C. B. M. v. Riel (Ed.), *Corporate communication: het managen van reputatie* (3rd ed.). Alphen aan den Rijn: Kluwer.

Kleinnijenhuis, J., de Ridder, J. A., & Rietberg, E. M. (1997). Reasoning in economic discourse: An application of the network approach to the Dutch press. In C. W. Roberts (Ed.), *Text analysis for the social sciences: Methods for drawing statistical inferences from texts and transcripts* (pp. 191–207). New York: Erlbaum.

Kleinnijenhuis, J., Oegema, D., de Ridder, J. A., van Hoof, A. M. J., & Vliegenthart, R. (2003). *De puinhopen in het nieuws.* Alphen aan de Rijn: Kluwer.

Kleinnijenhuis, J., van Hoof, A. M. J., & Oegema, D. (2006). Negative news and the sleeper effect of distrust. *Harvard International Journal of Press and Politics*, *11*(2), 86–104.

Knoke, D. (1990). *Political networks: The structural perspective.* Cambridge, England: Cambridge University Press.

Lippmann, W. (1922). *Public opinion.* New York: Free Press.

Lynch, R. (1997). *Corporate strategy.* London: Pitman Publishing.

Maynard Smith, J. (1983). *Evolution and the theory of games.* Cambridge, England: Cambridge University Press.

McCombs, M. E., Pablo Llamas, J.-P., Lopez-Escobar, E., & Rey, F. (1997). Candidate images in Spanish elections: Second-level agenda-setting effects. *Journalism and Mass Communication Quarterly*, *74*(4), 703–717.

McCombs, M. E., & Shaw, D. L. (1972). The agenda-setting function of mass media. *Public Opinion Quarterly*, *36*, 176–187.

Meijer, M.-M. (2004). *Does success breed success? Effects of news and advertising on corporate reputation.* Amsterdam: Aksant.

Meijer, M.-M., & Kleinnijenhuis, J. (2006). Issue news and corporate reputation: applying the theories of agenda setting and issue ownership in the field of business communication. *Journal of Communication*, *56*(2), 543–559.

Moloney, K. (2005). Trust and public relations: Center and edge. *Public Relations Review*, *31*(4), 550–555.

Monge, P. R., & Contractor, N. S. (2001). Emergence of communication networks. In F. M. Jablin and L. L. Scott (Eds.) *The new handbook of organizational communication* (pp. 440–502). Newbury Park, CA: Sage.

Monge, P. R., & Contractor, N. S. (2003). *Theories of communication networks.* Oxford, England: Oxford University Press.

Newcomb, Theodore M. (1953). An approach to the study of communication acts. *Psychological Review, 60,* 393–404.

Nowak, M., & Sigmund, K. (1993). A strategy of win-shift, lose-stay that outperforms tit-for-tat in the Prisoners' Dilemma game. *Nature, 364,* 56–57.

Pennings, P. J. M., Keman, J. E., & Kleinnijenhuis, J. (2006) *Doing research in political science.* New York, London: Sage.

Petrocik, J. R. (1996). Issue ownership in presidential elections, with a 1980 case study. *American Journal of Political Science, 40*(3), 825–850.

Petrocik, J. R., Benoit, W. L., & Hansen, G. J. (2003). Issue ownership and presidential campaigning, 1952–2000. *Political Science Quarterly, 118*(4), 599–628.

Pfau, M. (1995). Designing messages for behavioral inoculation. In *Designing health messages: Approaches from communication theory and public health practice* (pp. 99–113). Thousand Oaks, CA: Sage.

Popping, R. (2000). *Computer-assisted text analysis.* Newbury Park, CA, London: Sage.

Roberts, C. W. (Ed.) (1997). *Text analysis for the social sciences: Methods for drawing statistical inferences from texts and transcripts.* Mahwah, NJ: Erlbaum.

Sampson, S. P. (1968). *A novitiate in a period of change: An experimental and case study of social relationships.* New York: Cornell University.

Schattschneider, E. E. (1960). *The semi-sovereign people: A realist's view of democracy in America.* New York: Holt Rinehart & Winston.

Schellens, P.-J. (1985). *Redelijke argumenten: een onderzoek naar normen voor kritische lezers (Reasonable arguments. A study in criteria for critical reading).* Dordrecht: Foris.

Schrodt, P. A. (2001). *Automated coding of international event data using sparse data techniques.* Paper presented at the International Studies Association, Chicago, February 21–24, 2001.

Shin, J.-H., Cheng, I.-H., Jin, Y., & Cameron, G. T. (2005). Going head to head: Content analysis of high profile conflicts as played out in the press. *Public Relations Review, 31*(3), 339–406.

Sigelman, L., & Buell, E. H. J. (2004). Avoidance or engagement? Issue convergence in U.S. presidential campaigns, 1960–2000. *American Journal of Political Science, 48*(4), 650–661.

Skrondal, A., & Rabe-Hesketh, S. (2004). *Generalized latent variable modeling: multilevel, longitudinal, and structural equation models.* Boca Raton, FL: Chapman and Hall, CRC.

Snijders, T. A. B., & Bosker, R. J. (1999). *Multilevel analysis: An introduction to basic and advanced multilevel modeling.* Newbury Park, CA: Sage.

Toulmin, S. E. (1958). *The uses of argument.* Cambridge, England: Cambridge University Press.

Utz, S., Ouwerkerk, J. W., & Van Langen, P. A. M. (2004). What is smart in a social dilemma? Differential effects of priming competence on cooperation. *European Journal of Social Psychology, 34,* 317–332.

van Cuilenburg, J. J., Kleinnijenhuis, J., & de Ridder, J. A. (1986). Towards a graph theory of journalistic texts. *European Journal of Communication, 1,* 65–96.

van de Bunt, G. G. (1999). *Friends by choice. An actor-oriented statistical network model for friendship networks through time.* Groningen: Rijksuniversiteit Groningen.

van den Bergh, J. J. C. M. (2004). Evolutionary modeling. In J. Proops & P. Safonov (Eds.), *Modelling in ecological economics*. Cheltenham: Edward Elgar.

van Eemeren, F., Grootendorst, R., & Snoeck Henckemans, A. F. (2002). *Argumentation: Analysis, evaluation, presentation*. Mahwah, NJ: Erlbaum.

van Langen, P. A. M., Ouwerkerk, J. W., & Tazelaar, M. J. A. (2002). How to overcome the detrimental effects of noise in social interaction: The benefits of generosity. *Journal of Personality and Social Psychology, 82*(5), 768–780.

van Ruler, A. A. (2000). Communication management in the Netherlands. *Public Relations Review, 26*(3), 403–423.

Weenig, W. H., & Midden, C. J. H. (1991). Communication network influences on information diffusion and persuasion. *Journal of Personality and Social Psychology, 61*, 734–742.

Young, M. D. (2001). Building worldviews with Profiler+. In M. D. West (Ed.), *Applications of computer content analysis* (pp. 17–32). Westport, CT, London: Ablex.

5 Conceptualizing Quantitative Research in Public Relations[1]

James E. Grunig

1. Introduction

Public relations practitioners in the United States first became interested in measurement and evaluation in the 1970s, although discussion of the topic has exploded in the last ten years. The beginning of this explosion of interest occurred around October 10, 1996, when the U.S. Institute for Public Relations, the magazine *Inside PR*, and the Ketchum Public Relations Research and Measurement Department invited twenty-one leading U.S. public relations practitioners, counselors, researchers, and academicians to a summit meeting to discuss and then define minimum standards for measuring the effectiveness of public relations. The group developed and agreed on a report describing the state of the art in public relations evaluation (Lindenmann, 1997), and in 1998 the group formally became a Measurement Commission under the sponsorship of the Institute for Public Relations. Since that time, the Measurement Commission has met four times each year, issued a number of publications, and held annual Measurement Summits since 2003. At the same time, public relations firms and research firms have developed a number of tools to measure and evaluate communication programs; and discussion of metrics has dominated public relations periodicals and conferences.

I believe it is unfortunate, however, that the terms "measurement" and "metrics" have been used more often to describe this revolution in thinking about public relations than the term "research." Measurements are tools that researchers use to test their ideas. Public relations programs result from ideas developed by practitioners, just as research hypotheses result from ideas of academic scholars. As Manfred Rühl points out in Chapter 2 of this volume, measurement by itself has little value unless it is preceded by conceptualization. Measurement is only half of what a researcher does, and it probably is the least important half. More important is the ability to conceptualize—to think logically and systematically about concepts, definitions, measures, and the relationships among them.

Academic scholars have known how to measure and evaluate the effects of communication programs since the 1950s, and a new breed of scholars began to conduct theoretical research on public relations in the 1960s. Academic research on public relations has grown exponentially since that time, but there still are few public relations scholars compared to the numbers in other communication disciplines. Public relations practitioners today have access to an exploding number of research firms, research divisions of public relations firms, and in-house research departments. Many practitioners have training in research methods themselves. However, most public relations practice today still does not include research; and most of that research is limited to measuring the short-term effects of marketing communication and media relations programs. Although great progress has been made in academic research on public relations, most practitioners and applied public relations researchers do not seem to be aware of this research.

As a result, I believe, the greatest problem in public relations is not the lack of measurement but the lack of conceptualization. Metrics abound, but I believe that a large number of applied researchers and public relations practitioners use metrics without knowing what concepts they are measuring. For example, media monitoring is often used to try to show the value of the public relations function—a metric gathered at one level of analysis to show an outcome at a higher level of analysis. Therefore, if we are to use research to improve the practice of public relations we must improve our conceptualization of public relations itself and of the effects we are seeking when we practice it. In this chapter, I will explain conceptualization and how it can be used to identify relevant measures that can be used in quantitative research to formulate and evaluate public relations ideas. The process of conceptualization applies also to qualitative research, a topic addressed by L. Grunig in Chapter 6 of this book, so I will limit most of my discussion to quantitative research in this chapter.

I will begin this chapter by discussing differences between academic research on and for public relations and research that is conducted in the practice of public relations. Next, I will discuss the nature of conceptualization. The chapter then will develop a conceptual framework that can be used to guide research in the practice of public relations. It will conclude by describing ongoing academic research that has identified concepts and tools that can enhance public relations practice.

2. Research In, On, and for Public Relations

I believe there is a great deal of confusion among both practitioners and academic scholars in the public relations discipline about their differing roles and the extent to which their work complements each other. Practitioners often seem to believe that academics are practitioners like themselves who have chosen to teach and conduct research rather than practice. As a result, they often think that most academic research is useless because they see no way to apply it in their work. They also typically believe that academics should learn from practitioners and use what they learn in teaching the next generation of practitioners.

Academics, on the other hand, typically see themselves as critics and analysts of the public relations profession more than as practitioners. Although academics hope their criticism and analysis will improve the profession, they do not believe that all of their research must have practical applications. They express dismay when practitioners show little interest in research to develop the profession from a broad perspective. They generally believe that practitioners should learn from academics to improve or change their practice. Academic scholars are willing to help practitioners understand how to conduct research *in* the practice of public relations; but, for the most part, they are more interested in conducting basic theoretical research *on* the profession.

To overcome these misconceptions of each other, we must realize that public relations is a profession. In professional disciplines such as law, medicine, education, and management, academic researchers and practitioners interact and learn from each other. Each, however, contributes something different to the body of knowledge. When academic scholars conduct research *on* the profession, they often develop ideas *for* the profession—that is, ideas that flow from basic research that practitioners can use *in* the profession. To develop those ideas, however, academic scholars must understand the problems that practitioners' experience; and they must interact with practitioners to understand whether their ideas are useful in practice.

If we are to understand the nature of both academic research and applied research in public relations, therefore, we can begin by distinguishing among these three types of research:

- *Research in public relations* is conducted by practitioners as part of the practice of public relations or research conducted by professional researchers in research firms or research units in public relations firms or in-house public relations departments. Academic public relations scholars often conduct such research for public relations practitioners or train applied researchers to do it. However, research in public relations generally does not bring academic rewards such as promotion, tenure, or salary increases because it generally does not lead to a broad theoretical understanding of the public relations profession unless it is based on research *on* the profession.
- *Research on public relations* is usually conducted by academic scholars using a theoretical framework they construct. At times, professional associations, public relations firms, and trade publications conduct research on public relations, although they usually do not do so from a theoretical perspective. Most scholars who conduct research on the profession do so in order to identify best practices and to improve the profession. The most extensive such research project was the fifteen-year *Excellence* project that my colleagues and I conducted with funding from the International Association of Business Communicators (IABC) Research Foundation (L. Grunig, J. Grunig, & Dozier, 2002). Other scholars, who call themselves critical scholars in contrast to what they call instrumental

scholars, conduct research on the profession to expose its negative activities and what they believe to be weaknesses in the theories of scholars working to improve the profession (e.g., Curtin & Gaither, 2005; Durham, 2005; Holzhausen & Voto, 2002; Leitch & Neilson, 2001; L'Etang & Pieczka, 1996; McKie, 2001; Motion & Weaver, 2005). Usually, but not always (an exception is Holzhausen & Voto, 2002), critical scholars have little interest in conducting research *for* the profession.

- *Research for public relations* usually results from research on the profession, except for the research of critical scholars. For example, researchers have identified best practices in crisis communication, issues management, environmental scanning, and media relations and then diffused those best practices to practitioners. Others have developed theoretical ideas such as symmetrical communication or a strategic managerial role, as we did in the *Excellence* study and research that preceded it, and use such ideas in the teaching of new practitioners and diffuse them to current practitioners. These best practices and theoretical ideas then can be used and evaluated *in* the practice of public relations—thus fusing research *on* the practice, *for* the practice, and *in* the practice. Such fusion is the hallmark of a true profession.

The primary focus of the current discussion of metrics in public relations and of most of the chapters in this book is research *in* the profession. Most of the current research in the profession, however, lacks a basic conceptual foundation. In addition, most of it fails to use research *on* and *for* the profession to develop a conceptual framework. The next section, therefore, explains conceptualization; and the rest of the chapter conceptualizes how research *in* the profession can be conducted and how researchers working in the profession can use academic research conducted *on* and *for* the profession to improve their conceptualization of the independent and dependent variables they are measuring.

3. The Nature of Conceptualization

Conceptualization is the process of thinking logically and systematically about concepts, definitions, measures, and the relationships among them. First, researchers begin to conceptualize when they isolate and describe problems —both theoretical and applied—that are worthy of study. Second, they think logically about how to solve the problem by identifying a concept, which usually is called a dependent variable in quantitative research, whose presence or absence defines the problem. Third, they identify independent variables that have a logical effect on the dependent variable that can be changed to have an effect on the dependent variable—thus solving the problem. Most of this conceptualization takes place at an abstract, or theoretical, level. If researchers do not think theoretically before they measure something, their measurements usually turn out to have little or no value—other than measurement for its own sake.

Public relations people can apply the same kind of rigor to practice. They need to define problems, identify variables that can be changed to solve the problem, change these independent variables, and then measure to determine if the dependent variable has changed and the problem has been solved. Practitioners tend to behave historically rather than scientifically, however. They do what they have always done—or what others in their organization have done. As a result, they usually cannot explain why they do what they do or what effect it has when a skeptical top manager or client asks. Furthermore, they have difficulty working with professional researchers (who usually do not understand public relations) who need to have logically related variables to measure before they conduct either formative or evaluative research.

This is not to say that public relations practitioners do not have a theory. Nearly every human being can construct an explanation for his or her behavior if asked. The difference between a scientist (or other kind of scholar) and a layperson is that the scientist has systematically developed his or her conceptualization. In public relations, practitioner theories often include concepts such as image, reputation, brand, relationships, and issues. The word "management" is then attached to these concepts (such as reputation management) to suggest that the dependent variable (reputation) can be changed (managed). However, dependent variables can seldom be changed directly because they are outcomes of behaviors or processes (independent variables) that can be changed. Thus, we can manage the behaviors and processes that result in a reputation, for example; but we cannot manage the reputation.

3.1. The Conceptual Process

Theorists commonly use the diagram in Figure 5.1 to explain the process of conceptualization.[2] The two levels of this diagram describe two kinds of thinking. The top level describes theoretical or conceptual thinking. The bottom level describes operational thinking—applying measures to concepts.

At the conceptual level, a theory usually consists of at least two concepts, which are usually called "variables" in quantitative research (but not necessarily

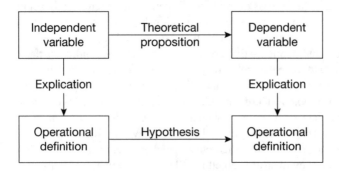

Figure 5.1 Components of conceptualization

so in qualitative research). We simplify the theory here by including only two concepts, although there can be more than two related independent or dependent variables in a theory. The theorist links these two concepts by stating a logical expected relationship—a theoretical proposition. The relationship can be causal but it does not have to be. The theorist only needs to say that the dependent variable is affected by (depends on) the independent variable.

The independent variable is independent of the other variable in the theory. It can be affected from outside the theory, however, by intervention of a researcher (such as in an experiment) or by a practitioner (who can engage in an activity that eventually affects the dependent variable). For example, in public relations the dependent variable might be *reputation*. The independent variable might consist of *messages* sent by public relations practitioners (a common assumption in public relations thinking) or it might consist of *management behaviors* (which I believe is more likely).

When one "manages" within this framework, he or she "directs, controls, or carries on" (*New Webster's Dictionary*) the independent variable. If one could "direct, control, or carry on" the dependent variable directly, it would not be a dependent variable. To continue with the example of reputation, a practitioner cannot manage reputation; he or she can manage only the messages or the management behaviors that have an expected theoretical relationship with reputation.

We move to the operational level of the diagram when we do research to test the theoretical proposition we developed at the conceptual level. Theories cannot be tested directly because they are abstract. To measure the concepts that are included in a theory, we have to operationalize them—specify how we can observe or measure the concept. For example, we can observe messages by counting the number or types of messages sent out. We can observe management behavior by classifying, describing, or counting what management did. Reputation has been measured by analyzing media coverage, by asking people what they think about the organization, or by asking financial analysts and CEOs to complete a survey of their attitudes.

We "explicate" a concept when we derive operational definitions of the concept. The operational definitions must be carefully thought through and be logically related to the concept. There may be several related operational definitions of the same concept, however, because the concept is more abstract than the definition. The concept must "cover" the operational definition. Philosophers of science call these explications "covering laws."

We call the relationship between operational definitions a "hypothesis." It must parallel the theoretical proposition at the conceptual level so that we can test that proposition by measuring empirically whether the operational definition of the independent variable affects the operational definition of the dependent variable in the way predicted by the proposition. Because the proposition is always more abstract than the hypothesis, many hypotheses can be developed to test the proposition. That is why scientists say you can never *prove* a theory by confirming a single hypothesis. You can *support* a theory by confirming a single hypothesis, but you must confirm many hypotheses over time before the weight of the evidence allows researchers to conclude that the theory is a good one—"good" meaning that managing the independent variable more often than not solves the problem by changing the dependent variable.

For research to be done well, the thinking and measuring processes that occur in the boxes and the relationships between the boxes of Figure 5.1 must meet high logical and empirical standards. First, theoretical variables must be *defined* well so that they have a single clear meaning. Chaffee (1996) called this "the disciplined use of words" (p. 20). He emphasized that the name we choose for a concept is crucial. Other scholars and practitioners should be able to grasp the meaning of the concept when they hear the name. It should contain the "essential features of an idea" (p. 21). If the name conveys different meanings to different people, it is not a good concept. Unfortunately, that is the case with popular public relations terms such as image and reputation. We determine the *validity* of research by comparing the operational definitions with the concepts they measure. We ask, does the operational definition "represent the concept as we have defined it . . . does the hypothesis represent a test of the theory?" (p. 24).

In addition to the conceptual processes described in Figure 5.1, the unit of analysis of a theory has particular relevance to theorizing in public relations. As Chaffee (1996) put it:

> A basic question that can be surprisingly tricky is, for what class of entities does this concept vary? Is it an attribute of individual persons, of aggregates such as communities or nations, of messages, of events, or of some other unit? Units of analysis should be the ones talked about in your theorizing and the ones that are observed and described in empirical work. Inconsistency in the unit of analysis is a common error in communication research.
>
> (p. 25)

The concept of image provides a good example of confusion over units of analysis. Practitioners often say that their organization has an image—therefore, defining the term as a property of an organization. Others talk about projecting, creating, polishing, or restoring images. Essentially, they are talking about communicating positive messages about their organization—the unit of analysis is the message. Others talk about images as residing in the minds of their publics—an individual, psychological unit of analysis. Still others define image as what the media say about an organization—so that a content analysis of media stories defines image operationally. Still others lump all these units of analysis together and define image as the "sum total" or "composite" of all of them—a certain problem of adding apples and oranges.

An unclear unit of analysis becomes particularly problematic when the independent variable is defined as a different unit of analysis than the dependent variable, or the operational definitions specify a different unit than the theoretical concepts. This is evident in the assertions of many media monitoring services that maintain that their analyses of media content are measures of public opinion—media *messages* are defined as measures of *collective* opinions.

3.2. An Example of a Conceptualization of the Public Relations Process

Although other theorists might conceptualize the process differently, I believe that a logical conceptualization of the public relations process states that public relations people manage *communication* with *top managers* and with *publics* (concepts are italicized) to contribute to the strategic decision processes of organizations. They manage communication between management and publics to build *relationships* with the publics that are most likely to affect the behavior of the organization or who are most affected by the behavior of the organization.

Communication processes can be managed (they are independent variables), and processes that facilitate dialogue among managers and publics can also contribute to managing *organizational behaviors*—although public relations people cannot manage organizational behaviors by themselves. Dialogue among managers and publics, in turn, can produce long-term relationships character-ized as communal relationships that result in higher levels of the indicators of the quality of a relationship my students and I (e.g., J. Grunig & Huang, 2000; J. Grunig & Hung, 2002) have identified and defined—trust, mutuality of control, commitment, and satisfaction. Relationships also are affected much more by the behavior of management than by one-way messages sent out by public relations or advertising people.

The independent variables, therefore, are *communication activities* conducted by public relations departments and *management behaviors* that result from strategic decisions. The key dependent variable is relationships. Relationships do influence dependent variables farther down the causal chain, such as reputations, images, attitudes, and brands. But these variables also are affected by other variables outside the control of public relations, such as financial markets, the state of the economy, or corporate behaviors over which public relations has little influence.

With this basic understanding of conceptualization, we can now move to develop a conceptual framework for research conducted *in* the practice of public relations.

4. Basic Concepts for Research in Public Relations

In their book, *Using Research in Public Relations*, Broom and Dozier (1990) described five approaches to the use of research in public relations programs. Three of these approaches do not include research as an integral part of the ongoing management of such programs. The first of these approaches is to use no research, which is all too common in public relations practice. A second is the use of informal research, such as talking to members of the public or the media, reading reports, or listening to unsolicited feedback from superiors or members of a public without systematically planning the research or analyzing the results. This is another common, but limited, approach.

A third is "media-event" research, in which organizations typically conduct a poll, for example, to determine how satisfied participants are with an organization or the extent to which they favor an organization's policies. The organization then publicizes the results if they are favorable in order to marshal support for the organization or policy. Organizations typically conduct the fourth type of research, evaluation-only research, to show managers or clients that programs have been effective. If the research shows that a program has not been effective, the organization typically downplays the results or is forced to discontinue a program. However, the research plays no role in planning or improving communication programs.

In contrast to these typical approaches to research in public relations, Broom and Dozier (1990) recommended what they called "the scientific management of public relations." Just as research in science is used to develop, test, and revise theories, so research in scientifically managed public relations is used to develop, test, and revise communication programs. With the scientific management of public relations, research also is a part of the communication process itself. Scientific management of public relations includes research at different levels, or units, of analysis; and it is based on research conducted both before and after a program is conducted. It can also be done with both quantitative and qualitative methods, although this chapter concentrates on quantitative methods.

4.1. Levels of Analysis in Public Relations Research

Public relations practitioners and scholars have strived for many years to explain the value of communication programs. Until recently, they have focused most of their efforts on the evaluation of individual communication programs, such as media relations, community relations, or employee relations. In fact, the root of "evaluation" is "value." Focusing only on the evaluation of individual programs is too narrow, however, although evaluation should be an ongoing part of the scientific management of all communication programs.

In the *Excellence* project (L. Grunig *et al.*, 2002), my colleagues and I searched the literature on organizational effectiveness for ideas that could explain the value of public relations beyond the effects of individual communication programs. We believed it was necessary to understand first what it means for an organization to be effective before we could explain how public relations makes it more effective. We learned that effective organizations achieve their goals, but that there is much conflict within the organization and with outside constituencies about which goals are most important. Effective organizations are able to achieve their goals because they choose goals that are valued by their strategic constituencies both inside and outside the organization and also because they successfully manage programs designed to achieve those goals.

Effective organizations choose and achieve appropriate goals because they develop relationships with their constituencies, which we in public relations call "publics." Ineffective organizations cannot achieve their goals, at least in part, because their publics do not support and typically oppose management efforts to achieve what publics consider illegitimate goals. Public relations makes an organization more effective, therefore, when it identifies the most strategic publics as part of strategic management processes and conducts communication programs to develop effective long-term relationships with those publics. As a result, we should be able to determine the value of public relations by measuring the quality of relationships with strategic publics. Furthermore, we should be able to evaluate individual communication programs by measuring their effects on indicators of a good relationship.

Organizations must be effective at four increasingly higher units of analysis— (1) the program level, (2) the functional level, (3) the organizational level, and (4) the societal level. Effectiveness at a lower level contributes to effectiveness at higher levels, but organizations cannot be said to be truly effective unless they have value at the highest of these levels. Research in public relations can be conducted to systematically plan how to increase effectiveness at each level and to evaluate the extent to which a public relations program has contributed to organizational effectiveness.

The *program level* refers to individual communication programs such as media relations, community relations, or employee relations that are components of the overall public relations function of an organization. Communication programs generally are effective when they meet specific objectives such as affecting the cognitions, attitudes, and behaviors of both publics and members of the organization.

The *functional level* refers to the evaluation of the overall public relations function of an organization, which typically includes several communication programs for different publics. Even though individual communication programs successfully accomplish their objectives, the overall public relations function might not be effective unless it is integrated into the overall management processes of an organization and has chosen appropriate publics and objectives for individual programs. The public relations function as a whole can be audited by comparing its structure and processes with those of similar departments in other organizations or with theoretical principles derived from scholarly research—a process called benchmarking. These audits can be conducted through self-review or peer review.

The *organizational level* refers to the contribution that public relations makes to the overall effectiveness of the organization. Public relations contributes to organizational effectiveness when it helps integrate the organization's goals and behavior with the expectations and needs of its strategic publics. This contribution adds value—sometimes monetary—to the organization. Public relations adds value by building good, long-term relationships with strategic publics; and research can be used to monitor and evaluate the quality of these strategic relationships.

Research at the *societal level* refers to evaluations of the contribution that organizations make to the overall welfare of a society. Organizations have an impact beyond their own boundaries. They also serve and affect individuals, publics, and other organizations in society. As a result, organizations cannot be said to be effective unless they are socially responsible; and public relations adds value to society by contributing to the ethical behavior and the social responsibility of organizations.

4.2. Formative and Evaluative Research

As Broom and Dozier (1990) pointed out, evaluation research alone is of limited value. Evaluation research measures dependent variables only and is conducted after programs have been implemented. In contrast, scientists conduct research both to formulate theories and, after theories are specified, to evaluate and improve those theories. The same procedures should be used in the scientific management of public relations programs. Both formative and evaluative research should be used at all four levels of analysis. Public relations departments often are asked to provide evidence of their value at the societal or organizational level. Too often, however, they respond by conducting evaluation-only research, such as media monitoring, at the program level.

Public relations departments, therefore, should conduct *formative research* to identify strategic publics, to determine how the organization can communicate best to develop quality relationships with those publics, to develop departmental structures that facilitate communication with strategic publics, and to determine how the organization can align its behavior with the needs of its publics. Public relations departments should conduct *evaluative research* both to pretest and to post-test those programs, structures, and organizational policies and behaviors.

4.3. Quantitative and Qualitative Research

Research in public relations too often has been confined to the extremes of quantitative and qualitative research—large-scale, highly quantified, expensive, and intrusive public-opinion surveys of the general population or undisciplined informal research of poorly chosen research participants. Neither is very useful in formulating or evaluating programs for specific publics or in developing, maintaining, and evaluating relationships with the publics that both need or are affected by an organization.

In contrast, public relations professionals should choose from a full menu of quantitative and qualitative methods, each of which might be appropriate in different situations and each of which is equally scientific. *Quantitative methods* include surveys of and experiments with members of scientifically segmented publics. *Qualitative methods* include focus groups; structured, semi-structured, or unstructured interviews with key participants; or observations of the behaviors of members of publics or of public relations professionals or other managers conducting their work.

Quantitative and qualitative methods do not work equally well at different levels of analysis or for both formative and evaluative research. For example, qualitative research (especially focus groups) is ideal for formative research at the program level, although it can also be used for evaluation at that level. Quantitative research can be especially valuable for segmenting publics and for evaluating outcomes at the program level. In many cases, both types of research can be used to provide complementary perspectives in both formative and evaluative research.

4.4. Process and Outcomes Evaluation

Public relations programs can be evaluated by measuring both the processes of communication programs and the outcomes of those programs. At the program level, *measures of processes* indicate how often and in what ways someone is communicating or his or her success in placing messages in a medium where *it is possible but not assured* that members of a public can attend to them. Often in the discussion of public relations metrics, process measures are termed measures of *outputs*. Program-level processes can be measured by counting whether messages are being sent, placed, or received, such as counts of press releases or publications issued or media placement and monitoring. At the functional level, auditors often measure processes by observing and counting what programs have been conducted, what personnel have been hired, and the amount of effort expended by program personnel.

It is important to point out that measures of communication *processes* must go beyond measures of *products.* Too often communication products (such as numbers of press releases or publications) are counted without understanding how those products fit into a strategic plan for communicating with a particular public. Sometimes, counting products might provide a good indicator that a process is being implemented. Too often, however, products are produced because the organization has always produced them and not because they are part of a consistent strategy.

Measuring process indicators can be very useful in evaluating public relations programs, but they must be preceded by research that demonstrates that the processes being measured or counted have had demonstrable and valuable *outcomes*—both in the short term and the long term. At the program level, we must demonstrate, first, that the processes have had short-term effects on the cognitions, attitudes, and behaviors of both publics and management—what people think, feel, and do. In addition, we need to determine whether those short-term effects continue over a longer period—that is, whether they have any effect on the long-term cognitive, attitudinal, and behavioral relationships among organizations and publics. At the functional, organizational, and societal levels, broad measures of effects of a public relations department on the long-term quality of relationships between the organization and its publics are essential. Short-term effects are not sufficient. These outcomes can be measured through quantitative survey methods or qualitative questions asked in interviews, focus groups, or similar methods.

A public relations department could validate process measures either by conducting outcomes research itself (or contracting with an outside firm), by using secondary research conducted by the public relations department of a different organization, or by analyzing research published by academic researchers.

A public relations department itself could conduct pre-test or post-test research to demonstrate that particular processes regularly have desired effects. For example, an educational relations program could be tested by measuring how much students who participated in the program learned (a cognitive effect) in a pre-test of the program or post-test of an ongoing program. If the students consistently learned from the program, then we could infer that students who participate in the program in the future also will learn; and we could evaluate the program by counting how many programs are held and the number of students who attend. In a community relations program, we might determine whether residents who attend an open house become less likely to call to complain about the organization or are more likely to say they support its objectives. If that outcome occurs, then we could measure the effect of the program by counting how many community residents attend open houses each year. This kind of research to confirm the effects of processes must be repeated from time to time, however—such as every three to five years—to demonstrate that the processes remain effective.

Organizations that conduct such validation research could help each other by sharing the results of their research or by collaborating in conducting the research. Perhaps most importantly, public relations departments often can find research to validate communication processes from research conducted *for* the profession in the academic literature, published in such journals as the *Journal of Public Relations Research* or *Public Relations Review* in the United States or the *Journal of Communication Management* in Europe.

I now will use these distinctions in types of research to provide a roadmap for how to conduct research to scientifically manage public relations programs. These suggestions are organized around the four levels of analysis.

5. Public Relations Research at the Program Level

This discussion of metrics for public relations begins with the program level because this is the level that most public relations professionals think of when they are asked to do research to demonstrate their effectiveness. However, keep in mind that a senior public relations officer should begin planning public relations programs at the organizational and societal levels so that specific communication programs relate to organizational goals and decisions, and to stakeholders who affect or are affected by organizational goals and decisions. As I discuss research at the program level, therefore, I also will explain how specific communication programs can be connected to effectiveness at the organizational and societal levels.

When most public relations professionals think of research, they think of research directly related to specific communication programs. For example, when they think of media relations, they think of monitoring the content of media. When they think of community relations, they think of a survey to determine the level of satisfaction that community residents have with an organization. When they think of employee relations, they think of an audit of employees' satisfaction with the organization, their jobs, or the quality of communication in an organization.

It is important to remember three things about these kinds of programmatic research, however. First, they are evaluation-only studies, which generally have not been preceded by formative research to help plan the program. Second, the studies typically do not measure carefully constructed objectives based on formative research or theoretical guidelines that categorize logical and measurable communication objectives. Third, the measures cannot be used directly to conclude whether public relations programs contribute to the effectiveness of the organization at the organizational or societal levels—the levels at which the return on investment (ROI) of public relations must be measured. Measures of processes and outcomes at the program level can be used to infer effectiveness at higher levels only if they are logically and empirically connected to broader organizational goals—most notably to developing quality long-term relationships with strategic publics—and the publics affected by the program are strategic to the organization.

In the *Excellence* study, we found that the most effective public relations departments participated in the making of overall strategic decisions in organizations. Less effective departments generally had the less central role of disseminating messages about strategic decisions made by others in the organization. By participating in organizational decisions, excellent public relations departments were in a position to identify the stakeholders who would be affected by organizational decisions or who would affect those decisions. Once they had identified stakeholders, excellent public relations departments strategically developed programs to communicate with them. They conducted formative research to identify potential issues and define objectives for programs to communicate with the stakeholders, they specified measurable objectives for the communication programs, and they used both formal and informal methods to evaluate whether the objectives had been accomplished. Less excellent departments conducted no formative or evaluative research and generally had only vague objectives that were difficult to measure.

5.1. Formative Research at the Program Level

In its initial stages, formative research at the program level cannot be separated easily from environmental scanning research at the organizational level. If a public relations department is to be effective, it must engage in continuous scanning of stakeholders and potential stakeholders so that the department builds up a base of knowledge about stakeholders that makes it possible to provide valuable information to strategic decision-makers about the consequences of organizational decisions and the consequences sought by stakeholders. Continuous formative research makes it possible for the public relations department to understand and predict the likely emergence of publics and issues.

Public relations programs should begin when formative research identifies a new or existing strategic public with which the organization needs a relationship. When a strategic public relations manager scans the environment, therefore, his or her first step should be to think broadly in terms of stakeholder categories, such as employees or community residents. Then he or she should use a theory of publics[3] to identify and segment active, passive, and latent publics from the non-publics that might also be present in the stakeholder category. It is important to segment active publics because active publics typically make issues out of the consequences of organizational decisions. This behavior may be individual or it may be collective—when members of publics organize into activist groups. Sometimes publics react negatively to harmful consequences of an organization's behaviors—such as pollution or discrimination. At other times, they act positively to try to secure a behavior from an organization that has useful consequences for them—such as a community public that wants cleaner air or water. At still other times, publics collaborate with organizations to secure consequences of benefit to both.

After identifying publics, the strategic communicator should do additional formative research to identify problems that publics want solved or that the organization creates for publics, issues that might result from these problems, and strategies that will help to build a successful relationship with these publics. Strategic public relations programs follow these four steps:

1. Develop short-term objectives specified as communication effects and long-term objectives specified as relationship indicators.
2. Plan a communication program to accomplish these objectives.
3. Implement the program.
4. Evaluate the program by measuring the extent to which the objectives have been accomplished.

In a scientifically managed public relations program, formative research should be an integral part of the first two steps, as well as serving the function of identifying publics, problems, and issues.

In two-way communication programs, many strategies designed to listen to publics or to seek information from publics can be described as informal research. That informal research can be made more scientific by using qualitative methods to structure these information-seeking activities and by using qualitative methods to analyze and interpret the information. Public relations professionals have used several kinds of formative research for these purposes. Some of these methods are based on qualitative research, on which more information can be obtained in the chapter by L. Grunig in this volume. The other methods use quantitative research methods.

Observations. Public relations personnel can attend meetings of community groups or other bodies in which publics might be represented to observe what they are saying and doing about the organization or their discussion of problems that might affect the organization even though the members of the groups do not specifically connect these problems to the organization.

Advisory groups. Many organizations have developed community advisory panels both as a means of seeking information from individual members of publics in the community or the organizations that represent them and for engaging publics in the solving of community problems and issues.

Interviews. Public relations professionals often interview community leaders, activists, and other key stakeholders formally or interact with them informally. Principles of rigorous qualitative interviewing can be used to plan and analyze these interviews.

Focus groups. Public relations professionals use focus groups to gain insights from publics and serve as a basis for program planning and policymaking. Focus groups are perhaps the most useful kind of formative research because they help public relations professionals grasp what motivates people and explain what people think and do in their own terms.

Questionnaires and survey research. Quantitative surveys of a population have been used for many years in public relations to segment publics and for measuring attitudes and opinions. Surveys, however, are expensive and intrusive when administered to a large number of people. Quantitative questionnaires generally are more useful for evaluative research than formative research because they generally ask people to respond to previously identified problems, issues, or programs.

Content analysis of media. The content of media coverage of an organization can be analyzed systematically to detect themes, problems, issues, and publics. Content analysis can be conducted quantitatively by developing categories and placing stories into those categories. It can also be conducted qualitatively by looking for patterns and impressions within the clippings.

Cyber analysis. A public relations staff can follow and analyze (qualitatively or quantitatively) the content of chat rooms, discussion groups, blogs, and listservs related to the interests of an organization and problems and issues that might be mentioned on these sites.

Naturally occurring information. Members of publics often provide information to an organization without any effort by public relations professionals or researchers. They make telephone calls, write letters, send e-mail messages, and talk to employees. A public relations department can develop a system to capture and analyze this information to identify problems, consequences, publics, and issues.

Databases. Databases are tools for analyzing, collecting, and using information gathered through the formal and informal research methods we have described in this section. Information should be classified by problems, publics, and issues, and then used for input into strategic decision processes.

5.2. Evaluative Research at the Program Level: Developing Objectives and Measuring Them

After formative research has identified the publics with which an organization needs relationships and the problems and issues that exist or might exist, public relations staff should formulate objectives for programs to communicate with these strategic publics. Since the value of public relations to an organization and society exists in the relationships developed with strategic publics, objectives should consist of *strategies to cultivate relationships* (independent variables) and the *relationship outcomes* (dependent variables) that the organization strives to achieve with these strategies. The theoretical expectation that cultivation strategies will lead to desired relationship outcomes is a hypothesis. Cultivation strategies can be specified as *process objectives.* Relationship outcomes can be specified as *outcome objectives.* Public relations staff can monitor both process and outcome objectives to evaluate its communication programs—as long as research has established that the process objectives do indeed lead to the outcome objectives.

Process Objectives and Measures

Most of the knowledge that public relations professionals possess has something to do with how to communicate with publics to cultivate a relationship with those publics. Not all strategies for cultivating relationships are equally effective, however. Therefore, we must recognize that not all public relations strategies, techniques, and programs are equally likely to produce quality relationship outcomes. Public relations researchers have identified and classified the strategies that research has shown to be most effective. Cultivation strategies that are symmetrical in nature generally are more effective than asymmetrical strategies. To be symmetrical means that the public relations staff communicates in a way that helps to balance the interests of both organizations and publics. To be asymmetrical means that the public relations staff strives for a relationship that benefits the organization but that it is less concerned about the interests of the public. Hon and J. Grunig (1999) provided a list of symmetrical and asymmetrical cultivation strategies derived from academic studies of relationships and conflict resolution.

Public relations staff can measure these process objectives to provide meaningful information in the short term that its communication programs are leading to desired long-term effects. For example, public relations managers can measure one of these objectives, disclosure of concerns by publics to the organization, by counting suggestions, complaints, inquiries, and other contacts that members of publics, the media, government, or leaders of activist groups make with the organization, rather than to regulatory bodies, legislators, or the media. Public relations practitioners can measure process objectives from the management side of the organization-public relationship by keeping a count of the times management seeks them out for advice or is willing to disclose its intentions, decisions, and behaviors to outside publics or the media through the public relations function. Other process indicators of effective cultivation strategies include counts of what management has done to show publics that their interests are legitimate, of contacts with networks of activist groups, or in social responsibility reports showing the extent to which management has worked on problems of interest to publics.

Outcome Objectives and Measures

The ultimate goal of communication programs such as community relations, media relations, or employee relations—and even of specific communication activities such as an open house, a media interview, or an employee publication —is a quality relationship with a strategic public. Relationships develop slowly, however, and a particular communication activity or short-term program can be expected to have only an incremental effect on the quality of a relationship. In most cases, that incremental effect will be too small to measure.

There are five short-term objectives that communication research (research *for* the profession) has shown can be attained through discrete activities and programs. Each can be measured either quantitatively or qualitatively, depending on the nature of the evidence desired to show the effect of the programs. Sometimes qualitative evidence is sufficient; at other times, management or a client demands quantitative evidence. In most of the communication literature, these objectives are defined as one-way effects—as effects on the public. These one-way effects can also be measured on management, however, to determine the effects of symmetrical programs. When we think of two-way effects, different terminology makes the objectives more meaningful.

The one-way effects are the following, with examples and measures included:

- *Exposure.* Members of a strategic public or of management receive a message. Stories are placed in the media and members of publics read them. Members of a public see an advertisement, attend a special event, go to a website, or read a brochure. Managers meet with public leaders, read the results of a public opinion survey, or view a videotape of a focus group. Exposure can be measured through such methods as readership surveys, attendance counts, web hits, or management attendance at meetings. Note that media monitoring alone usually is not a sufficient measure even of exposure because it cannot tell you if anyone has read or seen a news story.
- *Retention of messages.* Members of the public are not only exposed to a message, they also remember the message. Recipients of the message do not necessarily agree with the message or plan to do anything about it;

they simply remember what you said. This objective can be measured through questions about the recall of messages.

- *Cognition.* Recipients of messages not only remember messages but they understand them and develop new knowledge. To measure a cognitive effect, for example, survey participants could be asked a multiple-choice question testing knowledge of the organization.
- *Attitude.* Members of a public or of management not only receive and understand a message, they also evaluate its implications favorably and intend to behave in a way that is consistent with a message. Attitudes can be measured through conventional evaluative questions.
- *Behavior.* Members of a public or of management behave in a new or different way—changing the behavioral relationship of an organization and public, and the consequences that each has on the other. Behaviors can be measured by asking what publics have done that affect the organization or that management has done that affects a public. In situations in which a behavior of the public produces sales or revenue or reduces costs, it might be possible to compute a financial return on investment to a public relations program. However, a researcher must always take care to control for variables other than public relations that might have led to the increase in revenue or decease in cost, or that might interact with public relations to produce the financial effect.

The conventional wisdom in communication research has been that these five effects constitute a hierarchy of effects—that changes in behavior, for example, must be preceded by changes in exposure, message retention, cognition, and attitude. However, these effects can occur independently of each other or in a different order. For example, people often hold attitudes that are based on limited or no knowledge; or behavior sometimes changes before attitudes or cognition change. Therefore, a public relations manager should decide which objectives are most likely for each communication process that he or she wants to evaluate. The objectives become more difficult to attain as we move from exposure to behavior.

When a public relations department thinks of its objectives in two-way terms, it should use somewhat different terminology for the above five effects. Two-way objectives envision the effect of communication activities on management and publics simultaneously. Ideally, both change, although sometimes one must change more or less than the other. These two-way objectives are based on a theory of coorientation originally developed by McLeod and Chaffee (1973) and adapted for public relations by Broom (1977) and J. Grunig and Hunt (1984: 128).

- Exposure becomes *mutual awareness*. Both management and public are aware of the effect they have on the other.
- Message retention becomes *accuracy*. Both can accurately remember and repeat what the other said.

- Cognitive effect becomes *understanding*. Both have similar cognitions about a problem or issue or purpose of the organization.
- Effect on attitude becomes *agreement*. Both have similar evaluations of what the organization or public wants and intend to behave in a way that enhances their relationship.
- Effect on behavior becomes *symbiotic behavior*. Both behave in a way that serves the interests of the other as well as their own interests.

Public relations professionals should recognize that the main reason to measure short-term objectives is not so much to reward or punish individual communication managers or the entire public relations function for success or failure as it is to learn from the research whether a program should be continued as is, revised, or dropped in favor of another approach. If pre-testing is conducted of programs, rather than just post-testing, such decisions can be made before large expenditures of time and money are made on a program.

Over the long term, successful short-term communication activities and programs should contribute to the development and maintenance of quality long-term relationships with strategic publics. These relationships have value at the organizational level. To understand the nature of relationships and how to evaluate them, I will turn next to the organizational level of analysis because of its logical relationship to the program level. Then, I will return to the functional level to suggest ways of auditing the public relations department.

6. Public Relations Research at the Organizational Level

At the organizational level, the central concept for planning and evaluating public relations programs is the *relationship* between the organization and its publics. The concept is inherent in the term "public relations," which means managing *communication* to build *relationships* with *publics*. At the organizational level, the public relations staff contributes to strategic decision-making by using formative research as a means of environmental scanning to identify publics with which an organization needs relationships. Staff, too, can do formative research to assess the quality of relationships with these publics before it develops specific communication programs to establish, maintain, or improve relationships with publics. Finally, the staff should conduct regular evaluative research to assess the effects of its communication programs on these relationships with strategic publics.

6.1. Formative Research at the Organizational Level

At the organizational level, public relations staff should do formative research as an integral part of the environmental scanning that provides essential information for public relations to participate in the strategic-planning and decision-making processes of the organization. Traditionally, public relations managers have scanned the environment by monitoring the media and political processes. These sources are useful, although there are better methods of environmental scanning. By the time the consequences of a management decision hit the media and become political, it is too late to affect a decision. Then issues management becomes reactive—damage control. After scanning the media and political processes, public relations professionals most often use large-scale public opinion polls. They, too, typically identify issues too late.

What is better? Sources of scanning information can be internal or external—from sources inside the organization as well as from external publics. They can also be personal or impersonal—from published sources or directly from personal contacts. I recommend the following process of environmental scanning:

1. Begin environmental scanning by monitoring strategic decisions made by senior managers. Ask what stakeholders might be affected and what issues they might raise if certain decisions are made.
2. Do qualitative research on activists and personal contacts. Set up advisory boards and attend meetings of key stakeholders. Systematically monitor and classify problems, publics, and issues identified through these personal sources.
3. Monitor discussion groups, chat rooms, listservs, blogs, and websites on the Internet related to problems and issues of concern to your organization. Set up your own interactive forum on the web to allow publics to bring problems and issues to your attention.
4. Systematically interview boundary spanners in your own organization—managers with frequent contact outside the organization, other employees with community contacts, and people in divisions or functions with frequent contact with stakeholders.
5. Identify the stakeholders and publics most likely to be affected by and to actively do something about the problems and issues identified in the previous analysis.
6. Systematically content analyze and categorize all of the information and put it in a database—classified by type of management decision, problem, public, and issue. Use this database as research evidence to present to management during strategic deliberations and decisions.
7. Monitor the media and printed sources to track your effectiveness in dealing with publics and issues. In addition, do research systematically to assess and evaluate your relationships with publics.

6.2. Evaluative Research at the Organizational Level

Recently, academic public relations researchers have studied the literature on relationships in related disciplines such as interpersonal communication and social and organizational sociology to identify key characteristics of relationships and to develop measures *for the profession* of the quality of long-term organization–public relationships. In the discussion of the program level,

I described several process indicators that research shows are likely to lead to quality long-term relationships. To demonstrate that a public relations function has value to the overall organization, however, it also is necessary to develop and use long-term outcome indicators of the quality of relationships. My graduate students at the University of Maryland and I have identified two types of relationships (communal and exchange) and four relationship outcomes (trust, mutuality of control, satisfaction, and commitment) that define the quality of long-term relationships. These indicators can be measured to monitor the overall effect of public relations programs on each strategic public and, therefore, the value that the public relations function has to an organization.

We also have conducted research to develop valid and reliable measures of the six indicators of the quality of long-term relationships—the two types of relationships and the four relationship outcomes. Details of the research can be found in a report published by the Institute for Public Relations (Hon & J. Grunig, 1999). In addition to quantitative measures that can be used in survey research, we also have developed qualitative measures for the indicators that can be used both in formative and evaluative research on the quality of relationships (J. Grunig, 2002).

Public relations managers can use these measures as indicators of the quality of their relationships with strategic publics, such as community members, journalists, and employees. Although individual communication programs do not usually produce a short-term change in these indicators, communication programs have a cumulative effect on the indicators over time. Therefore, public relations professionals should measure these indicators periodically to monitor the quality of the relationships their organizations have developed with each of their publics and, therefore, the value that the public relations function has contributed to the organization. Ideally, relationships should be measured yearly. Minimally, they should be measured every three years.

In contrast to our emphasis on relationships in explaining the value of the public relations function, many business scholars (e.g., Fombrun, 1966; Fombrun & Van Riel, 2004) and research firms (for a summary, see Jeffries-Fox Associates, 2000a, 2000b) have argued that public relations has value because of its influence on the reputation of an organization. These researchers also have developed measures of reputation that can be used to demonstrate this value. J. Grunig and Hung (2002) reviewed the literature on reputation and concluded that existing conceptualizations of the concept are confused and that measures of it more often measure attitudes or evaluations than reputation. J. Grunig and Hung defined reputation as a *cognitive representation*—what people think, and subsequently say, about an organization. They measured reputation with an open-end question that asked participants in a survey to indicate what comes to mind when they hear the name of an organization. Using this measure, J. Grunig and Hung (2002), Yang and J. Grunig (2005), and Yang (2005) demonstrated that relationships are affected more strongly by communication with publics than is reputation and that relationships also affect a public's evaluation of organizational performance more than reputation. In addition, they showed that differences in reputation could be explained by the quality of relationships with a public.

Although we have provided a great deal of evidence that the value of the public relations function can be measured by measuring the quality of relationships with different stakeholder publics, many public relations professionals and researchers insist that we must be able to measure a monetary value of the relationships to demonstrate the ROI of the function. Indeed, the pursuit of the ROI of public relations currently occupies a great deal of time and attention among public relations researchers. As I mentioned in the discussion of measuring behavioral outcomes at the program level, it is sometimes possible to measure the financial values of behaviors that result from individual programs, such as a marketing communication program, as long as variables other than communication that affect behavior are included or controlled in the analysis.

However, the ROI of the overall public relations function can be measured only at the organizational level. Even still, measuring the monetary value of relationships is difficult for the following reasons:

- Relationships (and their product reputation) provide a context for behavior by consumers, investors, employees, government, the community, the media, and other strategic constituencies; but they do not determine this behavior alone. The behavior of these constituencies affects financial performance; but many other factors, such as competition and the economic environment, also affect that performance.
- Relationships save money by preventing costly issues, crises, regulation, litigation, and bad publicity. It is not possible, however, to determine the cost of something that *did not happen* or even to know that the negative event or behavior *would have happened* in the absence of excellent public relations.
- The return on relationships is delayed. Organizations spend money on relationships for years to prevent events or behaviors such as crises, boycotts, or litigation that *might* happen many years down the road.
- The return on relationships usually is lumpy. Good relationships with some constituencies such as consumers may produce a continuing stream of revenue, but for the most part the return comes all at once—e.g., when crises, strikes, boycotts, regulation, litigation, or bad publicity are avoided or mitigated. Similarly, relationships with potential donors must be cultivated for years before a donor makes a major gift. As a result, it is difficult to prorate the delayed returns on public relations to the monies invested in the function each year (L. Grunig *et al.*, 2002: 105).

Accountants tell us that an organizational function such as public relations has value if it (1) increases revenue, (2) reduces costs, or (3) reduces risk.

Good relationships produced by public relations may result in one or more of these three sources of value. The greatest contribution of public relations, however, most likely comes from reducing costs and risk, other than from marketing communication programs. For the reasons just mentioned, however, it is difficult to measure reductions of costs and risk in monetary terms.

In the *Excellence* study (L. Grunig *et al.*, 2002), we used the technique of compensating variation to estimate the value of relationships cultivated by public relations to the organization. Ehling (1992) developed the rationale for using this technique in the first *Excellence* book. With compensating variation, the researcher simply asks the people who benefit most from an activity to estimate its value to them. We asked CEOs to estimate the value of public relations, using several measures, and were able to show that CEOs valued excellent public relations functions more highly than less excellent functions. Although we could not measure ROI directly, our interviews with CEOs and senior public relations officers revealed numerous examples of how good relationships had reduced the *costs* of litigation, regulation, legislation, and negative publicity caused by poor relationships; reduced the *risk* of making decisions that affect different stakeholders; or increased *revenue* by providing products and services needed by stakeholders. Those examples provided powerful evidence of the value of good relationships with strategic publics. I doubt, however, that researchers will ever be able to place a precise monetary value on this evidence of the value of relationships. With the strong conceptual and empirical evidence we have produced of this value, it is not necessary to measure a monetary ROI to establish the value of public relations to an organization.

7. Public Relations Research at the Functional Level

At the functional level of analysis, a public relations department should conduct research to evaluate itself—how it is organized and what it does. Then it should ask whether the structure and behavior of the public relations function make it possible to contribute maximally to organizational and societal effectiveness. Research at the functional level is "benchmarking" research. Typically, benchmarking studies identify organizations that are believed to be leaders in an area of practice and then describe how these organizations practice public relations or some other management function. Such benchmarking studies are useful, but they would be even more useful if they were based on a foundation of scientific research that provides a theoretical rationale explaining *why* the practices of the benchmarked departments contribute to organizational and societal effectiveness.

Our study of excellent public relations departments (L. Grunig *et al.,* 2002) provides such a theoretical profile, a theoretical benchmark, of critical success factors and best practices in public relations. It is a profile that we initially constructed from past research and by theoretical logic. In addition, we gathered empirical evidence from more than 300 organizations in the United States, Canada, and the United Kingdom to confirm that this theoretical profile explains best actual practice as well as best practice in theory.

In most benchmarking studies, communication units compare themselves with similar units in their industry or with similar functional units inside the organization. The *Excellence* study, in contrast, is an example of what Fleisher (1995) called "generic benchmarking" in his book on public relations benchmarking, identifying critical success factors across different types of organizations. Generic benchmarking is most valuable theoretically because it is unlikely that one organization will be, in Fleisher's words, "a world-class performer across the board." In the *Excellence* study, only a few organizations exemplified all of the best practices, many organizations exemplified some of them, and others exemplified few of the practices. A theoretical benchmark does not provide an exact formula or detailed description of practices that a public relations unit can copy in order to be excellent. Rather, it provides a generic set of principles that such units can use to generate ideas for specific practices in their own organizations. The criteria we developed and tested in the *Excellence* study can be used as a theoretical benchmark for auditing a public relations function. This is an example of how research *on* the profession can result in useful concepts and tools *for* the practice of public relations.

The *Excellence* criteria require knowledge and professionalism by the public relations unit. They also require understanding of and support for public relations by senior management. They can be used both for formative and evaluative analysis of a public relations function, as prior research that can be used to plan and organize the function, and as a standard for reviewing the past structure and performance of the function.

The characteristics of an excellent public relations function fall into four categories, each of which contains several characteristics that can be used to audit a public relations function (for specific criteria, see L. Grunig *et al.*, 2002).

- Empowerment of the public relations function through participation in strategic management, providing public relations professionals access to key decision-makers, including women as well as men in senior public relations positions, and planning and evaluation of communication programs strategically.
- Organizing public relations as a managerial role rather than as a technical support activity for other management functions.
- Integrating all communication programs through the public relations function and not subordinating public relations to other management functions such as marketing, human resources, or finance.
- Practicing public relations as a two-way communication process and with a "symmetrical" purpose of using communication to foster collaboration between organizations and their publics.

8. Public Relations Research at the Societal Level

The value of public relations at the societal level results from the cumulative impact of what it does at the program, functional, and organizational levels. The value of public relations at the societal level is the long-term impact of good relationships identified at the organizational level and cultivated at the program level. As a result, research on the quality of relationships can also be used to establish the contribution of public relations to society. In addition, the public relations function should evaluate the ethics and social responsibility of the organization and serve as an ethics counselor to management as part of its role in strategic management.

The extent to which a public relations function performs in an ethical and socially responsible manner can be determined by comparing its behavior with two principles of ethics derived from the principal branches of ethical theory: teleological (or consequentialist) and deontological (or rule-based) approaches to ethics (J. Grunig & L. Grunig, 1996). Public relations programs should be assessed according to the extent to which they have considered two questions in their role in the management of an organization:

•   The teleological question: To what extent has public relations staff helped management address the consequences the organization has had on publics and addressed the needs of publics?
•   The deontological question: To what extent has public relations staff carried out its moral obligation to communicate with and disclose the organization's behavior to publics when it has consequences on them or the public expects consequences from the organization?

9. Conclusions about Research *in* Public Relations

Public relations should be an integral part of the management of every organization. The public relations function helps the organization interact with the stakeholders in its environment both to accomplish its mission and to behave in a socially responsible manner. An excellent public relations staff cannot serve this role, however, unless research and measurement are an integral part of the function. Formative research is necessary to identify strategic publics with which an organization needs a relationship and to determine how to develop and maintain relationships with those publics. Evaluative research is necessary to establish the effectiveness of public relations programs and their contribution to organizational effectiveness. Public relations functions as a whole can be audited by comparing them to a theoretical benchmark and by their contribution to the ethical and socially responsible behavior of the organization.

This section on conceptualizing research *in* the practice of public relations should provide a roadmap for public relations professionals who want to design and evaluate an excellent public relations function. In the last section of this chapter, I will highlight recent academic research that provides useful tools *for* the practice of public relations.

9.1. Recent Research for Public Relations

Since the completion of the *Excellence* study, scholars working in this research tradition, which features the strategic management role of public relations, have continued to conduct research *for* the profession that has resulted in concepts and ideas that public relations professionals can use to participate in strategic decision processes. I described this new research in an article published in a special issue of the *Journal of Public Relations Research* (J. Grunig, 2006). In addition, Toth (2007) has edited a book with chapters written by authors following this tradition who have developed new concepts and tools for use in different parts of the profession.

Additional information about these concepts and tools can be found in that article and book. Much of the new research has been on relationships, reputation, and evaluation of public relations—research already discussed in this chapter. In addition, research has provided new concepts and tools related to:

- *Environmental scanning.* Research to identify publics and issues and to evaluate information sources that can be used to bring information into the organization (e.g., Chang, 2000; J. Grunig & L. Grunig, 2000b).
- *Publics.* Research to further develop the situational theory of publics and to explain the social nature of publics (e.g., Aldoory, 2001; J.-N. Kim, 2006; Sha, 1995).
- *Scenario building.* Research to develop this technique for explaining the consequences of the behavior of publics to management and the issues created by the behavior of publics (e.g., Sung, 2004).
- *Relationship cultivation strategies.* Research to expand the concepts of symmetrical and asymmetrical communication to include a number of strategies to cultivate relationships (independent variables) that are most effective in producing high-quality relationships with stakeholder publics (dependent variables) (e.g., Hung, 2002, 2004; Rhee, 2004; Chapter 11 of this book).
- Development of an ethical framework for public relations practitioners to use as they participate in strategic management (e.g., Bowen, 2000, 2004).
- *Empowerment of the public relations function.* Research to clarify the nature of the dominant coalition in an organization and how public relations practitioners become part of or gain access to empowered coalitions (e.g., Berger, 2005).
- *Specialized areas of public relations.* Research to extend the generic principles of excellence, used as a framework for auditing the overall public relations function in this article, to specialized areas of public relations, such as fund raising (Kelly, 1991), investor relations (Shickinger, 1998),

employee relations (H.-S. Kim, 2005), community relations (Rhee, 2004), and government relations (Chen, 2005).

- *Global public relations and global strategy.* Research to develop a global theory of public relations, based on the theory that the principles of excellent public relations are *generic principles* that can be applied in many cultures and political-economic settings as long as *specific applications* are used to adapt them to different contexts (e.g., L. Grunig, J. Grunig, & Verčič, 1998; Verčič, L. Grunig, & J. Grunig, 1996; Wakefield, 1997, 2000). Recent research has applied this theory to a multinational organization (NATO) (Van Dyke, 2005), public diplomacy programs of governments in other countries (Yun, 2005), and globalized and localized strategies of multinational organizations (Ni, 2006).
- *Institutionalization of strategic public relations as an ongoing, accepted practice in most organizations.* No research has been conducted on institutionalization to date, but Yi (2005) has made a compelling argument that research is needed to learn how organizations come to understand and accept public relations as a strategic management function rather than solely as a messaging, publicity, and media relations function.

9.2. In Conclusion

Public relations practitioners today recognize the urgent need to include measurement in their practice. However, most measurement programs are not clearly conceptualized and fail to answer the questions and solve the problems they were developed to answer. Practitioners can improve their measurement programs by refining their conceptualization of the public relations function, public relations programs, and communication processes and of the effects these have in producing desired organizational outcomes. Practitioners can improve their research used *in* the practice of public relations most effectively by studying and making use of theoretical principles of conceptualization and by studying research that has been conducted *on* and *for* the practice of the discipline.

Notes

1 Portions of this chapter were adapted from J. Grunig (2005), J. Grunig and L. Grunig (2000a), and J. Grunig and L. Grunig (2001).
2 This diagram is similar to one in Chaffee (1996). The following discussion also is based in part on Chaffee's chapter.
3 I have developed such a theory, which I call a situational theory of publics. For basic information on the theory, see J. Grunig and Hunt (1984, Chapter 7). For more advanced information, see J. Grunig (1997).

References

Aldoory, L. (2001). Making health communications meaningful for women: Factors that influence involvement. *Journal of Public Relations Research, 13,* 163–185.

Berger, B. K. (2005). Power over, power with, and power to public relations: Critical reflections on public relations, the dominant coalition, and activism. *Journal of Public Relations Research, 17*, 5–28.

Bowen, S. A. (2000). *A theory of ethical issues management: Contributions of Kantian deontology to public relations' ethics and decision making.* Unpublished doctoral dissertation, University of Maryland, College Park.

Bowen, S. A. (2004). Expansion of ethics as the tenth generic principle of public relations excellence: A Kantian theory and model for managing ethical issues. *Journal of Public Relations Research, 16*, 65–92.

Broom, G. M. (1977). Coorientational measurement of public issues. *Public Relations Review, 3*(4), 110–119.

Broom, G. M., & Dozier, D. M. (1990). *Using research in public relations: Applications to program management.* Englewood Cliffs, NJ: Prentice-Hall.

Chaffee, S. H. (1996). Thinking about theory. In M. B. Salwen & D. W. Stacks (Eds.), *An integrated approach to communication theory & research* (pp. 15–32). Mahwah, NJ: Lawrence Erlbaum Associates.

Chang, Y.-C. (2000). *A normative exploration into environmental scanning in public relations.* Unpublished M.A. thesis, University of Maryland, College Park.

Chen, Y.-R. (2005). *Effective government affairs in an era of marketization: Strategic issues management, business lobbying, and relationship management by multinational corporations in China.* Unpublished doctoral dissertation, University of Maryland, College Park.

Curtin, P. A., & Gaither, T. K. (2005). Privileging identity, difference, and power: The circuit of culture as a basis for public relations theory. *Journal of Public Relations Research, 17*, 91–116.

Durham, F. (2005). Public relations as structuration. *Journal of Public Relations Research, 17*, 29–48.

Ehling, W. P. (1992). Estimating the value of public relations and communication to an organization. In J. E. Grunig (Ed.), *Excellence in public relations and communication management* (pp. 617–638). Hillsdale, NJ: Lawrence Erlbaum Associates.

Fleisher, C. S. (1995). *Public affairs benchmarking.* Washington, DC: Public Affairs Council.

Fombrun, C. J. (1996). *Reputation: Realizing value from the corporate image.* Boston: Harvard Business School Press.

Fombrun, C. J., & Van Riel, C. B. M. (2004). *Fame & fortune: How successful companies build winning reputations.* Upper Saddle River, NJ: Financial Times/Prentice-Hall.

Grunig, J. E. (1997). A situational theory of publics: Conceptual history, recent challenges and new research. In D. Moss, T. MacManus, & D. Verčič (Eds.), *Public relations research: An international perspective* (pp. 3–46). London: International Thomson Business Press.

Grunig, J. E. (2002). *Qualitative methods for assessing relationships between organizations and publics.* Gainesville, FL: The Institute for Public Relations, Commission on PR Measurement and Evaluation.

Grunig, J. E. (2005). Guia de pesquisa e mediçaõ para elaborar e avaliar uma funçaõ excelente de relações públicas (A roadmap for using research and measurement to design and evaluate an excellent public relations function). *Organicom: Revisa Brasileira de Communiçaõ Organizacional e Relações Públicas* (*Brazilian Journal of Organizational Communication and Public Relations*], *2*(2), 47–69.

Grunig, J. E. (2006). Furnishing the edifice: Ongoing research on public relations as a strategic management function. *Journal of Public Relations Research*, 18, 151–176.

Grunig, J. E., & Grunig, L. A. (1996). *Implications of symmetry for a theory of ethics and social responsibility in public relations*. Paper presented to the International Communication Association, Chicago (May).

Grunig, J. E., & Grunig, L. A. (2000a). Conceptualization: The missing ingredient of much PR practice and research. *Jim and Lauri Grunig's Research: A Supplement of PR Reporter*, 10 (December), 1–4.

Grunig, J. E., & Grunig, L. A. (2000b). Research methods for environmental scanning. *Jim and Lauri Grunig's Research: A Supplement of PR Reporter*, 7 (February), 1–4.

Grunig, J. E., & Grunig, L. A. (2001, March) *Guidelines for formative and evaluative research in public affairs: A report for the Department of Energy Office of Science*. Washington, DC: U.S. Department of Energy.

Grunig, J. E., & Huang, Y. H. (2000). From organizational effectiveness to relationship indicators: Antecedents of relationships, public relations strategies, and relationship outcomes. In J. A. Ledingham & S. D. Bruning (Eds.), *Public relations as relationship management: A relational approach to the study and practice of public relations* (pp. 23–53). Mahwah, NJ: Lawrence Erlbaum Associates.

Grunig, J. E., & Hung, C. J. (2002). *The effect of relationships on reputation and reputation on relationships: A cognitive, behavioral study*. Paper presented to the International, Interdisciplinary Public Relations Research Conference, Miami, Florida (March).

Grunig, J. E., & Hunt, T. (1984). *Managing public relations*. New York: Holt, Rinehart & Winston.

Grunig, L. A., Grunig, J. E., & Dozier, D. M. (2002). *Excellent public relations and effective organizations: A study of communication management in three countries*. Mahwah, NJ: Lawrence Erlbaum Associates.

Grunig, L. A., Grunig, J. E., & Verčič, D. (1998). Are the IABC's excellence principles generic? Comparing Slovenia and the United States, the United Kingdom and Canada. *Journal of Communication Management*, 2, 335–356.

Holtzhausen, D. R., & Voto, R. (2002). Resistance from the margins: The postmodern public relations practitioner as organizational activist. *Journal of Public Relations Research*, *14*, 57–84.

Hon, L. C., & Grunig, J. E. (1999). *Guidelines for measuring relationships in public relations*. Gainesville, FL: The Institute for Public Relations, Commission on PR Measurement and Evaluation.

Hung, C.-J. (2002). *The interplays of relationship types, relationship cultivation, and relationship outcomes: How multinational and Taiwanese companies practice public relations and organization-public relationship management in China*. Unpublished doctoral dissertation, University of Maryland, College Park.

Hung, C.-J. (2004). Cultural influence on relationship cultivation strategies: Multinational companies in China. *Journal of Communication Management*, *8*, 264–281.

Jeffries-Fox Associates (2000a). *Toward a shared understanding of corporate reputation and related concepts: Phase I: Content analysis*. Basking Ridge, NJ: Report prepared for the Council of Public Relations Firms (March 3).

Jeffries-Fox Associates (2000b). *Toward a shared understanding of corporate reputation and related concepts: Phase III: Interviews with client advisory committee members*. Basking Ridge, NJ: Report prepared for the Council of Public Relations Firms (June 16).

Kelly, K. S. (1991). *Fund raising and public relations.* Hillsdale, NJ: Lawrence Erlbaum Associates.

Kim, J.-N. (2006). *Communicant activeness, cognitive entrepreneurship, and a situational theory of problem solving.* Unpublished doctoral dissertation, University of Maryland, College Park.

Kim, H.-S. (2005). *Organizational structure and internal communication as antecedents of employee-organization relationships in the context of organizational justice: A multilevel analysis.* Unpublished doctoral dissertation, University of Maryland, College Park.

Leitch, S., & Neilson, D. (2001). Bringing publics into public relations: New theoretical frameworks for practice. In R. L. Heath (Ed.), *Handbook of public relations* (pp. 127–138). Thousand Oaks, CA: Sage.

L'Etang, J., & Pieczka, M. (Eds.) (1996). *Critical perspectives in public relations.* London: International Thomson Business Press.

Lindenmann, W. K. (1997). *Guidelines and standards for measuring and evaluating PR effectiveness.* Gainesville, FL: The Institute for Public Relations Research & Education.

McKie, D. (2001). Updating public relations: "New science," research paradigms, and uneven developments. In R. L. Heath (Ed.), *Handbook of public relations* (pp. 75–91). Thousand Oaks, CA: Sage.

McLeod, J. M., & Chaffee, S. H. (1973). Interpersonal approaches to communication research. *American Behavioral Scientist, 16,* 469–500.

Motion, J., & Weaver, C. K. (2005). A discourse perspective for critical public relations research: Life sciences network and the battle for truth. *Journal of Public Relations Research, 17,* 49–67.

Ni, L. (2006). *Exploring the value of public relations in strategy implementation: Employee relations in the globalization process.* Unpublished doctoral dissertation, University of Maryland, College Park.

Rhee, Y. (2004). *The employee–public–organization chain in relationship management: A case study of a government organization.* Unpublished doctoral dissertation, University of Maryland, College Park.

Schickinger, P. (1998). *Electronic investor relations: Can new media close the symmetry gap?* Unpublished M.A. thesis, University of Maryland, College Park.

Sha, B.-L. (1995). *Intercultural public relations: Exploring cultural identity as a means of segmenting publics.* Unpublished M.A. thesis, University of Maryland, College Park.

Sung, M.-J. (2004). *Toward a model of strategic management of public relations: Scenario building from a public relations perspective.* Unpublished doctoral dissertation, University of Maryland, College Park.

Toth, E. L. (Ed.) (2007). *Excellence in public relations and communication management: Challenges for the next generation.* Mahwah, NJ: Lawrence Erlbaum Associates.

Van Dyke, M. A. (2005). *Toward a theory of just communication: A case study of NATO, multinational public relations, ethical management of international conflict.* Unpublished doctoral dissertation, University of Maryland, College Park.

Verčič, D., Grunig, L. A., & Grunig, J. E. (1996). Global and specific principles of public relations: Evidence from Slovenia. In H. M. Culbertson & N. Chen (Eds.), *International public relations: A comparative analysis* (pp. 31–65). Mahwah, NJ: Lawrence Erlbaum Associates.

Wakefield, R. I. (1997). *International public relations: A theoretical approach to excellence based on a worldwide Delphi study.* Unpublished doctoral dissertation, University of Maryland, College Park.

Wakefield, R. I. (2000). World-class public relations: A model for effective public relations in the multinational. *Journal of Communication Management, 5*(1), 59–71.

Yang, S.-U. (2005). *The effect of organization–public relationships on reputation from the perspective of publics.* Unpublished doctoral dissertation, University of Maryland, College Park.

Yang, S.-U., & Grunig, J. E. (2005). Decomposing organizational reputation: The effects of organization–public relationship outcomes on cognitive representations of organizations and evaluations of organizational performance. *Journal of Communication Management, 9*, 296–304.

Yi, H. (2005). *The role of communication management in the institutionalization of corporate citizenship: Relational convergence of corporate social responsibility and stakeholder management.* Unpublished M.A. paper, University of Maryland, College Park.

Yun, S.-H. (2005). *Theory building for comparative public diplomacy from the perspectives of public relations and international relations: A macro-comparative study of embassies in Washington, DC.* Unpublished doctoral dissertation, University of Maryland, College Park.

6 Using Qualitative Research to Become the "Thinking Heart" of Organizations

Larissa A. Grunig

1. Introduction

In his acceptance speech for the Alan Campbell-Johnson Medal, Toni Muzi Falconi (2005) eloquently articulated what he considered two new challenges for the profession of public relations: "accountability to our clients and employers, and social responsibility to our stakeholders" (n.p.).[1] Rather than being the oxymoron they might seem, these challenges can be met at least in part through careful reflection and research.

As a teacher, I have long relied on metaphor to help explain. In fact, my first published paper as a graduate student in public communication was an analysis of the metaphors used to explain the dramatic loss of farmland in the United States to urban development (Schneider, a.k.a. L. Grunig, 1982). In this chapter I use metaphor to explain and, I hope, to inspire scholars and enlightened practitioners to conduct the kind of inquiry that truly has value. Much of that research, as readers will see, must be qualitative in nature. It hinges largely on exploring someone else's world and making sense of it.

Many metaphors have been used to characterize public relations, whose identity is confusing even to some of us who practice and study this field. Most of these metaphors do explain or describe the role or function. Too few have the inspirational element that I deem essential. For example, public relations practitioners often see themselves as the "conscience of the corporation." Inspirational? Perhaps, but to me this analogy seems too preachy. It positions public relations as the "nag" in the organization. Another typical metaphor is the "eyes and ears of the corporation," referring to the environmental-scanning function. Inspirational? Again, perhaps, but more utilitarian than stirring. We hear of public relations practitioners as "boundary spanners," especially in conjunction with our role in developing relationships with publics. Descriptive, yes, but inspirational? Not to me: I picture someone with one foot on either side of the invisible fence or boundary between the organization and its publics. It's not a comfortable position. Yet another metaphor is "spin doctor" or "spinmeister," an allusion to the hype that is characteristic of many press agents or publicists. Inspirational? Most certainly not, unless one is moved by the tabloid press.

In a professional development session at the Public Relations Society of America (PRSA) international conference several years ago, Hamashima (2002) of SAS called public relations the "Grand Central station" for communication about work–life issues in his software company. If you have ever waited for a train in New York City's Grand Central, you know how uninspiring this analogy is. The postmodern characterization of the public relations professional as "in-house activist" (Holtzhausen & Voto, 2002) may inspire some and turn others, the more conservative among us, off. Most recently, Odedele (2004) called practitioners "sociological physicians." In his comments on the 2005 World Public Relations Festival (WPRF) diversity manifesto, he extended his metaphor by saying that public relations people "need a good diagnosis of their organization's publics for effective application of public relations' medication on their 'diversity.'" Inspirational? Only if you like giving or taking medicine.

2. The Metaphor of the "Thinking Heart"

To me, the best metaphor for what public relations is or should be and do is the "thinking heart" of the organization. I believe that through research and teaching, a new generation of practitioners will consider themselves the thinking heart of their organization. The term "thinking heart"[2] comes from the diary of Etty Hillesum (1982), a Dutch Jew who died in Auschwitz in 1943. She seemed to sense that she would be sent there and that she would not return. She asked only that if she were imprisoned in the concentration camp, she could serve as the "thinking heart" of her barracks. Her diary reflects a profound connection between her people and herself.

Hillesum's (1982) writing also shows she was willing to subjugate her self-interest in order to connect with and to serve others. She managed to do this without eroding the dignity of those she helped. This sense of responsibility or service to others reflects the essence of the thinking heart. Social responsibility, similarly, must reflect more than mere charity to embrace the spirit of true responsiveness that grows from both thinking and feeling.

The question, of course, is how to create of the heart a thinking organ of perception. I believe the process begins with translating interest in "the other" into a spectrum of research methodologies—emphasizing the qualitative—that allow us to build knowledge about both the others and ourselves. At that point, the heart becomes active, engaging in such activities as communicating.

Communication is central to the work of public relations, so I begin to explain the thinking-heart metaphor[3] with a quote from the Talmud about openness: "As my mouth, so my heart." Public relations people at their most effective use their *hearts* when they legitimate the concerns of their publics, both external and internal.

Public relations professionals maintain their credibility within their organization when they use their analytical abilities to *think* through their plans (by doing formative research) and to measure whether they have been effective (by doing evaluative research). Chief executive officers (CEOs) appreciate communicators who use research to scan their environments. Results of the *Excellence* study (L. Grunig, J. Grunig, & Dozier, 2002) conducted for the Foundation of the International Association of Business Communicators (IABC) showed that using research (not guessing, not intuition, not gut reactions, not impressions alone) to provide a broad perspective was the main reason why members of the dominant coalition value and support public relations.[4]

We can pull apart the constituent elements of the "thinking-heart" metaphor and distinguish between "head knowing" and "heart knowing." Jung (as cited in Varughese, 2002) reported in 1925 that Native Americans in Taos, New Mexico, considered white people "mad" because they thought with their heads—a sure sign of mental illness to the Hopi. To others, "heart thinking" is inferior—a surrender of reason and a descent into what Varughese called "some level of gibbering infantilism." To me, neither way of knowing, however, is superior or at a higher level. Knowledge associated with the heart tends to be deep-rooted, certain, and holistic; it focuses on ethics, values, and behavioral choices. Knowledge associated with cognitive processes, by contrast, is measured and pragmatic. Decisions result from analysis, logic, and reason. In contemporary economics, the head seems to overshadow the heart when, for example, capitalism dictates that the best way to enhance the bottom line is by making employees redundant.

In the past, of course, theologians and physicians considered the *heart* the thinking organ of the body. A contemporary researcher, Pearsall (as quoted in Bennett and Sparrow, 2005), was convinced that the heart has its own form of intelligence. He believed that the heart processes information internal and external to the body through what he called an "info-energetic code" that goes beyond the circulatory system to serve as an information-gathering and distribution system. He likened the heart to a complex telephone network. He concluded: "We need the brain, and we need these brilliant scientists who are bringing their brain power to the world. But we want them to have heart . . ." (n.p.).

Neither by itself—heart nor head—is sufficient to the critical task of establishing and nurturing relationships with stakeholders. As Koper (2004) put it in his comment on the WPRF diversity manifesto, any aims of doing evaluative research, of being ethical and strategic, and of valuing diversity are:

> only good if this could be supported by clear evidence and the latter seems to be lacking. We are thus at danger to be not taken seriously . . . meanwhile these are essential elements for a sustainable occupation and practice and key to the development of the profession.
>
> (n.p.)

I have often used this metaphor of the thinking heart when lecturing on values. As the little prince of Antoine de Saint Exupéry said, "It is with the heart that one sees rightly; what is *essential* is invisible to the eye" (emphasis added, 1943: 73). What we value, what we consider essential, is what we should determine to measure. This implies that we share values, a communal enthusiasm for the most significant problems in our field.

3. The Nature of Qualitative Research

The question becomes, then, which methodological approach shows the most promise for studying those important problems. In an ideal world, perhaps all research would reflect triangulation, or a combined method that compensates for the weaknesses of one approach with the strengths of another. In actuality, most research emphasizes either the quantitative or the qualitative. And unfortunately, research in public relations too often has been confined to these extremes. The extremes are often characterized as "large-scale," "expensive," "artificial," and "intrusive" in the case of the former and "undisciplined," "soft," and "informal" in the case of the latter. However, each approach might be appropriate in a given situation; each is equally scientific. The dichotomous choice tends to reflect such considerations as the nature of the research question, time, cost, and preference and expertise of the researcher.

Qualitative researchers, interested more in the quality than the quantity of a phenomenon, tend to ask "how?" and "why?" rather than "how many?" or "to what extent?" questions. At the heart of their research is the desire to understand some condition (dissatisfied employees? protestors? overzealous government regulators? seemingly biased media?) and figure out how to eliminate what makes it a problem. Recognizing the connection between the person asking the question and those providing the answers goes a long way toward realizing the high quality of information necessary.

The ideological stance of qualitative scholars shares a lot with feminists—and with public relations scholars as well. For example, the aim of much feminist scholarship is to analyze a situation in order to figure out how to change it. Change often involves the empowerment of people in a one-down position vis-à-vis the dominant norm. To me, this is what much public relations research is all about.

One cannot discuss qualitative methodology in any field without touching on the issue of *credibility*. This type of inquiry has gained credibility in the academy only recently. This may be attributable in part to the fact that few qualitative procedures are rigorously defined; they are evolving. Even at this early stage, scholars understand that different standards of quality must be applied to qualitative research than to the quantitative. In addition to credibility—or the "truth value" of the portrait that emerges from the research—the most common alternatives to reliability and validity are *dependability* (the assurance that appropriate adaptations to the situation being studied have been made); *confirmability* (enough intersubjective agreement in the data analysis so that another researcher would likely come to the same conclusions); and *transferability* (the ability to apply this set of findings to a relevant new situation).[5]

The range of data-collection modes available to the qualitative scholar is wide: primarily interviews (long, active, elite, deep, structured, semi-structured, unstructured, and so forth), participant observation, content analysis,[6] focus groups, ethnography, Delphi technique, and case study. What tends to differentiate this research from the quantitative is the assumptions researchers bring to their work and the relationship they develop with those who participate. Key tenets[7] of qualitative research include the following.

• *Research and the people who create it are connected.* There are reciprocal influences between the parties. As a result, qualitative scholars place themselves in the middle of the topics and the people they study—rather than maintaining the "distance" or so-called "objectivity"[8] of their counterparts in quantitative research. This serves to democratize the relationship between the researcher and the researched—again, consistent with what most professionals consider the ideal relationship. In qualitative study, relationships take on special meaning and value. Open, egalitarian relationships between researchers and participants co-create a very high-quality knowledge.

• *Establishing rapport matters.* Because observation alone rarely brings about understanding, most qualitative methods involve participation as well. These methods grew out of many disciplines, but primarily the anthropological tradition of studying "alien" societies and societal culture. As a result, they have been widely adopted throughout the social sciences and, of course, public relations. Because the success of these research approaches rests on giving up a modicum of scientific control to the people being studied, I have come to appreciate the importance of establishing rapport with prospective and actual participants in the research. In fact, personal involvement is a strength of qualitative study.

Unfortunately, too many researchers ignore the ethics of getting close to the people they study; or, they may err on the side of "otherizing," deliberately distancing themselves from the researched. Perpetuating the dichotomy between the researched and the researcher sets up a false distinction that too often privileges the scholar and devalues the "other." So, although we typically refrain from developing close personal friendships with participants, we do listen attentively and try to connect with them. Not only does this approach value participants, but such collaboration also helps avoid misinterpretation of the data and subsequent write-up of results. (Interviewees may be unwilling to be candid with interviewers who are strangers to them, especially when certain responses are more socially acceptable than others.)

Along the way, many qualitative scholars avoid writing about the people who have cooperated in their investigations as "subjects" or "respondents." Those labels demean the nature of the relationship.[9] After all, the people we talk with typically do far more than simply respond to our questions. They actively participate in the process of giving and seeking information. As one communication theorist explained it, "[T]he researched are active participants in, rather than objects of," most qualitative research (Kauffman, 1992: 187). In other words, the process can be a kind of two-way symmetrical communication. So, in an effort to treat such people responsibly and with respect and to reflect the reciprocal nature of the relationship, we typically refer to them as "participants."

•   *Less may be more.* Qualitative studies typically pose fewer questions than in the traditional survey[10]—only those questions that are truly important and relevant. Researchers ask those questions in a way that respects the expertise of participants—more open-ended than closed-ended. As we on the *Excellence* team (L. Grunig *et al.*, 2002) described it, "We pared the 'ideal' list of Phase 2 [case studies] research questions and topic probes *rather brutally* . . ." (p. 43, emphasis added).

The time and energy required to develop relationships with research participants also suggest that small *samples* may be appropriate. Working longer and more cooperatively with a few people tends to produce richer data than does working more superficially with many. What the small sample sacrifices in breadth, it can make up for in depth. When measuring relationships, the aim may be to mine the opinions of a few key people rather than skimming the superficial view of many. Researchers can devote their time more to data analysis than to data collection.

•   *Reciprocity matters.* Qualitative research allows participants to express their views in their own words. Many people value this public voice and the chance to offer their own meanings, rather than having meanings supplied by a researcher as in closed-ended survey response options. Thus, quoting participants directly is critically important in the qualitative research report.[11] Participants are also able to speak for themselves when, pre-publication, researchers share drafts of their results with the people who supplied the data.

Additional benefits for participants include the validation of their life stories and experiences, being listened to, gaining insight from the questions asked, and possibly enhancing their practice as a result. To add to these reciprocal benefits, many qualitative investigators provide participants with an executive summary[12] of the study along with a letter of appreciation.

•   *People are diverse.* Qualitative scholars try to avoid stereotyping and over-generalizing. Rather than looking only at measures of central tendency, such as median and mean, they also explore the "outliers." They understand that people within groups, such as women or men, are not all the same. There is no single thing that all female employees or all male consumers want. I have come to acknowledge that since people (no matter how I may try to categorize them) come in different genders, ages, classes, races, sexual orientations, abilities, cultures, and even appearances, there is no such thing as "women's experience" or "men's experience." So, qualitative research tries to capture experiences in the plural. Doing less leads to research that is partial and exploratory at best. We must expect more complex analyses, but a firmer foundation on which to base future action.

• *Research is not neutral.* The personal involvement of researchers and the researched suggests another difference between qualitative and quantitative scholarship. The latter traditionally has assumed that scientists can and should produce value-free knowledge. By contrast, the former believe that values always are embedded, even in supposedly objective theories and knowledge. In fact, I consider objectivity a mythical concept, whether it is "objective" reporting or "objective" research.

• *Ethical issues abound.* Risk to research participants may be greater with quantitative studies such as experiments than with qualitative studies such as interviews or focus groups; but any methodology may risk damaging partici- pants' self-esteem, deceiving them, invading their privacy, creating a false sense of friendship, or exposing or identifying them. For example, confidentiality[13] is a key consideration. On the other hand, "anonymity" is not a relevant con- cept for qualitative work; because ethnographers conducting field studies such as participant observation or interviews know the identity of the people they study. So, the burden of protecting the identity and the comfort level of research participants weighs heavily on the ethical scholar.

Such ethical quandaries may present themselves at each stage of the data- analysis process: reduction, analysis, and interpretation. For example, the problem of data reduction is obvious when the qualitative scholar "eyeballs" his or her data and tries to compress lengthy video- or audiotapes or transcripts. This is a special problem in qualitative research where the researcher (rather than the computer) is the instrument of analysis. However, I believe that approaching the analytical process with a solid understanding of its ethical implications leads to a deep, comprehensive understanding of the phenomenon being studied. After all, what matters is not how much one describes but how well one describes it. Otherwise, what results may be *partial* in two senses of that word: incomplete and biased.

• *Reflexivity is a hallmark.* The thinking heart suggests that how we struc- ture a problem and examine a problem reflects our individual experiences, our culture, and our biases. Thus, one key consideration for any measurement effort is reflexivity, exploring and exposing those biases throughout the research and writing process. However, scholars are often rewarded (and sometimes criticized) for rationality, for rigorous attention to "fact." The United States and many other Western countries are brain cultures, not heart cultures.[14] The same might be said for the academic culture, where numbers tend to enjoy mythical properties. Thus we as researchers are perceived as people who are tempted to try to quantify everything.

The traditional advice for qualitative researchers serves all researchers well, in my opinion. Think about who you are and what you're doing. As an expert in the interview approach said, "A clearer understanding of one's vision of the world permits a critical distance from it" (McCracken, 1988: 33). He called this "taking stock" or intellectual capital, without which any data analysis is poorer.

Researchers and female practitioners alike may confound this perception because women are considered emotional, intuitive, and reliant on feelings more than the computer printout. However, if scholars, teachers, and practitioners serve as thinking hearts—combining the best of systematic, scientific research and concern for the people who make up our classrooms or publics— they make the greatest contribution.

• *Field studies are holistic.* Much qualitative research is done in the field, in context. The context is taken into account when analyzing the data. Thus, interviews, for example, are typically conducted in participants' offices or homes rather than a more artificial, laboratory-type setting. Observation of the context helps with the analysis. This holistic notion is often explained as researchers immersing themselves in the organizations they study. As the research team described the qualitative phase of the *Excellence* project (L. Grunig *et al.*, 2002), "We sought to contextualize the stark findings of the quantitative phase of the study" (p. 43). Adding context to the project's survey data was a major goal of that second phase. (Because of the standard of transferability, discussed above, qualitative researchers are obliged to make their context clear to other scholars who would transpose the results to a new situation.)

The holistic nature of the process typically requires *flexibility* in the field (including the willingness to be surprised) as the research progresses. For example, that qualitative stage of the *Excellence* study was designed "to maximize opportunities for the unexpected to occur" (p. 43). At times, holism requires a multiplicity of methods as well. The essence of the case method, for example, is its multiple sources of data collection (although in public relations, most case studies rely primarily on long interviews, and participant observation and document analysis only secondarily).

Readers of this chapter may not embrace all of the tenets listed above; they may also not agree that the topic areas and qualitative approaches listed next are critical for research in public relations. However, these have value for me; they speak to my heart. More specifically, I propose preliminary responses to what I consider four core questions.

4. Core Questions for Public Relations Researchers

4.1. What Are We Researching?

Developing a research agenda[15] is far beyond the scope of this chapter, but I will highlight just three critical and illustrative areas suggested by the recent WPRF conference held in Trieste in 2005—research foci most appropriate for qualitative approaches. First, I hope we agree to concentrate on new ways of thinking about *diversity* or *inclusivity*. Mcleod (2004), commenting on the WPRF diversity manifesto, cited K. Sriramesh in saying that "there are no books on this topic, no real teaching, and little by way to give us the canvass on which to base our communications advice and actions" (n.p.). Linking the gap in understanding of diversity and cross-cultural communication with public relations, Mcleod said: "This must be addressed and re-dressed as a matter of urgency, not only for the profession and practice of public relations, but *for society as a whole* for if we don't work at it, who will?" (n.p.).

Diversity has become a matter of international importance. Diversity in its many forms—racio-ethnicity, gender, age, class, physical ability, physical appearance, religion, sexual orientation, and so on—increasingly affects the global economy in general and the public relations profession in particular. As boundary spanners, people in public relations can contribute to organizational effectiveness in this era of growing heterogeneity within and around the organizations that employ them. As a result, I believe the nascent attention to multiculturalism goes well beyond "political correctness." It approaches the goals of accountability and social responsibility which Muzi Falconi (2005) considered so vital to the future of the field.

In the past, during the 1970s, companies in significant numbers around the world began to realize they would lose their best female employees if they failed to respond to the growing need to help women integrate family, work, and community life. Thus, gender has represented a business issue in the United States at least since the 1980s. What began as programs for women—programs often developed and promoted by the public relations or employee relations department—have morphed into programs to benefit all workers. Thinking has shifted. Some organizations have experienced true transformation of their culture, from what had been authoritarian to increasingly participative cultures that value employees as whole human beings. We have no perfect companies to point to as exemplars, no cookie-cutter approaches that work. However, we have case examples from the recent WPRF and, for the last three years, from the PRSA conference sessions sponsored by its Committee on Work, Life, and Gender Issues.

In her column "diversity dimensions" in PRSA's *The Strategist*, Ford (2004) pushed for "needs assessment" as the starting-point for effective diversity training. Do we have an audit instrument for assessing organizational, opera-tional, and personal needs, as she suggested, as a solid foundation for diversity programs that may cost hundreds of thousands of dollars?

However we develop such measures, I trust we will go beyond gut instinct when planning or evaluating public relations programs. U.S.-based research typically finds a significant gap between perceptions of executives and their employees on the question of whether their diversity programs are effective. The former are significantly more positive than are the rank-and-file workers. In essence, top-level decision-makers tend to view their companies through rose-colored glasses. As a result, we in public relations have an obligation to acquaint our dominant coalitions with the realities of the workplace, from employees' perspectives—or, for a second example, of the realities of the community from neighbors' perspectives. As Varughese (2002) put it: "Because it is ego-driven, head-thinking can often be delusory. Heart-thinking is focused on reality and therefore unlikely to go too wrong" (n.p.).

Similarly, the University of Oregon recently withdrew a diversity plan when its faculty members objected to what they considered a "frightening and offensive" effort by administrators to impose cultural competency. The proposed solution to this conflict is collaborative planning to narrow the gap between the view of the administration and the faculty (Staff, 2005).

Diverse publics bring with them the need for new ways of measuring *relationships*. As Koper (2004) stated flat out, "Limiting ourselves to communication alone is actually a short-termist behaviour *lacking* ambition" (n.p.). He explained, "Public relations practitioners will have to consider more than communication tactics alone if relationship management in a rich and diverse world is the practice it wants to pursue" (n.p.). J. Grunig (2002) has contributed to the profession a solid foundation for qualitative measurement of relationships.

But are we a "practice" or a "profession"? Reflecting on *public relations as a profession* is a third area ripe for study. Muzi Falconi (2005) recommended using the new information technologies for communicating *with* rather than communicating *to* publics. Technologies such as the World Wide Web, as well as the growing body of knowledge about diversity he mentioned, will allow for this kind of transformation from asymmetrical to symmetrical communication—a transformation he considered "more attuned to the activity inherent in the very name of our profession, public relations, or even better, relationships with publics" (n.p.). Such a shift would help balance the heart and the head in professional practice.

Unfortunately or, if one appreciates a challenge, fortunately for us, the researchable questions remaining in public relations are both legion and what cognitive psychologists call "ill-structured" problems:[16] problems that rarely can be solved quickly, that may have more than a single defensible solution, that may have multiple routes to one solution, and that typically have many sub-problems that must be solved before arriving at an answer. Although the so-called "well-structured problems" have a single answer and can be solved relatively quickly, they lack the "pulling power" of the more complex. Solving ill-structured problems such as those related to diversity, relationships, and professionalism of what has been largely a technical function can provide deep insight into this discipline. However, doing so often requires qualitative methodology because of its flexible, holistic, interactive, reciprocal, egalitarian, and reflective nature.

4.2. How Are We Measuring It?

Qualitative research is an eclectic methodology. Data-collection and analytical methods alluded to in my take on the nature of qualitative study included focus groups, long interviews, participant observation, content analysis, case studies, and *Delphi* technique. Here I elaborate on just three of these approaches that I consider especially relevant to the needs of public relations.

The *Delphi* study is an especially important qualitative method because it typically combines the contributions of educators and professionals. In this approach, a relatively small cadre of experts is queried (via the Internet, in the case of the recent project commissioned by the European Body of Knowledge project (van Ruler, Verčič, Flodin, & Buetschi, 2001)) and their responses typically are analyzed qualitatively rather than quantitatively. The research undergoes several iterations, building on the experts' opinions and experiences. Despite the fact that new communication technology should make the *Delphi* technique more attractive to researchers around the world, it remains under-utilized in our field (L. Grunig & J. Grunig, 2002a).

Interviews—either individual or group—are perhaps the most common type of qualitative research in public relations. Both are especially useful for assessing relationships because they help professionals grasp what motivates people. Personal interviews often involve community leaders, activists, journalists, government officials, and employees—all are important publics for organizations. Researchers can analyze interview data to explain what such critical stakeholders think and do *on their own terms*. These participants should be guaranteed (implicitly, if not explicitly) the chance to "speak" in their own voices. Thus, quoting participants, either individually or in groups, is critically important in the write-up of interview data.

Also important in interview-based research (as in fieldwork in general) is the relationship between the person guiding the inquiry and those he or she is talking with. Qualitative interviews are not one-way streets. They are two-way conversations. The richest data result from conversations that grow out of respectful and ethical approaches to establishing and maintaining rapport. They are characterized by listening and the faithful reporting and interpretation of what participants offered. Thus, participants enjoy reciprocity, rather than false promises or unmet expectations.

Qualitative researchers may face a special challenge in designing projects that meet the expectations of scientific rigor demanded by our quantitative colleagues. We need to consider and ultimately try to gain control of at least some of the vexing issues related to the ill-structured problems alluded to above. Standardizing interview protocols for dependable comparisons among responses of participants is one approach. So, too, is including multiple measures of the key concepts in the research, interviewing more than a single member of each stakeholder group, assuring participants of confidentiality, and inviting—rather than coercing—their participation.

In group interviews, a trained facilitator guides participants in a discussion that builds from the general to the specific, gradually focusing on the issue of concern. Such focus groups may bring together small numbers (typically six to twelve) of workers, consumers, or neighbors to ask questions about their satisfaction, buying behavior, attitudes and opinions, or relationships. The unique strength of focus-group research is the synergy of the group, making it especially useful for public relations (which is, after all, about collectives rather than individuals). Focus groups can develop an *interactive* view of a relationship, a view that is closer to the way members of publics actually behave in the real world. I believe focus groups are perhaps the most useful type of formative research, because they help practitioners base their plans on what actually motivates people. They are helpful, of course, in evaluative research as well.

Participants from both group and personal interviews should come away from the ethical experience feeling validated, not betrayed. What they have learned in the process may enhance their performance at work or in their community, but they should not expect to have problems solved or true friendships developed as a direct result of the research.

Another approach to data collection that typically relies on qualitative analysis is the *case study*. Although survey research was the backbone of the *Excellence* project to which I dedicated almost fifteen years of my academic life, I believe some of the study's most important insights—especially those concerning integrity, women, and people of color—emanated from the follow-up, comparative case studies (Dozier, with L. Grunig & J. Grunig, 1995; L. Grunig *et al.*, 2002).

Case study, of course, is not so much a method as a collection of methods. To qualify as a case study, it must draw on more than one source of information. Public relations researchers have used both individual and group interviews, participant observation, content analysis of organizational documents and media accounts, and even survey research when developing cases.

I argue for meta-analyses of case-study research—either surveys of cases or the case-comparison method. Take the instances of diversity initiatives and work–life integration alluded to earlier. No company has perfected an approach to such programs as flextime and elder- and childcare, so no one case is sufficiently explanatory for solid action. Whereas every case is unique, the best practices share elements and themes that can help illuminate the larger issue of how employers can attract and retain the best female practitioners of public relations. Collectively, case studies help develop theory and lead to progress in the profession, turning our vision of a nurturing organizational culture into reality. Too often, though, the case is considered stand-alone measurement of success or failure.

4.3. How Well Are We Measuring It?

We must develop a "culture of quality" for public relations research. Making continuous improvements to our research should become a priority. Some reviewers of the top papers at the Spring 2005 conference of the International Communication Association were "aghast," in the words of one reviewer, at the inadequacy of the faculty work being considered for highest honors. Criticisms included ethical concerns about methodology; over-emphasis on measures of one-way, asymmetric communication techniques such as the press release; studying "old news" such as information campaigns without cutting-edge insights or literature; artificiality of the quasi-experimental design using the ubiquitous undergraduate student as subject; framing the inquiry in literature that is irrelevant, outdated, or limited to a single country of origin; and exploration of topics that might or might not have anything to do with public relations. These included such issues as identity and marketing, with no clear links established between the literature cited (often sadly dated) and the literature of public relations. Similarly, submissions to a new journal of best practices in public relations have been disappointing in both quantity and quality (Toth, personal communication, April 2005).

Ways to enhance the quality of how and what we measure include striving for coherence, engaging in *programs of research* that build over time yet avoid the problem of "salami science"—another good metaphor—and working collaboratively. Team research can help overcome the limits any individual faces in terms of time, cost, bias, and barriers of geography and language. Collective efforts, in fact, may be necessary if we are to give respect to participants, empower them, share the research with them, study their myriad experiences, and let their voices—and hearts and minds—help guide the investigation.

Perhaps most importantly, working together necessarily provides diverse perspectives on the subject being studied. Remember that participants can be part of the team. In exchange for their time and collaboration, researchers need to offer incentives. These can be as modest as the assurance that the research is meaningful and will make a difference. Incentives can go as far as promising participants a summary of the findings.

Professional associations can help by building awareness of the pressing needs of the practice and by commissioning projects that address those concerns. Together, the scholars and the practitioners can create venues such as conferences for ongoing discussion and the development of meaningful research agendas and methodologies. I consider the annual Bled research conference in Slovenia a laboratory in which the best ideas are being distilled. Broadening the existing programs in rewards, recognition, and incentives also is important.

4.4. How Much Research Are We Doing—And Why?

In the United States, unrealistically rigorous standards for promotion and tenure (P&T) have led to a disturbing trend: assistant professors doing research for the purpose of P&T alone. Of course, productivity is important. However, choosing to do research because it is likely to get published is insufficient reason. I have already mentioned the problem of "salami science." Perhaps more egregious is the case of the person who revealed at the 2005 ICA conference in New York that she had accepted the directorship of a campus-based research center, not because she was passionate about its focus, but because she believed it would help her gain job security. Thinking, yes, but heart? No. Revealing the work of the center would reveal the identity of the assistant professor, so I will refrain from doing that. Let me just say that the mission of the center is so significant that it deserves a person of whole-hearted dedication and top-notch intellect.

5. Concluding Thoughts

Qualitative research seems especially appropriate for the kind of global studies in public relations that would help take this field from one that is overly parochial to one that can address the most pressing problems of organizations worldwide. These issues include responsibility for inclusivity and relationships with diverse publics as well as the accountability professionals owe to the society allowing them to operate, to their professional peers, and to the organizations that employ them.

To date, quantitative research has dominated studies that analyze data collected through formal means, primarily because numbers transcend the language barrier. (This is certainly the case with research published in U.S. journals (van Ruler & Verčič, 2002).) However, it may be possible to overcome the obstacles of language and cultural difference. Sha and Huang (2000) offered several useful suggestions. They include encouraging journals to publish translations of articles originally written in different languages, discussing methodological issues in cross-cultural research at special conference sessions, urging public relations firms and associations to contribute necessary funds for research dependent on international travel, encouraging U.S. scholars to study languages, collaborating with colleagues around the world, and developing a truly international journal in the field. In these ways, we may be able to create a fertile field for the propagation of more qualitative study in public relations.

Whatever we measure, however we measure it, and how often we do so, I hope our research helps us achieve the values important to public relations. One major value is contributing to a world whose society is collective. This kind of institution of community is a change that, I hope, can be brought about not by violence or even persuasion but by a thoughtful transformation of the heart.

Notes

1 Muzi Falconi defined the former as management's demand that investments in the function be demonstrably effective and the latter as the demand by stakeholders that organizational activities avoid undesirable consequences on the public sphere.

2 Of course, "thinking heart" has found its way into other contexts, such as: poetry ("A Thinking Heart," author unknown); short fiction ("A Naked, Thinking Heart" about Mr. Spock and the Vulcans, author unknown); business management (Ishmael & Mackinnon, 2002); New Age philosophy (Varughese, 2002); design (S. Danko, Associate Professor of Design and Environmental Analysis at Cornell University, offers a course called "Dancing Mind and Thinking Heart"); music (Nelson, 1982); and developmental disabilities (Pietzner, 2002).

3 A student in my graduate seminar in the ethics and philosophy of public relations, Jennifer Vardeman, explained the "thinking heart" as follows: understands the plight of others (heart part) and uses mind to solve problems (thinking part). She said (June 2005, personal communication): "We feel deeply for publics because we are responsible for presenting their attitudes, constraints, goals to the organization; [we] don't want to be perceived as 'soft.'. . ."

4 Expertise in crisis communication was mentioned second most frequently.

5 For a greater understanding of all four standards, see Lincoln and Guba (1985).
6 Manifest content can be analyzed systematically, if not quantitatively, by detecting themes, problems, issues, and publics. Published works, or those appearing in cyberspace (e.g., the content of chat rooms, discussion groups, listservs, websites, and so forth) also can be analyzed.
7 Portions of the section that follows come from L. Grunig and J. Grunig (1999) and L. Grunig and J. Grunig (2002b).
8 Feminists believe that objectivity inherently privileges the researcher over the researched (Keller, 1985; Muto, 1988; Kauffman, 1992).
9 Yet another way of devaluing or demeaning those who cooperate as participants in research is questioning their self-reports, or what they tell researchers.
10 In survey research, accuracy increases significantly with sample size up to 400. However, the intention of most qualitative research is not prediction (as in "how many people will buy this product?" or "how many people will vote for this candidate?"); the goal, more often, is action or change.
11 Direct quotes also add life to an otherwise boring account.
12 This can be considered both an incentive to take part in the project at the outset and compensation for cooperation at the end.
13 Participants may need to be reassured of confidentiality throughout the research process, especially if the information gathered is sensitive (as in queries about sexual harassment, job satisfaction, pay, promotion, morale, and so forth).
14 In other cultures (such as Hawaiian, Chinese, and Hopi), people believe that we only know truth through the heart (Pearsall, as quoted in Bennett and Sparrow, 2005).
15 The final chapter of the third book in the series on *Excellence* in public relations (L. Grunig *et al.*, 2002) suggests several of the most pressing areas for future research in our field. They include ethics and integrity, relationships and strategic management, globalization, and change and chaos theory.
16 For the prototypical ill-structured problem, see Cronbach and Furby (1970).

References

Bennett, H., & Sparrow, S. (2005). The thinking heart: An interview with Paul Pearsall. *Nature: Holistic Medicine*. Retrieved June 9, 2005, from www.ikosmos.com.
Cronbach, L. J., & Furby, L. (1970). How should we measure "change"—Or should we? *Psychological Bulletin, 74*, 68–80.
de St. Exupery, A. (1943). *The little prince* (translated by K. Woods). Paris: Gallimard.
Dozier, D. M., with Grunig, L. A., & Grunig, J. E. (1995). *Manager's guide to excellence in public relations and communication management*. Mahwah, NJ: Lawrence Erlbaum Associates.
Ford, R. L. (2004). Needs assessment helps ensure effective diversity training. *The Strategist* (July), 6.
Grunig, J. E. (2002). *Qualitative methods for assessing relationships between organizations and publics*. Gainesville, FL: The Institute for Public Relations, Commission on PR Measurement and Evaluation. Available online at www.instituteforpr.com/relationships.phtml?article_id=2002_relationships_org_public.
Grunig, L. A., & Grunig, J. E. (1999). What can we learn from a feminist approach to research? *Jim and Lauri Grunig's Research: A Supplement of PR Reporter*, 5 (August 23).
Grunig, L. A., & Grunig, J. E. (2002a). *The Bled Manifesto on public relations: One North American perspective*. Paper presented to the 9th International Public Relations Research Symposium, Bled, Slovenia, July.

Grunig, L. A., & Grunig, J. E. (2000b).. Ethical relationships in the conduct of PR research. *Jim and Lauri Grunig's Research: A Supplement of PR Reporter*, 15 (February 25).

Grunig, L. A., Grunig, J. E., & Dozier, D. M. (2002). *Excellent public relations and effective organizations: A study of communication management in three countries.* Mahwah, NJ: Lawrence Erlbaum Associates.

Hamashima, L. (2002). Remarks to the panel on work, life, and gender issues presented to the conference of the Public Relations Society of America, San Francisco (November).

Hillesum, E. (1982). *An interrupted life and letters from Westerbork.* New York: Henry Holt.

Holtzhausen, D. R., & Voto, R. (2002). Resistance from the margins: The postmodern public relations practitioner as organizational activist. *Journal of Public Relations Research, 14*, 57–84.

Ishmael, A., & Mackinnon, M. (2002). *Thinking heart, feeling mind: 10 business lessons from the compassionate workplace.* Distributed in the US and Canada by National Book Network.

Kauffman, B. J. (1992). Feminist facts: Interview strategies and political subjects in ethnography. *Communication Theory, 2*(3), 187–206.

Keller, E. F. (1985). *Reflections on gender and science.* New Haven, CT: Yale University Press.

Koper, E. (2004). *A comment by Eric Koper.* Retrieved February 8, 2005, from www.worldprfestival.org/eng/news.php?id=25.

Lincoln, Y. S., & Guba, E. G. (1988). *Naturalistic inquiry.* Beverly Hills, CA: Sage.

Mcleod, S. (2004). *Sandra Mcleod's Comments on the "Manifesto."* Retrieved February 8, 2005, from www.worldprfestival.org/eng/news.php?id=21.

McCracken, G. (1988). *The long interview.* Newbury Park, CA: Sage.

Muto, J. (1988). If I'm reading this, I must not be by the pool. *Women's Studies in Communication, 11*, 20–21.

Muzi Falconi, T. (2005). Acceptance speech, The Alan Campbell-Johnson Medal, London (June).

Nelson, B. (1982). *The love that whirls (Diary of a thinking heart).* Music album available at CD Universe.

Odedele, S. (2004). *Sunday Odedele's Comments on the "Manifesto."* Retrieved February 8, 2005, from www.worldprfestival.org/eng/news.php?id=13.

Pietzner, C. M. (2000). *The spiritual heart of service: Self-development and the thinking heart.* Proprietary report for the Fetzer Institute, Three Rivers, MI.

Schneider, L. A. [aka Grunig, L. A.] (1982). Farm lands brochure: Heavy artillery in the war between the bulldozer and the plow. *ACE (Agricultural Communicators in Education) Quarterly, 65*(1), 11–28.

Sha, B., & Huang, Y. H. (2000). *Research in international public relations: More easily said than done.* Paper presented to the Public Relations Division, International Communication Association, Acapulco, Mexico (June).

Staff (2005). University of Oregon diversity plan sparks criticism. *Chronicle of Higher Education* (June): A23.

van Ruler, B., & Verčič, D. (2002). *Reflective communication management.* Paper submitted to the Public Relations Division, Association for Education in Journalism and Mass Communication, Miami, FL (August).

van Ruler, B., Verčič, D., Flodin, B., & Buetschi, G. (2001). Public relations in Europe: A kaleidoscopic picture. *Journal of Communication Management, 6,* 166–175.
Varughese, S. (2002). *Moving from head to heart. Life positive.* Retrieved June 9, 2005, from www.lifepositive.com/mind/personal-growth/personal-growth/heartthinking. asp.

Part II
Public Relations Methods, Cases, and Specific Topics

7 The Corporate Communications Scorecard

A Framework for Managing and Evaluating Communication Strategies

Ansgar Zerfass

1. Introduction

At present, in the early 2000s, new tools for managing and evaluating communication strategies gain in importance all over the world. Beyond the traditional measurement of effects, they are mainly used to demonstrate how communication contributes to profitability and increase of shareholder value. This has been clearly demonstrated by the Global Benchpoint study (2004), which was based on interviewing 1,000 public relations professionals in over 25 countries (Gaunt & Wright, 2004: 37). Three-quarters of those interviewed state that new methods are necessary to determine the return on investment (ROI) of communication programs. This is considered an advantage in any internal competition for resources and competencies. A similar picture is described by the study "Best Practice in the Measurement and Reporting of Public Relations and ROI," published in 2004 by the British Institute of Public Relations. In the private sector, three out of four companies state that they evaluate their communication measures on a regular and proactive basis or at least sporadically (IPR, 2004). Fifty-nine percent plan to considerably improve in this area. However, so far they lack sustainable methods to do so.

This does not come as a surprise. There is agreement on the insufficiency of tools and methods currently used for PR evaluation (Lindenmann, 2003a, 2003b). This insufficiency is due to the fact that, up to now, the measurement of output, outtakes/outgrowth, and outcome has helped to improve only the effectiveness of communication. Whether in fact the goals, objectives, and accomplishments of the company or organization as a whole have been achieved cannot be proved. The crucial level of outflow of communication—the creation of economic value by building up reputation, stable relations to important stakeholders, room for maneuver, and other intangible values (Brønn, Roberts, & Breunig, 2004; Kaplan & Norton, 2004; Pfannenberg & Zerfass, 2005; Piwinger & Porák, 2005)—is not dealt with by current measurements.

2. Approaching the Balanced Scorecard

For the reasons given above, theory and practice have led to the suggestion that the balanced scorecard (BSC) should be used in corporate communications. This management tool has been widely approved in various areas of business administration. However, it should be treated with caution: most models adapting the BSC for corporate communications do not go far enough. For example, the PR/C-Scorecard of Fleisher and Mahaffy (1997) is restricted to optimize communication strategies on an operational level. This is equally true for the approach by Vos and Schoemaker (2004), who developed several criteria for improving communication management on the basis of the balanced scorecard. In fact, the approach they advocate is not a scorecard in the actual sense; it merely uses some of its dimensions to define communication quality. In contrast, the communication scorecard of the German and Swiss consultants Hering, Schuppener and Sommerhalder (2004) focuses on the link between communication and corporate strategy. Their approach, however, fails to specify the operational level and embed the tool in an overall concept of communication controlling.

Despite this rather meager theoretical basis, several companies across Europe presently have good experience with scorecards in communication management. Among companies quoted on the stock exchange in Germany, the use of this tool has doubled between 2002 and 2004 (Mast, 2005). Adopters of a scorecard method include renowned and successful companies such as Daimler, Bosch, Aventis, Siemens, and SwissRe, among others. In the following sections we will show how this know-how can lead to a theoretical framework that is able to overcome the limitations of current approaches. The corporate communications scorecard proposed in this chapter is an innovative method for managing and evaluating corporate communications. As a component it blends into an overall framework of communication controlling for companies and organizations (Zerfass, 2005a).

2.1. From Visions to Operational Objectives

The balanced scorecard was developed at the beginning of 1990s by Robert S. Kaplan and David P. Norton at the Harvard Business School (Kaplan & Norton, 1992). In a first step it was conceived as an extensive controlling system that would provide, apart from key financial indicators, a wide range of measurable figures for current and future performance. Later, the BSC was advanced to become a strategic management concept that, in addition to the operational measurement of success, would allow for a broad planning, control, and change of business strategy (Kaplan & Norton, 1996). It is this comprehensiveness which made BSC a very popular approach worldwide. Satisfaction is high: an extensive study of one hundred user companies in Germany has demonstrated that growth in comparison to their competitors has developed more positively and that BSC has led to an improvement in quality as much as to a decrease in costs (Horvath & Partner, 2003). Meanwhile, the basic model of BSC has been expanded by concepts for a strategy-focused design of the organization and its leadership (Kaplan & Norton, 2001) and for the development of immaterial values as a prerequisite for strategic readiness and sustainability of the company (Kaplan & Norton, 2004).

Kaplan and Norton (1996) point out that there is often a yawning gap between future-oriented management concepts and past-oriented controlling. This prevents a continuous management process and adjustment of strategies. The BSC as an integrated tool for control thus bridges vision, business strategy, and the single strategic programs of each business unit and sector. For this, one has to look at the company from different perspectives (financial, customer, process/internal business, potential/learning, and growth). For each of those perspectives, precise goals and factors of success are defined and value drivers are identified. For example, for a producer of household appliances, the crucial factor for a successful customer relationship can be the quality of the service offered. A value driver here would be a quick completion of repairs. Measurable key performance indicators are assigned to each value driver, which should, ideally, be both early indicators and classical, *ex post*, results. Further actions and measures should then be geared toward these indicators and resulting goals (such as average reaction time from customer call to technician's visit, average time until the problem is permanently solved, degree of subjective satisfaction from a customer's point of view).

By these means the BSC initiates a process with the help of which all actors can identify the effect of their own performance on business success, including possible interdependencies with other units and goals. Each member of staff should concentrate on value-raising activities and drop any unnecessary tasks. Whether goals have actually been achieved can be measured with the help of the key performance indicators. This allows for measuring success across different units as well as continuously adjusting the scorecard for the company and its business units. This is the reason why this method has become so popular in a short time and is nowadays widely used in many areas.

3. Using Scorecards Within Communication Management

The corporate communications scorecard (CCS) can be introduced into the management process of corporate communications (Cutlip, Center, & Broom, 2000: 341; Zerfass, 2004: 319; Zerfass, 2008) for both strategic and operational planning as well as evaluation. On the strategic level, the tool is used to ensure the coherence between overall goals of the company as a whole and communication objectives. It also helps to measure value-creation or outflow (see section 3.1). On the operational level, the scorecard can ensure that single activities within the media mix are linked to the communication goals. Moreover, it may help to focus all activities of a communication department on the ultimate goals (see section 3.2).

3.1. Corporate Communications Scorecards as a Strategic Management Tool

The corporate communications scorecard is a strategic management tool that blends into the balanced scorecard of a company. It extends it and allows for the management of communication programs. The starting-point is "Vision and Business Strategy," considered from various perspectives, as the balanced scorecard suggests (see Figure 7.1). A broad understanding of corporate communication already brings into account the importance of the socio-political sphere in terms of acceptance, image, and reputation. An extensive stakeholder approach (Andriof, Waddock, Husted & Sutherland, 2002, 2003; Grunig & Repper, 1992; Heath, 1994: 147) shows that partners from politics, local communities, NGOs, and the press are as important as the customers, employees, and shareholders mentioned in the basic model by Kaplan and Norton. It is reasonable, then, to add a socio-political view to the four classical perspectives of the BSC (finances, customers, processes, potentials). This extended balanced scorecard deduces for each perspective—as usual—factors of success, value drivers, key performance indicators, and strategic programs.

Figure 7.2 exemplifies what a scorecard for a chemical firm might look like and how to detect elements of the corporate communications scorecard (in the table these are highlighted in gray). For illustration, two perspectives have been singled out. Based on the business strategy (1), the most important strategic factors of success (2) are deduced. Because the socio-political dimension is taken into account, goals achievable by means of communication

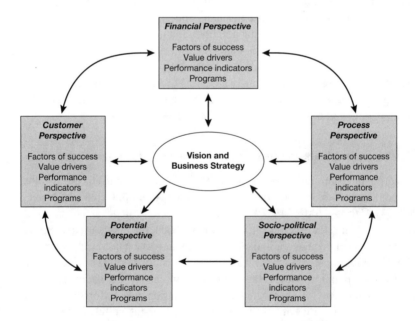

Figure 7.1 Five perspectives of the corporate communications scorecard

are considered already at this early stage—for example, the establishment of an all-embracing corporate citizenship. As a next step, all those value drivers are identified that have a direct and measurable bearing on factors of success and, accordingly, on company value (3). The example in Figure 7.2 makes clear that in the balanced scorecard, value drivers such as high profile and reputation play a decisive role in more than one perspective. Apart from the illustrated financial and socio-political perspective they also do so in the customer perspective (brand images; see Bentele, Buchele, Höpfner, & Liebert, 2004). On the other hand, socio-political goals like establishing mutual trust with local communities are not only influenced by professional communication; they may be reinforced or, rather, foiled by value chain activities, that is to say, production processes without any breakdowns and environmental pollution.

For each value driver, precise key performance indicators are defined and complemented by target measurements (4). On the basis of this, single strategic communication programs as well as defined measures can be generated (5). When applying the CCS, these target values are detected regularly in a quantitative measure and compared with the results quarterly. Here, key figures and evaluation methods established for public relations (such as image analysis, media response analysis, participant survey, and focus groups) are taken up, in the same way as newly defined values that have been developed with the company-specific scorecard are also taken up. Rather than being an alternative, the CCS is a supplement to today's already established measurement methods. They are still necessary but are now directly linked to the ultimate goals, objectives, and accomplishments of the company as a whole for the first time.

The scorecard is applied iteratively: one infers programs and actions, measures success and failure, so that the broader context is more easily discernible and the strategy may be adjusted where necessary. The gray boxes in Figure 7.2 clearly show which targets those in charge of communication are expected to meet, how this contributes to the company's profitability, and how their own efforts might be supported or foiled by other areas. At the same time, it demonstrates that communication is significant in so many areas that a thorough implementation of an integrated communication remains without alternatives (Bruhn, 2006; Kitchen & de Pelsmacker, 2004; Zerfass, 2004: 411).

The corporate communications scorecard is suitable for the strategic management of communication because it establishes a direct relation between business strategy and communication programs. It is not a tool used in isolation but acts in concert with financial, customer-, process- and potential-oriented considerations. Furthermore, the CCS is an extract from the overall scorecard, which has been widened by socio-political perspectives, focusing on the responsibilities and activities of communication management.

3.2. The Corporate Communications Scorecard at the Operational Level

Scorecards can also be used for the operational management of communication programs (micro-level). Concepts and campaigns can be put into action

Figure 7.2 Example of a corporate communications scorecard on a macro level (extract)

Business Strategy (1) ↓ deducing	Financial Perspective — Which goals are derived from the expectations of investors?		Socio-political Perspective — Which goals are derived from the expectations of citizens, residents, politicians?	
Strategic factors of success (2) ↓↑	Optimizing cost structure	Increasing stock quotation	Strengthening corporate citizenship	Ensuring the acceptance in local communities
Value drivers (3) ↓↑	a) Efficiency of administration	a) Image relevant for stock buying decisions	a) Publicity among NGOs and politicians	a) Relevance as employer
	b) Credit costs		b) Taking responsibility for the environment	b) Production without breakdowns
				c) Open-door policy
Key performance indicators and goals (4)	a1) Administration costs in relation to turnover Target < 6%	a1) Image profile among analysts Target: better than competitor X	a1) Public recognition of company name and values Target: 60%	a1) Jobs Target: > 850 fulltime, > 40 apprentices
	b2) Interest for outside capital Target < 9%	a2) Coverage in the financial press Target: monthly 10 articles/clippings	b1) Eco-audit Target: certifications according to EU standards	b1) Number of breakdowns Target: 0
↓↑				c1) Contacts with stakeholders Target: > 4 per citizen yearly
Strategic communication programs (5) ↑ measuring		a11) Expansion of analyst network a21) Investor relations press campaign	a11) Re-adjustment of lobbying and dialogue communication	c11) Community relationship program (sponsoring, press activities, events)

efficiently and operational measures in the media mix can be geared toward the communication goals. Moreover, the CCS may help us focus all activities of a communication department on common goals. See in particular Fleisher and Mahaffy (1997: 131) for examples. They highlight key factors of success, value drivers, and key performance indicators that have to be considered in the field of corporate publishing. For example, such factors need to be considered from the perspective of the communication department's customers and communication partners (newly acquired contacts, degree of credibility), from a process point of view (average production time of employees' magazines), for financial purposes (cost of magazine per reader), and from an internal potential point of view (innovative ideas per employee). Similarly, Fuchs (2003) demonstrates how value drivers and key performance indicators can be identified on the basis of the strategic factors of success by using examples from the field of marketing and financial communications. For example, the factor of success "Very high quality of capital market communication" is, among others, affected by the value driver "Quick availability of quarterly figures." In turn, precise key-performance indicators and target values can be derived, such as the date for the publication of quarterly figures on the Internet (less than five days after end of the quarter), dispatch date (less than fifteen days) and the error rate for any published information (less than 2%).

Figure 7.3 depicts a case study from business practice. It refers to the on-line communication of a German company that is publicly funded. Working as a center of excellence for the federal state of Baden-Württemberg, it runs an Internet portal featuring daily updates for the regional Information Technology and Media sector (www.doIT-online.de). The website has more than 10,500 subscribers. With this it is the market leader in the federal state, which has a population of about 10 million. However, it competes with national magazines that deploy a significantly higher set of personnel and financial resources. The service is run by in-house editors, who fall back on information supplied by several departments. It partly assigns available journalists and sources job and apprentice databases from other websites (on-line integration). In this particular case, the scorecard starts with the factors of success for the on-line communication strategy. On the basis of this, it is relatively easy to identify the most important value drivers, define key performance indicators for a given time frame, and derive concrete programs and actions. This procedure is suitable in particular for setting priorities, defining goals, and justifying size and breakdown of budget.

When applying the corporate communications scorecard on the operational level of programs and business units it is crucial to pay attention to not defining goals and factors of success in isolation but to derive them from the company's overall strategic scorecard. This helps to avoid a process optimization that does not support the overall business strategy but, in contrast, might even be counter-productive in that it reinforces department-specific agendas.

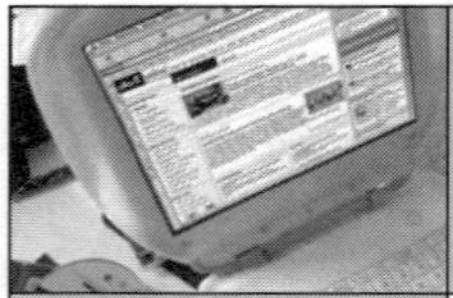	Financial	Customers/Recipients	Potentials	Processes	Socio-political
Factors of success	**Balanced Budget**	**Quality and Service**	**Power of Innovation**	**Workflow Optimization**	**Transparency**
Value drivers	a) Fees for freelancers b) Webhosting costs	a) Exclusiveness and additional benefit of features b) Up-to-date entries in the job database	a) Regular adoption of new elements	a) Cooperation of PR department and other functions b) Usability of Content Management Systems (CMS)	a) Privacy policy (e-mail addresses) b) Unbiased editorial policy
Key performance indicators and targets	a) Ø Fee for each article: < = 250 EUR b) Webhosting costs monthly < 400 EUR	a) Each feature contains 1 exclusive quotation or 3 links b) Last update: < = 3 days	a) Short-term actions (contests, games): 2 quarterly	a) Necessary corrections < = 2 monthly b) Ø activation time per entry: < 1 minute	a) Meeting standards of the branch association b) E-mails of complaint: = 0
Action programs	a) Introducing lump rates b) Checking change of provider	a) Training of freelancers and editors b) New partner for the job database	a) Setting up an internal task force "Actions/Add-ons"	a) Putting up an editorial agenda on the Intranet b) Licensing CMS update	a) Revising privacy infotexts b) Training of freelancers and editors

Figure 7.3 Example of a corporate communications scorecard at micro-level (online communication)

4. Toward a Multidimensional Concept of Communication Controlling

The presented considerations have demonstrated how the balanced scorecard can be of use for public relations research. As a matter of course, the concept described here can and should be further explored. In summary, for applying the scorecard in business practice, it is advisable to use it at the macro level (business strategy—strategic communication programs) as well as at the micro level (strategic communication programs—operational measures in the media mix). An optimization of communication activities in isolation does not make sense, though. For one thing, holistic considerations are necessary as much as incorporating communication politics into the overall process of company-wide strategy development (Steyn, 2002).

The presented corporate communications scorecard opens up new vistas for research and practice in several ways. Although the CCS is primarily a management tool, it can also be used for evaluating corporate communications. However, it cannot replace the widely tested tools that have been applied to operational impact control for many years now (surveys, media-response analyses, image profiles, cost benefit inquiries; see Lindenmann, 2003a, 2003b). In terms of strategic process control, it reveals how communication contributes to the company's profitability and helps to optimize the communication strategy. With this, the CCS blends in an overall evaluation model of corporate communication and public relations. Apart from classical approaches and methods of efficiency research, such a model comprises the management of communication processes as well as of the management processes itself (for more details, see Zerfass, 2005b; with a different focus, see Likely, 2000).

Figure 7.4 shows that such a multidimensional communication controlling provides a multitude of methods with which both strategic potentials for communication can be built up ("Doing the right things") and an efficient implementation of communication programs can be facilitated ("Doing the things right"). The method mix incorporates the well-established methods of *ex post* effect measurement as well as forecasts and interim evaluations. In addition, conventional measurements of public relations effects ("Which effect do PR measurements have on the target group?") should be supplemented by a systematic evaluation of PR usability ("Which use are PR measurements for the recipients?").

5. Theoretical Underpinnings: The Characteristics of Frameworks and the Limits of Evaluation

5.1. Applying Frameworks as "Linguistic Devices"

The previous examples have shown that the corporate communications scorecard—in contrast to many other methods of PR evaluation—is not an analytic model that represents interdependencies in a logical set of statements. Models

	Task	Perspective	Methods	Key Indicators
Strategic communication controlling	Managing and evaluating communication management	Process quality of CC from the top management's point of view (Potential)	Process analyses, i.e. > Communication audit > Audit of integration	> Rating > Acceptance rate
	Managing and evaluating communication strategies	Value creation through CC from the top management's point of view (Outflow)	Value determination, i.e. > Com. Due Diligence > Brand assessment Identifying value drivers, i.e. > Corp. Com. Scorecard	> Goodwill > Brand value > Degree of compliance
Operational communication controlling	Managing and evaluating communication programs	Program quality of CC from the communication management's point of view (Performance)	Program analyses, i.e. > Evaluation of concepts > Allocation of budgets	> Rating > Communication efficiency
	Managing and evaluating communication measures	Usability of CC from the recipients' point of view (Usability)	Success forecast, i.e. > Advert pretest > Web usability test Progress control, i.e. > Campaign's milestones	> Degree of sympathy > Solutions quota > Degree of fulfilment
		Effects of CC from the communication management's point of view (Output, Outcome)	Measurement of effects, i.e. > Attention > Media response analysis > Image analysis > Preference inquiry	> Recall value > Acceptance quotient > Reputation quotient > Ranking

CC = Corporate Communications

Figure 7.4 Multidimensional communication controlling

"deliver an analytical solution with clear results and action plans based on pre-determined criteria" (Scherer & Dowling, 1995: 234). When applied correctly in a model results are always the same, irrespective of users and their interests. They thus allow for a standardization and enhancement beyond company borders. An example in point is the media-response analysis, which has been continuously improved by researchers and service providers; it is now an established tool for efficiency research in PR. In the context of communication controlling, models fit best for well-structured processes. Here, all those involved agree on what the problem is, how to perceive the process on which the problem is based, and how to define interdependencies and success.

However, models have their limits when unstructured and complex matters are to be investigated. Evidently, this is the case at a strategic management level where solutions for success are sought. The definition of the situation already allows for numerous alternative ways of interpretation, which is even more true for describing processes and their interdependencies. With this, solutions are always dependent on actors involved, their interpretations and their interests. For this case, management research has introduced frameworks in which relations between variables are not determined (Porter, 1991). They are "linguistic devices" (Scherer & Dowling, 1995: 234) that support managers in the discussion process and decision-making but do not anticipate solutions in a "one best way" manner.

In this respect, the corporate communications scorecard as a linguistic device helps to professionalize the management of corporate communications. It allows for bundling the know-how of communication professionals and making it accessible for joint discussion and decision-making. Important side effects are an increased transparency and an objectification of arguments, for example when discussing budgets. In the end, however, the ones in charge of communication are responsible for decisions made and their ultimate success or failure. At the same time this makes clear that the design and implementation of a corporate communications scorecard cannot be delegated to consultants or service providers, in contrast to operational evaluation methods. A successful scorecard can hardly be adopted or bought. In fact, to become a strategic management tool it has to be tailor-made for each individual company. Naturally, in-house knowledge can be supplemented and enriched by the exchange with other professionals, researchers, and consultants.

5.2. Limits of Scorecards and Communication Metrics

The advantages of the corporate communications scorecard as presented in this paper are evident: setting methods like this into practice strengthens the role of communication because it displays how it contributes to the company's profitability and helps to optimize relevant processes. For these reasons we propose to increasingly use scorecards, identify typical value drivers and key performance indicators, and initiate a knowledge exchange with best practice examples on a European scale.

At the same time we should not ignore that the scope of communication control is limited by activities and processes that run counter to the overall business strategy and by the suppression of creativity. Looking at the downside of "marketing metrics" (Belz, 2004; Reinecke, 2004: 433), three fundamental dangers can be identified. First, by increasingly implementing control methods there is a tendency to design badly and abuse scorecards and systems of key indicators. Based on business practice, Paul (2004: 108) states "Two out of three companies misuse scorecards. They collect numbers like crazy, which turn out to be irrelevant at best, . . . and might even endanger the company altogether." Another frequent error is to design a detailed scorecard for part of the company or a single function without continuously linking it to the overall business strategy. Many of the well-intentioned activities to evaluate and optimize corporate communication degenerate into mere rituals of verification. Another problem poses the apparent objectivity of systems of key indicators, results of measurement, and numbers. Power (1997: 142) points out that they are not nearly as effective and neutral as commonly assumed. The connection between methods and key indicators is rarely scrutinized—"numbers seem to be objective. They are assigned a key position inwards as well as outwards and extensively shape all efforts and discussions" (Belz, 2004: 60). For this reason, methods are favored which are already established and easy to measure. Approaches, which are more creative and less orthodox, fade into the background even though they are an important source for sustainable competitive advantage. The selectivity of controlling methods constitutes a third problem area. By increasingly representing questions of the business practice with the help of frameworks and models one might lose sight with undirected strategic control (Reinecke, 2004: 434; Schreyögg & Steinmann, 1987). However, a challenge for communication management is to observe its environment in as wide a way as possible in order to spot technological, economic, and social changes at an early stage. This is true, for example, when looking at the rather neglected development of new and relatively self-contained publics on the Internet (virtual consumer communities) and within ethnic groups. In Germany, for instance, the number of print publications and radio programs in foreign languages has increased by 40% since 1990 and counts 2,500 titles today. This is an excellent way to reach the growing Turkish and Russian populations. Nevertheless, only companies and agencies that have a bird's-eye view of their environment will see this trend, and they will be more successful than those who serve the traditional media setting with sophisticated management and evaluation methods but fail to notice the change of general conditions.

To overcome these obstacles, the corporate communications scorecard shows how to link established methods of PR measuring to overall business objectives, and it highlights the ways in which communication contributes to a company's profitability. By doing so, it incorporates an intrinsic tension between control and creativity. This approach can be summarized in Albert Einstein's observation that "Not everything that counts can be counted, and not everything that can be counted, counts."

References

Andriof, Jörg, Waddock, Sandra, Husted, Bryan, & Sutherland Rahman, Sandra (2002, 2003). *Unfolding stakeholder thinking* (Vols. 1 and 2). Sheffield: Greenleaf Publishing.

Belz, Christian (2004). Gefahren der "Marketing-Metrics" (Risks of marketing metrics). *Thexis*, *21*(3), 60–63.

Bentele, Günter, Buchele, Mark-Steffen, Höpfner, Jörg, & Liebert, Tobias (2003). *Markenwert und Markenwertermittlung* (*Brand value and calculating brand values*). Wiesbaden: Deutscher Universitäts-Verlag.

Brønn, Peggy Simcic, Roberts, Hanno, & Breunig, Karl Joachim (2004). *Intangible assets, communication and relationships*. Paper presented at BledCom 2004, the 11th International Public Relations Research Symposium, July 2–4, 2004, Lake Bled, Slovenia. Available online at www.bledcom.com/ uploads/ documents/ Bled_Bronn. pdf.

Bruhn, Manfred (2006). *Integrierte Unternehmens- und Markenkommunikation* (*Integrated corporate and marketing communications*) (4th ed.). Stuttgart: Schäffer-Poeschel.

Cutlip, Scott M., Center, Allen H., & Broom, Glen M. (2000). *Effective public relations* (8th ed.). Upper Saddle River, NJ: Prentice Hall.

Fleisher, Craig S., & Mahaffy, Darren M. (1997). A balanced scorecard approach to public relations management assessment. *Public Relations Review*, *23*, 117–142.

Fuchs, Hans Joachim (2003). Welchen Wert schafft Kommunikation? (Which value is created by communication?). *Harvard Business Manager*, *25*(6), 37–45.

Gaunt, Richard, & Wright, Donald K. (2004). *Examining international differences in communications measurement. Benchpoint global measurement study 2004.* Paper presented at the PR Measurement Summit, September 21–24, 2004, Durham, NJ. Available online at www.measuresofsuccess.com/Speeches+and+Conferences/The+ Summit+on+the+Future+of+Measurement/Summit+2004/ Presentations & Downloads_ GetFile.aspx?id=504.

Grunig, James E., & Repper, Fred C. (1992). Strategic management, public, and issues. In J. E. Grunig (Ed.), *Excellence in public relations and communication management* (pp. 117–157). Hillsdale, NJ: Lawrence Erlbaum.

Heath, Robert L. (1994). *Management of corporate communication*. Hillsdale, NJ: Lawrence Erlbaum.

Hering, Ralf, Schuppener, Bernd, & Sommerhalder, Mark (2004). *Die Communication Scorecard* (*The Communication Scorecard*). Bern: Haupt.

Horváth & Partner (2003). *100 mal Balanced Scorecard. Studie bei Unternehmen in Deutschland, Österreich und der Schweiz* (*100 balanced scorecards. A study with companies in Germany, Austria and Switzerland*). Stuttgart: Horváth & Partner.

IPR Institute of Public Relations & The Communication Directors' Forum & Metrica Research (2004). *Best practice in measurement and reporting of public relations and ROI.* London: IPR.

Kaplan, Robert S., & Norton, David P. (1992). The balanced scorecard—measures that drive performance. *Harvard Business Review*, *70*(2), 71–79.

Kaplan, Robert S., & Norton, David P. (1996). *Balanced scorecard*. Boston: Harvard Business School Press.

Kaplan, Robert S., & Norton, David P. (2001). *The strategy-focused organization*. Boston: Harvard Business School Press.

Kaplan, Robert S., & Norton, David P. (2004). *Strategy maps.* Boston: Harvard Business School Press.

Kitchen, Philip J., & de Pelsmacker, Patrick (2004). *Integrated marketing communication.* New York: Routledge.

Likely, Fraser (2000). Communication and PR: Made to measure. *Strategic Communication Management, 4*(1). Available online at www.instituteforpr.com/pdf/SCM%20 Likely%20reprint%202000%20b.pdf.

Lindenmann, Walter (2003a). *Guidelines for measuring the effectiveness of PR programs and activities.* Gainesville, FL: The Institute for Public Relations.

Lindenmann, Walter (2003b). *Public relations research for planning and evaluation.* Palmyra: Lindenmann Research Consulting.

Mast, Claudia (2005). Werte schaffen durch Kommunikation (Creating values by communication). In Jörg Pfannenberg & Ansgar Zerfass (Eds.), *Wertschöpfung durch Kommunikation (Creating economic value through communication)* (pp. 27–35). Frankfurt: Frankfurter Allgemeine Buch.

Paul, Joachim (2004). Wenn Kennzahlen schaden (If figures do damages). *Harvard Business Manager, 26*(6), 108–111.

Pfannenberg, Jörg, & Zerfass, Ansgar (Eds.) (2005). *Wertschöpfung durch Kommunikation (Creating economic value through communication).* Frankfurt: Frankfurter Allgemeine Buch.

Piwinger, Manfred, & Porák, Victor (Eds.) (2005). *Kommunikations-Controlling (Communication controlling).* Wiesbaden: Gabler.

Porter, Michael E. (1991). Towards a dynamic theory of strategy. *Strategic Management Journal, 12* (Special Issue, Winter 1991), 95–117.

Power, Michael (1997). *The audit society. Rituals of verification.* Oxford, England: Oxford University Press.

Reinecke, Sven (2004). *Marketing performance management.* Wiesbaden: Deutscher Universitäts-Verlag.

Scherer, Andreas G., & Dowling, Michael E. (1995). Towards a reconciliation of the theory–pluralism in strategic management—incommensurability and the constructivist approach of the Erlangen School. *Advances in Strategic Management,* 12A, 195–247.

Schreyögg, Georg, & Steinmann, Horst (1987). Strategic control. A new perspective. *Academy of Management Review, 12,* 91–103.

Steyn, Benita (2002). From "strategy" to "corporate communication strategy": A conceptualisation. In Dejan Verčič, Betteke van Ruler, Inger Jensen, Danny Moss & Jon White (Eds.), *The status of public relations knowledge in Europe and around the world* (pp. 126–142). Proceedings of BledCom 2002 in conjunction with 2002 Euprera Annual Congress. Ljubljana: Pristop Communications.

Vos, Rita, & Schoemaker, Henny (2004). *Accountability of communication management. A balanced scorecard approach for communication quality.* Utrecht: LEMMA.

Zerfass, Ansgar (2004). *Unternehmensführung und Öffentlichkeitsarbeit. Grundlegung einer Theorie der Unternehmenskommunikation und Public Relations (Strategic management and public relations. A theory of corporate communication and public relations)* (2nd ed.). Wiesbaden: VS Verlag für Sozialwissenschaften.

Zerfass, Ansgar (2005a). Rituale der Verifikation? Grundlagen und Grenzen des Kommunikations-Controlling (Rituals of verification? Basics and boundaries of communication controlling). In Lars Rademacher (Ed.), *Distinktion und Deutungsmacht.*

Studien zur Theorie und Pragmatik der Public Relations (*Distinction and the power of interpretation. Studies dealing with the theory and pragmatics of public relations*) (pp. 181–220). Wiesbaden: VS Verlag für Sozialwissenschaften.

Zerfass, Ansgar (2005b). Steuerung und Wertschöpfung von Kommunikation (Managing communication and creating value). In Günter Bentele, Romy Fröhlich & Peter Szyszka (Eds.), *Handbuch der Public Relations* (*Handbook of public relations*) (pp. 533–548). Wiesbaden: VS Verlag für Sozialwissenschaften.

Zerfass, Ansgar (2008). Corporate communication revisited: Integrating business strategy and strategic communication. In Ansgar Zerfass, Betteke van Ruler, & Krishnamurthy Sriramesh (Eds.), *Public relations research, European perspectives and international innovations* (pp. 65–96). Wiesbaden: VS Verlag für Sozialwissenschaften.

8 Public Relations Is What Public Relations Does

Conclusions from a Long-Term Project on Professional Public Relations Modeling and Evaluation

Barbara Baerns

1. Introduction

This chapter discusses selected data from the final report of a long-term project searching for scientific approaches and developments in public relations conceptualization, strategy, and evaluation. At the same time it clarifies the range of an approach that deals with public relations as applied media and communication science (see also Baerns, 1995b). The study in question reconstructed and re-evaluated 493 of a total of 530 German public relations campaigns submitted between 1970 and 2001 for the *Goldene Brücke* ("Golden Bridge"), a prize then awarded by the German Public Relations Association (*Deutsche Public Relations-Gesellschaft e.V.*, DPRG, *Berufsverband Öffentlichkeitsarbeit*) for outstanding work in the field.[1] For more than thirty years it traced the advances in public relations within the German Federal Republic. There are indications that in other countries similar developments are under way (see, e.g., Xavier, Patel, & Johnston, 2005).

The 493 cases analyzed[2] represent 93% of the assessed entries for the Golden Bridge prize in the period under study (see Table 8.1). Within this framework, sixty-eight out of seventy-one award winners were included. More than half of the re-evaluated applications (262 cases or 53%) came from public relations agencies. Two hundred and fourteen cases (43%) originated in the public relations departments of larger organizations, including companies and public institutions. Seventeen campaigns were jointly submitted by in-house public relations departments and agencies. Over the years, agencies have substantially increased their participation in the competition, from only two applications in 1970 (12% of the analyzed cases for that year) to thirty-seven applications in 2000 (71% of the analyzed cases for that year). Agencies predominated in 1988 and from 1992 to 2001. Almost all applications (450 or 91%) concern relatively long-term campaigns, while the remainder represents single projects.[3] Three hundred and eight projects (63%) dealt with external relations, thirty-four (7%) with internal relations and 148 (30%) consisted of

Table 8.1 Cases submitted and cases analyzed (Goldene Brücke 1970–2001)

Year	Cases submitted	Cases analyzed	Winning cases
1970	26	17	3 (2)
1972	5	3	1 (0)
1974	26	16	3 (3)
1976	18	12	3 (3)
1978	6	3	2 (2)
1980	9	4	2 (1)
1985	11	10	3 (3)
1988	16	16	2 (1)
1990	14	14	3 (3)
1992	22	22	4 (4)
1993	15	15	4 (5)
1994	41	41	6 (6)
1995	57	56	5 (5)
1996	64	64	6 (6)
1998	56	56	8 (8)
1999	41	41	6 (6)
2000	52	52	5 (5)
2001	51	51	5 (5)
Total	530	493	71 (68)

a total communications project. The cases examined cover a broad spectrum of subject areas.[4]

"Public relations is what public relations does." Manfred Rühl's phrase, coined in 1992, has been taken literally, and thus can serve as the central theme of this study, recording how public relations through its own activity continually reconstructs and redefines itself. The analyzed output, a statistically non-representative selection of the public relations activities in Germany, seems especially informative since what we are dealing with is—at least in the perception of the professionals themselves—a particularly qualified sector of practical public relations.

The practitioners' self-concept served as a starting-point. Since 1994 at the latest, the international public relations associations have been widely dealing with problems of "quality" and "quality development" (Berth, 1996; Berth & Sjöberg, 1997; IPRA, 1994). In the context of that debate, which counts on the capacity of academia for constructive criticism,[5] we focused on (1) the problem-solving potential; (2) the reflective potential of public relations as necessary and appropriate standards of success and criteria of quality in this field; and (3) we were also searching for developments.

2. Problem Solving

For almost fifty years, practitioners who expressed themselves in public have presented a relatively simple decision-making model, proceeding from situation

Table 8.2 Explicit description of four strategic steps contained in a PR decision-making process (Goldene Brücke, 1970–2001)

	Yes	No	Not decisive
Situation analysis	421	64	8
Conceptualization	447	44	2
Implementation	411	73	9
Evaluation	389	98	6
Four steps of decision-making	323	161	9

analysis right up to the measuring of results by means of which a communication problem can be solved. This means that—based on a concrete situation—a communication process can be planned, managed, evaluated, and thus designed.[6] By reconstructing this decision-making process it should be possible to reveal and demonstrate the problem-solving potential of public relations.[7]

Following the assertions made by the authors of the analyzed public relations campaigns and measures, we observed that nearly all cases contain a situation analysis (421 or 85%). Almost all have undergone planning or conceptualization (447 or 91%). Most of the cases speak of implementation (411 or 83%); and also, in most of the cases, an evaluation, assessment, or review of the success had taken place according to the authors (389 or 79%). Again, according to the authors, in two-thirds of all cases (323), all stages of planning were considered separately before being carried out (see Table 8.2).

When we took the entire decision-making process into consideration more thoroughly, we arrived at a different result—again on the basis of the authors' own assertions (see Table 8.3). Twelve cases satisfy all requirements; six of these came from companies and institutions, five originated in public relations agencies and one was jointly submitted by an in-house public relations department and an agency. Significant differences between the material originating

Table 8.3 Explicit description of nine strategic steps contained in a PR decision-making process (Goldene Brücke 1970–2001)

	Yes	No	Not decisive
Situation analysis	421	64	8
Conceptualization	447	44	2
→ Objectives	371	108	14
→ Publics	213	270	10
Central idea	219	270	4
→ Selection of media	254	233	6
Time schedule	82	388	23
Budgeting	204	263	26
Implementation	411	73	9
Evaluation	389	98	6
Nine steps of decision-making	12	471	10

from public relations agencies on the one hand and from public relations departments on the other could not be identified.

The data reflect severe strategic deficits regarding particular goals, particular instruments, and particular publics:

(1) planning strategies require a concrete objective;
(2) they identify publics;
(3) these should be reached through the rational selection of media and other means.

In other words, if the different goals, which are conceivable, are to be achieved, this presupposes an adequately differentiated communication scenario, i.e., the judicious selection of suitable media and instruments. Furthermore, these communication scenarios may or may not include certain audiences. In fact, procedures involve interrelational decision-making.

Examining more closely the individual objectives that were formulated, it was possible to draw up a ranking list taking multiple coding into consideration. The following objectives were the most frequently formulated over the length of the research period:

(1) to inform (e.g., about institutions and businesses, or about products and services): 192 cases;
(2) to build or improve an "image" (e.g., of branches, businesses, other organizations, products, and services): 186 cases;
(3) to persuade (e.g., in favor of products, of political, social, or economic institutions and views): 99 cases;
(4) to initiate dialogue (e.g., in controversial questions, existing conflicts or as preventative measures): 67 cases;[8]
(5) several other objectives: 276 cases.

We looked into the question of which communication scenarios were actually developed in order to achieve these goals. With the cases we researched, it was in essence predominantly publicity or one-way communication: 76% (376 of 493 cases) were assigned to this information model. In nearly all these cases the press or media activities were involved. On the other hand, few cases communicated within the framework of a symmetrical model (eighteen cases or 4%). Besides, altogether ninety-nine candidates (20%) represented a two-way asymmetrical communication process since they showed interest in feedback. When these observations on communication scenarios are set against the manifold goals presented above, these are put into effect significantly much less frequently than intended (see Figure 8.1). This concurs with the finding that less than half of the projects explicitly dealt with the question of publics.

We grouped together the 376 cases with clear-cut scenarios of publicity or one-way information and the eighteen cases with clear-cut scenarios of

Explicit objective	Communication scenario
Information	One-way publicity and information
192 cases (38.9%)	376 cases (76.3%)
↕	↕
Dialogue	Two-way communication
67 cases (13.6%)	18 cases (3.7%)

Figure 8.1 Objective versus communication scenarios

symmetrical communication in order to cross-check their compatibility with the objectives once more. The result underlines the described findings: we found more divergence than concordance (see Table 8.4).

To sum up, the discussion of how intended communication processes should be prepared and presented, that is, which media infrastructure or which communicative instruments are needed in order to enable formulated goals to be achieved, was neglected in actual practice. These observations are in keeping with the hesitant use made of scientific methods as social techniques. But a relative majority of the cases submitted, which did indeed develop a proper communication scenario, applied scientific methods in their situation analyses and in their evaluations. The data reveal even a highly significant correlation between the use of scientific methods of evaluation and communication scenarios corresponding to objectives.[9]

In our research we took into account the following means of conducting a scientifically sound situation analysis and a scientifically sound evaluation. They were used by only 33% (162 cases) and 37% (182 cases) of the applications, respectively:

- media coverage analysis, that is to say, a content analysis of the achieved media coverage on the basis of a previously formulated frame of reference;
- special surveys commissioned for the public relations project in question;
- general public relations surveys, which, for a specific public relations project, are merely consulted;

Table 8.4 Correspondence of communication scenarios and objectives (re-evaluation Goldene Brücke 1970–2001, subgroup of 394 cases)

Communication scenario/objective	All cases	Cases with scientific methods of situation analysis	Cases with scientific methods of evaluation (p < 0,01)
Correspondence	157	55	63
No correspondence	237	69	66

- marketing surveys carried out for marketing purposes but still useful as a basis for public relations work;
- available survey findings, which, as data collections, are accessible for public relations work (we even went so far as to accept collections of data of uncertain origin as a scientific foundation);
- other scientific methods such as interviews with experts and experiments.

In contrast, far more than half of the applications conducting a situation analysis (287 cases or 58%) preferred unsystematic discussions with colleagues and clients or superiors and employees, documentations of press clippings, radio and television recordings and an unsystematic study of literature, which we regarded as unscientific. In due proportion, unscientific methods of evaluation like the following were widely employed by 53% (259 cases) of the applicants who were considering an evaluation:

- "media analysis" (ranging from the simple collection of articles to the counting of the clippings along with a statement on the estimated range and circulation);
- searching for "definite" results: sales figures, higher hotel-bed occupancy and a greater use of services are all examples of the indications belonging to this type of evaluation;
- praise and approval (extending from "positive feedback from top management" and "our agency got a follow-up contract" to "a lot of calls confirmed that we had done good work" and "enthusiastic onlookers lined the streets").

3. Reflection

The considerable discrepancies between what is said and what is done in public relations (i.e., between the way public relations characterizes itself and the way it actually fulfils its tasks and functions) had already made us a bit apprehensive in the past. In our search for convincing explanations we realized that the core of the problem might be the fact that to a large degree there was no reflection on how "successful" public relations can be defined (Baerns, 1995a:

9–29). Furthermore, the recent debate on the issue of evaluation, which has aroused great interest in public relations practice, concentrates on methods and procedures rather than standards. There is one exception to this. For most practitioners there is no doubt that success means managing to plant information on news desks—or to prevent it from getting there. This has been corroborated by every survey carried out among public relations professionals in Germany since 1973. Press and media work are considered to be the most important tasks of public relations practitioners with regard to the amount of time taken and/or the estimated value of the activity (Baerns, Klewes, & Tapper, 2000; Böckelmann, 1988, 1991a, 1991b; Deutsches Institut für Public Relations, 1973; Deutsche Public Relations-Gesellschaft e.V., 1990; Gumppenberg, 1991; Haedrich *et al.*, 1982; Haedrich, Jenner, Olavarria, & Possekel, 1994; Holscher & Jetter, 1980; Lüdke, 1988; Merten, 1997; Michels, 1986; Pracht, 1990; PR Executive Search, 1994; Riefler, 1988; Röttger, 2000; Strothmann, 1982, 1983; wbpr and LUMIS, 1997; Wienand, 2003; Wilke & Müller, 1979; etc.).

Whether the information given actually reaches its audiences—and if so, under which circumstances—is quite a different matter. Employees of media-analysis bureaus as well as press and information officers have probably been the most avid viewers, listeners, and readers. Communication processes with publics are thus not necessarily promoted! For example, in the late 1990s, the German communication scholar Margot Berghaus took pains to elucidate, on the basis of the present state of research, how little we can rely on the mass media in the shaping of communication processes. Interpersonal communication beyond the media is much more highly valued (see Figure 8.2). Quite a few research projects

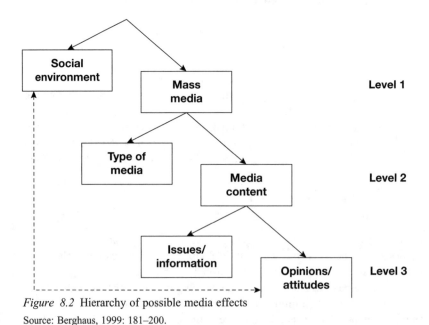

Figure 8.2 Hierarchy of possible media effects

Source: Berghaus, 1999: 181–200.

are now following this assumption. As a consequence, the search for standards of success for public relations not only has to unfold and factor in the state of knowledge of mass communication (even the term is misleading) but also the state of knowledge of interpersonal communication. From the point of view of media and communication sciences, reasonable strategies should orientate their planning—initially independent of organizations' aims as well as creative ideas and preferences—to communication objectives that are based on realistic expectations of success. In other words, communication managers are expected not only to provide and interrelate particular goals, particular media, and certain publics, but also beyond this, to systematically link particular objectives with specific knowledge about possible consequences and particular effects. This will also allow reasonable evaluation criteria or standards for what has actually been achieved.

Since effects were claimed to have been achieved by 365 or 74% of the projects submitted for the Golden Bridge prize, it appears justifiable to examine which models of effect—explicitly or implicitly, intended or unintended—were relevant. In a lot fewer than half of all strategies (198 cases or 40%) plausible models of effect could be assumed; in a third of all projects (167 cases or 34%) this was not the case, and in 128 cases (26%) there was no model of effect at all (see Table 8.5). As plausible models of effect we found and defined, for instance, the agenda-setting hypothesis (112 cases), the uses-and-gratifications approach (twenty cases), models of mutual understanding (fourteen cases), opinion leadership (twelve cases), and models of establishing relations (forty cases). An outdated stimulus–response model (forty-eight cases), several mutually exclusive models (twenty-five cases), and many approaches which we called "fantasy" models were regarded as unreasonable, imaginary, models of effect.

Again, an examination of the statistical significance is revealing: 82 out of 198 cases which were judged to be based on a plausible model of effect versus 48 out of 167 cases which were judged to be based on an unreasonable model, applied scientific procedures in drawing up their situation analyses; 116 out of 198 cases versus 119 out of 167 cases did not; 95 out of 198 cases versus 59 out of 167 cases with a plausible model of effect applied scientific methods

Table 8.5 Attributable models of effect (re-evaluation Goldene Brücke, 1970–2001)

Model	All cases	Cases with scientific methods of situation analysis ($p < 0.01$)	Cases with scientific methods of evaluation ($p < 0.01$)
Plausible models	198	82	95
Unreasonable models	167	48	59
No models of effect	128	32	28

of evaluation; 103 out of 198 cases versus 108 out of 167 cases did not. We thus discovered significant correlations.

4. Developments

Since 1970, the number of submissions for the Golden Bridge award has continually increased. The material accompanying the applications has become increasingly extravagant; further, throughout the years it has included many original design and other ideas. The instruments and media that were used in the public relations projects directly followed developments in information and communication technology. However, the increasingly elaborate media equipment does not necessarily provide a sufficient precondition for successful communication management in terms of problem solving and efficacy.

We have formulated two indices of quality which reflect, on the one hand, the problem-solving potential by means of procedures and, on the other hand, the potential for reflection with the assistance of scientific methods and models. In conjunction with the year of application, they provided clarity about qualitative progress over time. The first index consisted of adding up all characteristics indicating the existence of a strategy: situation analysis, setting objectives, defining publics, developing a central idea, selecting media, calculating time and costs, describing the implementation of the project, and describing the evaluation. These variables were counted according to their presence in the application submitted: explicit presence was assigned a value of 2, implicit presence a value of 1, and all other codings were assigned a value of 0. The sum of these values provided information about the characteristics of the relevant variables. The highest score that a case could achieve in this way was 18, meaning that all aspects were named explicitly. Twelve of the cases submitted achieved this value. At the other end of the scale, one application received a score of 0, with none of the criteria even implicitly fulfilled. A correlation calculation showed that a slightly positive correlation ($r = 0.37$)[10] existed between the quality of the applications (measured in terms of the strategic procedures) and the year in which the application was submitted. The second index in relation to the year of application was set up with reference to the application of scientific methods in situation analysis and evaluation, and the orientation to a sound model of effect. Again, explicit presence was assigned a value of 2, implicit presence a value of 1, and absence a value of 0. Accordingly, the highest possible score was 6. Altogether, fifty-two cases achieved this value. Seventy-two cases received a score of 0. The statistical analysis revealed that there was only a weak correlation ($r = 0.13$) between the quality of the submitted projects thus determined and the year of the submission.

Finally, it seems instructive to question and test the data once more for differences in the agencies' quality development in comparison to that of in-house public relations. In the case of the agencies the result is a significant and visibly greater positive correlation ($r = 0.43$) between the year and Index 1, and there is a rather low, but statistically unreliable correlation (r = 0.11) between the year and Index 2. This is probably largely due to the small number of cases and, at the same time, the sometimes great variability in the earlier years. Only from 1988 onward and, more distinctly, from 1993 can one observe a stabilization (see Figure 8.3). Thus, differences between PR agencies and organizations which it was worth singling out did not appear by this means.

Overall, it should be taken into consideration that information on the planning steps of public relations decision-making and strategy was explicitly provided as application criteria from 1994 onward. This means that it cannot be ruled out that applicants learned to adapt their applications to the jury's evident standards of examination. Speaking for this hypothesis is the stark contradiction between Indices 1 and 2. Whereas in the case of the first one a development or stabilization can be observed at a higher level, this is missing in the case of the second. Since, however, the strategic model is entirely dependent for its success or failure on the scientific methods used within its framework as well as on a planning based on well-founded expectations of its effects (i.e., the elements of Index 2), the findings must be qualified accordingly. Whereas the elements of the strategy model are relatively easily identified as the requirements for a successful application, this is not so evident with the elements of Index 2. Further, whereas a layperson in matters of communication and/or social sciences can work out the steps of the strategy model with relatively little effort, this requires the appropriate qualified specialist knowledge in the case of the elements of Index 2. And while it might be possible to mould,

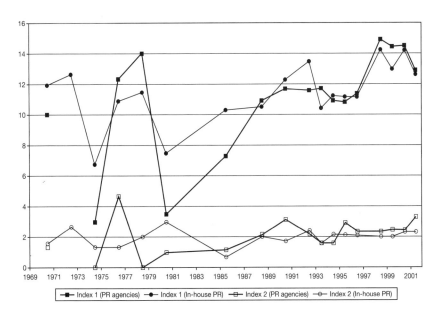

Figure 8.3 Development of indices (arithmetical means) per year of study

with moderate effort, an already completed campaign or action *ex post* on paper into the form required by the application with the steps of the strategy model, this is not so easily done *ex post* with the elements of Index 2.

Thus, on the basis of the data presented, one can contest whether there has been any notable improvement—in the sense defined here—in the conception and evaluation of public relations. There has always been a certain standard of quality in individual cases, but certainly not much more than this. When public relations is what public relations does, then it has performed in a quite stable and invariable manner throughout the decades.

Notes

1   In 2002 the Golden Bridge prize merged with The German PR Award (*Der Deutsche PR-Preis*), established by the F.A.Z. Institute of Management, Market and Media Information (*F.A.Z.-Institut für Management- Markt- und Medieninformationen GmbH*) in cooperation with the DPRG. The first announcement on the Golden Bridge was made in 1970: "Its purpose is to provide recognition for solutions to a task and a problem that can be regarded as outstanding and exemplary with regard to conceptualization, preparation, and execution, and also in view of the means and the costs involved. It may concern projects for a single task, campaigns for a certain purpose or for a certain period of time, or long- or short-term problems" (DPRG, 1970). Initially restricted to the members of the professional association, the competition was opened to all interested parties in 1978. From 1970 until 1980 the Golden Bridge prize was awarded every two years; later on, it was awarded at irregular intervals (in 1985, 1988, 1990, 1992 and 1993). In 1994 the text, until then only slightly altered, was thoroughly revised: "The purpose of the competition is to recognize and make known excellent PR campaigns and programmes of companies, organizations, institutions and public bodies as well as their consultants and agencies and to promote outstanding public relations . . . They are required to submit a summary . . . which features the following five points: initial situation, research, planning, implementation, and evaluation" (DPRG, 1994). There was no award in 1997. An independent panel of adjudicators, appointed by the DPRG and made up of experts from various professional areas, appraised the applications on the basis of a point system. The author acted as a member of the juries of the Golden Bridge prize and The German PR Award between 1984 and 2003.
2   Christoph Tapper, M.A., Dr. Juliana Raupp, Yvonne van Duehren, M.A., Victoria Olausson, M.A., Antje Rödel, M.A., Sandra Schwarzer, M.A., and Alexandra Stolle, M.A. participated in and contributed to the project.
3   From 1999 to 2001, the DPRG announced the Golden Column (*Goldener Pfeiler*) "for outstandingly realized tactical instruments and individual implementations in the area of public relations." The corresponding entries were not included in the study.
4   The chronological documentation of the subjects and authors of the campaigns and projects from 1970 to 2001 can be retrieved as a pdf file; please contact bbaerns@ zedat.fu-berlin.de.
5   "As critics of certification quite rightly observe, a reasonable service is by no means to be equated with a high-quality service. Thus, in general, the improvement of professional competence is a further factor which deserves attention. This includes the constant improvement of training as well as of ethics in the profession. This can be achieved only if the information exchange between theoreticians and

practitioners is intensified and work on joint projects is to become something quite normal in future. Public relations trainers must have practical experience and practitioners must avail themselves of theoretical experience if the quality process is to be driven forward" (Berth, 1996: 30).

6   The strategy model of public relations regards as substantial phases of decision-making the investigation of the initial position or the situation analysis; the conception (goal-setting, identification of publics, development of the guiding ideas, choice of media, time and cost plan); the realization; and the test of success or evaluation. Documentation and reappraisal of the experience and the evaluation within the work process should produce a cycle of constant improvement, as assumed.

7   The categories sought in the analyzed texts were designated by words ("explicitly named"), could be unequivocally read into the text ("implicitly named"), or were not to be found ("not named"). When none of these three designations could be unequivocally identified, the text was coded as "undeterminable," "not decisive". These decisions are illustrated in my presentation.

8   The objective "dialogue" appears throughout the entire research period although in the literature it has been expressly described as a recent acquisition (cf. Bentele, Steinmann, & Zerfaß, 1996: 11).

9   Fifty-five out of 157 applications whose communication scenario corresponded with the objective (compared with 69 out of 237 applications without this correspondence) applied scientific methods in the situation analysis. Sixty-three out of 157 applications whose communication scenario corresponded with the objective (compared with 66 out of 237 applications without this correspondence) used scientific methods to test the success or in the evaluation.

10 Pearson's correlation coefficient r, ranging from -1 to $+1$, provides us with a measure of association which produces information about the strength as well as the direction of the presumed relationship.

References

Baerns, Barbara (Ed.) (1995a). *PR-Erfolgskontrolle. Messen und Bewerten in der Öffentlichkeitsarbeit. Verfahren, Strategien, Beispiele (Assessing PR performance. On measuring and evaluating public relations. Procedures, strategies, cases).* Frankfurt am Main: IMK Institut für Medienentwicklung und Kommunikation GmbH in der Verlagsgruppe Frankfurter Allgemeine Zeitung GmbH.

Baerns, Barbara (1995b). Kommunikationsprozesse durchschauen und gestalten—Ein gemeinsames Projekt der Kommunikationswissenschaft und der Öffentlichkeitsarbeit (Understanding and shaping communication processes—A joint project of communication studies and public relations). *Public Relations Forum für Wissenschaft und Praxis (Nürnberg), 1*(1), 5–7.

Baerns, Barbara, & Raupp, Juliana (2002). Modelling and evaluating public relations campaigns. In Hans-Dieter Klingemann & Andrea Römmele (Eds.), *Public information campaigns and opinion research: A handbook for the student and practitioner* (pp. 21–35). London: Sage (State of Analysis: 1994).

Baerns, Barbara, Klewes, Joachim, & Tapper, Christoph (2000). *Was kann Kommunikationsmanagement heißen, was leisten? Berufsverständnis und Entscheidungsspielräume der Leiter (What can communications management mean, what can it achieve? Professional self-perception and scope for decision-making among senior managers).* FU Berlin, unpublished manuscript.

166   *Barbara Baerns*

Baerns, Barbara, & Klewes, Joachim (1996). Qualitätssicherung in der Öffentlichkeitsarbeit (Ensuring quality in public relations). In Barbara Baerns & Joachim Klewes (Eds.), *Public Relations 1996. Kampagnen, Trends und Tips (Public relations 1996. Campaigns, trends, and tips)* (pp. 9–19). Düsseldorf: Econ.

Bentele, Günter, Steinmann, Horst, & Zerfaß, Ansgar (Eds.) (1996). *Dialogorientierte Unternehmenskommunikation. Grundlagen—Praxiserfahrungen—Perspektiven. (Dialogue-oriented business communication. Fundamentals—Practical experience—Perspectives)*. Berlin: Vistas.

Berghaus, Margot (1999). Wie Massenmedien wirken. Ein Modell zur Systematisierung (On mass media effects. A model for systematization). *Rundfunk und Fernsehen, 47*(2), 181–199.

Berth, Kirsten (1996). Qualitätssteuerung ebnet den Weg zur Profession. Internationale Erwartungen, Erfahrungen und Ergebnisse (How quality control paves the way to professionalisation. International expectations, experiences and results). In: Barbara Baerns & Joachim Klewes (Eds.), *Public Relations 1996. Kampagnen, Trends und Tips (Public relations 1996. Campaigns, trends, and tips)* (pp. 22–32). Düsseldorf: Econ.

Berth, Kirsten, & Sjöberg, Göran (1997). *Quality in public relations*, Quality Public Relations Series 1, edited by The International Institute for Quality and Public Relations. Copenhagen: IQPR.

Böckelmann, Frank E. (1988). *Pressestellen in der Wirtschaft (Press offices in business and industry)*. Berlin: Wissenschaftsverlag Volker Spiess (Schriftenreihe der Arbeitsgruppe Kommunikation 28).

Böckelmann, Frank E. (1991a). *Die Pressestellen der Öffentlichen Hand (Press offices in the public sector)*. München: Ölschläger (AKM-Studien 35).

Böckelmann, Frank E. (1991b). *Die Pressearbeit der Organisationen (Press activities by organizations)*. München: Ölschläger (AKM-Studien 34).

Bundeszentrale für gesundheitliche Aufklärung (BZgA) (1999). *Evaluation—Ein Instrument zur Qualitätssicherung in der Gesundheitsförderung. Eine Expertise von Gerhard Christiansen, Bundeszentrale für gesundheitliche Aufklärung, im Auftrag der Europäischen Kommission, GD Gesundheit und Verbraucherschutz (Evaluation—An instrument for ensuring quality in public health promotion. An expert opinion by Gerhard Christiansen from the Federal Office of Public Health Promotion, commissioned by the European Commission, Division of Health and Consumer Protection)*. Köln: BZgA (Forschung und Praxis der Gesundheitsförderung 8).

Deutsche Public Relations-Gesellschaft, DPRG (1970). *Auszeichnung—Ansporn—Vorbild. Die Goldene Brücke 70 (Rewarding achievement—Giving incentive—Providing a model. The 1970 "Golden Bridge" award)*. Köln: DPRG.

Deutsche Public Relations-Gesellschaft e.V. (1990). *DPRG-Mitgliederumfrage 1989: Auswertung (DPRG membership survey 1989: Analysis)*. DPRG Bonn, unpublished manuscript.

Deutsche Public Relations-Gesellschaft e.V., DPRG Berufsverband Öffentlichkeitsarbeit and Gesellschaft Public Relations-Agenturen e.V. GPRA Verband führender PR-Agenturen Deutschlands (1990). *Das Berufsbild Öffentlichkeitsarbeit/Public Relations (Public relations—The profile)*. Bonn: DPRG.

Deutsche Public Relations-Gesellschaft e.V., DPRG Berufsverband Öffentlichkeitsarbeit (1994). *Der DPRG-Wettbewerb für ausgezeichnete Public Relations. Goldene Brücke 1994. Auslobung. Durchführungsrichtlinien (The DPRG competition for excellence in public relations. The 1994 "Golden Bridge" award. Announcement. Procedural guidelines)*. Bonn: DPRG.

Deutsche Public Relations-Gesellschaft e.V., DPRG Berufsverband Öffentlichkeitsarbeit (1996). *Das Berufsbild Öffentlichkeitsarbeit—Public Relations* (*Public relations— The profile*). Bonn: DPRG.

Deutsche Public Relations-Gesellschaft (2005). *Öffentlichkeitsarbeit/PR-Arbeit. Berufs- feld—Qualifikationsprofil—Zugangswege* (*Public relations. Occupational field— Qualification profile—Entrance*). Bonn: DPRG.

Deutsches Institut für Public Relations (DIPR) (1973). *Primärerhebung. Berufsbild Public Relations in der BRD* (*Primary data collection. The profile of public relations in the Federal Republic of Germany*). Köln: DIPR unpublished manuscript.

Duehren, Yvonne von (2001). *Qualitätsmerkmale praktischer Öffentlichkeitsarbeit. Ein Soll-Ist-Vergleich* (*Quality traits of practical public relations. Examining objectives and evaluation*). FU Berlin, unpublished Master's dissertation.

Grunig, James E., & Hunt, Todd (1984). *Managing public relations*. New York: Holt Rinehart & Winston.

Grunig, James E., Grunig, Larissa A., & Dozier, David M. (1996). Das situative Modell exzellenter Public Relations. Schlussfolgerungen aus einer internationalen Studie (The situational model of excellent public relations. Conclusions from an international study). In Günter Bentele, Horst Steinmann, & Ansgar Zerfaß (Eds.), *Dialogorienti- erte Unternehmenskommunikation. Grundlagen—Praxiserfahrungen—Perspektiven* (*Dialogue-oriented business communication. Fundamentals—Practical experience— Perspectives*) (pp. 199–228). Berlin: Vistas.

Gumppenberg, Dietrich V. (1991). Stellenwert und Instrumente der PR in unterschied- lichen Branchen (PR's status and tools in various branches). *prmagazin, 22*(4), 35–46.

Haedrich, Günther, Kreilkamp, Edgar, Kuß, Alfred, & Stiefel, Richard (1982). *Das Berufsfeld Öffentlichkeitsarbeit in der Wirtschaft. Organisatorische Einordnung, Mitarbeitersituation, PR-Ziele und -Tätigkeiten, Ausbildungsbedürfnisse. Ergebnisse einer schriftlichen Befragung* (*The job profile of public relations in business and industry. Hierarchies, staff situation, PR goals and activities, training needs. Results of a questionnaire survey*). Düsseldorf: Verlag für deutsche Wirtschaftsbiographien Heinz Flieger (Studien zu Theorie und Praxis der Public Relations 8).

Haedrich, Günther, Jenner, Thomas, Olavarria, Marco, & Possekel, Stephan (1994). *Aktueller Stand und Entwicklungen der Öffentlichkeitsarbeit in deutschen Unter- nehmen. Ergebnisse einer empirischen Untersuchung* (*State of the art and develop- ment of public relations in German companies. Findings of an empirical study*). Berlin: Institut für Marketing im Fachbereich Wirtschaftswissenschaft der Freien Universität Berlin (Arbeitspapier No. 29/94), unpublished manuscript.

Holscher, Claus, & Jetter, Ulrich (1980). *Public Affairs—PR fürs Gemeinwohl* (*Public affairs—PR for the common good*). Hamburg: SPIEGEL-Verlag Rudolf Augstein (Spiegel-Verlagsreihe 5).

Institut für industrielle Markt- und Werbeforschung (Strothmann) Hamburg (1982). *"Public Relations" im Urteil von Führungskräften. Spezial-Untersuchung im Auftrag des BDW Deutscher Kommunikationsverband* (*"Public relations" in the judgement of senior managers. Special study commissioned by the German Association of Advertisers, German Communication Federation*). Bonn: BDW Deutscher Kom- munikationsverband, unpublished manuscript.

Institut für industrielle Markt- und Werbeforschung (Strothmann) Hamburg (1983). *"Public Relations" im Urteil von Verbands-Geschäftsführern. Spezial-Untersuchung im Auftrag des BDW Deutscher Kommunikationsverband* (*"Public relations" in the judgement of Federation managers. Special study commissioned by the German Association of Advertisers, German Communication Federation).* Bonn: BDW Deutscher Kommunikationsverband, unpublished manuscript.

IPRA (1994). *Quality customer satisfaction public relations. New directions for organisational communication.* Geneva: International Public Relations Association (Gold Paper 10, April).

Lüdke, Jürgen (1988). *Diskussion, Verbreitung und Einsatz neuer Medientechniken— Eine Untersuchung zur "externen Kommunikation" von Großunternehmen der Investitionsgüterindustrie (The discussion, diffusion and deployment of new media technologies—A study of "external communications" in large companies of the capital goods sector).* Ruhr University Bochum unpublished Master's dissertation.

Merten, Klaus (1997). PR als Beruf. Anforderungsprofile und Trends für die PR-Ausbildung (Public relations as a profession. Requirements of profiles and trends for PR training). *prmagazin, 28*(1), 43–50.

Michels, Sabine (1986). Pressemitteilung oder Anzeige? Forschungsstand und Fallstudie zur Funktion verschiedener Instrumente in der Öffentlichkeitsarbeit (*Press release or advertisement? State of the research and a case study on the function of different PR tools*). Ruhr University Bochum, unpublished Master's dissertation.

PR Executive Search GmbH (1994). Umfrage zum Thema "Öffentlichkeitsarbeit" bei den 500 größten Unternehmen in Deutschland (Survey on the subject of "public relations" among the 500 largest companies in Germany). *prmagazin, 25*(9), 20–35.

Pracht, Petra (1990). *Zur Systematik und Fundierung praktischer Öffentlichkeitsarbeit. Versuch eines Soll-Ist-Vergleichs (On the systematics and fundamentals of practical public relations. An attempt at examining objectives and evaluation).* Ruhr University Bochum, unpublished Master's dissertation.

Riefler, Stefan (1988). Public Relations als Dienstleistung. Eine empirische Studie über Berufszugang, Berufsbild und berufliches Selbstverständnis von PR-Beratern in der Bundesrepublik Deutschland (Public relations as a service. An empirical study of entrance, job profile and professional self-awareness of PR consultants in the Federal Republic of Germany). *prmagazin, 19*(5), 33–44.

Röttger, Ulrike (2000). *Public Relations—Organisation und Profession. Öffentlichkeitsarbeit als Organisationsfunktion. Eine Berufsfeldstudie (Public relations— Organization and profession. Public Relations as an organizational function. A study of the occupational field).* Wiesbaden: Westdeutscher Verlag.

Rühl, Manfred (1992). Public Relations ist, was Public Relations tut. Fünf Schwierigkeiten, eine allgemeine PR-Theorie zu entwerfen (Public relations is what public relations does. Five difficulties in drawing up a PR theory). *prmagazin, 23*(8), 35–46.

Schwarzer, Sandra (2002). *Qualität in der Öffentlichkeitsarbeit—PR-Praxis auf dem Prüfstand. Inhaltsanalyse der Bewerbungen um den Preis "Goldene Brücke" 1998 und 2000 (Quality in public relations—PR practice put to the test. Content analysis of the cases submitted for the 1998 and 2000 "Golden Bridge" awards).* FU Berlin, unpublished Master's dissertation.

Stolle, Alexandra (2001). *Zum Problemlösungs- und Reflexionspotential der Öffentlichkeitsarbeit. Re-evaluation der Bewerbungen "Goldene Brücke" 1997 und 1999 (On the potential for problem solving and reflection in public relations. A re-evaluation of the cases submitted for the 1997 and 1999 "Golden Bridge" awards).* FU Berlin, unpublished Master's dissertation.

wbpr and LUMIS (1997). *Zweite Untersuchung zur unternehmensspezifischen Bedeutung von Public Relations. Eine Untersuchung der wbpr Gesellschaft für*

Public Relations und Marketing GmbH in Zusammenarbeit mit dem LUMIS-Institut der Universität-GH Siegen und dem Wirtschaftsmagazin Capital (*Second study on the company-specific significance of public relations. A study of the wbpr Association for Public Relations and Marketing GmbH in collaboration with the LUMIS-institution of the University GH Siegen and the business magazine "Capital"*). München, Potsdam, unpublished manuscript.

Wienand, Edith (2003). *Public Relations als Beruf. Kritische Analyse eines aufstrebenden Kommunikationsberufes* (*Public relations as a profession. A critical analysis of an aspiring communication profession*). Wiesbaden: Westdeutscher Verlag.

Wilke, Jürgen, & Müller, Ulrich (1979). Im Auftrag. PR-Journalisten zwischen Autonomie und Interessenvertretung (Under orders. PR journalists between autonomy and interest serving). In Hans-Mathias Kepplinger (Ed.), *Angepaßte Außenseiter. Was Journalisten denken und wie sie arbeiten* (*Conforming outsiders. What journalists think and how they work*) (pp. 115–141). Freiburg, München: Verlag Karl Alber (Alber Broschur Kommunikation 8).

Xavier, Robina, Patel, Amisha, & Johnston, Kim (2005). *Examining objectives and evaluation: How practitioners measure their success.* Paper presented to the 12th International Public Relations Research Symposium, Public Relations Metrics: Evaluation and Measurement, Lake Bled, Slovenia, July 1–3, 2005.

9 The Evaluation of Government Campaigns in the Netherlands

Wim van der Noort

1. Introduction

This chapter deals with government mass-media campaigns in the Netherlands, especially with the way they are managed and how their effectiveness is evaluated. For more than five years now the results of all government campaigns have been surveyed in a continuous tracking study. The resulting database of over 120 cases has proven to be very valuable for assessing the factors that contribute to successes and failures. Based on advanced multi-variate analyses of these data, a software tool has been developed, known as the Multimedia Tool. This unique tool provides campaign managers with guidelines on the budget they need for achieving their campaign objectives, the communication effects that they can expect from the campaign, and how best to allocate budgets to the various media types.

The systematic effect research has contributed to more effective and more cost-efficient government communication. For still further improvement, new standards for pre-testing are now being developed that can predict the performance of campaigns in an early stage when changes can still be made. An important new development in the coming years is the monitoring of free publicity. The inclusion of these data in the predictive modeling of campaign effectiveness could be a major step forward.

Every person and organization, including the government, wants to communicate effectively. This is particularly true of the central government, which has the task of informing its citizens and stimulating socially responsible behavior. Government communication must therefore be as effective and efficient as possible. Government spending on communication and media has increased over the years and now, in terms of media spending, it belongs to the top five advertisers in the Netherlands. All campaigns are paid from public funds. The expenditure must therefore be accounted for, and so the Prime Minister reports to the Lower House each year on how the communication budgets have been spent and how effective they have been. This obligation of accountability is the main reason why effect research is carried out. In this chapter, the role that evaluation plays in actually making government campaigns more effective and efficient is clarified. We will deal with the following aspects:

- the objective, structure, and content of media-effect research on government campaigns;
- the insights and lessons learned from such research, both for individual campaigns and for government campaigns in general;
- how the lessons learned are applied in the everyday practice of developing and conducting campaigns;
- the future plans for further improving the government communication.

2. The Development of Governmental Campaigning

2.1. Some Backgrounds on Dutch Government Communication

The importance of communication as an integral part of policymaking has been developing steadily over the past fifty years in the Netherlands. The staffing and financial resources of government communication services saw strong growth and, in line with these developments, the professionalism in the communication disciplines increased.

Shortly after World War II, "P.O. Box 51" was introduced as the central address where citizens could send their letters to if they had questions or needed information from the government. Most of the Dutch government's mass-media campaigns are run under the "P.O. Box 51" banner. Nowadays, it still is the name of the institute known to the public as the center of government information. A call center and (of course) the Internet are now the main means of communication with the public. P.O. Box 51 is also well known and appreciated by the public as the sender of information in mass-media campaigns. Every year about twenty-five campaigns are conducted by different ministries, using the common infrastructure of media buying and handling.

These campaigns have to meet certain criteria, the so-called *principles for government communication*. Public opinion, press and the Parliament are highly sensitive for elements of propaganda in communication activities of government. For instance, the subject should be non-controversial (i.e., part of an accepted policy) and priority is given to the government policy's main themes, such as national health, road safety, and the reduction of crime and violence. The Public Information and Communication Office of the Ministry of General Affairs plays a coordinating role and is also responsible for the media planning and buying, and since 1999 also for the evaluation of the effectiveness of campaigns.

2.2. The History of Effect Research for Government Campaigns

Government campaigns have been subject to systematic evaluation since the critical report, issued in 1991 by the Chamber of Audit [*Algemene Rekenkamer*], which concluded that there had been serious failures in accounting for the effectiveness of such campaigns. In 1993, the report led to guidelines being established for research on campaign effects, which became known as the "Silver Standard" [*Zilveren Standaard*]. In 1994, the Information Council decided to prescribe these guidelines for all campaign research.

The methodological design was ingenious in distinguishing properly between real communication effects and other influences that could account for changes measured. The Silver Standard still enjoys a certain fame among communication researchers today. In practice, however, the guidelines proved unworkable and, in fact, they were seldom or never applied (in full). There were various reasons for this, including the high cost of research and the lack of professional expertise to apply the guidelines satisfactorily. Other objections concerned the disproportionate emphasis on isolating communication effects, and the charge that the research offered inadequate explanations for the effectiveness of certain media and material. Concluding that a campaign has resulted in little or no effect is hardly satisfying if research also fails to explain the causes and the possibilities for improvement. The most important conclusion, however, was that the process in which the research was rooted had failed. As a result of the individual and *ad hoc* nature in which research was conducted, standardization and benchmarks for efficiency and effectiveness were lacking, so that it was impossible to draw lessons of a more general nature from the results.

The tracking tool used today investigates the effects of government campaigns more effectively and efficiently than in the past. The key aims of such investigations are:

1. to account for the effectiveness of public campaigns as policy instruments (*accountability*);
2. to contribute to improving and professionalizing government communication (*learning effects*).

Joint evaluation research has resulted in substantial cost savings, but, more importantly, the resulting systematic build-up of knowledge now provides a significant impetus for improving the quality and cost-efficiency of government campaigns.

2.3. The Research Design

We will briefly outline the tracking research structure used by market research agency TNS NIPO to evaluate government mass media campaigns since 1999. Until 2003, the research involved face-to-face interviews supported by CAPI (Computer Assisted Personal Interviewing). In early 2003, a hybrid method was introduced: the TNS NIPO Internet access panel, which is now used for 75% of the interviews, supplemented by face-to-face interviews with the 25% of the population who do not have a computer at home.

The research measures the reach, impact, message transfer, likeability and effectiveness of campaigns. It is divided into three phases for each campaign:

- pre-measurement (four weeks prior to the campaign; n = 400);
- intermediary measurement (six weeks of the campaign itself; n = 600);
- post-measurement (four weeks following the campaign; n = 400).

Each week, a representative sample of one hundred persons (aged 18 and older) is interviewed. The questionnaires cover multiple campaigns. In case the questionnaires of the campaigns involved in the survey exceed fifty minutes interviewing time, a parallel sample of one hundred persons is used. If the campaign is also aimed at youngsters, the interviews include an additional sample of young people aged between 13 and 17.

The pre- and post-measurements regard the objectives of the campaign with questions about knowledge, attitudes, and behavior on which the campaign focuses. The questionnaire used in these phases is largely specific to the particular campaign and differs from one campaign to the next.

The intermediary measurement looks at recognition of the ads, campaign recall, message transfer, and likeability. All the ads and the information provided during the campaign (TV and radio spots, advertisements, banners, etc.) are shown in full or played on the computer so that both reach and like-ability can be measured and differentiated per medium type. The questions used in this part of the investigation tend to be standard ones. As a result, an entire set of benchmarks is now available for measuring campaign performance.

3. Tracking Communication Effects

3.1. A Communication Model

The communication model shown in Figure 9.1 is used as a base for analyzing and understanding the communication effects. The aims of the campaigns are always stated in terms of specific objectives regarding (changes in) knowledge, attitudes, and/or behavior of the general public or a specific target group. The model shows that there are two important ways of managing campaigns in order to achieve and optimize the desired effects. The first is the campaign concept, that is, the creative interpretation and design of the communication objectives in the core campaign message and the campaign material. The second is the use of media, including both the media budget and the media mix. The greater part of the campaign budget is spent on these two items, and efficiency and effectiveness will therefore have to be improved, particularly in these two areas.

For a campaign to be effective, it must not only reach the target group, the information must also be noticed and processed properly—that is, generate sufficient impact, message transfer, and appreciation. These factors are best measured in a standardized and comparable way. Our research therefore involves measuring the following: recognition of the ads in order to determine the reach of the campaign per media type; spontaneous and aided recall as an indicator for impact and active perception of the campaign; spontaneous and

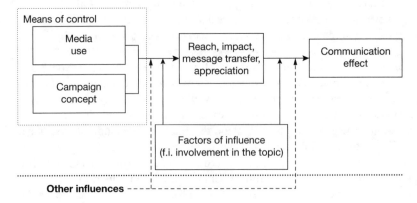

* Other policy
* Media attention
* Incidents

Figure 9.1 Communication model

aided message transfer; and likeability of the campaign, both generic (report mark) and on such dimensions as informative, clear, credible, striking, irritating, amusing, and appealing.

Finally, the model indicates that there are several factors related to the target group that influence the working of communication. For this reason, the research takes into account people's attitude toward and involvement with the campaign subject, as well as socio-demographic data. Finally—but importantly—external influences may play a role. One should think of other policy measures, media coverage on the campaign topics, and unexpected incidents that can have a great impact on the public perception of things. Note that the measurement of campaign effects is based on a pre-post design and that the influences speci-fied below the line are not measured. This means that changes in knowledge, attitudes, and behavior of the public during the campaign period cannot scientifically be interpreted as an effect (or the sole effect) of the campaign, since we do not control for these other influences. On the other hand, campaign managers are not primarily interested in science but in meeting their targets in the post measurement. Policy measures and (generating) publicity are all intrinsic part of their game. Naturally, these sorts of "external influences" are considered in a qualitative way when assessing the (lack of) effects of a campaign.

3.2. The Effects of Campaigns

The first question one might ask is, "Do government campaigns indeed have an effect on the knowledge, attitudes, and behavior of the public?" The answer is "Yes, for most of the campaigns we are able to demonstrate significant chances on primary objectives during the campaign period," but not always. On average, we see an increase of 10 percentage points in knowledge levels.

There are large differences, however, depending on the complexity of the communication task, the strength of the communication concept and the external influences that play a role. The transfer of information is nearly always one of the primary goals of government campaigns and the effects for this type of objectives are on average higher compared to attitudinal and behavioral changes.

The most successful campaigns are those that communicate rather simple and relevant messages. For instance, the loud testing of the national alarm system that warns the population in case of disasters in their neighborhood takes place once a month from 2003 onward, instead of once a year. In a short period of time, the campaign succeeded in conveying to nearly the whole population the exact time and day of the month when they should expect the test alarm. Another example is the campaign dealing with safety on the streets, which communicated successfully what to do when confronted with street violence.

The campaign accompanying new anti-smoking regulations (for a smoke-free working place) showed a big increase in basic knowledge about this new legislation. This was of course due to, among other things, the extensive coverage in the media and the public debate that these measures evoked—but then, it should be mentioned that managing this kind of "free publicity" is in fact an important and integral part of a campaign. Besides informing the public about the new rules, another objective of this campaign was to convince it that smoking damages the health of others who are present in the same room. In this respect, the campaign had no effect at all. This type of knowledge is more difficult to get accepted (especially among smokers) and it turned out that non-smokers were already convinced.

Apart from informing publics, most campaigns also try to change their attitudes. This proves far more difficult, at least in the period of one campaign. It will often require long-term communication efforts. A successful example was the introduction of the euro. An intensive one-year campaign created steadily growing support and acceptance of this new European currency.

Though changes in behavior are not often stated as direct communication goals, public information campaigns, especially in the field of road safety, together with policy measures and police control have demonstrable effects on good behavior and declining casualties. An example is the campaign to promote the use of child-restrainers on the back seats of cars. This has been a great success, not least thanks to the accompanying gadget called *Goochem* (Dutch for "smart"), the safety belt pet. With financial support from the EU, the campaign has now been adopted by ten other European countries.

3.3. Effect Predictors

The P.O. Box 51 campaign evaluations in 2002 and 2003 examined to what extent the factors specified in the communication model determine how effective campaigns are, based on causal analyses of the database of more than one hundred campaigns. Not all the analyses can be reported here, but a number of findings are worth mentioning.

Campaign Recall and Message Transfer

Campaign recall is a somewhat controversial effect indicator in the literature, but in government campaigns it appears to be a particularly important predictor for campaign effects. Campaign recall is measured weekly during the campaign and the highest level is reported. The results differ widely between campaigns (ranging from about 20% to 90%). These differences do really matter in sorting effect. The higher campaign recall, the stronger the effect ($r = 0.60$ for knowledge effects). The same goes for message transfer. Campaigns that are perceived by the public as having a clear message related to the objectives, have more effect ($r = 0.52$). Figure 9.2 shows the average campaign recall between 1999 and 2004. We see a strong rise from 38% on average in 1999 to 55% in 2004. This is a clear illustration of the improving communication strength of government campaigns in recent years.

Campaign Reach and Media Budget

As a basic preliminary for campaign recall and message transfer, the public has to be confronted (a couple of times) with the campaign. This is the task of media planning. As mentioned before, the reach of the campaign is measured in our survey with the recognition method. In 2004 the media budget on average was € 431,000. On average, 90% of the adult population recognized having seen one or more of the ads used in the campaign.

As shown in Figure 9.3, the average media budget for P.O. Box 51 campaigns declined in 2003 and 2004. Nevertheless, campaign reach has improved from about 80% to 90%.

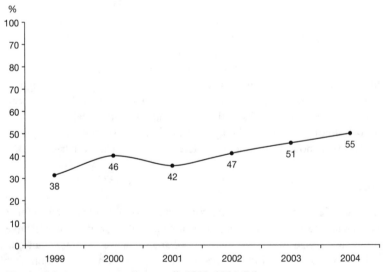

Figure 9.2 Average campaign recall, 1999–2004 (%)

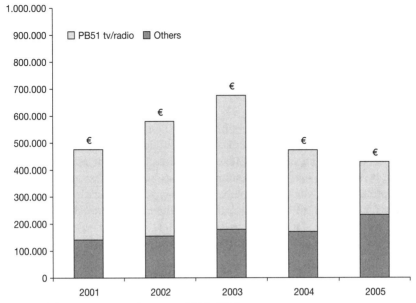

Figure 9.3 Average campaign costs, 2000–2004

Campaign Concept, the Role of Likeability

Different aspects of appreciation are measured related to form (amusing, striking), content (clear, informative, credible), tone of voice (irritating), and personal relevance (appealing). The overall mark is an indicator of the likeability of the campaign, which proves to be one of the most important predictors of campaign recall ($r = 0.52$) and message transfer ($r = 0.81$). So the higher the likeability, the more effect can be expected from a campaign.

On average, the campaigns are appreciated with a mark of 7.0 (both in 2004 and in 2003). Again, this is an improvement compared to former years, with an average score of 6.8. For getting high likeability and recall scores the campaign should above all be appreciated by the audience as clear and striking (attracting attention). The use of humor ("amusing") appears to be less decisive for successful government campaigns. Following the general trend in commercials, humor is increasingly used in government campaigns to get the attention of the public, but with varying results. As further research showed, the use of humor can easily interfere with getting a clear message through.

Interest In and Relevance of the Topic

Finally. an important factor influencing campaign effects is the way the target group relates to the campaign topic. Personal interest and perceived relevance ("it's good that the government is dealing with this matter") are crucial for a good campaign recall and message transfer (along with campaign appreciation and the level of campaign confrontation). Together, these factors can explain about 50% of the variance in campaign recall.

3.4. Practical Application of the Results

Although these research findings are interesting and informative, their value depends on whether they are actually used in daily practice and whether they are relevant to the issues that confront campaign managers in the throes of developing new campaigns. To make practical use of insights and learning experiences is an art in itself; after all, researchers and potential users often view the same topic from different angles. In our view, the government is an exception when it comes to actually conducting research, but here too, users often find research too expensive, time-consuming and difficult to apply to their own practice. Or could it be that they find it particularly threatening? Imagine that research reveals that a commercial that everyone liked at the ministry has had no effect whatsoever. By repositioning effect research and turning it from "a critical look back" to "a well-researched look ahead," we can remove part of this threat.

To enable campaign managers to use the research results to the best possible effect, we "package" the results in various products and services.

- The campaign manager receives written reports of the preliminary, intermediary, and subsequent measurements for each campaign. The results and recommendations from the final report are presented to the campaign managers and often to the relevant advertising and media agency.
- The main outcomes on reach and effects are reported online from the first campaign week to which the campaign manager has direct access. The graphs are supplemented each week by the most recent figures.
- Annual compilation and summary of all campaign evaluations, with general analyses based on the database and benchmark (*Evaluation of P.O. Box 51 Campaigns*).
- Availability of a multimedia prediction tool based on modelled data from the database.
- Learning experiences constitute input for discussions with communication consultants and for courses organized by the Academy for Government Communication.

Online reporting makes it possible to adjust the input during the course of the campaign. If, after two or three weeks of campaigning, campaign reach (recognition) proves to be inadequate, the campaign manager may be advised to increase media pressure on radio or television or to use daily newspapers, for example. In addition, campaign material that appears to have little impact may be exchanged for a version that has greater effect.

3.5. The Multimedia Tool

An actual "well-researched look ahead"—in the sense of making predictions prior to a possible campaign—requires an extra step. Research data and learning effects must be readily available outside the campaign context, and easily accessible for the right target group—communication consultants require benchmarks and a realistic method for quantifying the objectives of a specific campaign. These requirements led to the development of a multimedia prediction tool in 2002 in collaboration with Pointlogic. The tool was based on data drawn from more than one hundred campaigns in the database. The data were used to estimate models and response curves, with additional input by experts and based on lessons learned in workshops with communication and media strategists. The tool is updated regularly with new figures and new functionalities.

The multimedia tool provides the campaign manager with answers to questions such as:

- "What budget is required to achieve my objectives?"
- "What communication effects can I expect from this campaign?"
- "What is the best possible way of apportioning the budget between the various media types, and how do I divide the input over time?"

The campaign starting-points described in the communication plan constitute the input for the tool and include such aspects as the target group's familiarity with the subject, the budget and the campaign objectives (e.g., knowledge of a new law, encouraging a positive attitude or influencing behavior, energy awareness, traffic safety). The campaign manager enters the specific characteristics of the campaign via a simple data entry screen with slide bars. The government media consultant advises the manager during data entry and helps interpret the output.

The output is based on these campaign characteristics. It shows the ideal media type mix and forecasts the degree to which the formulated objectives will be achieved, according to the models. As a result, we progress from general benchmarks at database level to differentiated benchmarks for the campaign. The tool is now being used to help draw up campaign plans as well as to quantify objectives and substantiate budgets for each media type. Entering various scenarios makes the expected effect of budget changes or another media type mix immediately evident. Needless to say, the tool is nothing more than a handy aid ("a fool with a tool is still a fool"). The output provides a guiding principle; professional expertise and experience should be brought to bear when interpreting it. The manager can use the insights he has gained during his meetings with the advertising and media agency to arrive at a more strategic use of media and resources. Incidentally, showing the expected effects of a mass-media campaign also reveals what the campaign cannot achieve. Changing a negative attitude requires consistency and long-term thinking. A four-week TV campaign will not go very far. Such insights are helpful to communication consultants, particularly when discussing how to adjust overly ambitious objectives or to obtain larger budgets.

3.6. Future Developments

The systematic evaluation of government campaigns as described in this chapter is a good example of how central coordination and the interdepartmental sharing of insights and knowledge can lead to better results together with lower costs. Over the next five years, the Public Information and Communication Office, in co-operation with all departments, will continue on the path of sharing research and expertise to make further improvements possible. One way to achieve this is the organization and management of campaigns. In 2005, a pilot scheme was started for the build-up of a central unit with specialists in managing mass-media campaigns. In this way expertise, which is now rather fragmented and divided over different ministries, can better be bundled.

In the field of research, interesting developments take place as well. In addition to campaign effect research, a standard for concept testing and pre-testing has been introduced and will be further developed. Two agencies, both specialized in this kind of qualitative in-depth research, will be selected after a tender to do these tests for all ministries, coordinated by the Public Information and Communication Office.

Another form of pre-testing that has been adopted is a system of quantitative research based on dynamic eye tracking (Verify). This system registers whether people are willing to pay attention to the ads and whether relevant elements are actually seen by them. Expectations are that these forms of pre-testing, combined with the results of the effect research, will have good predictive value. An early diagnosis of strengths and weaknesses of the campaign makes adequate adaptations possible in the ads. In addition, it is possible to monitor *wear-out* to prevent media budgets being spent on adverts that are no longer working.

Further important new developments will be the systematic monitoring and content analysis of the media coverage of main policy issues (*media analysis*). A test was conducted in 2004 and is now continued, including the coverage in national and regional newspapers and some main broadcast news outlets. In this way, the amount of media attention can be measured and analyzed in terms of key messages, framing, positive and negative tenor, etc. The possible inclusion in the coming years of these kinds of data in the predictive modeling of campaign effectiveness could be a major step forward in assessing the value of free publicity in combination with mass media campaigns.

References

Bronner, A. E., & Reuling, A. (2002). Improving campaign effectiveness: A research model to separate chaff from campaign wheat. In G. Bartels & W. Nelissen (Eds.), *Marketing for sustainability* (pp. 150–159). Amsterdam: IOS Press.

Bronner, F., Noort, W. van der, Ross, R., & Tchaoussoglou, C. (2003). *The Netherlands live with water: Exciting, efficient, effect research.* Boston: Worldwide Readership Research Symposium (pp. 73–82).

Foley, T., & Kloprogge, P. (2003). *Data to decision: A channel planning solution for the public sector.* Esomar/ARF Worldwide Audience Measurement (WAM) Media Mix Conference.

Foley, T., & Kloprogge, P. (2004). How channel-planning tools can deliver ROI (and still allow innovation). *Admap*, March (issue 448).

Gerritsen, M., & Noort, W. van der (2005). De effectiviteit van overheidscampagnes; De resultaten van 5 jaar systematisch onderzoek (The effectiveness of government campaigns: Results of five years' systematic research). In MarktOnderzoekAssociatie, *Ontwikkelingen in het marktonderzoek (Developments in market research)* (pp. 49–66). Haarlem: De Vriesenborch, Jaarboek.

Montfort, P. van, & Kleuver, E. de (2001). Trackingonderzoek naar overheidscampagnes (Tracking research to government campaigns). In B. Dewez, P. van Montfoort, & E. Voogt (Eds.), *Overheidscommunicatie. De nieuwe wereld achter Postbus 51 (The new world behind P.O. Box 51)* (pp. 93–103). Amsterdam: Boom.

Rijksvoorlichtingsdienst (2005). Vijf jaar campagne-effectonderzoek (Five years of campaign evaluations). *RVD-communicatiereeks*, no. 3.

RVD/Publiek en Communicatie (2003). Jaarevaluatie Postbus 51 campagnes 2002 (Annual Report, P.O. Box 51 Campaigns 2002).

RVD/Publiek en Communicatie (2004). Jaarevaluatie Postbus 51 campagnes 2003 (Annual Report, P.O. Box 51 campaigns 2003).

Veenman, Jan, & Volmer, Fred (2002). Government communication in the Netherlands: Coordination and planning. In G. Bartels & W. Nelissen (Eds.), *Marketing for sustainability* (pp. 150–159). Amsterdam: IOS Press.

Veldkamp (1993). *Naar een zilveren standaard: Een aanzet tot richtlijnen voor effectonderzoek naar campagnes van de rijksoverheid (Toward a silver standard: An outline for guidelines for effect research on governmental campaigns)*. Amsterdam: Veldkamp.

10 The Role of Research in Shaping and Measuring Communication

London's Bid to Hold the 2012 Games

Claire Spencer and Julia Jahansoozi

1. Introduction

The public relations industry has long been searching for the "holy grail" in evaluation of communications. According to Lindemann (2005: 2) "there is no one, simplistic all-purpose tool that can be used to measure PR effectiveness." Instead, there is a range of evaluation tools and techniques that practitioners can employ in order to evaluate effectiveness. The Chartered Institute of Public Relations (CIPR) is in agreement and concluded in its recent policy paper on measurement and evaluation that while there is no "silver bullet" approach, public relations "can be measured and evaluated" (CIPR, 2005). The policy paper cites how public relations can be measured and evaluated on four levels (CIPR, 2005: 2):

- "in terms of its contribution . . . to organization performance (to business success or organizational, to better decision making . . .);
- as a process (of communication, relationship and reputation building) and as part of program development and implementation;
- as a practice with a contribution to make to social and economic development;
- in terms of the contribution and competencies of individual practitioners".

It is recognized that "what matters in measuring and evaluating public relations is the 'impact of public relations'" (Burson Marsteller, 1984, cited in CIPR, 2005: 5). Such evaluation "depends on good use of research for program development (formative research), for diagnostic purposes, to check that programs are being effective (diagnostic research), and for program evaluation (evaluative research)"(CIPR, 2005: 5). Public relations programs and campaigns are designed to achieve specific objectives, usually to change or reinforce a particular behavior. Good public relations campaigns are therefore designed to "cause observable impact" (Broom & Dozier, 1990: 73), which allows for effective measurement and evaluation.

Communication campaigns target individuals within defined publics in order to reinforce or change particular attitudes and linked behavioral outcomes. Measuring and evaluating outcomes involves looking at "whether target audience groups actually *received* the messages directed at them . . . paid *attention* to them . . . *understood the messages* . . . and *retained* those messages in any shape or form" (Hon & J. Grunig, 1999: 4). This understanding of outcomes mirrors Hovland's approach to message-learning theory (Hovland, cited in Bettinghaus & Cody, 1994: 63–64), which is discussed further on.

Measuring and evaluating outputs is the most basic level in assessing the success or failure of a campaign as opposed to measuring the success of a strategy. Outputs are a campaign's visible results, such as press releases, newsletters, and feature articles. Measuring and evaluating outcomes (such as attitude and behavioral change) provides a far more sophisticated look at whether the persuasive communication message was successful.

This chapter builds on the evidence of the "impact of public relations" (Burson Marsteller, 1984, cited in CIPR, 2005: 5), using a case-study approach where research has been applied in formative, diagnostic, and evaluative ways mentioned in the CIPR policy paper (2005). The case study also demonstrates how public relations can be measured and evaluated as a "contributor to organization performance," "process of communication, relationship and reputation building" and "practice with a contribution to make to the wider society" in accordance with the CIPR 2005 policy paper on measurement and evaluation.

The CIPR has identified the need for the industry to adopt a "measurement tool that can directly link communication outputs with changes in the attitudes and perceptions of target audiences" (Gregory, 2004). In this case study, public relations activity was measured and evaluated using a specific measurement tool—i to i tracker®—which provided the linkage between communication outputs and outcomes, namely changes in attitudes, perceptions and intended behavior. The i to i tracker® tool was developed by Claire Spencer, and launched by Publicis company, i to i research, to measure the impact and influence of public relations. It is recognized that most tools available to public relations practitioners tend to stop at measuring communication outputs, while what is needed is a tool that provides the linkage between outputs and outcomes. Moreover, this tool was developed in order to have an increased understanding and insight into the contribution of public relations in a holistic setting where other communication disciplines (such as advertising and promotions) were being used. The i to i tracker® tool is currently used by a number of corporations and government and non-government organizations globally to measure public relations and other marketing activities, such as advertising and promotions.

2. Introducing the Case: London's Bid to Host the 2012 Olympic Games

2.1. Making the Case for Britain

Since the creation of the Olympic Movement in 1894, Britain has been a strong protagonist, playing host to the Games in 1908 and 1948, and sending hundreds of British Olympians to compete. In the intervening years, Britain made two unsuccessful bids before London was nominated Official Candidate City for the 2012 Games in May 2004. In 2004 and 2005, the 2012 organization produced a compelling case for London to host the 2012 Olympic Games in what Mike Lee, Director of Communications, called the "most competitive ever bidding procedure mounted by the IOC" (Lee, 2005).

It was crucial that the London 2012 team convinced the 117-strong IOC (voting) members that London had the potential to deliver on the five selection criteria: the best Olympic Plan; low-risk delivery; an enthusiastic country; clear benefits of Games in London; a professional, likeable, and trustworthy team. In order to persuade the 117 IOC members that London met the five selection criteria, the London 2012 organization embarked on a large-scale communications program both internationally and within the UK. This case concentrates on the research and measurement activities around the communication targeted at the British public, with particular emphasis on London.

2.2. The Role of the Communication

Underpinning all communication was the need to portray "an enthusiastic country," where Britons—and particularly Londoners—were seen to be supportive of the Games being held in their country. The twin goals for the 2012 organization were: building and maintaining levels of support for the Games (attitudinal measure), and driving registration of a "vote" of support (behavioral measure). By setting these goals, it was recognized that support was a prerequisite for registration. The communication mix chosen was advertising (mostly posters and billboards posted in and around public transport hubs) and public relations. Given that there were no funds for marketing as all advertising hoardings and airtime were given free of charge to the 2012 marketing effort, a strong reliance was placed on non-paid for media space—that is, public relations—to communicate much of the campaign messaging.

The overarching theme developed for the campaign was "Make Britain Proud," a theme that was carried through the advertising strap line and seeded through public relations messaging.

The following objectives for communication were identified: engender a sense of *pride* around London's bid; communicate the *need* to register your vote of support (via texting, email, etc.); build knowledge around the benefits of London hosting the bid; inspire confidence that London could actually be the winning city. These objectives were set with measurement in mind.

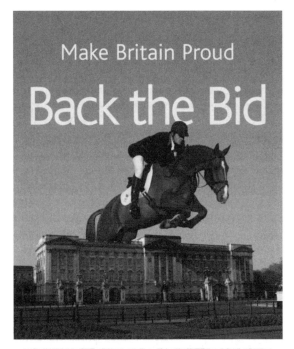

London, New York, Paris, Madrid and Moscow are in the race to host the 2012 Olympic and Paralympic Games.
They will be awarded to the city that wants them most. With your support we can win.

**Make Britain Proud. Back the Bid at London2012.com
or text LONDON to 82012**

MAYOR OF LONDON   Transport
for London

Figure 10.1 The advertising campaign for London

i to i research was brought in at the beginning of 2005 to help shape the communication at a key juncture of the campaign—the lead up to the IOC decision—and to measure the effectiveness of the advertising (see Figure 10.1) and public relations components in delivering the communication objectives. This timing was critical as persuasive messages lose their impact after some time (O'Keefe, 2002: 258). In order to prevent message decay or avoid its impact on the communication campaign, it was crucial to continue with the persuasive communication messages right up until the IOC made its final decision. It was also expected that London's bid would attract negative publicity, and it was i to i research's role to advise on the extent to which the general public picked up negative messages.

2.3. The Role of the Research

Research has, throughout the bidding process, played a critical role in tracking public "enthusiasm" for the Games being hosted in London. Initial research informed the direction of the communication campaign. At the start of the bid campaign, benchmarking research was conducted using opinion polls and qualitative focus groups in order to identify emotive themes for the campaign. As a result of the qualitative research "national pride" was identified as an emotive theme that would engage the British public. This was developed further into the "Make Britain Proud" theme that was consistent in all communications. As one of the five key selection criteria was to prove that Britain was "an enthusiastic country," all communications had to clearly reflect this emotional state. "Enthusiasm" was tracked using "support" as the key measure of success. Support was measured at two levels: at the attitudinal level—"Would you like London to be chosen as the host city of the 2012 Olympic Games?"—and at the behavioral level "Will you, or have you, registered your support?" In addition, the 2012 organization kept a database tracking the number of people who registered their support for the bid.

In the early stages of the bid, the objective of the research was to track attitudinal support for the bid. Olympic bids are generally characterized by fluctuating levels of support, and London proved to be no exception to the rule. Typically, when a city bid is announced, public support runs high, but

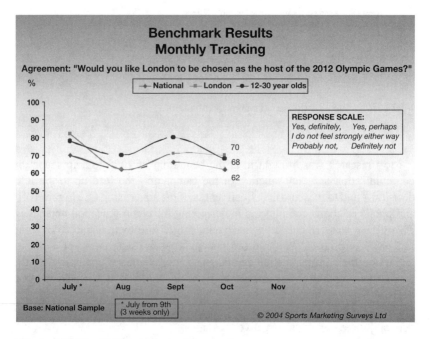

Figure 10.2 The 2004 monthly tracking results

this is soon followed by a dip in support as costs and public inconvenience come to the forefront. As is evidenced from tracking research undertaken by Sports Marketing Surveys, public support levels did peak and trough in the initial phases of the bid, between July and November 2004, both in London and in the rest of the country (see Figure 10.2).

However, the definitive poll was the one undertaken by MORI on behalf of the IOC in November 2004 as part of London's Candidate File submission. This showed that public support was in the high sixties, a level deemed acceptable by the IOC.

Having satisfied the IOC that Britain was largely supportive of London's bid, it then became critical over the next six months to continue the momentum behind the campaign in order to ensure that support levels did not dip as Londoners came to grips with the impact the Olympic Games would have on their lives (in terms of construction disruption, transport links and taxpayer costs). Encouraging Londoners to register their support of the Games also became more critical at this stage of the campaign as this would unequivocally demonstrate to the IOC that London really wanted the Games.

It was during this phase of the communications program that i to i research was brought in specifically to provide research-based advice on the communication efforts. i to i research used three categories of research (formative, diagnostic, and evaluative). The formative research identified any areas of weakness that might impact upon the campaign outcomes, which could then be immediately addressed. The diagnostic (or monitoring) research provided insight as to whether the communication campaign was on track and had the desired impact, while the evaluative research was done at the end and examined the final outcomes in order to see if the overall goals and objectives were realized.

For the 2012 campaign the specific research objectives were:

- *formative*: anticipate any wavering support, and any "weak spots" for London's bid that communication needed to shore up;
- *diagnostic*: provide some insight around how well the communication— advertising and public relations—was helping to maintain support levels, build registration and deliver key messages. This was to enable the communications plan to be honed prior to the IOC visit, and in the final months leading up to the IOC vote;
- *evaluative:* how well the campaign delivered the goals of the 2012 organization.

3. The Research

3.1. Research Approach

The i to i tracker® measurement tool was applied, as it evaluates the "impact" and "influence" of communication. The tool isolates the effect of communication and provides some understanding of how different components—in this

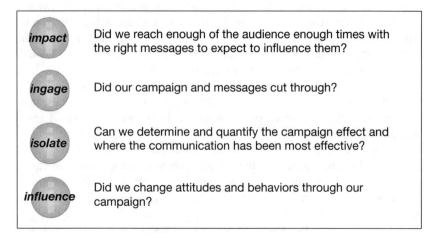

Figure 10.3 The i to i tracker® methodology

case advertising and public relations—achieved the campaign objectives. The i to i tracker® proprietary approach to evaluation includes four separate modules —"impact," "ingage," "isolate," and "influence"—which each answer the questions shown in Figure 10.3 about an organization's communication.

The impact module evaluates communications output at two levels: exposure and content. At the exposure level, the model measures reach and frequency for the campaign as a whole and for individual disciplines. Rather than using gross impressions (a common metric used by public relations practitioners, that does not reflect the actual reach of a campaign as it does not factor in overlap in exposure), the model uses media exposure analysis to calculate the true reach and frequency for public relations. This data is also collected for advertising.

The impact module also evaluates the content of public relations materials and uncontrolled messages in the media. Unlike advertising, there is no control of messages communicated via public relations activities, and the content analysis establishes answers to the following questions:

- Which messages were communicated through the media?
- What were the possible consumer out-takes from the public relations activities?
- What was the general tone of the media coverage?
- What was the context of this coverage?

The following three modules are all based on quantitative primary survey research with the target audience. Part of the approach measures the target audience's level of "ingagement" with the communications. This is measured in four ways:

- Unaided communications recall—does the target audience remember seeing or hearing anything about the campaign?
- Unaided playback of communications—what was it they saw? These answers are analyzed in detail to ascertain whether respondents are describing the current communications.
- Prompted communication recognition—do respondents remember specific communication initiatives, such as specific advertisements or public relations led stories?
- Message takeout—what messages did they take out from the communications?

The "ingagement" module is designed to isolate the effect of communications. In the most basic form, it does this by creating similar groups of publics (or media consumers) who share the same level of contact (behavior) and connection (attitudes) with the brand or issue. Segmenting publics this way reduces inherent biases in consumers and better isolates the influence of communications.

Finally, the research measures the key "relationship" and "response" indicators (KRIs) that the campaign is designed to influence. These would include measures such as brand preference, information-seeking actions and purchase intention. Significant changes in KRIs resulting from the campaign can be translated into "hard numbers" by calculating the "incremental" number of people who are feeling, or responding, in a certain way following the campaign.

The theoretical underpinnings behind the i to i tracker measurement tool link back to Hovland's research on message learning in the 1940s and 1950s (Bettinghaus & Cody, 1994: 63–64). Hovland proposed that four underlying processes resulted in successful persuasion: attention, comprehension, yielding, and retention. First, the persuasive message must gain the receiver's attention. The message then needs to be easily understood and also provide information regarding the "benefits" or "rewards" for complying. Finally, the message must be remembered. According to Hovland, it is after these four internal processes are engaged that persuasion is more likely to occur.

As well as Hovland's research, the Elaboration Likelihood Model (ELM) developed by Petty and Cacioppo (1986, cited in O'Keefe, 2002: 137–167) also partially underpins the i to i tracker® approach. The ELM posits that, depending on different conditions, receivers will vary the amount of engagement they have with a persuasive message. As a result of this varying cognitive engagement there are two routes to persuasion: the central and the peripheral route. The central route requires a high level of engagement with the message. The receiver carefully considers the message and reflects on the arguments presented. Public relations activities and campaigns strive to promote cognitive elaboration. In this particular case the public relations activities centered on explaining the benefits of having the 2012 Olympics. The peripheral route requires a low level of engagement with the message. Here the message is reliant on peripheral cues, such as images or source characteristics such as attractiveness or celebrity. This route is often used in advertising and in the case of the 2012 Olympic Bid the posters and billboards fall into this category. For the particular case of the 2012 Games bid it was not possible in practice to apply all of the i to i approach on account of the scale and outreach of the 2012 campaign (this is explained in section 4).

3.2. Research Design for 2012

As mentioned earlier, the research approach included the three categories of research. *Formative* research was conducted to help define the context for support. *Diagnostic* research was done in order to hone the communications plan and finally, *evaluative* research was carried out to assess how the campaign delivered overall against the goals set. The research design was quantitative and the methods adopted were content analysis and online surveys. Content analysis of newspaper coverage of both of the 2012 proactive public relations activities and the uncontrolled media was conducted.

For the online surveys (Ciao panel) a sample population of adults aged 18–64 was selected and the data was weighted on age and gender within London and the UK, excluding London (rUK). Two surveys were conducted: Wave 1 in late January 2005 (n = 1,753 for London, and n = 706 for rUK) and Wave 2 at the beginning of May 2005 (n = 1,509 in London, and n = 550 for rUK). Significant differences were noted in the data between the London sample and the rUK sample, reflecting the proximity of the former to the hosting city and differing levels of communication exposure in the two areas. Because the Games would affect Londoners the most, the focus on this case study is on the London research results.

i to i research waves were timed around one of the key milestones for the bid, the visit of the IOC to London in February 2005 (see Figure 10.4). There was no baseline measure established given that the bid was launched from a standing start in 2003. Opinion polls helped inform 2012 on support levels for the bid in the intervening period.

4. The Research Findings

The research findings are reported for each of the i to i modules, using a simple "Question and Answer" reporting. The data are from Wave 1 of the research (January), with the exception of the "influence" module where Wave 1 and 2 comparisons were needed to see how the needle had shifted on the key measures of success for the campaign. The role of the research at Wave 1 was to provide an indication of how well support levels were holding up. Opinion polls had shown that support had levelled off after an initial show of enthusiasm, and there was concern that there could be a dip in support the more Londoners learned how the Games would impact on their lives. There was also a need to use the research findings diagnostically, ahead of the visit of the IOC to London

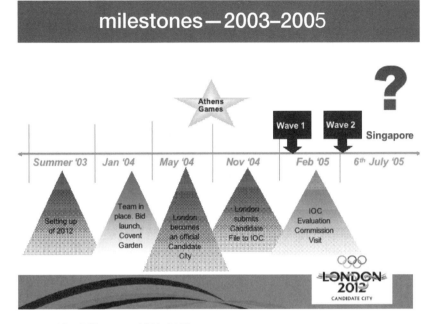

Figure 10.4 Milestones, 2003–2005

in the February, to check how effective the communication was in shaping opinion and in driving support and registration. Wave 1 research results were used to refine the communications plan between February and May 2005.

Question—Did this campaign "impact," or reach enough of the right people, enough times with the right messages to expect the communication to cut through and engender support, and drive registration?

i. Reach and Frequency Analysis (Advertising and Public Relations)

Given that the poster hoardings and a limited amount of TV airtime were donated free of charge, it was difficult to calculate exposure for the advertising. However, based on a UK government (the media was coordinated through the government's communications agency, the Central Office of Information) estimate of the value of the space, and airtime donated to 2012, the cost would have been in excess of £15,000,000 in London alone. Equating this to exposure levels, it is likely that the advertising would have been seen by almost all Londoners at least ten times.

The same applies to the public relations outputs, where all Londoners had the chance to see the communication several times through TV, radio, and press. The coverage gleaned by the 2012 campaign equates to the scale of coverage normally only achieved by a general election. Brand, or even issue-based campaigns never reach this level of exposure. A comparison of this level of reach and frequency to i to i research normative data shows that this campaign tops the scale.

Question—Did London have a chance to see the campaign?
Answer—YES.

ii. Media content analysis (editorial coverage only)

What is more interesting than the reach and frequency of the 2012 campaign is an evaluation of the media content of both the *proactive* public relations and the *uncontrolled media* attracted by London's bid (see Figure 10.5).

The objective of this analysis was to give an indication, based on content of the print articles, what messages Londoners were *likely* to be taking out of the media coverage, and how negatively or positively they were likely to feel. The messages were designed to support the four communication objectives: sense of pride, need to register, benefits, and confidence London could win. Much of the public relations effort was about communicating specific benefits, such as: the Games will provide a lasting legacy; improved transport and infrastructure; regeneration of East London; provision of sports facilities; the Games will benefit the whole of the country, not just London.

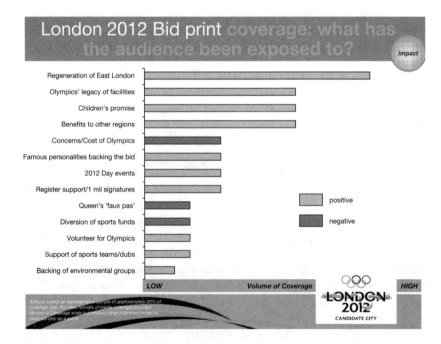

Figure 10.5 London 2012 bid-print coverage

The analysis of print coverage shows that there was a high volume of articles referencing these benefits. However, some of these messages were being diluted by stories publicizing the potential cost of the Games to Londoners.

Many of the stories initiated by the 2012 communications team—such as famous personalities supporting the bid and the "Children's Promise"—were picked up well by the media.

Question—Were key messages being picked up by the media?
Answer—Some, but not all. Some negative publicity, but less than one might expect for a campaign of this sort.

 Key question—Did the campaign messages cut through? How were advertising and PR contributing?

First, with 98% of Londoners able to recall either advertising or public relations, it was clear that the communication had entirely saturated London. Furthermore, both advertising and public relations activities had in their own right cut through the noise, with 87% and 94% aided recall, respectively. Comparing these results to i to i research norms, we can conclude that these are extremely high levels, particularly for public relations activity.

What was more important was to understand how well the communication messages were cutting through, and to glean some understanding of how advertising and public relations were contributing to getting the messages across. As shown in Figure 10.6, over a third of those seeing the advertising were playing back the "pride" message, reflecting the salience of the advertising strap line "Make Britain Proud."

With regard to Hovland's message-learning approach, the first process "attention" is clearly achieved as the target public paid attention to the persuasive communication.

However, while the advertisements were successfully instilling in Londoners a sense of pride and a need to support the bid, it appeared to be doing little to drive home the need to register, with only 7% mentioning this spontaneously.

The advertising also appeared to be doing little in communicating some of the benefits to London of hosting the Games. This is where public relations activities scored better; as shown in Figure 10.7, messages on the benefits of hosting the Games in London cut through reasonably well.

The public relations activities also helped the cut-through on the message that London could win over competing cities. However, some of the negative stories around the potential cost were also entering the psyche of Londoners. Again, referring back to Hovland's message-learning approach, the second process (comprehension), the third process (yielding), and the final process (recall) were also achieved. The target public understood the messages, weighed up the arguments and recalled them. It should be noted here that it is to be expected that public relations outputs will achieve a lower level of recall of messages at the unaided level, bearing in mind the low frequency delivered

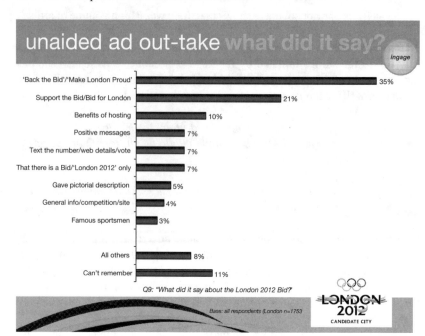

Figure 10.6 Unaided ad out-take

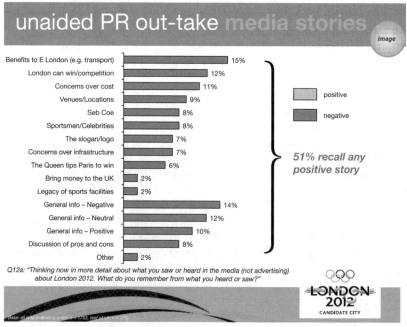

Figure 10.7 Unaided PR out-take

by any one media story (a newspaper is unlikely to run the same story twice).

Ordinarily, the i to i methodology evaluates the contribution of advertising and public relations separately and collectively; this is done by modelling groups of people who have seen combinations of "Advertising" or "PR" only, "Both advertising and PR" or "Neither." Attitudes and behaviors of these groups are then compared and contrasted, typically over several waves of research. However, this was not possible with the 2012 bid, as the communication saturated London to such a great extent that making the base size of seen "Neither" too small to work with.

An overwhelming 83% of people had seen both advertising and public relations outputs, showing how well each discipline had saturated London in its own right: i to i research norms put this overlap at a very high level.

The i to i model was used to see if there were any significant differences in those claiming to have seen only one discipline—advertising or public relations—versus both, as this would provide insight into the role that each was playing. This revealed that those who had only seen advertising represented a cohort of people who felt largely negative about the Games, and who were showing lower levels of agreement to the perceived benefits of hosting in London (see Figure 10.8) and higher levels of agreement on the disadvantages (see Figure 10.9).

key indicators positive attitudinal statements, top 3 box agreement 1) *influence*

"Hosting the 2012 Games in London will...

	Ad only	PR only	Both	Total
...establish the UK on the world stage in terms of sport"	10%	31%	38%	36%
...become a source of national pride "	14%	34%	52%	48%
...improve the standard of sports facilities available to the public"	14%	40%	49%	46%
...inspire children to participate in sport, & therefore create wider health benefits within the community"	16%	36%	50%	47%
... boost local employment in industries such as construction, IT and hospitality"	19%	44%	54%	51%
...generate a legacy of affordable housing for thousands of people in East London"	5%	20%	28%	26%
... improve transport links in and around London"	6%	34%	43%	26%
...benefit the whole UK and not just London"	7%	22%	38%	30%

LONDON
2012
CANDIDATE CITY

Figure 10.8 Key indicators, positive attitudinal statements: combined advertising and PR effect on perceived benefits of hosting

key indicators negative attitudinal statements, top 3 box agreement 2) *influence*

"Hosting the 2012 Games in London will...

	Ad only	PR only	Both	Total
... be a waste of taxpayers' money"	63%	35%	29%	31%
... leave London with unused sports stadia"	57%	26%	26%	27%
... lead to too much congestion in and around London"	82%	53%	50%	51%

Q31: "To what extent do you agree with the following statements other people have made regarding the possible impacts of hosting the 2012 Games in London?..."

LONDON 2012
CANDIDATE CITY

Figure 10.9 Key indicators, negative attitudinal statements: advertising and PR not closing on the negatives

The hypothesis that i to i research formed was that people who had seen only advertising represented a group of people who were opposed to London's bid, who could not help but see the advertising, but who chose not to "consume" the PR. This hypothesis is supported by Cognitive Dissonance Theory (Festinger, 1957, cited in O'Keefe, 2002: 77), especially with regard to the selective exposure to information. Dissonance is considered to be a highly unpleasant cognitive state, so it makes sense that individuals will do their utmost to avoid putting themselves in situations that cause it. O'Keefe (2002: 85) explains that the dissonance theory's selective exposure hypothesis posits that people seek out media sources that support, confirm, and reinforce their attitudes and behavior and avoid those that do not.

Coupled with the finding that 59% of Londoners claimed to have had a conversation with a colleague, friend, or family member about the bid, it was recognized how powerful word of mouth was in this campaign. Of greater concern was the fact that a third had had a conversation that was negative. Given the importance of shoring up support at this critical stage of London's bid, it was important to know more about this group. Using the "isolate" module of i to i it was possible to validate this hypothesis.

Question—Had the messages cut through?
Answer—Yes, but other "noise" had as well.

Advertising was engendering a general feeling of national pride and support but not communicating the need for, and importance of, registration.

Public relations activity was filling in the gaps by communicating benefits. However, the effect of negative publicity was to dilute the benefits.

Additional finding—those seeing advertising only were more negative than any other group.

The "isolate" module was applied to provide a deeper understanding than the opinion polls had provided of how support panned out among Londoners. The hypothesis was that there might have been a group of people who were not in support of the bid and who were "infecting" others with their opinions. From a research standpoint, the ideal approach would be to track individual opinions and behaviors over time. This is not ideal, bearing in mind that in surveying a respondent he/she is predisposed to noticing future communication. The i to i approach is to "isolate." This is done by controlling for differences and segmenting people into groups who think and act similarly. The segmentation is created by using attitudes and behaviors that are deep-seated and that the communication is unlikely to shift. Through segmentation it was possible to establish if, and where, there were any weak links in terms of support for London's bid.

Question—Where is support likely to be strongest/weakest?

In the case of 2012, Londoners were segmented and sized on two sets of measures: engagement in sports and attitudes toward Britain holding events in general. A battery of attitudinal statements was used relating to interest and participation in sports for one axis and viewership of Olympics and other Games for the other axis. The resulting segmentation placed Londoners in four quadrants, as Figure 10.10 shows.

Those who showed the strongest support for the Games being hosted in London—the strong supporters—ranked high on both measures. Conversely, those rejecting the Games ranked low on both measures. Two further groups, the swing voters and the skeptics, were high–low or low–high. These groups were then sized and profiled (see Figure 10.11). This exercise showed that the two groups who showed the weakest support for the Games—the skeptics and the rejecters—were not only sizeable but that they were most likely to feel negative on two key issues surrounding London's bid: confidence in the government to spend money effectively (the cost issue was one that research had shown to be of concern), and sense of national pride about London potentially hosting the Games. There was a high concentration of rejecters and skeptics among people who had only seen the advertising. Not only were the weaker supporters likely to be more negative, but they were also more likely to breed negativity through word of mouth, as Figure 10.12 shows. The concern at

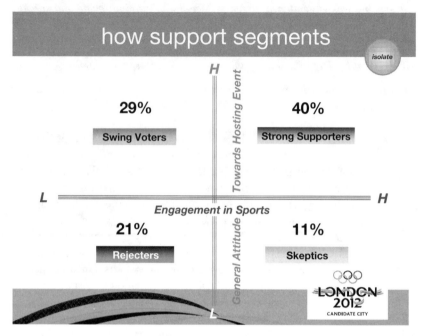

Figure 10.10 How support segments

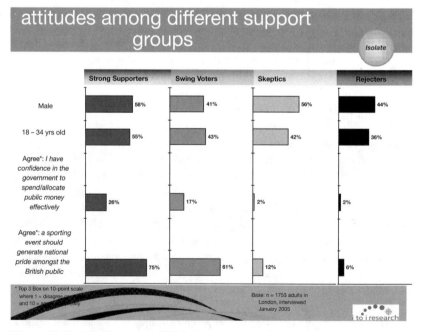

Figure 10.11 Attitudes among different support groups

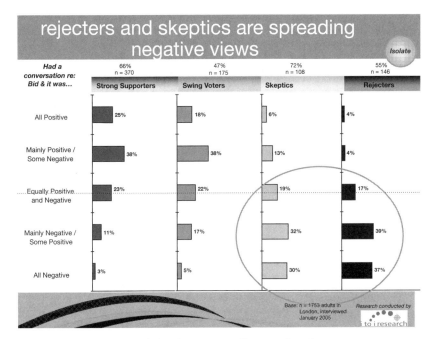

Figure 10.12 Rejecters and skeptics are spreading negative views

this stage of the campaign (end of January 2005) was that the swing voters—representing 29% of Londoners—could be "infected" and influenced by the negative opinion expressed by the skeptics and the rejecters. This could have had an adverse effect on support, and could have slowed registration.

Question—Where is support likely to be strongest/weakest?
Answer—Support was thought to be weak among the important swing-voter group who could be susceptible to the negative opinion being expressed by the rejecters and the skeptics. Older people and women were shown to be more likely to be rejecters, as they are less involved with sports and more likely to have concerns about the costs of the Games.

 The i to i approach to "influence" is to evaluate the effect of communication on "KRIs"—Key Relationship and Key Response Indicators. Here it is necessary to compare Wave 1 and Wave 2 results.

Question—Did the communication shift the KRIs?

For the 2012 Bid, the Key Relationship Indicators, which the communication was designed to shift, concerned attitudes about, and support for, the bid.

Following Wave 1 of the research, there was a need to shore up support among the swing voters, and ensure that no attrition occurred within this important, but vulnerable group.

Comparison of Wave 1 and Wave 2 data shows that perceptions of benefits of the bid remain largely unchanged, and that the swing voters have not been negatively influenced. Attitudes were compared on six key statements (see Figures 10.13 and 10.14). A similar picture emerges on support for the bid, which remained fairly constant across all groups (see Figure 10.15).

The Key Response Indicator, which the communication was designed to shift, was registration. As can be seen in Figure 10.16, claimed registration levels did increase overall over the two waves. This is corroborated by figures from 2012's own registry of support, which showed that registrations jumped from one million at the beginning of the year, to three million by July.

And, importantly, increases were not just seen among the strong supporters but also among the swing voters and the skeptics (Figure 10.17). Much of this movement can be attributed to an increased awareness—most likely driven by the communication—of the bid Support Registry.

To answer the key question, "Did the communication shift the KRIs," it proved necessary in this case to extrapolate from the research. Usually in this type of evaluation, i to i research relies on modelling the different groups of communication aware and unaware, within the segments, to look for any

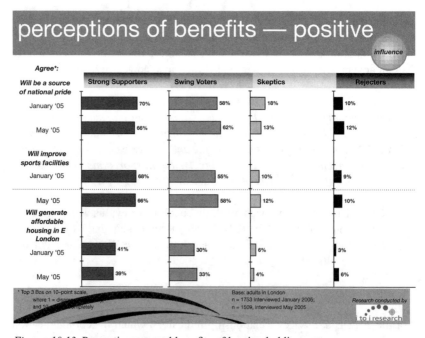

Figure 10.13 Perceptions around benefits of hosting holding up

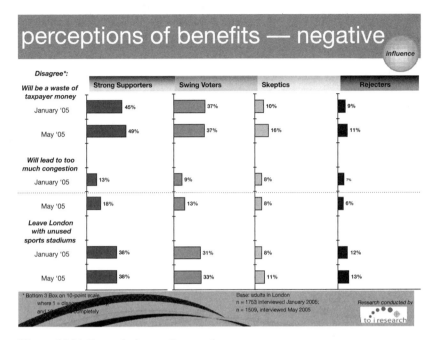

Figure 10.14 Some closing on the negatives

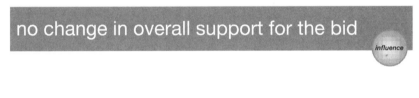

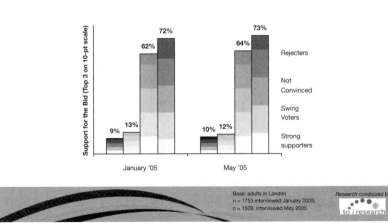

Figure 10.15 No change in overall support for the bid

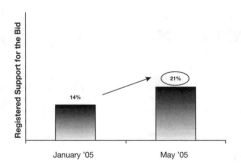

Figure 10.16 Claimed registration has increased

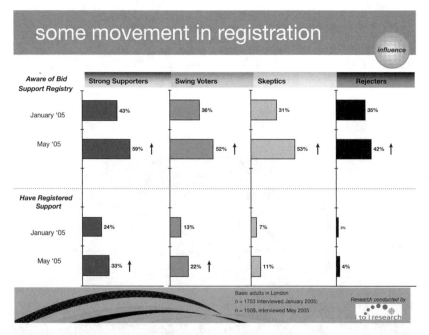

Figure 10.17 Some movement in registration: awareness of bid registry driving registration

differences. However, with the 2012 bid, few had not been exposed to communication, making any robust comparison impossible. Instead, this case study reviews to what extent the public relations activities that were rolled out subsequent to January 2005 (after Wave 1) helped to ameliorate some of the weaknesses.

5. How Communication Contributed to Success

The Wave 1 research had pinpointed a number of areas where communication needed to work harder. Given budgetary constraints and the reliance on long lead-time poster media, it was not possible to make any copy changes to the advertising. This meant that there was a greater reliance on public relations to get the messages out. Between Waves 1 and 2 of the research, the public relations effort was intensified with a focus on strengthening messaging around why it was important to register support, and the wider benefits of London hosting the Games, such as improved facilities and transport. By feeding the media with a spread of good news stories around the bid, the positive public relations messaging was able to drown out negative media, and to shore up potentially wavering support (see Figures 10.18 and 10.19).

The visit of the IOC to London in February provided the ideal opportunity for the 2012 communications team to showcase London as the ideal candidate city in the media, thereby influencing the British public as well as the IOC through the "trustworthy" source of media. Using the same i to i approach as in Wave 1, the output of communication between February and May 2005 was evaluated.

Communication continued to saturate London during this period. The media-content analysis showed that there was not only a greater volume of positive media, but also that the wider benefits of hosting the Games in London were being communicated effectively. From the primary research it can be seen that the media not only reported more positive stories, but also that the general public were able to recall, on an un-aided basis, more positive stories. By May, 63% of Londoners were able to cite something positive about London's bid without prompting, which was a considerable improvement on Wave 1.

The other weakness of the previous communication had been a lack of understanding of why it was important to register support for London's bid. By May 2005, 67% of Londoners understood that the main purpose of registration was to "show the IOC that there is public support." The researchers suggest that the focus of communication on the IOC's visit clarified for many why a public demonstration of support was important, and with this greater understanding, a greater degree of confidence was established that London could actually win the Games. At Wave 2, 58% believed London was likely to win, and 28% believed that London's chances of winning were better following the IOC's visit.

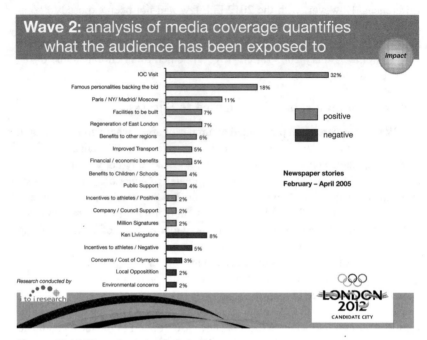

Figure 10.18 Wave 2: analysis of media coverage

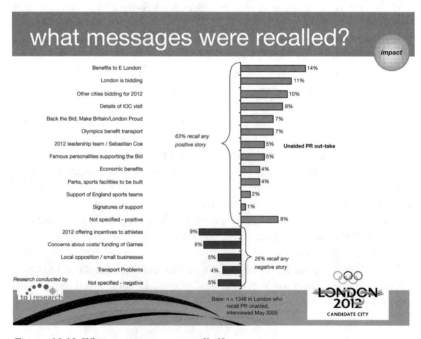

Figure 10.19 What messages were recalled?

6. Summary and Conclusions

The 2012 case illustrates how public relations can be evaluated at four levels "for its organizational contribution, contribution at the process and program levels, its contribution to society, and through the performance of individual practitioners" (CIPR, 2005: 2). This case study exemplifies in particular the triple role that research can play in communication: formative, diagnostic, and evaluative. Given that the key goal of this campaign was to build and maintain support for the bid (by securing attitudinal support for the bid, the required behavioral support—registration—would follow), it was important to have formative research in order to understand where there were weak links among the general public. The resulting public segmentation showed that there were two groups, or publics, which felt less positively about the Games—the skeptics and the rejecters, who had the potential to "infect" the swing voters who could waver. As a result of this formative research, communication was directed at strengthening support among wavering supporters.

Diagnostic research provided by the Wave 1 findings helped identify the weak spots of the campaign—specifically, the need to better communicate the importance of registration. The research indicated that the advertising was doing this less effectively than the public relations activities.

Communication was strengthened between the two waves of research to seed messages around the IOC's visit, and its significance in the context of demonstrating public enthusiasm for the Games being held in London. Public relations was relied upon heavily, given the constraints on advertising budgets, and was used to deal effectively with identified weak spots.

Following the Wave 2 research, it was possible to evaluate the success of the communication overall and shifts in some of the measures between the two waves. What was particularly encouraging was that support levels were maintained overall, and any wavering support among swing voters had been strengthened. Registration levels showed increases between waves, and confidence about London's chances improved. It is possible to extrapolate from the research, given the evidence of improved media messaging (output measure) and public perception (out-take measure) that the communication had contributed to these results.

For the 2012 campaign, Hovland's message-learning processes (Bettinghaus & Cody, 1994) as well as Petty and Cacioppo's Elaboration Likelihood Model (1986, cited in O'Keefe, 2002: 137–167) were engaged. The advertising and public relations campaign ensured that the target public was exposed to the key messages via a combination of posters, billboards, and news and editorial coverage (so via the central and peripheral routes). The persuasive messages used were simple and clear for easy comprehension. The public relations messaging went further than the advertising as it included an account of the many benefits the 2012 Games would bring. Finally, the messages were developed to be memorable and unaided recall was achieved. The persuasive communication resulted in behavioral change: increased registration of support for the 2012 London Bid.

On July 6, 2005 the IOC voting members selected London as the host city for the 2012 Olympic Games. The London bid beat stiff competition from Paris, New York, Moscow, and Madrid. The London bid successfully convinced the IOC voting members that it offered the best Olympic plan, the lowest delivery risk, an enthusiastic and supportive country, clear benefits from hosting the Games, and, finally, a professional, likeable, and trustworthy team. The communication program was an essential part of the London bid and played a large part in gaining the successful outcome of London being chosen as the host city for the 2012 Games.

Acknowledgments

Research team at i to i research; Brooke Hempell, Associate Director; Robert Bullock, Senior Research Executive; 2012 team; Michael Lee—Director of Communications.

References

Bettinghaus, E. P., & Cody, M. J. (1994). *Persuasive communication.* Fort Worth, TX: Harcourt Brace.

Broom, G. M., & Dozier, D. M. (1990). *Using research in public relations.* Englewood Cliffs, NJ: Prentice-Hall.

CIPR (2005). *Measurement and evaluation: Moving the debate forward.* CIPR Policy Paper.

Gregory, A. (2004). Verbal communication at the CIPR Communication Directors meeting.

Hon, L. C., & Grunig, J. E. (1999). *Guidelines for measuring relationships in public relations.* Paper presented to the Institute for Public Relations, Gainsville, FL. Available online at www.instituteforpr.com, accessed December 2005.

Lee, Mike (2005). Presentation at the "Brand building through public relations" conference, May 20, 2005.

Lindenmann, W. K. (2005). *Putting PR measurement and evaluation into historical perspective.* The Institute for Public Relations, Gainsville, FL. Available online at www.instituteforpr.com, accessed December 2, 2005.

O'Keefe, D. J. (2002). *Persuasion: Theory and practice.* Thousand Oaks, CA: Sage.

11 Organization–Stakeholder Relationships, Crisis Responsibilities, and Crisis-Response Strategies

Iris Wong and Chun-ju Flora Hung

1. Introduction

March 2003 was an atypical period to all Hong Kong people, with an atypical outbreak and epidemic spread of an unknown killer disease (i.e., atypical pneumonia or Severe Acute Respiratory Syndrome, SARS), atypical broadcasts of SARS news, an atypical response to health crises from the Hong Kong Special Administrative Region Government (also abbreviated as SAR, HKSAR or Hong Kong Government), professionals, publics, and the whole community. In response to the sudden outbreak of this communicable life-threatening disease and the dramatic rise in death tolls in just a few weeks, the Hong Kong Government took some measures to control the spread of the SARS to allay the public's fear over the epidemic.

Despite these measures, however, the epidemic grew uncontrollably in magnitude, extent, and speed. Most people blamed the government for this crisis, even after the SARS had gone. The criticism focused on how sluggish, unprepared, and indecisive the government's response had been. For example, there were accusations of the lack of comprehensive contingency planning, deficiencies in communication within the healthcare delivery system, ambiguities in their roles and functions, as well as inexperience in crisis handling and management. Few critics, however, have touched on the effects of these responses on the whole community.

In addition, as Broom, Casey, and Richey (2000) and L. Grunig, J. Grunig, and Dozier (2002) contended that the value of public relations to an organization is to build and cultivate long-term quality relationships, numerous studies have been done echoing their calls for the new research direction (e.g., Brunner, 2000; Kim, 2001; Hung, 2002, 2004, 2005). Yet, not much attention was paid to the influence of an organization's relationship with publics to crisis communication. The purpose of this study, therefore, is to explore how an organization's crisis response affects the relationships with the publics; in addition, by studying how the crisis-response strategies affect the relationship outcomes, we hope to provide some insights for the government in handling crises in future.

2. Conceptualization

The purpose of this study is to explore how crisis-response strategies affect the relationship between organizations and publics. To do so, we incorporate the concepts of relationships, crisis responsibility, and crisis-response strategies in this section.

2.1. Relationship

By definition, relationships arise "when organizations and their strategic publics are interdependent and this interdependence results in consequences to each other that organizations need to manage" (Hung, 2005: 396). "Relationship" is a dynamic concept, that is, it will change over time and vary with the interactions of the organization–stakeholders. It should be noted that, apart from being dynamic, relationships are also subjective. In other words, it is the feeling of the organization and the stakeholder about their relationships. Different stakeholders have different feelings about their relationship with the organization. Therefore, what we are going to investigate in this study is the subjective perception of the organization–stakeholder relationships.

The relationship with stakeholders is the core value in public relations (Chen & Hung, 2002; Hon & J. Grunig, 1999; L. Grunig *et al.*, 2002; Hung, 2005), no matter whether the organization is in crisis or not. Current events or crises do not exist in isolation but are viewed as part of the larger relationship (Ledingham, Bruning, & Wilson, 1999). As Coombs (1999a) said, "crises are episodes in the ongoing relationship between an organization and its stakeholders" (p. 73). We interpret crisis as "the result of not paying enough attention to existing or emerging issues and of neglecting stakeholders" (Lerbinger, 1997: 318). Undoubtedly, relationships play a crucial role in crisis management, partly because they affect how stakeholders interpret current events and crises and partly because they influence how the organization handles the crisis (Coombs & Holladay, 2001).

Hon and J. Grunig (1999) developed guidelines for measuring the concepts by focusing on six very precise elements or components of the relationships. These are:

1. Control mutuality—The degree to which parties agree on who has the rightful power to influence someone. Although some imbalance is natural, stable relationships require that, over time, organizations and publics each have some control.
2. Trust—One party's level of confidence and willingness to open themselves up to the other party. There are three dimensions to trust: (a) integrity: the belief that an organization is fair and just; (b) dependability: the belief that an organization will do what it says it will do; and (c) competence: the belief that an organization has the ability to do what it says it will do.

3. Satisfaction—The extent to which each party feels favorably toward the other because positive expectations about the relationship are reinforced. A satisfying relationship is one in which the benefits outweigh the costs.
4. Commitment—The extent to which each party believes and feels that the relationship is worth spending energy on to maintain and promote it. Two dimensions of commitment are (a) continuance commitment, which refers to a certain line of action, and (b) affective commitment, which is an emotional orientation.
5. Exchange relationship—In an exchange relationship, one party gives benefits to the other only because the other has provided benefits in the past or is expected to do so in the future.
6. Communal relationship—In a communal relationship, both parties provide benefits to each other because they are concerned with each other's welfare—even when they get nothing in return (Hon & J. Grunig, 1999: 2–3).

2.2. Crisis Responsibility

The term "crisis responsibility" was introduced by Coombs and Holladay (1996). It simply represents "the degree to which stakeholders blame the organization of the crisis event" (Coombs, 1998: 180). The stronger the crisis responsibility that publics perceive, the more the stakeholders blame the organization for the crisis. This means that it is the stakeholders, not the organization, who are to interpret the causes of the crisis. In fact, crises are subject to interpretation. The causes of one crisis can be interpreted differently by different people. For example, some people think that the SARS outbreak of 2003 was caused by the news coverage of the Chinese authorities; others think it was caused by the Hong Kong Government's negligence. According to Coombs and Holladay (1996: 282), "a crisis is an event for which people or publics seek causes and make attributions. More specifically, people evaluate organizational responsibility for a crisis when they determine the cause of a crisis."

Attribution theory explains what affects people's attribution of the causes to events or crises. Generally speaking, a crisis is the result of many factors. In reality, however, in the attributional process, people may not, or may not be able to consider all possible causes to a crisis thoroughly and comprehensively, and they would not give each cause "equal proportion" in contributing to the crisis. Attribution theory is therefore based on the assumption that people spontaneously search for the causes of events. Unexpected events and failures tend to stimulate causal thinking (Weiner, 1985; Wong & Weiner, 1981; Coombs, 1999a).

People's judgments of a crisis are affected by many factors. Coombs and Holladay (2001) examined several crisis situations that were believed to affect stakeholder perceptions of crisis responsibility, namely (a) control over the crisis; (b) frequency of the crisis; and (c) relationship between the organization and its stakeholders. Some support was found for (a) control over the crisis (i.e., the more the crisis is caused by the organization, the stronger the crisis responsibility people perceive), and (b) frequency of the crises (i.e., when crises occur more frequently, it is felt that the organization should take more responsibility) (Coombs, 1998).

Interestingly, no support was found for the correlation between pre-crisis relationship between organization and stakeholders and the crisis responsibility (Coombs & Holladay, 2001)—that is, people in favorable relationship conditions will not necessarily attribute less crisis responsibility to the organization than those in the unfavorable or neutral conditions.

From the factors mentioned here that influence people's perception of crisis responsibility, we want to concentrate on the influence of the organization–stakeholder relationship on crisis responsibility. One reason to do so is that the participants in Coombs's (2001) research were not the actual stakeholders in the crisis (the participants were only the undergraduate students in his research). Therefore, the results were merely others' perceptions of the stakeholder perception of crisis responsibility, which might affect the validity in findings. Another reason is that, apart from Coombs's research, the correlation between the organization–stakeholder relationship and crisis responsibility has gone untested but it is assumed to be a potentially important aspect in crisis communication.

Crisis responsibility serves as an independent and a dependent variable in this study. Crisis responsibility is assumed to be influenced by the organization–stakeholder relationship on one hand, and to affect the government crisis-response strategies, on the other hand. Crisis responsibility is important because it not only reflects how people feel and behave toward the organization involved in the crisis, but it also affects the way the organization responds to crisis.

From the discussion on the attribution theory, we therefore develop the first research question (RQ) and hypotheses (H) as follows:

- RQ1: What is the relationship between the stakeholders' perception of their relationship with the government at the pre-crisis stage and crisis responsibility?
- Hypothesis H1a: Favorable stakeholders' perception of their relationship with the government at the pre-crisis stage will attribute less (weak) crisis responsibility to the organization.
- H1b: Unfavorable stakeholders' perception of their relationship with the government at the pre-crisis stage will attribute more (strong) crisis responsibility to the organization.

2.3. Crisis Response Strategies

Crisis response strategies are the actions (verbal or non-verbal) taken by the organization to respond to the crisis. They have been widely discussed in the literature (see, for example, Allen & Caillouet, 1994; Benoit, 1992; Hobbs, 1995; Ice, 1991). In this study, we adopt Marcus and Goodman's (1991) categorization of crisis-response strategies. Marcus and Goodman (1991) divided the crisis responses into accommodative and defensive ones. By definition, accommodative strategies accept responsibilities, take remedial actions, or both, whereas defensive strategies claim that there is no problem or try to deny responsibilities for the crisis. The crisis-response strategies are placed on the accommodative–defensive continuum, which encompasses the strategies of attacking the accuser, denial, excuse, justification, ingratiation, corrective action, and full apology.

Full apology is "the most accommodative because it involves taking responsibility for the crisis and asking forgiveness. The organization must accept the crisis responsibility and ask stakeholders to forgive its misstep with some compensation such as money or aid" (Coombs, 1999b: 123). At the opposite end of the continuum is attacking the accuser, which is the most defensive strategy because "it goes beyond denial to attacking some stakeholder group. The organization is attacking stakeholders who claim a crisis and victims exist" (Coombs, 1999b: 125). The accommodative–defensive continuum links the crisis-communication/response strategies together. Different crisis-communication strategies affect stakeholders' perceptions of a crisis.

Different kinds of crisis response strategies have been widely discussed in the literature. Nevertheless, very little attention has been paid to the types of situation in which these strategies should be used. Coombs (1998) said, "Defensive strategies are most useful when crisis responsibility is weak, whereas accommodative strategies are more useful when crisis responsibility is strong" (pp. 188–189). We agree that different crises require different strategies to respond, but we also have different views with Coombs. Crisis responsibility is one of the determining factors affecting the choice of crisis response strategies, and this is what our study aims to investigate. We believe that accommodative strategies can apply to most, if not all, crises, no matter how big the crisis responsibility is.

We consider defensive strategies cannot be used if the crisis responsibility is strong. First, when perceptions of crisis responsibility are strong, the crisis managers must address the needs of victims, take responsibility and/or rectify the situation and be accommodative. Second, defensive strategies such as denial and justification become less effective when the organization is perceived as responsible for the crisis (Benoit, 1995; Coombs, 1999b). Third, defensive strategies are not necessarily effective if the crisis responsibility is weak. However, accommodative strategies can be used for most of the crises, regardless of the crisis responsibility.

Many scholars (such as Dionisopolous & Vibbert, 1988; Coombs, 1999b; Benoit, 1995; Hearit, 1994) argue that the main purpose of crisis response strategies is to protect organizational reputation and image. Nonetheless, taking into account that reputation and organization–stakeholder relationship are interrelated (J. Grunig & Hung, 2002; J. Grunig & L. Grunig, 2002), we believe the crisis-response strategies can be used to protect and repair the organization–stakeholder relationship at the same time.

From this discussion on the choice of crisis response strategies, we develop the second research questions and hypotheses as follows:

- RQ2: What is the relation between crisis responsibility and the choice of crisis response strategies?
- H2a: Defensive strategies are more effective when the crisis responsibility is weak.
- H2b: Accommodative strategies are more effective when the crisis responsibility is strong.

We believe that the three variables of organization–stakeholder relationship, crisis responsibility, and the choice of crisis-response strategy are related to one another. In what follows, we examine (a) the impact of the government's SARS response on organization–stakeholder relationships and (b) the effect of pre-SARS relationships on stakeholder perception of the crisis responsibility and on the government's choice of response strategy. Figure 11.1 shows the correlations between relationships, crisis responsibilities, and crisis-response strategies.

Based on this framework, we develop the third and fourth research questions and hypotheses as follows:

- RQ3: How do stakeholders' perceptions of their relationship with the government in the pre-crisis stage and crisis responsibility affect the government's choice of crisis response strategy?

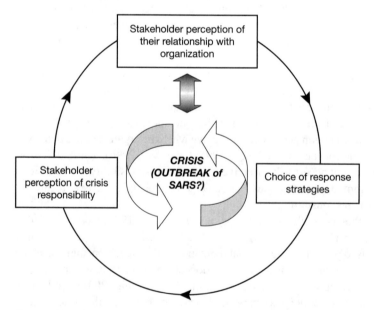

Figure 11.1 Correlation among the three variables in this study

- H3: Stakeholders' perceptions of their relationship with the government in the pre-crisis stage and crisis responsibility contribute to the government's choice of crisis response strategy.
- RQ4: How do stakeholders' perceptions of their relationship with the government in the pre-crisis stage, crisis responsibility, and the government's crisis-response strategies affect the relationships with the stakeholders after the crisis?
- H4: The stakeholders' perceptions of the relationships with the government in the pre-crisis stage, crisis responsibility, and the government's choice of response strategy contribute to the effect of organization–stakeholder relationships after the crisis.

2.4. Method

A self-administered survey was adopted to obtain people's perception toward the government's response to SARS and their attitudes toward or feelings about their relationship with the government. In all, 265 questionnaires were distributed to publics in three major districts in Hong Kong: Wan Chai (in Hong Kong Island), Kwun Tong (in Kowloon), and Tai Po (in New Territory) on public holidays and weekends in March and April, 2004. A total of 240 questionnaires were returned and the response rate was 91%.

3. Findings

3.1. Findings on Relationship

Respondents were asked whether or not they agreed with the statement that "my relationship with government is good overall." Table 11.1 shows the

Table 11.1 Frequencies on the overall organization–stakeholder relationship before and after SARS outbreak

	My relationship with the government is good overall (before SARS)		*My relationship with the government is good overall (after SARS)*	
	Frequency	*%*	*Frequency*	*%*
Strongly disagree	8	3.3	20	8.3
Disagree	32	13.3	64	26.7
Slightly disagree	16	6.7	52	21.7
Neutral	80	33.3	48	20.0
Slightly agree	36	15.0	12	5.0
Agree	56	23.3	36	15.0
Strongly agree	12	5.0	8	3.3
Total	240	100.0	240	100.0
Mean	*4.33*	*3.45*		

Table 11.2 Paired samples test for the organization–stakeholder relationship in pre-crisis and post-crisis period

	Paired differences					t	df	Sig. (2-tailed)
	Mean	Std. deviation	Std. error mean	95% Confidence interval of the Difference				
				Lower	Upper			
Pair 1								
- My relationship with the government (before SARS)	0.883	1.737	0.112	0.663	1.104	7.880	239	0.000
- My relationship with the government (after SARS)								

Table 11.3 Frequencies on six components of relationships before and after SARS outbreak

Frequency	Control mutuality (before SARS)	Control mutuality (after SARS)	Trust (before SARS)	Trust (after SARS)	Commitment (before SARS)	Commitment (after SARS)	Satisfaction (before SARS)	Satisfaction (after SARS)	Exchange relationships (before SARS)	Exchange relationships (after SARS)	Communal relationships (before SARS)	Communal relationships (after SARS)
Valid	240	240	240	240	240	240	240	240	240	240	240	240
Missing	0	0	0	0	0	0	0	0	0	0	0	0
Mean	4.22	3.77	4.22	3.97	4.65	4.33	4.45	3.95	4.23	4.28	4.48	4.48
Change of mean	0.45 (↓)		0.25 (↓)		0.32 (↓)		0.5 (↓)		0.05 (↑) *		No change	
Std. error of mean	0.328	0.348	0.414	0.459	0.333	0.403	0.375	0.394	0.318	0.334	0.292	0.337
Std. deviation	5.075	5.396	6.409	7.111	5.161	6.249	5.816	6.097	4.929	5.180	4.527	5.214
Variance	25.756	29.117	41.081	50.571	26.632	39.052	33.828	37.176	24.297	26.827	20.495	27.190

Note: Since each component of a relationship is measured by different numbers of questions, in order to eliminate this factor, mean (individual) is arrived at.
* Although there is a rise in the mean of exchange relationships, it should be noted that a higher mean implies that respondents think the government demands something in return when doing people a favor.

findings on the organization–stakeholder relationship in the pre-SARS and post-SARS periods in general. In this study, relationships in the pre-SARS period refers to the period before the outbreak of SARS in Hong Kong (that is, March 2003); relationships in the post-SARS period refer to the period after the removal of Hong Kong from the SARS list by the WHO on June 23, 2003.

Overall, respondents found that their relationship with government in the pre-SARS period (mean 4.33) was better than that in the post-SARS period (mean 3.45). The paired sample t-test in Table 11.2 compares the means of the relationship between organization and stakeholder in the pre-crisis and the post-crisis stage.

The findings show that the difference between the two means of overall pre-crisis and post-crisis organization–stakeholder relationship is statistically significant. We then examined the six relationship components individually, based on Hon and J. Grunig's (1999) indicators on relationship outcomes: control mutuality, trust, commitment, satisfaction, exchange relationships, and communal relationships. Respondents were requested to "rate" their relationship with government before and after the SARS outbreak. Table 11.3 sets out the details of the six components.

On the whole, before the SARS outbreak, people had reasonably good feelings about their relationship with the government, with the highest score from commitment (mean 4.65), followed by communal relationship (mean 4.48), and satisfaction (mean 4.45). In other words, in the pre-SARS period, people thought that both government and people had been trying to commit to each other.

On the other hand, after the SARS outbreak, we can see a worsening trend for all the relationship components, except the communal relationships (with no change). In particular, the mean of satisfaction before and after the SARS outbreak declined sharply (a 0.5 decrease). The big fall in satisfaction after SARS needs examining here. Most respondents found that they became less

Table 11.4 Frequencies on the change of organization–stakeholder relationship before and after the SARS outbreak

What is your feeling toward your relationship with the government in the post-crisis period as compared with the pre-crisis period?	*Frequency*	*%*
Much worse	32	13.3
Worse	32	13.3
Slightly worse	60	25.0
No change	48	20.0
Slightly improved	36	15.0
Improved	24	10.0
Strongly improved	4	1.7
Missing/Refuse to answer/Don't know	4	1.7
Total	240	100.0
Mean	*3.47*	

Table 11.5 People's perception of the appropriateness of the government's response
strategies to SARS

Overall, government response to SARS was appropriate	Frequency	%
Strongly disagree	4	1.7
Disagree	44	18.3
Slightly disagree	48	20.0
Neutral	76	31.7
Slightly agree	20	8.3
Agree	40	16.7
Strongly agree	8	3.3
Total	240	100.0
Mean	*3.90*	

happy with the government after SARS and did not enjoy dealing and interacting with the government. This might relate to the performance of the government during the SARS period. More than half of the respondents thought that the government was not open to communication with the people and that the government refused to listen to advice (detailed findings can be found in Tables 11.6 and 11.7).

Control mutuality, with the lowest score (mean 3.77 in the post-SARS period), is another relationship component we have to pay attention to. Control mutuality means that both the government and the community agree on the distribution of power in their relationship. It is established in several ways; one aspect, for example, is mutual satisfaction about the decision-making process. After SARS, people found that control was not well balanced. This might be a result of the government's performance during the SARS period. For instance, seeing more and more healthcare staff and members of the public getting infected in mid-March 2003, people urged the authorities to close the schools. Arthur Li Kwok Cheung, the Secretary for Education and Manpower, still insisted that closing all schools would not reduce the risk of contracting the virus, despite parents' anxieties over student-to-student transmission.

The falling trend of the organization–stakeholder relationship is also verified with the question we asked, "What is your feeling about your relationship with government in the post-crisis period as compared with the pre-crisis period?" Table 11.4 shows how people think about their relationship with the government in the post-SARS period, compared with the pre-SARS period.

About 25% (i.e., 60) of the respondents thought that their relationship with the government had slightly worsened after the SARS outbreak. In total, over 50% of the participants thought that their relationship with the government had worsened. On the other hand, nearly 27% of the participants found that their relationship with the government was better after SARS. This result concurs with the previous finding on the worsening relationships after SARS.

Table 11.6 Participants' perceptions of the government's accommodative strategies during SARS

Statement	Our government assumed full responsibility in handling SARS		Our government tried its best to find every possible solution		Our government was open to communicate with the public		Our government apologized when it had done something inappropriate		Our government tried to release all the information about SARS to the public	
Opinion	Frequency	%	Frequency	%	Frequency	%	Frequency	%	Frequency	%
Strongly disagree	8	3.3	4	1.7	28	11.7	40	16.7	8	3.3
Disagree	20	8.3	28	11.7	60	25.0	44	18.3	24	10.0
Slightly disagree	40	16.7	12	5.0	52	21.7	32	13.3	12	5.0
Neutral	32	13.3	52	21.7	48	20.0	60	25.0	52	21.7
Slightly agree	60	25.0	48	20.0	36	15.0	36	15.0	40	16.7
Agree	72	30.0	80	33.3	16	6.7	28	11.7	96	40.0
Strongly agree	8	3.3	16	6.7	0	0	0	0	8	3.3
Total	240	100	240	100	240	100	240	100	240	100
Mean	4.52		3.22	3.38	4.72					

Table 11.7 Participants' perceptions of the government's defensive strategies during SARS

Do you agree with the measures taken in the SARS period ?	At the SARS outbreak, our government confronted others who claimed that SARS existed		In mid-March, our government insisted SARS had not broken out		Our government shifted its responsibility in handling SARS to others		Our government stated that the perceived damage associated with SARS might not be serious		At the initial stage of the outbreak, our government refused to listen to advice in dealing with SARS	
	Freq.	%	Freq.	%	Freq.	%	Freq.	%	Freq.	%
Strongly disagree	20	8.3	56	23.3	16	6.7	24	10.0	4	1.7
Disagree	60	25.0	56	23.3	48	20.0	92	38.3	72	30.0
Slightly disagree	40	16.7	16	6.7	44	18.3	48	20.0	44	18.3
Neutral	76	31.7	52	21.7	68	28.3	40	16.7	56	23.3
Slightly agree	16	6.7	28	11.7	16	6.7	12	5.0	20	8.3
Agree	20	8.3	16	6.7	20	8.3	16	6.7	24	10.0
Strongly agree	8	3.3	12	5.0	28	11.7	8	3.3	20	8.3
Missing/Refuse to answer/Don't know	0	0	4	1.7	0	0	0	0	0	0
Total	240	100	240	100	240	100	240	100	240	100
Mean	3.42		3.15		3.80		3.02		3.70	
Sum	820		744		912		724		888	

3.2. Findings on the Government's Choice of Strategy: Accommodative and Defensive Strategies

In the first half of 2003, the Hong Kong Government took various measures to cope with the epidemic. Some of these were accommodative (such as taking corrective actions); other measures were defensive (such as denying the SARS outbreak). Overall, about 40% of the participants did not agree that "the government's response to SARS was appropriate," while about 28% thought the response strategies were appropriate. Table 11.5 sets out the findings of this topic.

3.3. Findings on the Accommodative Strategies

Respondents were asked how far they agreed with these statements, which describe the government's actions during the SARS crisis in 2003. Relevant issues are, for example, taking full responsibility in handling SARS; paying greatest efforts in handling SARS; readiness to communicate with the public; apologizing for doing something inappropriate; releasing information on SARS to the public. Table 11.6 summarizes the results.

We can conclude that people thought that the government had used some accommodative strategies during the SARS period. Other than these measures, people did not think that the government was open to communication or apologized satisfactorily when they did something inappropriate.

3.4. Findings on the Defensive Strategies

The HK government also took defensive measures during the SARS period. Table 11.7 shows the results. These reflect that most people did not agree with the government's defensive strategies during the SARS outbreak. Probably because of the "miss-use" of the government's crisis response strategies, the relationship between the government and the general population has worsened.

Table 11.8 Participants' perceptions of the government's crisis responsibility

Our government should be solely responsible for the SARS outbreak	Frequency	%
Strongly disagree	8	3.3
Disagree	16	6.7
Slightly disagree	40	16.7
Neutral	36	15.0
Slightly agree	48	20.0
Agree	48	20.0
Strongly agree	44	18.3
Total	240	100.0
Mean	4.75	

3.5. Findings on the Crisis Responsibility

Table 11.8 describes participants' perception of the government's responsibilities for SARS. Fifty-eight percent of the participants considered that the government should be responsible for the SARS outbreak.

4. Examination of Research Questions and Tests of Hypotheses

4.1. Research Question 1

What is the relation between the stakeholders' perception of their relationship with the government at the pre-crisis stage and crisis responsibility?

H1a and H1b were developed to explore RQ1. Correlation coefficients were used to examine the correlations between the pre-SARS relationship and crisis responsibility. Apart from running the correlation coefficients between the overall relationship (before SARS) and crisis responsibility, we also took a more detailed look at whether or not there are any different effects from the six individual relationship indicators (i.e., control mutuality, trust, commitment, satisfaction, exchange relationships, and communal relationships) on crisis responsibility. The correlation table is presented in Table 11.9.

Not all the correlations are significant in our study; only those with the probability level equal to or lower than 0.05 are significant. With small correlation coefficients (which are closer to the absolute value of 0) of the relationship variable (including its six components) and the crisis responsibility variable, their correlations are not strong or with no correlations.

All six relationship components are negatively related to crisis responsibility. For instance, the correlation coefficient between trust (pre-SARS period) and crisis responsibility is −0.286, which means that the higher the trust, the weaker the crisis responsibility people perceive.

However, the overall pre-SARS relationship is positively related to crisis responsibility. Since the significant level is greater than 0.05, the results are likely due to chance. What we can say here is that the correlation coefficient (0.078) is insignificant (as the significance level is great than 0.05); this is shown in Table 11.9. The findings here cannot provide a "true" picture of the correlation between these two variables. One of the reasons may be that when asking the respondents whether they thought the government should be solely responsible for the crisis, most of them agreed. Their answers may be a combination of many reasons, apart from relationship, such as the government's response strategies. The results cannot therefore reflect the impact of other factors.

To counter-check the results generated from the correlation coefficient, we also asked the participants whether their relationship with the government

Table 11.9 Correlations between relationship variable (including its six relationship components) and crisis responsibility variable

Variable	2	3	4	5	6	7	8
My relationship with the government is good overall (before SARS)	0.369** 240	0.386** 240	0.531** 240	0.481** 240	-0.264** 240	0.149* 240	0.078 240
Control mutuality (before SARS)		0.706** 240	0.505** 240	0.580** 240	-0.236** 240	0.200** 240	-0.249** 240
Trust (before SARS)			0.600** 240	0.635** 240	-0.267** 240	0.272** 240	-0.286** 240
Commitment (before SARS)				0.731** 240	-0.278** 240	0.128* 240	-0.137* 240
Satisfaction (before SARS)					-0.295** 240	0.174** 240	-0.165* 240
Exchange relationships (before SARS)						0.199** 240	-0.125 240
Communal relationships (before SARS)							-0.030 240
Our government should be solely responsible for the SARS outbreak							

Note: * Correlation is significant at the 0.05 level (2-tailed). ** Correlation is significant at the 0.01 level (2-tailed).

before the outbreak of SARS affected their perception of the government's responsibility to SARS. Table 11.10 shows that about 36.7% of the respondents did not think that their relationship with the government before SARS would have any impact on their perception of crisis responsibility. At the same time, however, around 10% thought that their pre-SARS relationship with the government would affect their perception of crisis responsibility to a very large extent. Specifically, more than 40% of the respondents thought that their relationship with the government (before SARS) would affect their perception of crisis responsibility.

Tables 11.11 and 11.12 show the results of whether there are any differences in the perception of crisis responsibility between those with a positive relationship with the government (before SARS) and those with a negative relationship. We cannot draw any solid conclusion from Tables 11.11 and 11.12, since the significance level in both tables is greater than 0.05. Findings show that there is no correlation between the organization–stakeholder relationship (before SARS) and crisis responsibility. Thus, Hypothesis 1 is rejected.

Attribution theory posits that during a crisis people search for causes of events in a variety of domains and that crisis responsibility is the focal causal attribution. A relationship, developed between an organization and stakeholders, is assumed to be one of the crucial factors affecting the stakeholders' perception of crisis responsibility in times of crisis because relationships are considered to be vital to the survival of an organization (J. Grunig & Hung, 2000; Chen & Hung, 2002; Hon & J. Grunig, 1999). As a result, it is natural to assume that the pre-crisis relationship is closely connected to crisis responsibility during an emergency.

Consistent with the previous research by Coombs and Holladay (2001), the correlation between the pre-crisis relationship and crisis responsibility is weak. Coombs and Holladay (2001) found that people in a favorable relationship will not necessarily attribute less crisis responsibility to the organization. On the other hand, they found that people in an unfavorable relationship will attribute more crisis responsibility to the organization than those with a favorable or a neutral relationship (Coombs & Holladay, 2001). We therefore conclude that pre-crisis relationships are not strong predictors of crisis responsibility.

Although weak in correlation, we can interpret the findings from the following perspective. The SARS incident broke out suddenly and spread quickly in the early 2003. However, most people blamed the government for its sluggish, indecisive, and inappropriate measures. Most of the attention focused on the government's measures rather than the relationship with government in the pre-SARS period. Thus, relationship may not be the first and the foremost, or most powerful, factor in accounting for the crisis responsibility in this case. Instead, government response strategies might become a more powerful or significant factor in affecting stakeholders' perception of crisis responsibility.

Table 11.10 Frequency of participants' perception of the influence of the relationship with the government to the perception of the government's responsibility for SARS

How far do you think your relationship with the government before the outbreak of SARS will affect your perception of the government's responsibility for SARS?	Frequency	%
To a very large extent	24	10.0
To a large extent	32	13.3
To a slight extent	44	18.3
No impact	88	36.7
To a slightly small extent	28	11.7
To a small extent	20	8.3
To a very small extent	0	0.0
Missing/Refuse to answer/Don't know	4	1.7
Total	240	100.0
Mean	3.53	

Table 11.11 Correlation between positive relationship (before SARS) and crisis responsibility

Variable	2
1. Relationship before SARS (positive)	−0.056
	104
2. Our government should be solely responsible for the SARS outbreak	

Table 11.12 Correlation between negative relationship (before SARS) and crisis responsibility

Variable	2
1. Our government should be solely responsible for the SARS outbreak	−0.031
	56
2. Relationship before SARS (negative)	

4.2. Research Question 2

What is the relationship between crisis responsibility and the choice of crisis-response strategies?

RQ2 addresses the correlation between crisis responsibility and the choice of crisis-response strategies. Two hypotheses were developed and tested by using correlation coefficients. Before analyzing the correlation coefficient, it should be stressed that not everybody agreed with the defensive strategies taken by the government. This led us to divide the defensive strategies into two groups— the strategies that people agreed with and those that people rejected. The reason for this two-way division is that defensive strategies are not necessarily "un-welcome," and we can get a clearer picture of how these two groups of people perceive crisis responsibilities. The results are shown in Table 11.13.

The correlation between disagreement with defensive strategies and crisis responsibility is negatively related (–0.242). In other words, the stronger that people felt about the government's crisis responsibility, the more they disagreed with the defensive strategies. This confirms our hypothesis that defensive strat-egies are not effective when public perception of the government's responsi-bility with regard to the crisis is strong.

For Hypothesis 2b, Tables 11.14 and 11.15 show the correlation of accom-modative strategies and crisis responsibility. Again, we divided the accommo-dative strategies into two groups—those that people believed and those that they did not believe the government had taken.

In Table 11.15, the correlation coefficient is –0.623 (which is significant with a significance level less than 0.05). The correlation is strong and these two variables are negatively related. This means that the accommodative strategies are effective when the crisis responsibility is weak, which partially supports Hypothesis 2b.

Some support is found for Hypothesis 2b that "accommodative strategies are more effective when crisis responsibility is strong" while no support is found for Hypothesis 2a, "defensive strategies are more effective when crisis responsibility is weak" (results are shown in Tables 11.14 and 11.15). Instead, for Hypothesis 2a we can conclude only that defensive strategies are ineffective when crisis responsibility is strong.

In fact, it is not difficult to assume that defensive strategies are ineffective, especially in relation to the Hong Kong Government, which people consider as a weak one. Instead, for a weak organization, accommodative strategies would be more effective or appropriate. It is no surprise, then, that no correla-tions are found between crisis responsibility and the choice of crisis-response

Table 11.13 Correlation coefficient between defensive strategies and crisis responsibility

Variable	2	3
1. Defensive strategies (disagree with these strategies)	.(a) 16	–0.242(**) 192
2. Defensive strategies (agree with these strategies)		0.147 60
3. Our government should be solely responsible for SARS outbreak		

** Correlation is significant at the 0.01 level (2-tailed).
(a) Cannot be computed because at least one of the variables is constant.

Table 11.14 Correlation coefficient between accommodative strategies that people believe that the government had implemented and crisis responsibility

Variable	2
1. Accommodative strategies (people believe that the government had implemented these strategies)	−0.116 120
2. Our government should be solely responsible for the SARS outbreak	

strategies. From this, we cannot conclude that crisis responsibility is a very powerful determinant for the choice of crisis-response strategies. There may be other factors that have a greater impact on the choice of crisis-response strategies; further investigation into these factors should be made in later studies.

This study also suffers from the limitation that only the policy-receivers (i.e., the general population) were interviewed. Since the response strategies were made and implemented by the Hong Kong Government, we should also have interviewed those who make decisions on the choice of response strategies, such as government officials.

4.3. Research Question 3

How does the stakeholders' perception of the relationship with the government before the crisis and crisis responsibility affect the choice of crisis-response strategies?

RQ3 examines the impact of stakeholders' perception of their relationship with the government before the SARS crisis and crisis responsibility for the choice of crisis-response strategies. Linear regression was used to examine the correlations among the various variables (including the relationship before and after SARS, crisis responsibility and crisis-response strategies). Tables 11.16a through 11.16c show the results.

Table 11.15 Correlation coefficient between accommodative strategies that people do not believe the government had implemented and crisis responsibility

Variable	2
1. Our government should be solely responsible for the SARS outbreak	−0.623** 36
2. Accommodative strategies (people do not believe that the government had implemented these strategies)	

** Correlation is significant at the 0.01 level (2-tailed).

In Table 11.16a, the R square is 0.004, which indicates that only 0.4 of the variance in the dependent variable is explained by the independent variable in the model. Table 11.16c also shows that the two independent variables (the relationship with the government before SARS and crisis responsibility) is not related to the dependent variable of crisis-response strategies, with coefficients of 0.034 and –0.057, respectively. In other words, both the relationship variable and the crisis-responsibility variable have no impact on the choice of response strategies. Thus, Hypothesis 3 is not supported.

4.4. Research Question 4

How does the stakeholders' perception of their relationship with the government before the crisis, crisis responsibility, and crisis-response strategies affect their relationship after the crisis?

RQ4 focuses on the impact of stakeholders' perceptions of their relationship with the government in the pre-SARS period, crisis responsibility, and the effects of crisis-response strategies on the post-SARS organization–stakeholder relationship. H4 was developed to explore this research question. Tables 11.17a through 11.17c show the coefficients of (a) the relationships with the government before SARS; (b) the government's ability in handling the SARS emergency; (c) the government's response strategies; and (d) stakeholders' perception of crisis responsibility and of their relationship with the government after SARS.

The R Square (0.264) in Table 11.17a indicates that 26.4% of the variance in the dependent variable is explained by the independent variable in the model. From Table 11.17c, we find that the relationship with government before SARS gets the highest coefficient (standardized coefficient 0.379) among other independent variables, which means that the relationship before SARS has a stronger correlation with relationships after SARS as compared with other variables of crisis responsibility, response strategies, and the government's ability. This result cannot therefore fully support H4, since not all these independent variables are of equal variance in explaining their effects on the post-SARS organization–stakeholder relationship.

5. Conclusions

Figure 11.2 illustrates the correlations among the variables tested in this study.

5.1. Correlation between Pre-Crisis Relationship and Crisis Responsibility (H1a and H1b)

As discussed in the previous section, pre-crisis organization–stakeholder relationships may not be strong predictors of the crisis responsibility and the correlations between them are very weak. This can be explained with the

Table 11.16a Model summary (dependent variable: crisis-response strategies)

Model summary	R	R square	Adjusted R square	Std. error of the estimate
1	0.064(a)	0.004	−0.004	1.612

(a) Predictors (constant): Our government should be solely responsible for the SARS outbreak. My relationship with the government is good overall (before SARS).

Table 11.16b ANOVA (dependent variable: crisis-response strategies)

ANOVA (b)		Sum of squares	df	Mean square	F	Sig.
1	Regression	2.518	2	1.259	0.485	0.617(a)
	Residual	615.815	237	2.598		
	Total	618.333	239			

(a) Predictors (constant): Our government should be solely responsible for the SARS outbreak. My relationship with the government is good overall (before SARS).
(b) Dependent variable: Our government took appropriate measures.

Table 11.16c Linear regression coefficients (dependent variable: crisis-response strategies)

Coefficients (a)	Unstandardized coefficients		Standardized coefficients	t	Sig.
	B	Std. Error	Beta		
1 (Constant)	4.186	0.415		10.083	0.000
My relationship with the government is good (before SARS)	0.036	0.068	0.034	0.522	0.602
Our government should be solely responsible for the SARS outbreak	−0.054	0.062	−0.057	−0.873	0.384

(a) Dependent variable: Our government took appropriate measures.

Table 11.17a Model summary (dependent variable: relationship with the government in the post-SARS period)

Model summary	R	R Square	Adjusted R Square	Std. error of the estimate
1	0.514(a)	0.264	0.251	1.420

(a) Predictors (constant): Our government should be solely responsible for the SARS outbreak. My relationship with the government is good (before SARS). Generally, the government's response to SARS was appropriate. Our government was competent in dealing with SARS.

Table 11.17b ANOVA (dependent variable: relationship with the government in the post-SARS period)

ANOVA (b)	Sum of squares	df	Mean square	F	Sig.
1 Regression	169.804	4	42.451	21.064	.000(a)
Residual	473.596	235	2.015		
Total	643.400	239			

(a) Predictors (constant): Our government should be solely responsible for the SARS outbreak. My relationship with the government is good (before SARS). Generally, the government's response to SARS was appropriate. Our government was competent in dealing with SARS.
(b) Dependent variable: My relationship with the government is good (after SARS).

Table 11.17c Linear regression coefficients (dependent variable: relationship with the government in the post-SARS period)

Coefficients (a)	Unstandardized coefficients		Standardized coefficients	t	Sig.
	B	Std. error	Beta		
1 (Constant)	1.088	0.477		2.279	0.024
My relationship with the government is good (before SARS)	0.407	0.061	0.379	6.656	0.000
Our government was competent in dealing with SARS	0.144	0.073	0.140	1.973	0.05
Generally, the government's response to SARS was appropriate	0.174	0.079	0.155	2.215	0.028
Our government should be solely responsible for the SARS outbreak	−0.122	0.058	−0.125	−2.119	0.035

(a) Dependent variable: My relationship with the government is good overall (after SARS).

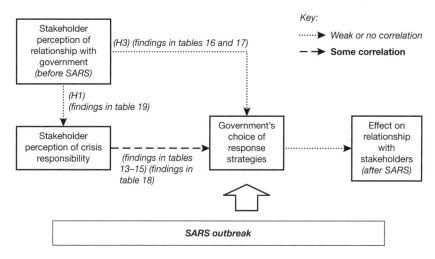

Figure 11.2 Correlations among the three variables in this study

attribution theory. According to this theory, people tend to seek causes for an event or crisis, and certain conditions may help prompt the search for certain causes. With regard to the SARS outbreak in Hong Kong in 2003, there were many causes leading to the rapid spread of the epidemic. To name just a few: (a) poor communication and insufficient information exchange between Hong Kong and China; (b) the government's slow response in controlling the spread of the epidemic at its outbreak; (c) lack of knowledge about SARS; and (d) the suddenness of the outbreak. All these were regarded as immediate causes, which sparked off or accelerated the spread of SARS. On the other hand, the pre-crisis organization–stakeholder relationship was seen as a "background" cause because relationships could not be built in one day. Because of the sudden outbreak of the crisis, people tended to blame the immediate causes of the outbreak, instead of looking at the background causes. This might be one of the reasons why pre-SARS relationships are not strong indicators of the crisis responsibility in the SARS epidemic.

5.2. Correlation Between Crisis Responsibility and Crisis-Response Strategies (H2a and H2b)

Hypotheses 2a and 2b are partially supported. Hypothesis 2a assumes that "defensive strategies are more effective when crisis responsibility is weak." Hypothesis 2b assumes that "accommodative strategies are more effective when the crisis responsibility is strong." Although these hypotheses are not confirmed, the results support the opposite—that is, defensive strategies are ineffective when the crisis responsibility is strong. It is generally believed that the Hong Kong Government is a weak one, so it is not difficult to imagine that defensive strategies would not be supported, no matter whether the crisis responsibility was strong or not. Therefore, for a weak organization, defensive strategies should not be used in times of crisis even though the crisis responsibility may be weak.

During the SARS epidemic, the Hong Kong Government made another mistake that might have undermined the effectiveness of its strategies, even though it used appropriate strategies to deal with the crisis itself. Many people blamed the government for its indecisive and slow action in handling SARS and its refusal to disclose essential information about the disease to the public at its outbreak. The choice of crisis-response strategies might be impacted by numerous factors other than stakeholders' perception of crisis responsibility, such as the power of the organization; this needs investigation in future studies.

5.3. Impact of Pre-Crisis Relationship and Crisis Responsibility on the Choice of Strategies (H3)

Hypothesis 3 cannot be supported from the findings because of sampling, which takes only the general population (i.e., the policy receivers) as the targets. However, crisis response strategies were made, selected, and implemented by government officials (i.e., the policy-makers). In order to explore the impact of the pre-crisis organization–stakeholder relationship on the choice of crisis-response strategies, it would be more appropriate to ask the policy-makers what affected their choice of strategies.

5.4. Impact of Pre-Crisis Relationship, Crisis Responsibility, and Crisis-Response Strategies on Post-Crisis Relationship (H4)

Hypothesis 4 cannot be supported. Findings show that the correlation among these variables is weak and none are strong predictors of the post-crisis relationship. There might be some other factors affecting the choice of response strategies and the relationship outcomes. The SARS incident which broke out in the first half of 2003 affected people from all walks of life. The epidemic killed 300 and infected 1,755 people in just three months. In response to the sudden, fast-spreading epidemic, which was difficult to fight, the Hong Kong Government took numerous measures to combat this disease. However, their success rate was poor, and the number of infections and deaths continued to rise rapidly. Many blamed the government for the quick spread. Specifically, the government's sluggish responses were targeted.

5.5. Limitations and Future Research

This study has the following limitations. The topic is quite sensitive to some participants who might be unwilling to disclose their true perceptions. For instance, some feel uncomfortable when asked about their relationship with the government and their perception of crisis responsibility. Another weakness is its restricted scope; it would have been more representative if opinions from the policy-makers could have been obtained; after all, this study aims at exploring how response strategies are selected.

This study provides some hints for future research. Additional testing is required to determine the effect of crisis responsibility and the choice of crisis-response strategies by including the opinions of policy-makers. Moreover, further research is needed to disclose the connection between various variables, such as the nature of the crisis, the power of the organization, the stakeholders' perception of crisis responsibility, the choice and use of crisis-response strategies, and the state of relationships after the crisis.

References

Allen, M. W., & Caillouet, R. H. (1994). Legitimate endeavors: Impression management strategies used by an organization in crisis. *Communication Monographs*, *61*, 44–62.

Benoit, W. L. (1992). *Union Carbide and the Bhopal tragedy*. Paper presented at the Annual Meeting of the Speech Communication Association, Chicago (November).

Benoit, W. L. (1995). *Accounts, excuses, and apologies: A theory of image restoration strategies*. Albany, NY: State University of New York Press.

Broom, G. M., Casey, S., & Richey, J. (2000). Concept and theory of organization-public relationship. In J. Ledingham & S. Brunig (Eds.), *Public relations as relationship management: A relational approach to the study and practice of public relations* (pp. 3–22). Mahwah, NJ: Lawrence Erlbaum Associates.

Brunner, G. (2000). *Measuring students' perceptions of the University of Florida's commitment to public relationships and diversity*. Unpublished doctoral dissertation, Gainesville, FL.

Chen, Y. R., & Hung, C. J. (2002). *Organizational behavior, stigma, and organization-public relationships*. Article submitted to the proceeding of the 10th BledCom Conference.

Coombs, W. T. (1998). An analytic framework for crisis situations: Better responses from a better understanding of the situation. *Journal of Public Relations Research*, *10*(3), 177–191.

Coombs, W. T. (1999a). Crisis management: Advantages of a relational respective. In J. A. Ledingham and S. D. Brunig (Eds.), *Public relations as relationship management: A relational approach to the study and practice of public relations* (pp. 73–94). Mahwah, NJ: Lawrence Erlbaum Associates.

Coombs, W. T. (1999b). *Ongoing crisis communication: Planning, managing, and responding*. London: Sage.

Coombs, W. T., & Holladay, S. J. (1996). Communication and attributions in a crisis: An experimental study in crisis communication. *Journal of Public Relations*, *8*(4), 279–295.

Coombs, W. T., & Holladay, S. J. (2001). An extended examination of the crisis situations: A fusion of the relational management and symbolic approaches. *Journal of Public Relations Research*, *13*(4), 321–340.

Grunig, J. E., & Hung, Y. H. (2000). From organizational effectiveness to relationship indicators: Antecedents of relationships, public relations strategies, and relationship outcomes. In J. A. Ledingham & S. D. Bruning (Eds.), *Public relations as relationship management: A relational approach to the study and practice of public relations* (pp. 23–54). Mahwah, NJ: Lawrence Erlbaum Associates.

Grunig, J. E., & Hung, C. J. (2002, March) *The effect of relationships on reputation and reputation on relationships: A cognitive, behavioral study.* Paper presented at the International Communication Association Conference, Miami, FL.

Grunig, J. E., & Grunig, L.A. (2002). A new definition and measure of reputation. *PR Reporter*, 16.

Grunig, L. A., Grunig, J. E., & Dozier, D. M. (2002). *Excellent public relations and effective organizations: A study of communication management in three countries.* Mahwah, NJ: Lawrence Erlbaum Associates.

Hearit, K. M. (1994). Apologies and public relations crises at Chrysler, Toshiba, and Volvo. *Public Relations Review, 20*(2), 113–125.

Hobbs, J. D. (1995). Treachery by any other name: A case study of the Toshiba public relations crisis. *Management Communication Quarterly, 8*, 323–346.

Hon, L. C., & Grunig, J. E. (1999). *Guidelines for measuring relationships in public relations.* Gainesville, FL: The Institute for Public Relations, Commission on PR Measurement and Evaluation.

Huang, C. J. F. (2002). *The interplays of relationship types, relationship cultivation, and relationship outcomes: How multinational and Taiwanese companies practice public relations and organization–public relationship management in China.* Unpublished doctoral dissertation, College Park, MD.

Huang, C. J. F. (2004). Cultural influence on relationship cultivation strategies: Multinational companies in China. *Journal of Communication Management, 8*(3), 264–281.

Huang, C. J. F. (2005). Exploring types of organization–public relationships and their implications on relationship management in public relations. *Journal of Public Relations Research, 17*(4), 393–426.

Ice, R. (1991). Corporate publics and rhetorical strategies: The case of Union Carbide's Bhopal crisis. *Management Communication Quarterly, 4*, 341–362.

Kim, Y. W. (2000). *How can we measure the organization–public relationships? Developing a valid and reliable instrument.* Paper presented at the Public Relations Society of America, World Congress, Chicago (October).

Ledingham, J. A., Bruning, S. D., & Wilson, L. J. (1999). Time as an indicator of the perceptions and behavior of members of a key public: Monitoring and prediction of organization–public relationships. *Journal of Public Relations Research, 11*, 167–183.

Lerbinger, O. (1997). *The crisis manager: Facing risk and responsibility.* Mahwah, NJ: Lawrence Erlbaum Associates.

Marcus, A. A., & Goodman, R. S. (1991). Victims and shareholders: The dilemmas of presenting corporate policy during a crisis. *Academy of Management Journal, 34*, 281–305.

Rowley, T. J. (1997). Moving beyond dyadic ties: A network theory of stakeholder influence. *Academy of Management Review, 22*(4), 887–910.

Weiner, B. (1985). An attribution theory of achievement motivation and emotion. *Psychology Review, 92*, 548–573.

Wong, P. T. P., & Weiner, B. (1981). When people ask "why" questions, and the heuristics of attributional search. *Journal of Personality and Social Psychology, 40*(4), 650–663.

12 The Case Study as an Evaluation Tool for Public Relations

Mafalda Eiró-Gomes and João Duarte

1. Introduction

According to Dozier and Repper (1992), evaluation is to be understood in the conceptual framework of public relations research. Different from the environmental scanning research, which helps in the problem-definition stage, evaluation research "is designed to determine how well public relations programs work" (Dozier & Repper, 1992: 186). Environmental scanning research would then be exploratory, adequate to allow early detection of emerging problems, and suited for qualitative research techniques. On the other hand, evaluation research would belong to a "highly structured field" with "experimental designs."

In many landmark texts in public relations theory, program evaluation has been positioned as the fourth stage of the PR process. However, evaluation has been growing complex in techniques and challenges, and has become some sort of "holy grail" that allows PR people to demonstrate their value and their work to top management, and, ultimately, even to legitimate the existence of and the need for public relations. This "results orientation," imposed by companies and clients in need of measurable results to present to the executive board, is mainly directed at showing the extent to which previously defined objectives are achieved. Even though many PR people still do not budget for research or see research as an integral part of the process, the fact is that evaluation is now becoming of pivotal importance to the majority of public relations practitioners.

2. Evaluation in Public Relations

2.1. Traditional Evaluation Areas

Traditionally, evaluation research has been understood as ". . . the systematic application of social research procedures for assessing the conceptualization, design, implementation and utility of social intervention programs" (Rossi & Freeman, quoted by Cutlip, Center, & Broom, 1994: 410). This approach configures the three main areas of evaluation: (a) program conceptualization and design; (b) program implementation; and (c) program impact and efficiency. During program preparation, the main preoccupation is to understand if the underlying theory of the program has been accurate. "Clearly evaluation of the preparation phase of the program includes a mix of subjective and objective assessments of (1) the adequacy of the background research, (2) the organization and content of program materials, and (3) the packaging and presentation of the program materials" (Cutlip *et al.*, 1994: 420).

The second traditional evaluation area is program implementation, that is, how well the program is implemented and communications are disseminated to target publics. This is essentially a quantitative evaluation, measuring how many messages were distributed, placed, how many people potentially received those messages, and how many of those belong to our intended audience and how many attended to the messages.

In the third evaluation area, program results are to be assessed by measuring the extent to which outcomes stated in the objectives of the program were achieved. These types of specific criteria for evaluation have traditionally included the number of people who learnt the message content, who changed their opinions, attitudes, and behavior. The ultimate criterion for evaluation is the extent to which all these changes contribute to a positive social and cultural change.

2.2. The Framework of Social Sciences Evaluation

We believe that public relations must also be understood in light of the social sciences, which is why we would like to suggest that the most important results of PR work may not be those that we usually assume but those that, in a certain sense, remain beyond our campaigns and our evaluation of their outcomes. However, these are not the kinds of changes that can be measured in the short term. As Dozier and Ehling put it more than a decade ago, "significant changes in the knowledge, attitudes and behaviours of publics are not likely to be achieved in the short term" (1992: 182). Of course, evaluation in the social sciences cannot produce the only explanation for the results and the changes produced—that is, searching for explanations we must not forget one of the most important concepts of the social sciences, namely, understanding.

As public relations professionals we should, then, reject simple explanations and deterministic accounts of phenomena, and that is why evaluation should go beyond summative research, i.e., beyond merely showing that program effects did or did not occur, and should include formative research. This formative kind of research allows practitioners to learn from their research, both to make corrections to their programs when they are running and to gather basic information for the next program cycle. This kind of approach is one that Cutlip *et al.* called the "Benchmark Model" (1994: 427), which we want to explore in this chapter. We believe that a good way to provide useful information for future program cycles is to create tools that allow us to document the whole strategic process, and not only the outputs, outtakes, or even outcomes.

3. The Case Study as an Evaluation Tool for Public Relations

In spite of their frequent association with teaching—as a way to create frameworks for discussions—case studies can and should be used in the professional practice for research purposes as well. We believe that the case study can be used as an evaluation tool for PR insofar as it allows the practitioner to get a good overview of the work accomplished and incorporate inputs for future campaigns. As it is acknowledged in many other social sciences, evaluation also means re-planning and planning for continuity, and case studies can help perform this kind of evaluation. The difference between case studies for teaching purposes and those for the professional practice lies in the degree of accuracy in the presentation of the data collected.

3.1. Basic Principles

A case study is basically an empirical study that researches phenomena in their real-life context in order to get a better understanding of those phenomena at their various levels of analysis. In fact, it may be said that the purpose of doing case studies is to analyze processes and their results, emphasizing the dynamic nature of the phenomena. "The essence of a case study, the central tendency among all types of case study, is that it tries to illuminate a decision or set of decisions: why they were taken, how they were implemented, and with what result" (Schramm, quoted by Yin, 1994: 12).

There is no consensus on a possible case studies' categorization. Maybe two of the best known categorizations are those referred to by Yin (1994) and Tellis (1997). Yin (1994) mentions exploratory, explanatory, and descriptive case studies. Exploratory case studies are normally considered to be the prelude of bigger social research projects, while explanatory case studies may be used for causal investigations. Descriptive case studies, on the other hand, require the development of a theory or basic framework prior to the description itself. Tellis (1997) prefers to talk about intrinsic, instrumental, and collective case studies. Intrinsic case studies are those where the researcher has an interest in the case; instrumental case studies are those in which the case is used to understand more than what is obvious to the observer; and the term "collective" is used when a group of cases is studied. In short, the case study's importance derives from its strategic dimension by helping to better understand the decision-making processes. The selective nature of the case studies allows the researcher to identify one or two issues that are fundamental for the understanding of the system being examined.

3.2. Information Sources

Case studies use different information sources, which corroborate impressions and allow the confirmation of insights and hypotheses. Among the most widely used sources are documentation, archival records, interviews, direct observations, and participant observation. Documentation includes all kinds of letters, memos, proposals, reports, previous studies or evaluations, newspaper clippings, clippings of articles published in internal or external communication outlets, etc. More than literal recordings of events, documents are analyzed as complementary to other sources of information. Nevertheless, we must acknowledge some difficulties with access to documentation (it may be unavailable), especially if there are agencies' or clients' documents involved. Archival records include all forms of secondary data, such as service records, organizational records, data collected in previous surveys, or personal records. This kind of source can be difficult to access when the case study is prepared by an external agency, or even when PR professionals need to access the records of other departments. Interviews, on the other hand, are useful to corroborate certain views; they are especially useful when they make use of good inquiry techniques and when their inputs are adequately synthesized. Direct observation can be used in case studies that are not about purely historical phenomena. This is the kind of input that agencies may have difficulty in collecting, especially if they do not spend time with clients in their own organizational setting. If they do manage to collect such data, then the discussion with the client (as another different observer) is very interesting and can be of great value.

While all the aforementioned sources of information are suited for a passive investigator—one without the capability to control events—the participant-observation source entails that observers may actually assume a variety of roles and participate in the events being studied. The ability of PR staff to accede events or groups, to perceive reality from "inside" the case study, and to control minor events, is a great help when evaluating public relations campaigns. Nevertheless, the kind of information obtained from participant observation must be filtered because the staff member has less ability to work as an external observer (being more "participant" than "observer") and may have to assume advocacy roles, thus becoming a supporter of the organization being studied.

3.3. Uses, Advantages, and Weaknesses of Case Studies

The case study is a powerful tool to apply in a context of strong learning potential or in situations that configure uncommon challenges and demand new approaches from PR practitioners. However, in order to be effective as an evaluation tool, the case study should not be confused with other evaluation tools. PR professionals must continue to assess program preparation, program implementation, and program impact; they can improve those evaluations with the case-study approach.

In fact, the case-study approach is stimulating and interesting for several reasons. First, investing in a case-study database of the most important PR strategies can provide quick, effective, and low-cost training for PR professionals entering the organization. Second, keeping a record of case studies can also show that the work of the PR people is based on sound theoretical principles, instead of common sense insights or ad-hoc problem-solving techniques. Third, from an ethical point of view the case-study approach is interesting in that it emphasizes more than just the results produced, thus allowing a panoramic and dynamic view of all the strategic management processes and decisions. Finally, the data collected for a case study may well lead to specific benchmark indexes that can be used to gauge the outputs and outcomes of PR campaigns.

On the down side, one of the drawbacks of case studies is that data collection, analysis, and reporting are time-consuming. For this reason, they are frequently neglected as a tool in a campaign's evaluation. Another problem with case studies, especially the ones conducted by agencies for their clients, is that they require the researcher to spend some time in the organizational environment, perceiving processes and collecting important data, which may add an important cost to the service. From a theoretical point of view, it has also been pointed out that case studies have some weaknesses, especially in their capability to produce data suited for generalization.

However, we can say that case studies are useful to gain an understanding of situations and for the production of guiding principles for future action, not necessarily for predicting or anticipating future events. Case studies are, then, an interesting way to illustrate examples of PR in action and may serve as schematic models for students, linking theory with practice.

4. A Case Study

The remainder of this chapter is dedicated to exploring a possible case-study methodology applied to a real situation. Our description follows the four traditional steps of the PR process and looks for specific results for each of the strategic publics considered as interlocutors in the campaign. The case study's application requires sound background knowledge of the organization, its strategy, and the business itself, but also a thorough understanding of the situation and of the publics involved.

4.1. The Context

This case is about a PR campaign to support the launch of the first mortgage financial product for non-EU citizens in Portugal. This campaign was put up by a financial institution, specialized in providing mortgages through real-estate agents. This campaign interested us because it overcame the traditional marketing communications approach and focused on mobilizing key participants. If we take into account that this campaign was implemented by the PR department of a financial company, used to much more instrumental campaigns, we find a relevant shift in the PR approach, one that we consider as one of the possible criteria for the application of case studies.

The Company

The financial company studied is part of an international group founded by a joint venture between two of Europe's biggest and most important financial groups. The business began in France in the 1950s and makes financial mortgage products available in real-estate agents' offices. The focal company was implemented in Spain and arrived in Portugal in 1999, becoming the only financial entity specializing in mortgage solutions exclusively available through real-estate agents. As a specialist, the corporate mission is: *To provide leading mortgage solutions and a premium service that helps our partners to boost their business, and that allows our clients to fulfil their life projects.*

Although it is a financial institution, this company is not a bank, as it does not deal with savings accounts or any other financial products apart from mortgages. The company strives to be: "the best specialist mortgage provider of the market"; "the privileged partner of the real-estate agents when it comes to recommending a financial institution to their clients"; "an innovative player in the market, introducing new financial services to address growing market needs"; and "a dynamic and attractive company to our employees."

As it is virtually a business-to-business player, this company's strategy is not wide in scope, but aimed at a niche: the distribution channel of real-estate agents. It focuses on the introduction of innovative products aimed at market niches with a strong communication potential.

The Mortgage Market in Portugal

Using Michael Porter's five-competitive-strengths model, we can try to give a portrait of the industry in which our company operates. Among its main competitors we find all the national banks, which outrank the company in size, market share, number of clients, and communication investment. Rivalry among competitors in the market is high, and although the company had introduced some products that other banks had to copy, it had not been considered as a serious competitor by the major players due to its small size and reduced market share (about 4%). There are not many possibilities for new entrants in the market due to legislative constraints and to the mergers-and-acquisitions strategies of major banks. However, recent players such as GE Money (part of General Electric group) or Primus Bank (part of Credit Foncier group) have appeared in the market with a niche positioning and with specific products aimed at high-risk clients.

In this industry the real alternative to the mortgage credit market is a competitive house rental market, which in Portugal is quite underdeveloped. So the pressure of alternative products is not very high and the negotiating power of suppliers is not significant as a competitive force. However, if it is true that suppliers (house valuation companies, for example) do not have much bargaining power in this industry—as they are mostly working exclusively with one or other bank, thus not being independent—the power of real-estate agents as prescribers is underlined by the fact that they have the means to recommend products from several financial institutions.

Among the main driving forces of the market is product innovation: this is the best resource for any of the competitors to gain competitive advantage. Closely associated with this driving force is the marketing innovation as a way to improve the presence in the real-estate agent's office and to become more visible to the potential clients.

The Business Opportunity

Following a legislation change that clarified the legal situation of immigrants from non-EU countries in Portugal, and with the information gathered by the company's commercial network, the company started to analyze the possibility of creating a new financial product aimed at immigrants. After checking the legal background and the procedures needed in order to assure a risk policy for this type of client, it was decided that the launch of the product would be given serious consideration. As the financial studies began, the company also began the communication and preparation of the public relations strategy.

The PR Opportunity

The situation could have been considered a classic case of marketing communication. The launch of a new and innovative financial product, which had not any parallel in Portugal, was attractive enough for a company willing to obtain public recognition as the only specialist in mortgage solutions. But the PR people, in their environmental scanning activity, found a new set of opportunities. Immigrant issues were widely covered in the media, especially those issues related with housing problems. A national conference had been promoted by supporters of immigrant issues, newspapers and magazines had front-page reports about the issue, TV and radio programs interviewed immigrants and spoke about housing problems, and so it was considered that this campaign should also highlight the company's social responsibility by introducing this new financial solution that would reduce social inequalities. But this social responsibility demanded that the PR department engage in community-relations activities and do a comprehensive media relations campaign in order to obtain product recognition and get the endorsement of immigrant communities. So the PR opportunity was stated as the need to benefit from the creation of the first mortgage product aimed at non-EU citizens in order to reinforce the company's specialist positioning, and to cooperate with the various publics in order to emphasize the business opportunity and the social responsibility of the company in launching the new product.

4.2. Research and Environmental Scanning

The research objectives were aimed at understanding the main immigrant communities and environments from which potential customers could be sourced, and from which potentially active and engaged publics could emerge. This was done in two different ways. First, by studying pilot financial operations already done by the company with immigrants and, second, by studying how these communities had settled in the country. With this research it was also possible to identify key publics and to understand how to deal with them.

The financial transactions already made with immigrants revealed a consistent growth between 2002 and 2004. The growth was noted in almost all of the geographical areas. In some areas these financial operations grew from 3% to 14%. When trying to learn which immigrant communities were the most representative, it was shown that Portuguese-speaking African countries led the way, followed by Brazilians. Nevertheless, Eastern Europeans represented the biggest growth since 2003, even overtaking EU citizens. In terms of countries, Brazil was the best represented, followed by Cape Verde, Angola, the Ukraine, Guinea Bissau, the United Kingdom, Spain, Mozambique, São Tomé and Príncipe, and Bulgaria.

This diversity was consistent with the situation in the country. Since the 1970s, mainly due to its past colonies, Portugal has received many flows of emigrants from Portuguese-speaking colonies such as Cape Verde, Angola, Mozambique, Guinea Bissau, and São Tomé and Príncipe. More recently, from the 1980s, the Brazilian community and the Eastern European countries (the Ukraine, Russia, and Romania) have provided the biggest flows of migration to Portugal. The Chinese community has also been growing, but still only reaching residual levels. The total number of immigrants in Portugal doubled between 1980 and 1990, when it surpassed the 100,000 mark. Some eleven years after, when the 2001 census was produced, that number was already above 300,000 and, in 2003, the estimated number of immigrants was almost 500,000 (for comparison, Portugal has 11 million inhabitants). If we take into account those having a legal resident status in Portugal (excluding all those who have permanency authorization or temporary visas and, of course, the illegal immigrants), in 2003 there were some 250,000 foreign citizens in Portugal (about 4.5% more than in the previous year). Table 12.1 sets out the main foreign communities in Portugal and highlights the fact that five of those ten communities are from Portuguese-speaking countries.

As to the geographical distribution of these immigrant communities, they are mostly concentrated near the main urban centers and extend from the south to the north coast (see Figure 12.1). More than half of the total foreign residents in Portugal are based around Lisbon (in the Lisbon and Setúbal districts) as well as in the Algarve.

The point, then, for the PR research was: how do these communities organize themselves and how are they capable of acting collectively? As happens in many other immigrant-receiving countries, these groups are special because they are strongly connected and have many communicative links between them. Whether we refer to a daily newspaper edited in their own language, to specific TV channels and programs, to websites, blogs, and other on-line platforms, or to simple physical and regular encounters in specific public places, these

Table 12.1 The ten largest foreign communities in Portugal

Country of origin	%
Cape Verde	21.5
Brazil	10.6
Angola	10.2
Guinea Bissau	8.1
UK	6.7
Spain	6.1
Germany	5.0
France	3.5
USA	3.2
São Tomé and Príncipe	2.9

Source: National Statistics Institute (INE).

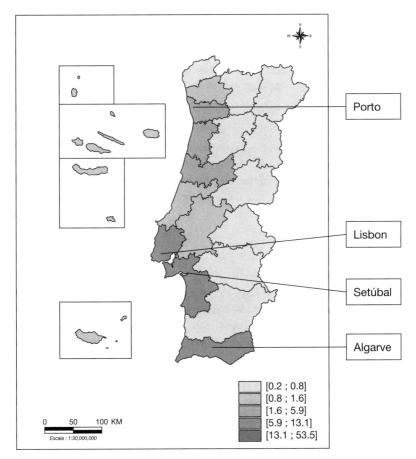

Figure 12.1 Geographical distribution of immigrant communities in Portugal

Source: National Statistics Institute (INE).

communities clearly constitute their own public spheres and become publics, whether organizations acknowledge them or not. In Portugal's case, these communicative communities (especially Brazilians and Africans, which comprise more than 50% of the total number of immigrants) share the same language, and that was clearly identified as an important opportunity for the PR campaign. Due to budget constraints, and to the experimental character of the situation, it was decided not to translate any of the communication outlets into other languages but to communicate entirely in Portuguese. The collection of all this information allowed the PR people to clarify the context in which the publics could be understood.

4.3. The Publics

In this PR strategy, publics were understood not as what we may designate as an organization-centred construct, but as communicative communities with their own interests, already participants in immigration issues, and with their own agenda. The company positioned itself as another participant in these issues; it proposed something new and valuable, and intended to "communicate/ cooperate with" publics rather than to "speak to" them. The strategic map of the publics that the PR campaign approached included the following.

Real-Estate Agents

They were the most interested party in the marketing communication as well as in the product itself, which allowed them to sell more houses and make more money. As prescribers of the mortgage, they were given special attention and received many direct communication inputs, consistently reinforced by regular visits of commercial agents.

The Company's Commercial Agents

They are full-time employees specializing in mortgages who deal closely with a number of real-estate agents. They are responsible for collecting the mortgage applications, preparing the processes, and submitting them to the national headquarters for risk analysis and approval. They were the first to know about the product and the main information source for the real-estate agents. They were also the points of contact with potential clients and members of other institutional publics.

Public Entities Related with Immigration

Research showed that one of the most active publics in these issues were the official agencies. The High Commission for Ethnic Minorities and Immigration (a governmental institution) was one of the potentially interested interlocutors in the field, as well as its Immigration Observatory. Besides being present in the field with several immigrant support centers across the country, both had important and powerful communication tools for reaching citizens. To avoid any kind of conflict and deal with potential problems of attracting illegal immigrants, the Foreigners and Frontiers Services departments were also informed.

NGOs

NGOs like the International Migrations Organization, the Portuguese Association for the Citizens Rights, the Jesuit Centre for Refugees, and other mixed-motive NGOs supporting immigrants in legal, economical, cultural, or religious aspects of their lives were considered as interested parties and potential information disseminators.

Embassies and Consulates

The identification of the most important immigrant communities led to the inclusion of the embassies and consulates of the countries mentioned as privileged publics to be kept informed; they were also asked to provide any further information if required.

Immigrant Associations

A set of officially recognized immigrant associations was also taken into account. As these associations have great potential to disseminate information and to start opinion-leading movements, representatives of these organizations were identified and considered for PR purposes. As the researchers were to find out, no campaign can ever succeed at this level without engaging these organizational publics; they can be of great help. We can say that they were the key participants from the point of view of a communicative approach that exceeded the marketing communication approach.

The Media

Being a classical category in almost every PR campaign, and even the *raison d'être* of many communication strategies, the media were considered in three different ways for this campaign. First, research identified a set of key journalists from national mainstream media that had recently been covering immigration issues, and the first approach was aimed precisely at these professionals. From the editorial point of view, they were mainly society journalists, and not economics journalists, although the latter were also considered in order to get the necessary publicity for the financial product and to reinforce the specialist positioning of the company. Second, news agencies and communication outlets (radio, TV, Internet) from the foreign countries mentioned earlier as the most important were identified, so that they could be sent

246 Mafalda Eiró-Gomes and João Duarte

information about the possibility for their country's citizens to buy property in Portugal with access to credit. Finally, targeted communication media, specially produced and delivered for the immigrant communities in Portugal, were identified and contacts were established. From a strategic point of view, this was the critical point to reach the non-Portuguese-speaking immigrants in their own language.

4.4. Campaign Implementation Tactics

In this chapter we mentioned the importance of the case study as an evaluation tool to document the PR processes and understand the decisions made. This is why case studies should include descriptions of campaigns' tactical dimensions.

PR from the Basics: Communication Materials

The first step was the production of all communication materials, including developing a product brand that was easy to recognize. After several brainstorming sessions and informal tests with different names, the product's name was determined with a clear reference to the idea that this new mortgage product would "open doors" for immigrants in Portugal. Then, different communication tactics were compared and tested before the final decision was taken. The company then produced 40,000 leaflets, 2,500 commercial displays, and 500 posters.

The communication outlets were presented in the first place to the commercial agents' network in a general meeting. The campaign then turned to the real-estate agents. They were given a personalized presentation of the product by their commercial agent and received the communication materials. It was decided that targeted distribution would be made, emphasizing those real-estate agents with better access to immigrant clients. The segmentation criterion was the density of immigrant communities in the catchment area of the real-estate agent. Other communication tools used to communicate the product were the company's magazine, produced exclusively for its real-estate agents, and the extranet exclusively available to all registered partners.

Placing the Issue in the Agenda: Media Relations Tactics

After securing this first step in the communications strategy, the company decided to anticipate the media relations campaign in order to profit from the presence of the immigrant housing issue on the media agenda. The media efforts had initially been planned after the institutional publics were involved, but due to the appearance of a series of news reports and to the work of opinion leaders, the company decided to act promptly. The society editors provided most of the coverage of the immigrant issues, but the journalists who normally covered the company's issues belonged to economics editorial offices. Therefore, the media relations campaign was aimed at these two different editorial offices. The first approach was with the Portuguese news agency (Lusa), which immediately produced a news report and widely diffused it. Daily national newspapers (mainstream and economic, printed and on-line), weekly newspapers, magazines, and websites (portals, web logs, issue-oriented, among others) were then targeted. Special attention was given to Russian-language newspapers edited in Portugal and to informative outlets from the countries of origin of the most representative communities. This targeted campaign reinforced the idea that the company wanted to focus the innovative character of the product as well as its social responsibility significance. The press materials included news releases and a press kit containing background information about the product, a company profile, and information about other products.

Public Involvement: Reaching Different Interlocutors

Information kits were also produced to communicate with institutional inter-locutors identified as potential partners in disseminating the message. Public entities related to immigration, NGOs, embassies and consulates, and immi-grant associations received these kits and not only acknowledged the organ-izational work but also accepted it as a key partner in their own strategies of social inclusion and citizenship. The company expected to begin a dialogue with these constituencies in order to find common interests and potential cooperation areas.

4.5. Results

As with many other PR campaigns, their results cannot be completely explained in the short term and their impact cannot be reduced to mere facts and figures. Different PR campaigns can produce effects in different ways through time, and this has mainly to do with the nature of the business itself. In this specific business, for instance, the time frame is very important; a lot of time can pass between the mortgage application (the initial stage of the process) and the mortgage deed (which marks the completion of the transaction), and that is why our explanation of PR results must be consistent with the specific business language and metrics.

Real-Estate Agents/Commercial Network

The feedback collected from the real-estate agents was extremely positive. During the first wave of the communication efforts they got to know the product and started their own communication efforts in order to attract immigrant clients. In less than two months, the initial stock of communication materials was almost totally distributed, and the company had to reprint them in order to maintain the flow of communication.

The number of mortgage applications from immigrants increased strongly, as did the number of mortgage deeds. Some real-estate agents reported that they had more than doubled their turnover thanks to the publicity that the company and the product received.

Another key indicator very much appreciated by the top management was the fact that new real-estate agents initiated cooperation protocols with the company because they heard about this new product and wanted to be able to sell it to their own clients.

Public Entities

Of the twenty-seven entities or departments that the PR strategy reached with the information kit, positive feedback was received in the form of additional information requests and website postings. One of the most active entities was the High Commissioner for Ethnic Minorities, whose Centers for the Support of the Immigrant are central meeting points for immigrants. They displayed the product's communication outlets and dealt with many information requests from the immigrants, which made them request further information about the product.

Also interesting in this third party endorsement activity was the fact that the High Commissioner for Ethnic Minorities was the most active public in immigration issues and also had an editorial responsibility in a national TV show specifically aimed at immigrant communities. In this context they also produced a program entirely dedicated to the issue of immigrant housing problems in which the product was widely discussed.

NGOs

The ten most important relevant NGOs were also informed about the financial product. Although they were not very active in the public sphere, they spread information throughout their own networks of relations; there was evidence that some people bought a mortgage after receiving information from one of these NGOs.

Embassies and Consulates

Embassies and consulates posed a challenge for the PR campaign. Although they could be seen as privileged information sources for their countries' citizens, there were some restrictions on their endorsing a financial product. The PR people therefore did not expect much activity from these important publics. Nevertheless, employees of the fifty-five embassies and consulates reached were among the first clients to show interest for the product.

Immigrant Associations

A group of thirty associations was chosen from a list of officially recognized associations, which turned out to be the one of the most active and important publics. The cooperation obtained ranged from displaying product information in their offices to signing cooperation protocols with the company in order to act as promoter of the product. Many of these associations responded to the information kit, asking for further information to supply their associates. Some of these publics acted in really creative ways, placing information in their websites, organizing meetings and presentations, and developing their own printed communications as third-party endorsement for the product. The most relevant association was the immigrant association for Eastern European countries, which gathered citizens from Russian-speaking countries. Their internal networks of communication quickly and effectively spread the word about the product from north to south and boosted the mortgage applications.

The Media

Although the media-relations campaign generated the most important press coverage for the company ever in Portugal, decisively contributing to the PR campaign tactics for the other publics, the PR evaluation considered that the most important contribution of the campaign was the goodwill it generated among journalists. As some PR people acknowledged, the company gained recognition among journalists, some journalists wrote about this company for the first time and the editorial coverage made by society journalists reinforced the social responsibility behind the financial product.

From the total press coverage attributed to media relations' efforts, 33% had to do with specialized media outlets in the economy/real-estate area, while the majority was placed on general media outlets. Forty percent of that press coverage was due to journalists who had not previously written about the company, which meant a qualitative improvement of the media-relations database. Besides, the content of the press coverage highlighted the innovative character of the product as the most important aspect (70%). When we compare the press coverage of this campaign with that of other financial products, however, this campaign proved more effective since the social aspect of the product was visible, with 10% of the coverage focusing on the social significance of the product.

Without any advertising in this campaign, the media relations tactic was pivotal in reaching the almost two million people believed to have been able to relate to the message. Nevertheless, these indicators should not be perceived as an end in themselves, but as positive contributions for the achievements described earlier.

4.6. Case-Study Assessment

We believe that evaluation in PR should deal not only with specific campaigns or actions, but also with the continuity of organizational activities. Learning from what we did, and how and why we did it, can then be understood as equally important as showing what we achieved.

The specific campaign analysis confirmed the value of thorough research about the context in which the publics evolve. This enables a better understanding of each public as a specific social actor. What initially could have been thought of as a relatively simple marketing communication campaign turned out to be an added-value corporate-identity campaign. Thanks to the PR research and the design of the campaign, publics were involved in cooperative ways and chose to position the organization as their partner.

In this case study, the compatibility was shown of a business-oriented evaluation report and a PR evaluation report centered on the campaign's achievements for each of the publics. Relevant campaign achievements from the PR point of view included not only the growth of the number of mortgage applications and mortgage deeds, but also the increase in journalists who wrote about the company for the first time, the fact that immigrant associations wanted to establish cooperation protocols with the company, and the fact that public organizations acknowledged the social validity of the product and endorsed it.

If it is true that this PR campaign managed to involve the publics in creative ways, it is also true that they have clearly shown how powerful and fruitful the cooperation between publics and organizations can be, and how much can be learnt.

5. Final Considerations

From the point of view of those involved in the situations analyzed—that is, the actors—our description of the case study showed its value as a tool to complement traditional evaluations by PR practitioners. We said that case studies should preferably be applied to non-ordinary campaigns that break the normal standards. This is not to say that they should be limited to successful campaigns, but that they are preferably done in situations with strong learning potential.

However, we strongly believe that case studies are also useful learning tools for agents not directly involved in specific situations. By illustrating the PR process in action, case studies allow those entering the practice to link theoretical contents to real-life problem-solving situations.

Besides these two rather PR-centered perspectives, we might risk saying that case studies are a good basis for multi-disciplinary research and learning. People from other fields of study and/or practice can use case studies to match their own strategies with the ones used by PR professionals. And this is perhaps a good aid for a benchmark approach to the professional practice by which we state our willingness to show our work to others and to learn from their work. Is this not a sound guiding principle in our modern complex societies, organizations, and professions?

References

Broom, Glen M., & Dozier, David (1990). *Using research in public relations: Applications to program management.* Englewood Cliffs, NJ: Prentice Hall.

Cutlip, S., Center, A., & Broom, G. (1994). *Effective public relations* (7th ed.). Englewood Cliffs, NJ: Prentice Hall.

Dozier, David, & Ehling, Willian (1992). Evaluation of public relations programs: What the literature tells us about their effects. In James Grunig (Ed.), *Excellence in public relations and communications management.* Hillsdale, NJ: Lawrence Erlbaum Associates.

Dozier, David, & Repper, Fred (1992). Research firms and public relations practices. In James Grunig (Ed.), *Excellence in public relations and communications management.* Hillsdale, NJ: Lawrence Erlbaum Associates.

Feagin, J., Orum, A., & Sjoberg, G. (Eds.) (1991). *A case for case study.* Chapel Hill, NC: University of North Carolina Press.

Grunig, James, & Hunt, Todd (1984). *Managing public relations.* Orlando, FL: Harcourt Brace Jovanovich.

Lesly, Philip (1997). *Lesly's handbook of public relations and communications.* Lincolnwood, IL: NTC Business Books.

Rossi, Peter, & Freeman, Howard (1993). *Evaluation: A systematic approach* (5th ed.). Newbury Park, CA: Sage.

Stake, R. (1995). *The art of case research.* Newbury Park, CA: Sage.

Tellis, Winston (1997). Application of a case study methodology. *The Qualitative Report, 3*(3) (September). Available online at www.nova.edu/ssss/QR/QR3-3/tellis2.html.

Yin, Robert K. (1994). *Case study research: Design and methods* (2nd ed.). Thousand Oaks, CA: Sage.

13 Public Relations Research and Evaluation in Africa

Ronél Rensburg

1. Introduction

Africa as a continent finds itself increasingly left behind as globalization takes center stage. The world's developed economies are becoming unwilling to pull Africa out of its strife and underdevelopment, and they will not continue to support it unconditionally. The time has come for Africa to take responsibility for its own development and for the contribution that it can make on the global stage and to international bodies of knowledge. There are challenges, but there are also opportunities—in all areas of research, but particularly in the social sciences, of which public relations as a discipline forms a part. While exploring the challenges of renewal that confront the African continent, scholars in Africa should take full cognizance of the changing contexts, conditions, and forces shaping Africa today (see Yieke, 2005). Issues such as African nationalism; the role of intellectuals in the African quest for renewal; ethnicity and citizenship; movementocracy and democracy; transient mobile "nations" and nationhood; the challenges of nationalism, regionalism, and the promotion of pan-African ideals as well as questions of language—all this must be addressed, also by public relations scholars.

Before analyzing the evolution of the continent's public relations research and its evaluation, we need to sketch the background of social science research in Africa.

2. The Problem with Social Science Research in Africa

There are numerous problems that face social science research (in all its disciplines) in Africa. The importance of public relations as a social science, as an academic discipline, and as a practice might be recognized fully in Africa (particularly in South Africa, Kenya, Nigeria, and Tanzania, and through the Federation of African Public Relations Associations (FAPRA)), but there are some obstacles. World wide, social science research in Africa has been omitted from the research agendas for some time. One effect of this is the omission of the African experience from much of the analyses where the intent is global—mainly because of the lack of information about Africa in general.

The position of social science in Africa can be seen as a function of the status of knowledge in African societies and the resources available to governments for knowledge production. Africa is a region where underdevelopment prevails and poverty still characterizes the condition of the majority of the people. If research is funded by agencies and completed (public relations research as well), we can expect that the outcomes of the research would improve the lives and circumstances of the majority of people. How to deal with poverty, underdevelopment, and the AIDS problem seems to affect perceptions and determine African research priorities (Sall, 2003: 11). The short span of Africa's independence and post-colonial history makes this issue even more critical. African researchers and scholars are attempting to make sense of increasingly complex local and global phenomena and are actively involved in the creation and development of a modern public sphere, which may or may not overlap with the sphere of the state (government) and/or of individual communities. The development of social science teaching and research in Africa can be seen as closely linked to the birth and evolution of the post-colonial state (Sall, 2003: 15). The expressions of "national priorities" and "development needs" are still rife in the discourse of African scholars. They believe their role is to make sense of local, regional, national, and global social processes and transformation.

2.1. The Need for Transformation in Social Science Research

Although the term "transformation" has become a buzzword for academic and political correctness in Africa, it appears that the process and the results expected of transformation and change are not clear. The views on transformation in social science research in Africa appear to be that interpretative and culturally sensitive researcher-centered approaches should be advocated. *Interpretativism* embraces subjectivity and qualitative procedures that are often incompatible with *positivism* (objectivity and quantification). African development should first and foremost be about creating and validating knowledge of Africa that is relevant to Africa's needs. African development requires research methods that are compatible with African cultures and contexts. Transformation in research is therefore needed, whereby institutions and researchers refrain from seeking just international recognition, learn about and understand local cultures and belief systems, and develop local research paradigms that cater for local contexts, cultures, and experiences (cf. Muwanga-Zake, 2000).[1] During BledCom 2005, Naudé reported on the complexities regarding her research on measurement and benchmarking in the South African mining industry (Naudé, 2005), which is typical of the experiences of social researchers in Africa.

The development of social science research and the teaching of the social sciences (particularly communication and public relations) in Africa is very much a post-colonial phenomenon. Now, however, "transformation" is affecting the social research environment. Among the different types of transformation that characterize the context of public relations teaching and research in Africa, the following five seem to be of paramount importance: (1) economic transformation; (2) social transformation; (3) political transformation; (4) transformation in information and communication technologies (and the lack of infrastructures); and (5) transformation in and of social institutions (cf. Allen, 1986; Aina, 1998; UNESCO, 1999; World Bank, 2001).

2.2. The Discourse of Social Science Research in Africa

Social science discourse is experienced by some African scholars (see Muwanga-Zake, 2000) as a tool used by institutions (universities, research institutions, business, and industry) to control the processes and, unintentionally— it is hoped—the outcomes of research. Dictionaries such as the *Cambridge International Dictionary of English* (March, 1999) define "discourse" as "communication in speech or writing." Michel Foucault viewed discourse in terms of *knowledge production* and *power*, and discourse has been interpreted by, *inter alia*, Mphahlele (1996), as a way of constituting knowledge, together with social practices, forms of subjectivity, and power relations. Foucault viewed discourse as a tool that controls the production and structure or constitution of knowledge (the way the world and reality are viewed); knowledge systems (or "epistemes," in Foucault's terms); social dynamics, and strategies (how people organize the world and themselves, including their thinking and emotions and how they fit into society); as well as acceptable, permissible or desirable practices. This view forms the basis of Pinkus's (1996) question about discourses that have acquired "international" status, dominating the world, shaping and creating meaning systems that have the status and currency of "truth." The question here remains: can a discourse be specific to a particular context and yet lead to universal truths and paradigms? The experiences of African scholars in social science research seem to be a struggle against contemporary discourse and its foreign-based paradigms, and a sign of the possibility of alternative discourse. Public relations scholars in Africa find that this increasingly happens during their research.

2.3. Social Science Research in Africa: In Search of a New Paradigm?

Is there then a need for a complete social science research paradigm shift (which will include public relations research) for Africa? According to Kuhn, paradigms are "general ways of seeing the world." Paradigms determine "normal science" and therefore also the kind of analysis that is made of a given social phenomenon. A paradigm shift occurs when, as a result of the evolution of social phenomena and/or developments within a science itself, new general ways of seeing the world emerge (cf. Kuhn, 1975; Abercrombie, Hill, & Turner, 1994). However, a real empirical base for social science research remains.

There appears to be a general belief that all research must be based on certain underlying assumptions that validate research and the selected methods. Those assumptions are described by paradigms; the choice of a paradigm thus appears fundamental in research discourse. According to Breton and Largent (2000), the term "paradigm" was originally used in classic times by the Greeks to refer to an original archetype or ideal. The definition given by Guba and Lincoln (1994: 107) is best related to the classical use, referring to a paradigm as a set of basic beliefs that deals with ultimate or first principles. It represents a worldview that defines, for its holder, the nature of the world, the holder's place in it, and the range of possible relationships to that world and its parts. Guba and Lincoln (1994) believed that any given paradigm represents simply the most informed and sophisticated view that its proponents have been able to devise, given the way they respond to: (1) the *ontological* aspect—the form and nature of reality and what can be known about it; (2) the *epistemological* aspect—the nature of the relationship between the knower or would-be knower and what can be learnt about it; (3) the *methodological* aspect—how the inquirer (researcher) can go about finding out whatever he or she believes can be known. Schwandt (in Denzin & Lincoln, 1994: 118) indicated that meanings of paradigms are also shaped by the intent of their users. Since discourse controls all aspects of paradigms listed above, it follows that discourse controls paradigms—the understanding, the choice, and the use of paradigms. It is important to emphasize that paradigms are human constructs or inventions based on faith, and are therefore subjective in terms of human characteristics and interests such as race, politics, economics, gender, religion, and culture. The subjectivity of paradigms and discourse opens the way for speculation. For example, as with discourse, a paradigm ought to be relevant in a specific context, and assumptions underlying a paradigm must be matched as closely as possible to the context in which it is used.

Given the dominant paradigms and their close connections with post-independence development processes, social science research in Africa was primarily intended to serve state (government) and national development purposes, themselves conceived in very statist terms. The state was there-fore not only the key theme in social science research, but also the main user of the research. In the post-colonial era, research has become more diversified to include social movements, civil society organizations, business, etc. Among the key issues of research that emerge in debates on both theories and para-digms in public relations in Africa are personal and cultural identity, Africanity, ethnic identities and ethnicity, and race; Africa in the world economy; social movements; activism; structural adjustments; gender issues; authoritarianism, democracy, democratic transitions, corporate governance and citizenship, chal-lenges in democracy; conflict and conflict resolution; rural and agrarian issues; business incubation; entrepreneurship, small and medium enterprises; black empowerment; urban processes; regional integration; endogenous knowledge and research-based global knowledge; reputation management; development communication and nation-building; corruption, and HIV-Aids.

Paradigms are sometimes *foreign* which can compromise the validity and reliability of social science research in African contexts. The argument is based on the experience of how the discourse of institutions control choices of terminology, paradigms, methods, style of writing, and interpretation of findings, which, as a result of their foreignness, might wipe out some of the participants' experiences. It is therefore also proposed that there should be transformation in social science research so that it becomes more valid for African contexts. This is true also for public relations research and evaluation.

2.4. Context, Paradigms, Discourse, and Public Relations Research

In the African environment, more so than elsewhere in the world, public relations researchers must thoroughly understand the context (including the respondents) that they are researching and all the paradigms, if they want to make informed paradigm choices. Problems are likely to arise when the researcher, the people, paradigms, and contexts are foreign and removed from one another. It is often noted that in Africa, social science researchers (and public relations researchers, too) do research on a community whose culture, language, and context they hardly can relate to or understand. In such cases, the researchers might misinterpret the context and community that are investigated. Can Africa claim to have distinctly different contexts from those of America and Europe? Can a paradigm be the property of a continent, a culture, or of a specific time and space? Can Africa strive to evolve its own paradigms suitable for its unique contexts? Can a paradigm and accompanying methods of research that evolved out of the international public sphere and its social dynamics be used to legitimately do research in a context foreign to their origins, without compromising validity and reliability (or verisimilitude)? The way that developed countries define their life styles differs from Africa where there are still distinct life styles, knowledge systems, and cultures, which justify African paradigms. Paradigms outside Africa are applied in African contexts and emphasize the search for how paradigms can be modified for Africa without changing into alternative paradigms. According to Gay (1995 quoted in Atwater, 1996: 823), wrong paradigms can lead to inaccurate knowledge construction, which in turn can become universal or global "truths." It is possibly due to similar inaccuracies that in Africa, knowledge produced from research may not be relevant to its needs and contexts, and cannot be developed further, and yet held as the scientifically proven truths.

Curbing the *paradigm addiction* for concepts from the developed world may require the use of Foucault's concept of a *subversive genealogy* which, according to Denzin (1991) in Denzin and Lincoln (1994: 579), is a strategy that refuses to accept those "systems of discourse (economic, political, scientific narrative)" that ignore who people are collectively and individually. The need cannot be overemphasized for cultural or contextual sensitivity when adopting or developing research and bodies of knowledge (Ogunniyi, 1996: 275), particularly not in public relations research in Africa.

2.5. Different Metrics for Public Relations Research in Africa?

In November 1998, the CODESRIA Small Grants for Thesis Writing Selection Committee analyzed trends in the social science disciplines on the basis of 418 dossiers (Sall, 2003: 42). They found that most research studies are defined by interests that express curiosity toward daily experiences and social transformations in Africa. The themes that are based on the realities of the day mirror the pluralism and dynamism of the emerging social science research community. These are attempts to adapt the disciplines to local African conditions, not merely through the study of local phenomena, but also by attempting to revisit certain theories and research methodologies. Scholars all over Africa are looking to indigenize disciplines (cf. Niang, 2000). As an indigenized discipline, public relations could, for example, study the following: (1) African communication themes or issues of particular interest to Africa; (2) conceptual frameworks and research paradigms in communication developed by African scholars; (3) particular African innovation in public relations research methodologies such as *settlu,* a traditional method of observation that does not disturb the observed. It is common knowledge that, for numerous reasons, "developed" metrics such as interviews and questionnaires are not always effective in collecting data in Africa (from low literacy through to cultural taboos). For example, in many African societies, the question–answer format is problematic, as African respondents prefer to draw the interviewer into a dialogue (cf. Sall, 2003). The methodology to be developed here, then, will take such a relation between the interviewer and respondents into account (cf. Niang, 2000 for a discussion regarding problems associated with data collection by questionnaire in African communities).

South African scholars, in particular, are very interested in and geared toward public relations research and public relations theory-building (cf. Mersham, Rensburg, & Skinner, 1995). Research is taken very seriously in all tertiary institutions in South Africa and most universities offer public relations somewhere in their curricula. Most of the African literature on public relations comes from South Africa. The position is strongly held—by the Public Relations Institute of Southern Africa (PRISA) and scholars—that public relations has already developed (in South Africa at least), as a separate research field, utilizing the discourse, methods, and tools of the developed world.

Research on the education, measurement, and body of knowledge of public relations in Africa has been done extensively by Ferreira (1998). Ferreira's investigation was executed between 1994 and 1998, and was aimed at the whole of the African continent except South Africa, but including the islands of the Southern African Development Community (SADC) region. The study covered a total of forty-seven countries. The research was exploratory and a literature review of what had been written down about public relations in Africa has been recorded. Data was collected by means of correspondence. The next encompassing study by van Heerden—on public relations practice in Africa

—was completed in 2004. Both studies were hampered by various logistic problems. Consequently, reports on these studies do not contain information on all the African countries contacted as not all responded. The main problems were due to lack of infrastructure—such as the absence of access to information technology. Language was also a problem as many African countries speak French or Arabic, or their own indigenous languages, while their English is poor.

When doing research on respondents on the rural African environment, Murangwa-Zake (2000), for example, found the following:

(1) Individuals conferred with their colleagues before committing themselves to an answer during structured interviews. Therefore, what appeared like individual responses were in fact community responses, in which individual opinions had been compromised. Such conferring would seem to concur with *social constructivism*. However, social constructivism assumes full participation of the researcher in the construction and requires a fair degree of knowledge of the social dynamics of all the participants.

(2) Interviews were more successful if respondents could trace the roots (background) of the researcher. This required that the researcher was representing a certain group or clan. Respondents weighed what to say and how to say it based on who the researcher was. Researching required the researcher to become part of that community, which would isolate him or her from using a foreign paradigm at the same time.

(3) Socializing was sometimes essential before settling down to the actual research business. Thus, the formal structuring of interviews was not very acceptable.

(4) Researchers do not always have access to modern research equipment, laboratories, and information-technology infrastructures.

(5) The field-research area may consist of rural villages whose traditions do not always feature in university curricula and whose experiences are most often factored out by the discourse or by "formal" research.

(6) Discourse demands potentiality for defining trends and generalizations, regardless of the unique social setting and individual differences.

Other factors outside the interview schedules that may affect research in Africa are the following:

(1) The influence of traditional belief systems and suspicions about what will happen to responses.

(2) The political history of researchers and respondents, and how these influence their participation in research. Researchers often have to stretch or re-interpret the definitions of the approaches to cover the research context and unexpected experiences. In rural Africa, for example, research is not a "natural" process, and almost always there will be tensions when researchers try to align their paradigms with the context at hand.

(3) Research experiences are the influence of traditional belief systems; credibility often requires reliving the researcher's experiences via his or her references. Referencing, for example, can also be documented as a problem in the African research context. To record the experiences of the respondents is rarely seen as "scientific." Institutional and internationally recognized research demands "sources" for the statements and experiences.

(4) Literature is mostly from the developed world, and as the African experiences are not written up, due to strong oral traditions where stories and legends are transmitted from generation to generation, findings are not seen as valid. The mastery of Western concepts, paradigms, and methodologies are required by institutions for students to obtain their degrees and for researchers to complete their research on a world stage. African scholars should be allowed to break new ground and discover new methods or paradigms while acquainting themselves with mastering established research methods. Mphahlele (1996: 246) indicated that participants in the research process are individuals with unique personalities. African research findings and contributions are often betrayed by leaving out certain realities due to adhering to acceptable scientific global discourse that does not always relate to local contexts—where findings or responses are interpreted as "unscientific" according to the paradigm at hand. According to Lincoln and Denzin (1994: 578), paradigms and language (particularly research terminology) are the most controversial and controlling tools in research discourse because they are not natural integral parts of the context and of the respondents' culture. This could cause uncertainty, according to Kincheloe and Steinberg (1993: 296). They found that there is no "democracy" in selecting and applying research paradigms. The "truth" is seen as procedural, methods have to be "objective," and researchers demand "precise results" and "recognized sources." Lack of direct translations and wrong spoken and written English are also research impediments in Africa. Similar language concerns are echoed by Solomon (1994: 5). The discourse relationship to the African reality of the research done in African communities (the verisimilitude of the research) remains questionable.

   The parochial nature of current public relations research in Africa is in the choice of research objects, themes, and tools. As to research methods being used, public relations and communication as practiced in South Africa are as universal as they are anywhere else in the world. Moreover, as scholars like Mamdani (cf. 2001) have argued, African scholars have always studied "Africa in the world." The tendency to select topics close to the continent is probably part of a more global postmodern shift away from grand theory and grand systems. However, certain topics (also in public relations and communication) can be universally convergent in nature.

   There are currently many public relations research topics that have been identified by African scholars and students. The methods that are used range from observational research through to experimental and survey research. There are public opinion research, image surveys, needs and perception surveys, corporate communication research, reputation management research, and content/discourse analyses of public relations message content. The classified types of research that are used by scholars include, *inter alia*, basic, applied, introspective, tactical, strategic, quantitative (empirical), and qualitative research. The purposes for doing research range from the description of phenomena, via their explanation, to predictions. Research on corporate communication strategy (cf. Steyn & Puth, 2000) has been well publicized. The work of Skinner and Mersham on various issues in public relations in Africa is also well documented. Current ongoing research by De Beer (on corporate governance and corporate reputation management), Chaka (on government communication and nation-building), and Leonard (on communication and activism) will be completed soon. Scholars and students alike, in all the universities offering public relations as an academic discipline, are embarking on various areas of research in the field. A comprehensive book on public relations in Africa—to which scholars from all over Africa will contribute—will soon be available.

3. The Way Forward: The Need for an African Public Relations Philosophy

The academic respect for global trends should never be discarded but may be detrimental to the full development of local methods. There is a shortage of local references because Africa has neglected its own knowledge base and methods. The advent of globalization seems to have increased the impact of "international" ways of doing things. Africa must create a paradigm in which its scholars are able to solve the unsolvable problems of the old paradigm. It is possible that some of the First World discourses (and paradigms) could be useful in African contexts. However, it seems that a concerted effort is called for to use them with a clear understanding of their origins, and to critically assess how they fit into contexts in which they are used. The first step to developing Africa is to transform research toward using African discourse and paradigms, and to use foreign paradigms only when they perfectly fit African contexts.

Kwasi Wiredu, a leading African philosopher, also advocates a re-examination of current African epistemic formations in order to subvert un-savory aspects of tribal cultures embedded in modern African thought, as well as to deconstruct the unnecessary epistemologies of the developed world that are found in African philosophical practices (Osha, 2005).

4. Conclusion

Among the most important constraints faced by the African social science research community are the extremely volatile political environment and the very precarious economic and social conditions in which it has to operate. The rapid changes now also pose considerable challenges for institutions and scholars alike, and the challenges facing the community are many and varied. Social reality in Africa is becoming increasingly complex. Keeping up with the academic debates globally in the respective disciplines (also in public relations) is a major challenge for African scholars. The drive toward "marketability" is a global phenomenon, which causes major questions about agenda setting for social science research carried out on the African continent. The information technology revolution in particular brings along its own cohort of opportunities and risks for Africa.

5. Epilogue

The Ubuntu concept (people exist because of and with other people) may naturally fit into local research processes and may enable mutual interpretation of results by all participants. Rather than a "paradigm shift," a transformation is needed that will replace paradigms handed down to Africa with African paradigms. Efforts in research also require cooperation between African countries, and, as Ogunniyi (1996) suggested, collaboration is needed to share African experiences and avoid duplication, and to ensure the free flow of information. Africa and its issues can become a green field for research for international scholars, as well as in public relations.

Note

1   Note that though the phenomenon of having to do country-relevant research applies to all countries, there is a significant degree of difference in Africa because of the levels of underdevelopment and illiteracy that still prevail in the continent.

References

Abercrombie, N. S., Hill, S., & Turner, S. (1994). *Dictionary of sociology* (3rd ed.). London: Penguin.

Aina, T. (1998). *The state of social sciences in contemporary sub-Saharan Africa: A status report.* Mimeo, n.p.

Allen, C. H. (1986). A review of social science research in Eastern, Southern and some Western African states. *Report to SAREC.* Stockholm: SAREC (June).

Atwater, M. M. (1996). Social constructivism: Infusion into the multicultural science education research agenda. *Journal of Research in Science Teaching, 33*(8), 821–883.

Breton, D., & Largent, C. (April 20, 2000). Available online at www.trufax.org/paradigm/welcome.html.

Cambridge International Dictionary of English. (March, 1999).

Chaka, M. (2006). *Public relations in nation-building: A development communication perspective for South Africa.* Ph.D. dissertation, in progress.

Denzin, N. K., & Lincoln, Y. S. (Eds.) (1994). *Handbook of qualitative research.* Thousand Oaks, CA: Sage.

Ferreira, E. (1998). *The state of public relations in then rest of Africa: A report.* Unpublished MA dissertation, Nelson Mandela Metropolitan University, Port Elizabeth, South Africa.

Foucault, M. (2000). *Ethics: Subjectivity and truth, the essential works of Michel Foucault, 1954–1984.* London: Penguin.

De Beer, E. (2006). *The measurement of corporate reputation management in organizations within the framework of corporate governance principles.* Ph.D. dissertation, in progress.

Guba, E. G., & Lincoln, Y. S. (1994). Competing paradigms in qualitative research. In N. K. Denzin & Y. S. Lincoln (Eds.), *Handbook of qualitative research.* Thousand Oaks, CA: Sage.

Kincheloe, J. L., & Steinberg, S. R. (1993). A tentative description of post-formal thinking: The critical confrontation with cognitive theory. *Harvard Educational Review, 63*(3) (Fall).

Kuhn, T. S. (1975). *The structure of scientific revolution* (2nd ed.). Chicago: University of Chicago Press.

Lincoln, Y. S., & Denzin, N. K. (1994). The fifth moment. In N. K. Denzin & Y. S. Lincoln (Eds.), *Handbook of qualitative research.* Thousand Oaks, CA: Sage.

Mamdani, A. (2001). *Understanding the crisis in Kivu.* Report of the CODESRIA mission to the Democratic Republic of Congo. Dakar: Senegal (September 1997).

Mersham, G. M., Rensburg, R. S., & Skinner, J. C. (1995). *Public relations, development and social investment: A Southern African perspective.* Pretoria: Van Schaik.

Mphahlele, M. K. (1996). *Supervision of science education research: Critique of the discourse.* Proceedings of the Fourth Annual meeting, January, 25–28. South African Association for Research in Mathematics and Science Education.

Muwanga-Zake, J. W. F. (2000). *Experiences of the power of discourse in research: A need for transformation in research in Africa.* Durban: University of Natal, Centre for the Advancement of Science & Mathematics Education, Edgewood School of Education.

Naudé, A. (2005). *Stakeholder management and sustainable development reporting: Measurement and benchmarking of the South African mining industry.* Paper delivered at BledCom.

Niang, A. (2000). *"Settlu," technique traditionelle d'observation.* Mimeo. Saint-Louis: Université Gaston Berger.

Ogunniyi, M. B. (1996). Science, technology and mathematics: The problem of developing critical human capital in Africa. *International Journal of Science Education, 18*(3), 267–284.

Osha, S. (2005). *Kwasi Wiredu and beyond: The text, writing and thought in Africa.* Senegal: CODESRIA (May).

Pinkus, J. (1996). *Foucault.* Available online at www.massey.ac.nz/~ALock/theory/foucault.htm

Sall, E. (2003). *The social sciences in Africa: Trends, issues, capacities and constraints.* New York: Social Sciences Research Council.

Schwandt, T. A. (1994). Constructivist, interpretivist approaches to human inquiry. In N. K. Denzin & Y. S. Lincoln (Eds.), *Handbook of qualitative research* (pp. 118–137). Thousand Oaks, CA: Sage.

Solomon, J. (1994). The rise and fall of constructivism. *Studies in Science Education, 23,* 1–19.

Steyn, B., & Puth, G. (2000). *Corporate communication strategy.* Sandown, Johannesburg: Heinemann.

UNESCO (1999). *World social science report.* Paris: UNESCO.

Van Heerden, G. (2004). *The practice of public relations in Africa: A descriptive study.* Unpublished MA dissertation, University of Pretoria, South Africa.

World Bank (2001). *Constructing knowledge societies: New challenges for tertiary education. A World Bank strategy.* Washington. DC: The World Bank Education Group, Human Development Network.

Yieke, F. A. (Ed.) (2005). *East Africa: In search of national and regional renewal.* Dakar: CODESRIA.

14 Adapting Communication Satisfaction and Relationship Scales to a Third-World Country

Tanya le Roux

1. Introduction

There is no communication-related measurement scale suitable for all circumstances (Devlin, 2003). J. Grunig (2001) supported this view by arguing that variables such as the political system, the economic system, culture (including language), the extent of activism, the level of development, and the media system should be taken into account when applying communication management and communication research to any specific context.

This means that measurement scales need to be adapted to their particular context of use. This chapter will show how current first-world internal organizational communication satisfaction and employer–employee relationship measurement instruments had to be adapted in order to be used in a third-world country context such as South Africa's mining industry.

When faced with a problem to be researched, researchers need to find a measurement scale that suits their research goals and takes the research context into account (Agarwal, 2003; Devlin, 2003). They can thus select to develop a new measurement scale, or adapt an existing scale to their research context. This chapter will focus on the challenge of adapting an existing scale to a specific research context.

When using an existing scale whose reliability and validity have been tested, and adapting it, one should note that reliability and validity once again become a concern (Clampitt, 2000, as cited in Hargie & Tourish, 2000). However, there is little documentation on procedures outlining how to adapt measurement scales for research and how to keep them reliable and valid (McGorry, 2000). Research articles seem to focus on problems and outcomes, not specifically on the adaptation of the scales that were used.

This chapter aims to provide some background on how a researcher should go about adapting scales in light of a case study based in the South African mining industry with unique challenges such as historical issues, cultural diversity, illiteracy, and much more.

The objectives of the chapter are as follows:

- To report briefly on the challenges of administering research questionnaires in a third-world country context such as the South African mining industry.
- To report on the methodology followed in adapting the communication satisfaction of Francis and Woodcock and the International Communication Association (ICA)[1] and the Grunig–Hon[2] relationship scales to the specific third-world country context in which it was to be used.
- To evaluate the reliability and validity of the adapted scales.
- To provide guidelines for the future adaptation of these scales for use in a third-world country context such as the South African mining industry.

2. Research Methodology

2.1. Case Study Context

A South African mining organization urgently needed to understand the factors influencing the employer–employee relationship. The excellence theory and relationship management theories were used as meta-theoretical approaches.

The mining organization studied, although committed to corporate account-ability, did not have a good relationship with its employees and other stake-holders (Naudé, Fourie, Le Roux, Van Heerden, & Venter, 2004). According to the excellence theory and relationship management theory, the level of satis-faction with the mutually beneficial organizational–stakeholder relationships is created and determined by two-way symmetrical communication, symbolic activities focusing on enhancing the organization's image, and expectations of behavior from both parties in the relationship and relationship history (Bruning & Galloway, 2003; Bruning & Ledingham, 1999; J. Grunig, cited in Ledingham & Bruning, 1998; Ledingham, 2003; Ledingham & Bruning, 1998).

Unfortunately, there was not a standardized measuring scale pertaining to the South African context that would answer to the research goals (Clampitt as cited in Hargie & Tourish, 2000). Therefore, organizational communication and the deteriorating employer–employee relationship were measured by using focus groups and an adaptation of the tested and existing questionnaires to which a section on demographic details of the respondents was added.

2.2. Research Design

To provide contextual input into the adaptation of the questionnaires, semi-structured interviews with selected managers were conducted prior to the final-ization of the measurement instruments. This was followed by the focus groups and adapted questionnaire to a stratified quota sample of 650 literate, semi-literate, and illiterate employees. The sample was stratified according to gender, race, business unit, place of work (underground, surface dusty, or surface), and job level. The final response rate was 551 completed questionnaires. The data were stored and analyzed with *Statistica*, a statistics program, using descriptive statistics common to social sciences research.

2.3. Practical Problems and Solutions

One of the circumstances for which the scales had to be adapted was the literacy level of the respondents. In South Africa, only 6% of people over twenty have twelve years or more of schooling, 50% fewer than nine years of schooling, and 15% never had any schooling (Rule, cited in Thatcher, Shaik, & Zimmerman, 2005). Semi-literate and illiterate miners lack basic numeric, business, technological, and business-language skills. Furthermore, miners migrate from outside South Africa and various provinces within South Africa to find work at one of the many mines in the North West province. This brings with it a wealth of problems in terms of a conglomerate of different cultures and languages, communication expectations, and communication styles in one workplace.

This implied that the length and complexity of the scales had to be adjusted in order to accommodate the literacy level and short attention span of the respondents (Clampitt, cited in Hargie & Tourish, 2000). The wording and any cultural specific content in the scales had to be adapted to accommodate all the cultures participating (Agarwal, 2003; Devlin, 2003; McGorry, 2000). A translated questionnaire was found to be unsuccessful due to the fact that the languages are spoken and read on different levels, and because there are many dialects of the same language. Semi-literate and illiterate employees also had to be assisted in one-on-one interviews conducted by interpreters fluent in six languages (McGorry, 2000).

The researchers added a section to the survey to ascertain the demographics of the respondents (Clampitt, cited in Hargie & Tourish, 2000). They suspected that problems could be isolated according to certain demographic details; for instance, underground workers might not get information through meetings and illiterate employees do not experience communication positively when it is written. Language, race, gender, education level, department, job level, age, and time spent with the company—all these were added.

The organizational background was also taken into account in order to assist the researchers in evaluating the best possible method of administering the scale (Clampitt, cited in Hargie & Tourish, 2000). Union involvement and the large number of employees involved in the study had the potential to severely impact the mine's productivity. The researchers limited the impact on production by randomly selecting employees already present at the training centers. The training centers were found to be the most ideal research locations as employees were most relaxed and felt safe there, and interruptions were limited.

2.4. Questionnaire Problems and Solutions

Adaptations were used of the Francis–Woodcock and the ICA communication satisfaction questionnaires, and the Grunig–Hon relationship questionnaire. The structure of the combined questionnaire was as follows:

- demographic data;
- relationship history: comparison of the current employer–employee relationship with the past employer–employee relationship;
- questions on organizational behavior;
- an adaptation of J. Grunig and Hon's relationship questionnaire;
- an adaptation of Francis and Woodcock's communication satisfaction questionnaire;
- an adaptation of the ICA communication satisfaction questionnaire, with added questions on specific methods of communication as requested by the management.

3. Existing Scales

3.1. The Francis and Woodcock Communication Satisfaction Questionnaire

Francis and Woodcock suggested that blue-collar workers should complete their questionnaire only if the pilot trials proved satisfactory (Francis & Woodcock, 1994a). In this study it was crucial that both white-collar and blue-collar workers completed the questionnaire, as the researchers anticipated a big difference between the views of these two groups on organizational communication and wanted to compare the findings. A pilot trial was undertaken and it became apparent that the five-item Likert scale was too complex for the respondents to understand. The researchers then decided to revert to a four-point Likert scale.

Francis and Woodcock (1994b) centered their questionnaire on four concepts, each divided into three constructs with six questions, measuring each construct. In the combined questionnaire, selected statements from four of the concepts—namely, persuasive management, downward communication flow, upward communication flow, and prejudice—were included; see Table 14.1 for the reasoning behind selecting the listed four constructs for the combined questionnaire. Because of the length of the questionnaire, the number of questions dealing with the selected constructs was narrowed down to thirteen for the four constructs selected. The wording of the statements were adapted to accommodate the literacy levels of the respondents and abstract statements, statements that were too complex, and negatively phrased statements, were eliminated (McGorry, 2000). Table 14.2 depicts the difference between the statements proposed by Francis and Woodcock, and those used in the combined questionnaire.

3.2. The ICA Communication Satisfaction Questionnaire

The original ICA questionnaire consisted of 122 questions divided into eight major sections (Clampitt, in Hargie and Tourish, 2000). In the original questionnaire, respondents were asked to rate their answers on a Likert scale

Table 14.1 Constructs from the Francis and Woodcock questionnaire included in the combined questionnaire

Francis & Woodcock (1994b) concepts and constructs	Definition of the constructs	Inclusion in the combined questionnaire
1. Sharing vision		
1. Sensitivity to the external environment	Organization interaction with the environment.	Not included. A complete survey of the external environment was done during phase one of the study.
2. Compelling vision	Defining the future of the organization.	Not included. Teams at the platinum mine are managed by clear production objectives.
3. Persuasive management	Management communication skills.	Included in the combined questionnaire. In the initial interviews, it was found that managements' general communication skills limited their ability to send messages.
2. Integration of efforts		
4. Integration mechanisms	Business units should work together by using set communication mechanisms.	Not included. This was not the focus of our research brief.
5. Helpful geography	The local geography should assist communication.	Not included. The mine operations are geographically separated. This is a known factor that limits the integration of organizational communication.
6. Downward flow	Power is centralized at the top of the hierarchy, not two-way symmetrical.	Included in the combined questionnaire as the organization did not seem to practice two-way symmetrical communication.
3. Sustaining a healthy community		
7. High trust	People can rely on one another.	Not included. Trust is already measured as part of the relationship determinants.
8. Lack of prejudice	Principle of fairness.	Included in the combined questionnaire as a diverse workforce is employed and there are reported problems with prejudice.
9. Supportive teamwork	Teamwork adds to the success of the organization by providing people with a sense of personal worth and support.	Not included. At the organization employees work in teams to accomplish tasks and attain their goals.
4. Intelligent decision-making		
10. Upward flow	Management needs to establish two-way symmetrical communication with employees in order to be successful.	Included in the combined questionnaire as the organization did not seem to practice two-way symmetrical communication.
11. Apt administration	Channels of communication can enhance or delay communication.	Not included. The channels of communication are questioned by using the ICA questionnaire.
12. Communication skills	Written and spoken communication skills used by management can help to express them more clearly.	Not included. Communication channels and methods were measured in the ICA questionnaire.

of one (very little) to five (very great) for information they received. In a parallel scale, respondents rated the amount of information they would like to receive. A difference score was then calculated comparing employees' information needs with the amount of information they actually receive.

Three major changes were made to adapt the ICA questionnaire to the context in which it was going to be used. First, the researchers collapsed the parallel scales of "amount of information employees received" and "amount of information employees would like to receive," into a single question in which respondents had to make a value judgment on whether they thought that they received enough information. The results were enhanced by information from the focus groups. Second, open-ended questions and questions in which respondents would have difficulty interpreting subtle semantic differences were not used in the combined questionnaire. In some cases, questions were combined with other similar sections. Finally, the language of the original questionnaire was adapted to suit the respondents' literacy levels (see Table 14.3).

3.3. J. Grunig and Hon's Relationship Scale

An adaptation of J. Grunig and Hon's relationship measurement scale (J. Grunig & Hon, 1999), was used to determine the employer–employee relationship. The scale measures six relationship constructs—trust (integrity, dependability and competence), control mutuality, commitment, satisfaction, communal relationships, and exchange relationships. J. Grunig and Hon (1999) suggested that researchers could use a shorter scale, including twenty-six of the forty-six questions in order to increase the completion rate of the questionnaire.

J. Grunig and Hon (1999) originally asked respondents to rate their answers on a nine-point Likert scale. A four-point Likert scale was used in the combined questionnaire in order to accommodate the semi-literate and illiterate respondents.

Only fifteen questions from J. Grunig and Hon's shortened questionnaire of twenty-six questions were included in the combined questionnaire. This was because of concerns about the length of the questionnaire and the inability of the respondents to distinguish between small semantic differences in the questions. The language of some questions had to be adapted and negatively phrased questions needed rephrasing. Table 14.4 lists the adapted statements used in the combined questionnaire.

Finally, two questions, using a four-point Likert scale, were added to the combined questionnaire to test the respondents' perception of the employer–employee relationship history. In the first question the respondents had to rate their historic relationship with the organization ("How would you rate your relationship with the company when you joined?"). The second question focused on the current employer–employee relationship ("How would you rate your current relationship with the company?"). The ratings of the two questions were then compared in order to indicate a perceived improvement or deterioration in the employer–employee relationship over time.

Table 14.2 Francis and Woodcock statements used in the combined questionnaire

Francis and Woodcock (1994c) statements	*Combined questionnaire statements*
Persuasion	
• The top management group is persuasive when communicating to employees	1. Management/team leaders/supervisors are convincing when communicating to me
• Managers, at every level, get their message across to the whole organization	
• When changes are made, great efforts are made to explain the reasons	2. When changes are made, great efforts are made to explain the reasons for the changes
• Managers can be relied upon to put forward clear proposals which are supported by strong arguments	3. Managers/team leaders/supervisors forward clear suggestions/instructions supported by strong arguments
• Managers at every level are good at selling ideas	
• Management skillfully uses a wide variety of media to communicate its message	
Downward communication flow	
• There are effective systems for conveying information from top management down through the organization	
• Top managers have direct lines of communication right down the organization	4. Everyone is frequently updated with news about the success of the organization
• Everyone is frequently updated with news about the fortunes of the organization	
• There are frequent presentations to everyone to tell them what is happening in the organization	
• In the last month I have been given a formal briefing from my manager about what is going on in the organization	
• People in this organization are kept well informed of changes which influence them	

Francis and Woodcock (1994c) statements

Combined questionnaire statements

Prejudice

- People feel comfortable about communicating between different status levels
- Men and women are treated as equals here
- There is a genuine dialogue between representatives of the workforce and management
- Everyone had equal treatment regardless of race, color, sex, or creed
- The organization really is an 'equal opportunity employer'
- People are promoted on merit, regardless of their social origins

5. People working for this organization feel comfortable about communicating between different status levels
6. Men and women are treated as equals here
7. There is a genuine conversation between representatives of the workforce and management
8. Everyone has equal treatment regardless of race, color, sex, or creed
9. The organization really is an 'equal opportunities employer'
10. People are promoted on merit, regardless of their social origins

Upward communication flow

- Information flows easily up the organization
- Managers at every level make great efforts to keep in touch with everyone who works in their department
- Those lower down in the organization feel that top management fully understand their difficulties
- There are systems which ensure that any employee's ideas are carefully considered
- Top managers talk frequently with people throughout the organization
- Managers frequently collect information on the thoughts and feelings of the workforce

11. Those lower down in the organization feel that top management/team leaders/supervisors fully understand their problems
12. Top managers/team leaders/supervisors talk frequently with people throughout the organization
13. Managers/team leaders/supervisors frequently collect information on the thoughts and feelings of the workforce

Table 14.3 Sections of the ICA questionnaire included in the combined questionnaire

Original ICA sections and questions (Clampitt in Hargie & Tourish, 2000)	Questions included in the combined questionnaire
Section 1: Strengths and weaknesses in communication (open-ended questions)	Not included.
Section 2: How do you feel about the amount of information you are receiving vs. the amount you would like to receive? (parallel scale question)	Only a single scale question was included. This section was combined with section 9 in order to shorten the questionnaire and limit confusion as the sections were perceived as very similar. *Q: How do you feel about the amount of information you are receiving on the following issues?* *A: Never enough, seldom enough, mostly enough, always enough*
Section 3: How do you feel about the amount of information you are receiving from the following sources vs. the amount you would like to receive from the following sources? (parallel scale question)	Only a single scale question was included. *Q: How do you feel about the amount of information you are receiving from the following sources?* *A: Too much, enough, too little*
Section 4: How much information are you receiving through these channels and how much information would you like to receive? (parallel scale question)	Only a single scale question was included. *Q: How would you rate the amount of information usually received through the following methods?* *A: Too much, enough, too little*
Section 5: How do you feel about the amount of information you are sending vs. the amount you would like to send? (parallel scale question)	Only a single scale question was included. This section was combined with section 10. *Q: How often do you have the opportunity to send information about the following topics?* *A: Never, seldom, often, always*

Original ICA sections and questions (Clampitt in Hargie & Tourish, 2000)	Questions included in the combined questionnaire
Section 6: How do you feel about the action taken on information you are sending vs. the amount of action needed? (parallel scale question)	Only a single scale question was included. *Q: If you did report a problem (or did send some information) how would you describe the action taken by the relevant people/department? A: Always satisfactory, sometimes satisfactory, rarely satisfactory, never satisfactory*
Section 7: How quickly do you get information from the following sources? (single scale question)	Not included. The timeliness of communication was already established as a problem.
Section 8: Working relationships (single scale question)	Included and adjusted to the mining context. This question correlates with Grunig and Hon's trust questions. *Q: How much to you trust each of the following in terms of working together? A: Always, often, rarely, never*
Section 9: How much information do you receive on important issues facing your organization vs. the amount of information you would like to receive? (parallel scale question)	Not included. This section was combined with section 2.
Section 10: How much information do you send on important issues facing your organization vs. the amount of information you need to send? (parallel scale question)	Not included. This section was combined with section 5.
Section 11: Communication experience (short and open-ended questions)	Not included.
Section 12: The challenges ahead (open-ended questions)	Not included.
Section 13: Suggestions for making communication better (open-ended questions)	Not included. This was discussed in the focus groups.

Table 14.4 Grunig and Hon's (1999) relationship statements on integrity and dependability

Grunig and Hon (1999) statements	Combined questionnaire statements
Trust—integrity • This organization treats people like me fairly and justly • Whenever this organization makes an important decision, I know it will be concerned about people like me	1. This organization treats me fairly and justly 2. Whenever this organization makes an important decision, I know it will be concerned about me
Trust—dependability • This organization can be relied on to keep its promises • I believe that this organization takes the opinions of people like me into account when making decisions	3. This organization can be relied on to keep its promises 4. I believe that this organization takes my opinions into account when making decisions
Trust—competence • I feel very confident about this organization's skills • This organization has the ability to accomplish what it says it will do	5. This organization has the ability to accomplish what it says it will do
Control mutuality • This organization and people like me are attentive to what each other say • This organization believes the opinions of people like me are legitimate • In dealing with people like me, this organization has a tendency to throw its weight around • This organization really listens to what people like me have to say	6. In dealing with me, this organization has a tendency to boss me around 7. This organization really listens to what I have to say
Commitment • I feel that this organization is trying to maintain a long-term commitment to people like me • I can see that this organization wants to maintain a relationship with people like me	8. I can see that this organization wants to maintain a relationship with me

Grunig and Hon (1999) statements	Combined questionnaire statements
• There is a long-lasting bond between this organization and people like me	
• Compared to other organizations, I value my relationship with this organization more	
Relationship satisfaction	
• I am happy with this organization	9. I am happy with this organization
• Both the organization and people like me benefit from the relationship	10. Both the organization and I benefit from the relationship
• Most people like me are happy in their interactions with this organization	
• Generally speaking, I am pleased with the relationship this organization has established with people like me	
Communal relationship	
• This organization does not especially enjoy giving others aid	11 This organization usually helps non-employees
• This organization is very concerned about the welfare of people like me	12. This organization is very concerned about my welfare
• I feel that this organization takes advantage of people who are vulnerable	13. This organization only uses people to reach their goals
• I think that this organization succeeds by stepping on other people	
Exchange relationships	
• Whenever this organization gives or offers something to people like me, it generally expects something in return	14. Whenever this organization gives or offers me something, it generally expects something in return
• Even though people like me have a relationship with this organization for a long time, it still expects something in return whenever it offers us a favor	
• This organization will compromise with people like me when it knows that it will gain something	
• This organization takes care of people who are likely to reward the organization	15. This organization takes care of people who are likely to reward the organization

4. Findings

In order to judge whether the combined questionnaire (adapted scales) provided consistent results and overcame the South African mining environment's limitations, it was necessary to investigate the questionnaire's reliability and validity.

4.1. Scale Validity and Reliability

Validity, the extent to which the measurement adequately reflects the true meaning of the concept under consideration, was determined by using expert panel validity (Baxter & Babbie, 2004), factor analysis, and triangulating the questionnaire's findings with focus-group outputs and the results of other phases of the study. Factor analysis determines if the questions did test the construct at hand and explain possible variations in interpretation of the questions in third-world countries like South Africa. The analysis and triangulation provided consistent results.

Reliability, the ability of the questionnaire to generate similar answers from a similar group of respondents, was measured by calculating the Cronbach alpha coefficient (Baxter & Babbie, 2004). J. Grunig and Hon (1999) state that a shorter questionnaire might not measure such high Cronbach values as a longer questionnaire, as the more questions one asks, the more reliable the index is. There is no set level for the Cronbach alpha, but the closer the scale is to 0.90 the more ideal.

4.2. Adapted Francis–Woodcock Questionnaire

When grouping the adopted statements on the concepts together, as defined by Francis and Woodcock (1994a), persuasive management communication delivered a Cronbach alpha of 0.68, statements on prejudice delivered a Cronbach alpha of 0.76, and a Cronbach alpha of 0.74 was calculated for the three statements on the upward flow of communication. However, only one statement was included to measure the downward flow of communication, so a reliability score could not be calculated. These scores indicated that three of the four concepts tested by the Francis–Woodcock questionnaire were reliable.

However, factor analysis showed that respondents attributed statements 1, 2, 3, 11, and 13 (as shown in Table 14.2) to persuasive management, although statements 11 and 13 were originally about upward communication flow. The Cronback alpha for the five statements was 0.75. It can be argued that this shows that management is perceived as persuasive if they also take the views of the employees into account.

Through factor analysis, question 4—the only statement on the downward flow of information—was grouped together with statements 5 to 7 on prejudice and statement 12 on the upward flow of information. The Cronbach alpha calculated as 0.74. This grouping of statements could be explained by the fact that people view the flow of communication as part of the prejudice issue; for instance, people withhold information because they do not like other people.

Statements 8 to 10 were grouped together through factor analysis and resulted in a Cronbach alpha of 0.75. Note that the statements on prejudice divided into two concepts after factor analysis. The two concepts could be described as questions relating to prejudicial communication and equal employment. The eigenvalue for the three factors was greater than one, showing that the three concepts were relatively independent from one another.

Table 14.5 shows that the scale was reliable and valid in terms of measuring persuasive management, as Francis and Woodcock intended. It is interesting to note that respondents made a distinction between prejudice (communication) and prejudice (equal employment), as equal employment is a burning issue in this environment. Downward communication flow and upward communication flow could not be clearly distinguished from the other concepts.

The factor analysis may also show that the concepts as defined by Francis and Woodcock (1994a) may need to be renamed for this particular environment.

4.3. Adapted ICA Questionnaire

The reliability and validity of the adapted ICA questionnaire was proved by triangulating the results of the combined questionnaire with other phases of the project and management interviews. Furthermore, through factor analysis on sections 3, 6, and 8, a difference was noted between the options for those people close to the employee (immediate work colleagues, team leader, and supervisors) against that of management (middle management, senior and top management, and human resources department). The Cronbach alpha for the

Table 14.5 Difference between the concept grouping of original questions and questions grouped together with factor analysis

Concept	Statements in the adapted questionnaire	Cronbach alpha for the adapted questionnaire concepts	Statements grouped together with factor analysis	Cronbach alpha as per the factor analysis
Persuasive management	1–3	0.68	1–3, 13	0.75
Downward communication flow	4	–	–	–
Prejudice (communication)	5–10	0.76	4–7, 11, 12	0.74
Prejudice (equal employment)	5–10		8–10	0.75
Upward communication flow	11–13	0.74	–	–

278 *Tanya le Roux*

two factors that were identified was in all cases more than 0.70. These findings correlate with cross-tabulations done on the data.

The training department was the only option that could be considered as part of either group. These results were confirmed by the focus groups and cross-tabulation results that management is seen as a threat, that the training department is viewed more positively, and that workers prefer to talk to those closest to them (immediate work colleagues, team leader, or supervisors).

Section 2 focused on the question of the amount of information received on various issues. These issues divided into three main concepts through factor analysis:

- job-related issues: job performance; decisions that affect my job; pay, benefits, and appraisals; organizational goals; job contribution to the organization (CA = 0.81);
- job-progress issues: career development opportunities and training;
- current issues in the community: health and safety; environmental, social, and human-rights issues (CA = 0.83).

The Cronbach alpha for job progress issues could not be determined as it only contained two questions. It did, however, match with the focus-group findings.

In section 4, which measured the amount of information that employees received through certain methods delivered, four concepts were identified through factor analysis. These concepts were labeled according to the unavailability of methods to the average worker:

- Limited access methods: these are formal methods that are distanced from the employees through which they can get information. Examples are annual reports, induction programs, policy statements, and billboards in the community (CA = 0.83).
- Less limited access methods: these formal methods are closer to the employees and required literacy, for instance, email and newsletters (CA = 0.64).
- Fairly available methods: informal methods for which literacy is not required; examples are video and information from unions. (Cronbach alpha could not be calculated as there were only two items.)
- Available to all methods: informal methods close to the employees, not requiring literacy; for instance, informal face-to-face contact and telephone conversations. (Cronbach alpha could not be calculated as there were only two items.)

Through factor analysis it was clear that section 5—on sending information— was seen as one concept, with a Cronbach alpha of 0.91. In all the above cases an eigenvalue of greater than 1 was calculated.

Due to the fact that respondents answered the items consistently, the researchers can do *post hoc* concept identification. These concepts are similar to that which the researchers intended to measure; this implies that this scale is valid and reliable.

4.4. The Adapted J. Grunig and Hon Questionnaire

At first the researchers tried to group the statements as close to the concepts as defined by J. Grunig and Hon (1999) and then calculate the Cronbach alpha, in order to prove the reliability of the scale. All the statements measuring trust in the combined questionnaire, except "I believe that this organization takes my opinions into account when making decisions," were used to calculate a Cronbach alpha coefficient of 0.81. This correlates with the Cronbach alpha coefficient that J. Grunig and Hon (1999) obtained in their study. Therefore, it can be argued that the adapted J. Grunig and Hon scale on trust is reliable. Unfortunately, the individual elements of trust could not be measured.

The statement allocated to trust—"I believe that this organization takes my opinions into account when making decisions"—was combined with the two statements on control mutuality. They produced a Cronbach alpha coefficient of 0.39, which proved to be unsatisfactory.

The Cronbach alpha coefficient on commitment and satisfaction could not be established as only one question per construct was included in the combined questionnaire. However, the information gathered from control mutuality, commitment, and satisfaction correlated with the other phases of the project and the qualitative data gathered.

The statement "Both the organization and I benefit from the relationship" was added to the statements on the communal relationship. It proved to be reliable, calculating to a Cronbach alpha coefficient of 0.63. The statement "This organization only uses people to reach their goals," together with the two exchange relationship statements, delivered a Cronbach alpha coefficient of 0.60. Thus, the statements on these constructs proved to be reliable.

However, with factor analysis a very different picture emerged. According to factor analysis, statements 1 to 12 were all part of factor 1 with a Cronbach alpha of 0.85. This means that the concepts of trust, control mutuality, commitment, relationship satisfaction, and communal relationship were not clearly distinguished from each another. Factor 2, with a Cronbach alpha of 0.61, consisted of statements 13 to 15, which proved that the concept of exchange relationship was clearly identified. Once again, the eigenvalues for all of the above factor analyses was more than one.

The factor analysis could indicate that the formulation of the statements, or the fact that statements were left out, or the uniqueness of the respondents, could have influenced the matching of the findings to the previously defined concepts.

5. Recommendations and Future Research

Most of the scales used in the study proved to be reliable and valid on a satisfactory level. The Cronbach alpha coefficients were lower than those obtained in studies that included more questions. However, this can be expected since the alpha coefficient decreases as the number of questions decreases. Factor analysis also provided insight into the concepts as interpreted by the respondents. Furthermore, the following recommendations can be made:

- In the Francis–Woodcock scale, more items should be included and tested on the concepts of downward and upward communication flow; prejudice, too, should be tested in terms of the two concepts it was divided into.
- More work is needed to test the four concepts on the amount of information employees received (section 4) in the ICA questionnaire, and to test the three concepts of section 2 on the amount of information received on various issues.
- Future studies should include more statements on the constructs making up trust in the Grunig–Hon relationship questionnaire in order to test the reliability and validity of the adapted scale of integrity, dependability, and competence. Attention should also be paid to the adapted items measuring commitment, relationship satisfaction, control mutuality, and communal relationships.

In this study, we had to combine the questionnaires in order to meet the client's expectations. More work on the separate testing of each of the scales within this research context needs to be completed in order to make recommendations on the adaptation of these scales to South African mining. The ideal would be to provide a benchmark for measuring communication, organizational behavior, and relationships with semi-literate and illiterate respondents in the South African mining industry.

The general recommendations derived from this study are:

- Researchers in the South African mining industry should be sensitive to the effect of their audit on the employees. After such a study, employees tend to expect almost immediate changes and improvements in their circumstances.
- Adapting existing questionnaires is not an easy process. One should consider any changes carefully and manage them scientifically in order for the scale to maintain their reliability and validity.
- There is a great need for standardized scales that apply to various different research contexts. The importance of employer–employee communication and the resulting relationship will depend on how successfully it can be measured and tracked with a set scale. However, it can only be achieved by researchers using tested scales and adapting them to the context at hand.

We hope that this chapter will inspire researchers to start adapting scales to specific research contexts, in order to provide future researchers with scales applicable to their research goals and context.

Notes

1 Questionnaire printed with the permission of the International Communication Association (ICA).
2 The Grunig–Hon questionnaire was compiled for the Institute for Public Relations' Commission on Public Relations Measurement and Evaluation.

References

Agarwal, S. (2003). The art of scale development. *Marketing Research*, (Fall) 10–12, (electronic version).
Baxter, L. A., & Babbie, E. (2004). *The basics of communication research*. Belmont, CA: Wadsworth.
Bruning, S. D., & Galloway, T. (2003). Expanding the organization–public relationship scale: Exploring the role that structural and personal commitment play in organization-public relationships. *Public Relations Review*, *29*, 309–319 (electronic version).
Bruning, S. D. and Ledingham, J. A. (1999). Relationships between organizations and publics: Development of a multi-dimensional organization-public relationship scale. *Public Relations Review*, *25*(2), 157–170 (electronic version).
Devlin, S. J. (2003). The science of scale interpretation. *Marketing Research*, *44–45* (Winter) (electronic version).
Francis, D., & Woodcock, M. (1994a). *The audit of communication effectiveness: Guide*. Aldershot: Gower Publishing.
Francis, D., & Woodcock, M. (1994b). *The audit of communication effectiveness: Scoring and explanation exercise*. Aldershot: Gower Publishing.
Francis, D., & Woodcock, M. (1994c). *The audit of communication effectiveness: Questionnaire*. Aldershot: Gower Publishing.
Grunig, J. E. (2001). *The role of public relations in management and its contributors to organizational and societal effectiveness*. Speech delivered in Taipei, Taiwan, May 12 (electronic version).
Grunig, J. E., & Hon, L. (1999). *Guidelines for measuring relationships in public relationships*. Gainsville, FL: The Institute for Public Relations (electronic version).
Hargie, O., & Tourish, D. (2000). *Handbook of communication audits for organizations*. London: Routledge.
Ledingham, J. A. (2003). Explicating relationship management as a general theory of public relations. *Journal of Public Relations Research*, *15*(2), 181–198 (electronic version).
Ledingham, J. A., & Bruning, S. D. (1998). Relationship management in public relations: Dimensions of an organization–public relationship. *Public Relations Review*, *24*(1), 55–56 (electronic version).
McGorry, S. Y. (2000). Measurement in a cross-cultural environment: Survey translation issues. *Qualitative Market Research: An International Journal*, *3*(2), 74–81 (electronic version).
Naudé, A. M. E., Fourie, L. M., Le Roux, T., Van Heerden, L., & Venter, A. (2004). *Research report: Employee survey conducted as phase 2 of a stakeholder perception survey*. Unpublished research report.
Thatcher, A., Shaik, F., & Zimmerman, C. (2005). Attitudes of semi-literate and literate bank account holders to the use of automatic teller machines (ATMs). *International Journal of Industrial Ergonomics*, *35*, 115–130 (electronic version).

15 Applying Stakeholder Thinking to Public Relations

An Integrated Approach to Identifying Relationships That Matter

Nigel de Bussy

1. Introduction

The terms "stakeholder" and "public" are often used interchangeably, despite what some public relations scholars claim are subtle differences (J. Grunig & Repper, 1992). Whether or not a distinction can be made between the two designations, the importance of the underlying concept they represent is undeniable. J. Grunig, L. Grunig, and Ehling (1992: 76) described these "organized bodies" as "the raison d'être for public relations." In recent years, beyond the relatively narrow confines of the public relations literature, "stakeholder" has become the more widely favored expression. Numerous academic papers devoted to stakeholder theory have appeared, largely to be found in journals of management and the related fields of business ethics, and business and society (Donaldson & Preston, 1995; Gibson, 2000). Few, if any, mention public relations or acknowledge the term "publics" as a plausible alternative to "stakeholders." With some exceptions (e.g., Black & Hartel, 2004; Bronn & Bronn, 2003), public relations scholars have been relatively slow to take into account the burgeoning field of stakeholder theory in their own research despite its obvious relevance.

This chapter addresses one of the most contentious issues in the entire stakeholder debate—the question of who (or what) a stakeholder is. The concepts of legitimacy (Phillips, 2003; Suchman, 1995) and stakeholder responsibility (Windsor, 2002) are posited as central considerations. Clarification of this fundamental issue is as important to public relations practitioners and scholars as it is to the field of stakeholder management. Indeed, I argue that an integrated approach, drawing on concepts developed in both areas, is essential.

The chapter proceeds as follows. We begin with a brief introduction to the stakeholder concept, including the emergence of three distinct strands of stakeholder theory—instrumental, normative, and descriptive (Donaldson & Preston, 1995). The long-standing problem of defining who exactly is a stakeholder is then discussed, highlighting the discrepancies between the so-called broad and narrow definitions (Freeman & Reed, 1983). Next, the concept of legitimacy (Phillips, 2003; Suchman, 1995) is reviewed in some detail given its potential significance in identifying who is a stakeholder. An analysis of the theory of stakeholder identification and salience (TSIS) (Mitchell, Agle, & Wood, 1997) follows—one of the few substantial contributions to the stakeholder literature from a descriptive perspective. Previously unacknowledged parallels between TSIS and situation theory from the public relations field (J. Grunig & Hunt, 1984) are noted. An apparently small but highly significant revision of Freeman's classic definition of a stakeholder (Freeman, 1984) is then proposed. A framework based on the notion of stakeholder responsibility is presented as a guide to assist managers assess the legitimacy of potential stakeholders and, consequently, to identify who should be accorded stakeholder status.

2. The Stakeholder Concept

It is now more than two decades since the publication of R. Edward Freeman's landmark book *Strategic Management: A Stakeholder Approach* (Freeman, 1984). During that time, the word *stakeholder* has emerged from relative obscurity to become one of the most widely used and discussed terms in the contemporary discourses of business academe, corporate management, and even political campaigning. In their seminal 1995 article, Donaldson and Preston estimated that more than 100 articles and around a dozen books focusing primarily on the stakeholder concept had been published since the appearance of Freeman's work (Donaldson & Preston, 1995). Since then, the pace of publication has quickened yet further. Gibson (2000) found that over 200 articles on stakeholder theory had appeared between 1998 and 2000. The stakeholder economy was a defining theme of the British Labour Party's highly successful 1997 general election campaign (Sternberg, 1999). As Donaldson put it recently, "today the term has arrived" (Donaldson, 2002: 107). Yet, despite this plethora of publications, or indeed partly because of it, there exists today widespread confusion about the stakeholder concept, the nature of stakeholder theory (or theories), and its proper role in management practice (Stoney & Winstanley, 2001). Freeman and Phillips (2002) have recently argued that stakeholder theory is better understood not as a monolithic theory, but rather as a genre of stakeholder theories.

Donaldson and Preston critiqued the already considerable volume of stakeholder-theory literature available in 1995 and created a framework for much subsequent debate. The key aspect of their analysis was to identify three distinct types or strands of stakeholder theory, which, Donaldson and Preston argued, had always been implicit in the stakeholder debate but had hitherto simply been lumped together inappropriately. The authors sought to make these three strands—descriptive, instrumental, and normative-stakeholder theory— explicit and to devote separate analyses to each. Descriptive-stakeholder theory attempts to describe and sometimes explain aspects of corporate and stakeholder behavior. It is concerned with what managers and organizations actually do. Instrumental-stakeholder theory relates to the potential connections between certain stakeholder management practices and the achievement of traditional corporate objectives such as profitability and growth. Normative-stakeholder theory focuses on ethical guidelines for the operation and management of corporations. It endeavors to tell managers what they *should* do (Donaldson & Preston, 1995).

Identifying exactly who is a stakeholder has become one of the most contentious and problematic issues of the entire stakeholder debate (Mitchell *et al.*, 1997). The apparent failure of stakeholder theorists to reach consensus on the definition of the term has provided an opportunity for critics to ridicule the entire stakeholder project (Sternberg, 1999). This paper argues that the concept of legitimacy is a vital consideration in identifying stakeholders (Mitchell *et al.*, 1997; Phillips, 2003; Suchman, 1995). Only those who can *legitimately* affect or who are affected by the organization should be taken into account as stakeholders.

2.1. The Narrow Versus the Broad Definition of a Stakeholder

The term *stakeholder* was originally defined by the Stanford Research Institute as "those groups without whose support the organization would cease to exist" (Freeman, 1984: 31). This was taken to mean such groups as shareholders, employees, customers, suppliers, lenders, and society. In addition to launching the voluminous and long-running debate on the stakeholder concept, Freeman also dramatically widened the definition and scope of "stakeholder." The Stanford Research Institute definition cited here has come to be known as the narrow definition. Freeman (1984: 25) proposed a much broader conceptualization, defining a stakeholder as "any group or individual who can affect or is affected by the achievement of the firm's objectives." In other words, virtually anyone—even a terrorist (Freeman, 1984: 53)—can be considered a stakeholder. Specifically, Freeman talked about governments, local community organizations, consumer advocates, competitors, the media, special interest groups, and environmentalists as stakeholders in addition to owners, customers, employees, and suppliers. Others subsequently took the notion yet further, extending the notion of stakeholder to non-human entities such as the environment (Starik, 1995).

Clarkson (1995: 106) defined stakeholders as "persons or groups that have, or claim, ownership, rights, or interests in a corporation and its activities, past, present, or future." He added that stakeholders with similar interests could be classified into groups such as employees, shareholders, and customers. A primary stakeholder group in Clarkson's view is one without whom the corporation cannot survive, which is essentially the original Stanford Research Institute definition. Specifically, Clarkson referred to shareholders, employees, customers, suppliers, and "the public stakeholder group" defined as governments and communities. He used Freeman's concept of groups who affect or are affected by the corporation—but are not engaged in transactions with the organization and are not essential to its survival—as the basis of his definition of secondary stakeholder groups. Examples include the media and special interest groups.

As Mitchell *et al.* (1997: 853) observed, "stakeholder theory . . . offers a maddening variety of signals on how questions of stakeholder identification might be answered." They went on to present a table containing no fewer than twenty-seven definitions of stakeholder that have appeared in the literature over the past forty years. Phillips and Reichart (2000) correctly described the problem of stakeholder identity as a "glaring shortcoming" of stakeholder theory, adding, "this inability to distinguish stakeholders from non-stakeholders threatens the very meaningfulness of the term" (p. 185). As might be expected, comments from critics of stakeholder theory on this issue are even more forthright. Sternberg (1999) highlighted problems with the relatively simple category of "employees." Should temporary employees be included or just permanent staff? Should part-timers be treated on the same basis as full-timers? What about pensioners, former employees, probationary trainees, and potential recruits? As noted above, Clarkson (1995) suggested that stakeholders with similar interests could be classified into groups. Sternberg (1999), however, questioned that assumption. What if some employees want higher wages while others prefer shorter hours? Some employees may regard more responsibility as a benefit, others as a burden. Who is to be regarded as the authoritative voice of stakeholder opinion if there are competing representative groups? If individuals belong to more than one group, should they be treated primarily as an employee, a shareholder, a member of the local community, or as whatever other stakeholder category they may fit?

It has frequently been pointed out that Freeman's famous definition of a stakeholder as "any group or individual who can affect or is affected by the achievement of the firm's objectives" (1984: 25) is extremely wide ranging. Under this definition virtually anyone—legitimate or otherwise—may be regarded as a stakeholder. Only those unable to affect the organization (i.e., those with no power) *and* who are unaffected by it (i.e., have no claim, interest, or relationship) are non-stakeholders (Mitchell *et al.*, 1997). In addition, Starik (1995) has argued that non-human nature should be regarded as a stakeholder in its own right and not merely be represented through proxies such as environmental activist organizations. While Clarkson is widely viewed as an advocate of a relatively narrow definition of "stakeholder"—based on the notion of risk—in defining the term he refers to claims, rights and interests, "*past, present, or future*" (emphasis added) (Clarkson, 1995: 106). If these contentions are accepted, it would be possible to assert, based on the literature, that a stakeholder can be virtually any living organism—human, animal, or plant (including the Earth itself)—that has ever lived, is alive now, or might be alive in the future. Sternberg observed that stakeholders can include "virtually everyone, everything, everywhere." With the clear objective of ridiculing the stakeholder concept, she wrote, "terrorists and competitors, vegetation, nameless sea creatures, and generations yet unborn are amongst the many groups that are now officially considered to be business stakeholders—by major businesses as well as by misguided academics and special interest groups" (Sternberg, 1999: 13).

2.2. Strategic and Moral Stakeholders

Freeman's differentiation between those affecting and those affected by the organization has been elaborated upon to create a distinction between *strategic* stakeholders (those with the power to affect the organization) and *moral* stakeholders (those affected by the organization) (Frooman, 1999), or as Mitchell *et al.* (1997: 859) put it, "influencers" and "claimants." The possibility that an individual or group can both affect *and* be affected by an organization is apparent (Kaler, 2002); arguably, most stakeholders would fall into that category. In general terms, theorists who wish to narrow the definition of stakeholders (e.g., Clarkson Centre for Business Ethics, 1999; Phillips, 1997; Kaler, 2002) put greater emphasis on claimant than influencer definitions. Kaler (2002) has recently argued that at least as far as business ethics is concerned, "influencer" and combinatory definitions are redundant. Stakeholders in a business should be regarded only as those with a claim on its services. On the other hand, those who wish to retain a broad definition (e.g., Mitchell *et al.*, 1997) acknowledge the value of identifying influencer stakeholders to the strategic planning process.

One problem with the concept of moral stakeholders is the difficulty of establishing how they differ qua stakeholders from any other individual or group upon whom an organization may impact. In other words, with regard to those affected by the organization, does stakeholder theory add anything of value to more conventional (non-stakeholder) ethical analyses? Kaler (2002) identified this problem, highlighting in his discussion of claimant stakeholder definitions that claims must be role-specific or they would indeed create no duties over and above those required toward anyone. Unfortunately, he did not elaborate this point further. The key problem with Kaler's analysis is the same problem which besets normative-stakeholder theory in general—namely, the assumption that business must serve the interests of all its stakeholders as opposed to merely taking the interests of non-shareholder stakeholders into account while focusing on firm value maximization. If the assumption is accepted, then stakeholder theory does indeed create claimants whose interests must be satisfied. Even the narrowest definition of a stakeholder would lead to enormous difficulties for business on this basis, since the theory offers little guidance on how the often conflicting wishes of (at a minimum) shareholders, employees, customers, the community, and suppliers are to be satisfied or co-ordinated. There appear to be no criteria to determine where the balance should be struck. If the broad definition is applied, normal business activity would simply become impossible; the critics (e.g., Sternberg, 1999) are quite correct on this point.

2.3 The Principle of Stakeholder Fairness

Phillips, a supporter of normative-stakeholder theory, has acknowledged the practical difficulties inherent in applying the theory while upholding a very broad definition of a stakeholder (Phillips, 1997; Phillips & Reichart, 2000). In order to narrow down the definition of stakeholder, Phillips proposed an approach predicated on Rawlsian notions of fair play (Phillips, 1997; Phillips & Reichart, 2000). Phillips's principle of stakeholder fairness states:

> Whenever persons or groups of persons voluntarily accept the benefits of a mutually beneficial scheme of cooperation requiring sacrifice or contribution on the parts of the participants and there exists the possibility of free-riding, obligations of fairness are created among the participants in the cooperative scheme in proportion to the benefits accepted.
>
> (Phillips, 1997: 57)

If it is accepted that the term "cooperative scheme" includes conventional commercial corporations, then the Phillips principle looks remarkably similar to the ethical framework of one of stakeholding's severest critics, Elaine Sternberg. Sternberg (1994, 1999) proposed a libertarian version of distributive justice as the cornerstone of ethical business practice. Those who contribute to the success of a business enterprise should share fairly in its profits, to the extent merited by their individual contributions. Phillips (1997) and Phillips and Reichart (2000) argued that it is not human interaction per se which creates obligations but the act of voluntarily accepting benefits. He also pointed out that these obligations cut both ways—stakeholders who voluntarily accept benefits from a corporation are under an obligation to consider the well-being of the firm (Phillips & Reichart, 2000).

The next part of Phillips's argument appears superficially to put considerable distance between himself and Sternberg, as he contended the task of management is to find the middle ground in the distribution of limited resources from among a finite number of stakeholder groups with legitimate but often competing interests. In practice, however, using Phillips's principle, a stakeholder accepting a benefit would presumably have an obligation to make a contribution to the enterprise commensurate with the size of the benefit received—very much along the lines proposed by Sternberg. On this interpretation, Phillips's principle of stakeholder fairness does not seem to provide moral stakeholders with additional rights over and above those Sternberg (1994, 1999)—or indeed any reasonable person—would acknowledge are owed anyway to those affected by the actions of an organization. If that is the case, why then employ the term "stakeholder" at all as opposed to simply using the term "human"? Ironically, Phillips and Reichart (2000) used precisely this argument with regard to strategic stakeholders in the context of their rebuttal of Starik's advocacy of the natural environment as a stakeholder in its own right (Starik, 1995). Phillips's principle of stakeholder fairness (Phillips, 1997) does not appear to provide a rationale for treating moral stakeholders *as stakeholders* over and above simply as human beings.

2.4. The Significance of Legitimacy

In more recent work, Phillips (2003) seems in effect to have joined the broad stakeholder definition camp albeit by a circuitous route and without explicit acknowledgment. The notion of legitimacy has long been recognized in the literature as a key consideration in the identification of stakeholders. Freeman (1984) wrote, "stakeholder connotes legitimacy . . . legitimacy can be understood in a managerial sense implying that it is legitimate to spend time and resources on stakeholders, *regardless of the appropriateness of their demands*" (p. 45, emphasis added). It is this interpretation of legitimacy, which enabled Freeman, as discussed previously, to include terrorists as potential stakeholders. Legitimacy is one of the three core constructs in the stakeholder identification and salience model developed by Mitchell *et al.* (1997)—the others being power and urgency. For Mitchell *et al.* (1997), legitimacy is a variable that stakeholders may possess to differing degrees or not at all. For example, the groups that Mitchell *et al.* (1997) described as dangerous stakeholders are those possessing both power and urgency but not legitimacy (terrorists would presumably be an example). Demanding stakeholders possess urgency, but neither legitimacy nor power (Mitchell *et al.*, 1997).

Derivative Legitimacy

Phillips (2003) ostensibly took a very different position, arguing that there may be no such thing as an illegitimate stakeholder. A person or group falling into that category would be a "non-stakeholder." However, Phillips (2003) has moved considerably in the direction of a more expansive definition of stakeholders than he envisaged previously (Phillips, 1997; Phillips & Reichart, 2000). He has done this while remaining consistent with his earlier philosophical underpinnings by delineating a special category of legitimacy which he called "derivative legitimacy" (Phillips, 2003). According to Phillips (2003: 31), derivative stakeholders are "those groups whose actions and claims must be accounted for by managers due to their potential effects upon the organization and its normative [moral] stakeholders." Phillips (2003) continued to argue that normative or moral stakeholders are owed additional obligations of stakeholder fairness over and above those due to any human being. What is significant here, however, is the conferral of derivative legitimacy on those referred to elsewhere in the literature as strategic stakeholders or influencers. It appears highly likely that Phillips's (2003) notion of derivative legitimacy leads to a de facto acknowledgment of the broad definition of a stakeholder. If any individual or group who can affect an organization has derivative legitimacy, and any individual or group who is affected by an organization has normative legitimacy, the upshot is that just about anyone possesses legitimacy and, therefore, just about anyone is a stakeholder.

The issue of who is a non-stakeholder brings the question into focus. Phillips stated that non-stakeholders are important, but, unfortunately, he gave few examples of who they may be. If non-stakeholders possess neither normative nor derivative legitimacy, then who are they, if not merely the same groups excluded from Freeman's broad definition on the grounds of their inability to affect the organization and the fact that they are unaffected by it? In their rebuttal of Starik's (1995) claim for the natural environment as a stakeholder, Phillips and Reichart (2000) argued that the ability to affect the organization does not create moral obligations above those owed to all humans. They wrote, "it therefore appears possible for 'stakeholder' to lose all significance under the 'can affect' criterion" (p. 189). Yet Phillips's introduction of the notion of derivative legitimacy appears to have exactly the same effect. The useful purpose served by the recent work of Phillips (2003) is to provide a normative justification for taking into account those with the power to affect organizations; previously, this was thought of largely as a strategic matter. Normative-stakeholder theory argues that managers have obligations to a diverse range of moral stakeholder groups. Therefore, Phillips contended that those with the ability to affect the interests of moral stakeholders must be taken into account, not just for reasons of self-interest, but because of their potential to impact morally legitimate stakeholders (Phillips, 2003). To this extent Phillips, through the notion of derivative legitimacy, has refined the basis on which strategic stakeholders are afforded legitimacy, a status first accorded to them by Freeman more than twenty years ago.

Traditions and Types of Legitimacy

Before examining Mitchell *et al.*'s (1997) theory of stakeholder identification and salience in more detail, it is necessary to scrutinize further the key construct of legitimacy. The foregoing discussion has already highlighted its relevance to this debate. Phillips (2003) criticized Mitchell *et al.* (1997) on several grounds, one of the most crucial of which concerns legitimacy. Mitchell *et al.* contended that power and legitimacy are separate, if overlapping, constructs. Phillips, however, argued that power and legitimacy cannot be separated in the manner proposed by Mitchell *et al.* According to Phillips, only legitimacy matters in this regard; power is merely one avenue through which legitimacy is acquired.

The most comprehensive recent overview of the concept of legitimacy in the management field was produced by Suchman (1995), whose observation that "many researchers employ the term legitimacy, but few define it" (p. 572) can be fairly applied to much of the stakeholder literature. Suchman defined legitimacy as "a generalized perception or assumption that the actions of an entity are desirable, proper, or appropriate within some socially constructed system of norms, values, beliefs, and definitions" (p. 574). This definition calls into question the arguments of Freeman (1984) and Phillips (2003), discussed above. It may well be legitimate for managers to take into account "entities" that are undesirable, improper, or inappropriate in order to protect others with legitimate—i.e., desirable, proper, or appropriate—interests. However, it is questionable, to say the least, whether this then entitles one to describe such entities as "legitimate," as Freeman (1984) did, without much further rational-ization, and which Phillips justified by appealing to "derivative" legitimacy. (To be fair, Phillips did make clear that managers are under no obligation to treat "derivative" stakeholders in the same way as normative stakeholders.)

Suchman (1995) identified two broad traditions in the organizational legitimacy literature—strategic legitimacy and institutional legitimacy. Strategic legitimacy refers to "the depiction of legitimacy as an *operational resource* that organizations extract—often competitively—from their cultural environments and that they employ in pursuit of their goals (Suchman, 1995: 576; emphasis in the original). Many public relations activities can be construed as strategic legitimation endeavors by managers attempting to control often-symbolic resources in order to win the support of stakeholders. For example, Heugens, Van Den Bosch, and Van Riel (2002) identified various types of legitimacy as potential organizational benefits resulting from correctly applied stakeholder-management strategies. By contrast, institutional legitimacy refers to the view that legitimacy is a set of constitutive beliefs (Suchman, 1995: 576). Rather than organizations extracting legitimacy from the environment, institutional legitimacy researchers view the concept as a function of the influence of external institutions on organizations. Prevailing cultural norms will determine how the organization is structured and managed as well as how it is perceived (Suchman, 1995). Stakeholder management is of relatively minor significance to the institutionalist but a focal theme for strategic legitimacy researchers. An institutional perspective would lead to a cautious view on the potential efficacy of much "traditional" stakeholder management.

In addition, Suchman identified three basic types of legitimacy—pragmatic, moral, and cognitive—each predicated on a different behavioral dynamic. Pragmatic legitimacy rests on the self-interested calculations of an organization's most immediate audiences, at its simplest, boiling down to a sort of "exchange" legitimacy (Suchman, 1995: 578). Related to this is "influence legitimacy," which is similar but involves organizations being responsive to what stakeholders perceive as their larger interests, rather than being based on specific favorable exchanges. Suchman noted that influence legitimacy can often be obtained through an organization's willingness to relinquish some measure of authority to the constituency in question. A third form of pragmatic legitimacy is "dispositional legitimacy," where the audience accords legitimacy to those organizations which it perceives as having its interests at heart, sharing its values, or considers honest, decent, and trustworthy (Suchman, 1995). Moral legitimacy refers to positive normative evaluations of the organization and its activities irrespective of whether a given activity is perceived to benefit the evaluator, in other words, to whether the audience believe that the organization is "doing the right thing" (Suchman, 1995). Moral legitimacy can be divided into four types: consequential (based on moral outcomes), procedural (related to moral processes), structural (connected with types of activity and/or organization), and personal (founded on perceptions of organizational leadership) (Suchman, 1995). Finally, there is cognitive legitimacy, a very different concept from the first two basic types in that it is not based on audience evaluations. According to Suchman, cognitive legitimacy has two significant variants: legitimacy based on comprehensibility, and legitimacy based on taken-for-grantedness. The latter, suggested Suchman, is the most subtle and powerful source of legitimacy of all the various types discussed. If alternatives are unimaginable (or at least unimagined), opposition is inconceivable. However, Suchman noted that in practice, such taken-for-grantedness is difficult or impossible for managers to obtain. Indeed, to move from pragmatic to moral to cognitive legitimacy becomes progressively harder for managements to achieve. Suchman contended that researchers employing the legitimacy-construct need either to address the full range of the phenomenon or specify which aspect(s) they have in mind—pragmatism, morality, or cognition. In addition, when considering legitimation strategies, Suchman showed the need for drawing a clear distinction between efforts to gain, maintain, and repair legitimacy. In short, legitimacy is a highly complex, multi-dimensional construct, which, arguably, has been discussed hitherto in the stakeholder literature in an overly simplistic manner.

While acknowledging the cautionary implications of institutional legitimacy research, stakeholder theory is best understood within a strategic legitimacy framework. Instrumental-stakeholder theory, in particular, belongs in an environment concerned primarily with gaining, maintaining, and repairing (when necessary) the three major forms of pragmatic legitimacy—exchange, influence, and dispositional legitimacy. Traditional, transaction-oriented, product and services marketing to customers belongs in the domain of exchange legitimacy, although it could be argued that some higher-order services involve the notion of influence legitimacy. Corporate level public relations is very much concerned both with influence and dispositional legitimacy.

Applying Suchman's (1995) legitimacy taxonomy to organizational stakeholders, as opposed to focal organizations themselves, is potentially enlightening. If, as Mitchell *et al.* (1997) contended, legitimacy is a key variable in understanding stakeholder salience, it may well be that salience is influenced by the type of legitimacy which managers perceive the group in question to possess. Some primary stakeholders (e.g., shareholders) may possess cognitive legitimacy for managers—a legitimacy based on "taken-for-grantedness"—whereas suppliers may be perceived to possess merely exchange legitimacy. Government and community groups may be salient to managers for reasons of influence legitimacy. In other words, the application of the legitimacy construct to stakeholder identification and salience may be far more complex than Mitchell *et al.* allowed for. Stakeholders may vary in the eyes of managers, not only in terms of the overall level of legitimacy, but also with regard to the type of legitimacy. Perhaps a given value of cognitive legitimacy would be a more powerful attribute in determining managerial salience than the same level of exchange legitimacy. These questions are worthy of further investigation.

2.5. The Theory of Stakeholder Identification and Salience

Considerable reference has already been made to Mitchell *et al.*'s (1997) theory of stakeholder identification and salience (TSIS). As Jawahar and McLaughlin (2001) acknowledged, TSIS was one of the few substantial pieces of descriptive-stakeholder theory prior to their own publication. TSIS is actually intended to be a contribution to both normative and descriptive theory, in that the framework for identifying stakeholders falls into the realm of the normative, while salience is an aspect of descriptive theory (Mitchell *et al.*, 1997). Mitchell *et al.*'s core argument is that managerial perceptions of stakeholder salience are based on the perceived stakeholder attributes of power, legitimacy, and urgency. After reviewing the broad versus narrow debate, as well as numerous other definitions falling somewhere between the two extremes, Mitchell *et al.* opted to base their theory on Freeman's (1984) broad definition, which has been so widely cited in the literature. Their justification appears to be that an exhaustive list of stakeholders is needed, based on whether managers are motivated by conventional strategic considerations (i.e., maximizing long-term financial performance) or by a desire to balance the various claims and interests within the firm's social system. The application of a broad definition to the latter approach would indeed, in the words of Phillips (2003: 32), "drive the framework straight back into the abyss of stakeholder proliferation and intractability." However, if the purpose of the firm is restated as long-term value maximization, as proposed by Jensen's "enlightened stakeholder theory" (Jensen, 2002), adoption of the broad definition becomes not only manageable but essential.

Mitchell *et al.* described the presence of an underlying strategic intention in stakeholder management programs as a "public-affairs approach" (p. 859). This reference to public affairs is interesting: a theoretical model, situation theory, had been developed by J. Grunig and Hunt (1984) more than a decade before the publication of Mitchell *et al.*'s article, and bears some striking similarities with TSIS. This appears to be another case of researchers from separate but related areas operating on parallel lines without paying attention to developments in the other field (de Bussy & Ewing, 1998). As stated above, TSIS is predicated on three key variables—power, legitimacy, and urgency. Situation theory is also based on three key variables, namely, problem recognition, constraint recognition, and level of involvement. Power and constraint recognition are clearly parallel. The former refers to managerial perceptions of the ability of stakeholders to affect their organizations; the latter refers to the self-belief of the publics themselves to do so. Equally, urgency and level of involvement have striking conceptual similarities. Mitchell *et al.* (1997) made clear that "urgency" in the context of their discussion refers both to time-based urgency and the degree of importance which managers believe that stakeholders attach to an issue—a very similar concept to the level of involvement.

One potential problem with Mitchell *et al.*'s use of legitimacy as a variable in their model has been highlighted above, namely, the failure of TSIS to take into account fundamentally different types of legitimacy. Another is the relationship between the constructs of legitimacy and power. As noted earlier, Mitchell *et al.* held that legitimacy and power are separate but overlapping constructs, whereas Phillips (2003) argued that legitimacy and power cannot be separated in this manner, contending that power is but one avenue through which legitimacy can be acquired. If Freeman's broad definition is accepted, then it is clear that power must be an important criterion in identifying stakeholders; after all, what else can be understood by the "can affect" component of the definition other than that the individuals or groups in question possess some form of power? However, if the second variable in the model (legitimacy) overlaps with the first (power), as Mitchell *et al.* themselves acknowledged, it should be immediately apparent that TSIS is a less than ideal conceptualization. Robust theoretical models should be comprised of mutually exclusive independent variables.

Apart from this methodological issue, conceptually, the notion of a "non-legitimate" stakeholder seems at odds with the entire thrust of the stakeholder project. The very term "stakeholder" was coined in the first place to imply that groups other than shareholders have rights, claims, and interests that should be paid attention to by management. If the stakeholder concept means anything at all, it surely must imply that managers should give stakeholders more consideration and better treatment than non-stakeholder groups. This contention appears to make little sense if those rights, claims, and interests lack legitimacy. Individuals and groups lacking legitimacy should not logically or ethically be given any favorable treatment. As Freeman (1984: 45) wrote, "stakeholder connotes legitimacy." Phillips (2003) claimed that there is no such thing as a non-legitimate stakeholder. A number of leading stakeholder theorists actually include the term "legitimate" in their definition of a stakeholder (e.g., Brenner, 1993, cited by Mitchell *et al.*, 1997; Donaldson & Preston, 1995; Hill & Jones 1992).

Legitimacy as used in TSIS is ultimately unsatisfactory because *all* stakeholders should be legitimate or they are not stakeholders at all. Nor is it necessary to claim as Phillips (2003) did that groups lacking legitimacy in the accepted sense of the term (Suchman, 1995) may be accorded derivative legitimacy if they have the power to affect the organization. Such groups may be considered illegitimate non-stakeholders with terrorists, burglars, and extortionists falling into this category. The current understanding of stakeholder theory stresses interactive, mutually engaged and responsive relationships (Andriof, Waddock, Husted, & Sutherland, 2002). The idea of engaging in a mutually responsive manner with terrorists and extortionists is palpably absurd. Families must take into account the possibility of being affected by a burglar and take appropriate precautions, but they do not normally seek to establish a mutually supportive relationship with such criminals. Similarly, organizations must take into account the possibility of being affected by those wielding illegitimate power, but it would be a grave mistake to call them "stakeholders," whether derivative or otherwise. Both Freeman's (1984) and Phillips's (2003) according of stakeholder status to terrorists—albeit with caveats—merely provides ammunition to the likes of Elaine Sternberg who seek to ridicule the whole notion of stakeholding.

2.6. Redefining Who Is, and Is Not, a Stakeholder

In view of the confusion in the literature, this chapter proposes to redefine a stakeholder as "any individual or group who can affect *legitimately*, or is affected by, the achievement of the organization's objectives." "Legitimate" is used here in the broad sense encompassing the entire construct delineated by Suchman (1995). Closely related to the foregoing discussion is the issue of stakeholder responsibility, long acknowledged in the literature (e.g., Bowie 1991) but until recently relatively little examined. Indicative of the blossoming interest in this topic, however, was a 2002 special issue of the *Journal of Corporate Citizenship*. Just as Carroll's (1979) model of corporate social responsibility requires both legal and ethical behavior of corporations, so it would be reasonable to extend these dimensions as a minimum to evaluate the behavior of stakeholders. Windsor's paper in the *Journal of Corporate Citizenship* special issue discussed the need for stakeholder responsibilities to be separated from general moral and citizenship obligations (Windsor, 2002), highlighting, in particular, inherent difficulties with the notion of consumer responsibilities. Stakeholder responsibilities, Windsor pointed out, require that managers first conduct themselves morally. He also distinguished between strong and weak forms of the stakeholder-responsibility thesis. Even the weak form would surely have to encompass ethical and legal behavior by stakeholders as a minimum. It is not necessary for the purposes of this argument to assume the strong form that might demand discretionary stakeholder responsibilities. Assuming ethical behavior by management, a simple two-by-two matrix based on the notion of stakeholder responsibility can be constructed to assist managers in distinguishing between legitimate stakeholders and illegitimate non-stakeholders.

As discussed above, terrorists and the like would fall into the bottom right-hand quadrant, classified as illegitimate non-stakeholders. Using Clarkson's RDAP (Reactive, Defensive, Accommodative, Proactive) scale (Clarkson, 1995), the appropriate managerial strategy for this group would be reaction or defence. Equally clearly, groups and individuals who behave both legally and ethically (top left-hand quadrant) must be regarded as legitimate and therefore qualify for stakeholder status (assuming, of course, that they can either affect or are affected by the achievement of the organization's objectives). The ambiguous quadrants are top right (stakeholder actions ethical but illegal) and bottom left (stakeholder actions legal but unethical). Here, management must exercise judgment as to whether to recognize the group or individual in question as legitimate and therefore worthy of stakeholder status.

An example of the former (ethical but illegal) could be some form of direct action by a special interest group. In Australia in late 2003, public controversy was generated over the issue of the live-sheep export trade and the alleged animal cruelty it entails. One animal-rights activist contaminated a sheep-feeding lot with pork meat in the knowledge that the sheep were destined for the Middle East where any suggestion of such contamination would render the animals completely unacceptable (Ray, 2003). Clearly, the action was illegal; however, some may regard it as ethically justified under the circumstances. As Humber (2002) pointed out, legality should be distinguished from

Table 15.1 Using the concept of stakeholder responsibility to identify
non-stakeholders

	Potential stakeholder actions legal	*Potential stakeholder actions illegal*
Potential stakeholder actions ethical	Legitimate stakeholder	Legitimacy must be considered on a case-by-case basis
Potential stakeholder actions unethical	Legitimacy must be considered on a case-by-case basis	Illegitimate non-stakeholder

ethicality. In this instance, the industry would need to make a judgment on whether to engage the animal rights activists in a dialogue (i.e., treat them as legitimate stakeholders) or regard them as non-legitimate "criminals."

An example typifying the bottom left-hand quadrant (legal but unethical) could be the behavior of some sections of the media, which distort facts to portray companies, governments, and individuals in the worst possible light. Examples of such abuses by the Australian media have been comprehensively documented in a recent book by a senior journalist (Sheehan, 2003). Faced with conduct of this nature, once again managers would need to make a judgment about whether or not to accept the media concerned as legitimate and therefore worthy of "stakeholder" treatment, which implies the adoption of, at a minimum, the strategy of accommodation on the RDAP scale (Clarkson, 1995). It should be apparent that the matrix in Table 15.1 is explicitly normative or prescriptive in character. No claims of a descriptive nature are being made.

2.7. Integrating Stakeholder Thinking into Public Relations

The basis of the subtle distinction made in the public relations literature between the terms "public" and "stakeholder" lies in the implications of J. Grunig's situation theory (J. Grunig & Hunt, 1984; J. Grunig & Repper, 1992). J. Grunig & Repper (1992) accepted Freeman's broad definition of a stakeholder as their starting-point and proposed the preparation of a stakeholder map as the essential first step in the strategic management of publics. They then recommended applying the situation model with its key variables of problem recognition, constraint recognition, and level of involvement to segment recognized stakeholders into active and passive publics. In other words, publics are segmented subsets of stakeholder groups. The strategic implication of this process for managers is obviously that active publics should be prioritized, although J. Grunig and Repper (1992) pointed out that passive stakeholders should not be ignored since they always have the potential to become active. Unfortunately, the subtleties of this distinction have often been confused. A typical example can be found in the popular text book *Public Relations: A Values-Driven Approach* (Guth & Marsh, 2006). Guth and Marsh (2006: 5) defined a public as "any group of people who share common interests or values in a particular situation" and went on to state that "when a public has a relationship with your organization, the public is called a stakeholder," that is, stakeholders are segmented subsets of publics rather than vice versa. To add to the confusion, they stated elsewhere in their text that "[t]he word *stakeholder* often substitutes for the word *public*, but the two words aren't interchangeable" (2006: 93, emphasis in the original), later contradicting themselves (p. 206) by defining "stakeholder research" as focusing on the identification of the "specific *publics* important to the success of the client" (emphasis added).

Rather than try to maintain a tortuous and artificial distinction between the terms "public" and "stakeholder," the way forward for public relations is to adopt stakeholder thinking. Outside the relatively small world of public relations scholarship, the term "stakeholder" commands considerable prominence (Donaldson, 2002). Referring to stakeholders rather than publics (in the narrow technical sense of the term) can help demystify the frequently misunderstood role of public relations. Of all the major management functions, public relations is the best placed to facilitate the adoption of the stakeholder concept by organizations. However, this is often not appreciated, resulting in the limitation of public relations to its traditional press agentry function. Public relations scholars and practitioners can help others to better understand their field by making clear that the focus of their discipline is stakeholder relationships.

Similarly, the now blossoming field of stakeholder theory needs to be better used in the specialist public relations literature, and public relations researchers should make greater efforts to publish in management and business-ethics journals. The potential for fruitful cross-fertilization is apparent. The obvious parallels between the theory of stakeholder identification and salience (Mitchell *et al.*, 1997) and situation theory (J. Grunig & Hunt, 1984) are a case in point. As noted earlier, both theories emphasize the importance of perceptions of stakeholder power and level of involvement/urgency. These variables can be used both to predict the salience of a particular stakeholder group in the eyes of management and the likely behavior of those stakeholders. To insist on referring only to active *publics*, rather than active *stakeholders*, is both pedantic and not in the best interests of the public relations discipline for reasons explicated above. In summary, an "active stakeholder" may be regarded as a group or individual who first of all possesses legitimacy through acting in a responsible manner and who, in addition, has both the perceived power to affect the organization and the motivation to do so as a result of a high level of involvement with the organization or issue in question. The problem-recognition variable of the situation model may be regarded as somewhat redundant or rather as an implicit precondition of limited importance by itself, since stakeholders are highly unlikely to perceive that they have the power to affect a situation, and/or to feel highly involved in it, unless they first recognize that it exists.

2.8. Moral Stakeholders: A Justification

It remains necessary to justify the inclusion of the "is affected by" clause in the definition of a stakeholder. In this regard, it must be demonstrated that organizations should give additional consideration to those individuals and groups they affect *in their capacity as stakeholders*—over and above the normal ethical responsibilities any person or organization must accept if their actions affect others. In other words, it must be shown that organizations have *role-specific* obligations to stakeholders (Kaler, 2002). It is important to appreciate that what is under consideration here is the existence and extent of organizational *responsibilities toward* those groups and individuals it affects. This is very different from assumptions in the normative-stakeholder theory literature that organizations should be somehow *responsible for* their stakeholders (Kaler, 2002), in the same way presumably that parents are responsible for their children, or *responsible to* their stakeholders (Alkhafaji, 1989, cited in Mitchell *et al.*, 1997). Let it be assumed that stakeholders are adults with the freedom to act as they wish within the constraints of the law and ethical norms, including the ability to enter into agreements—or not, as the case may be—voluntarily and without coercion or deception. Working under this assumption, organizations cannot and should not be *responsible for* their stakeholders. To think otherwise would be to adopt an irredeemably paternalistic and condescending attitude. To regard organizations as being *responsible to* their stakeholders is to assume the validity of multi-fiduciary stakeholder theory, the fundamental weaknesses of which have been comprehensively expounded by Marcoux (2003).

There is little doubt that stakeholder analysis is a very powerful and convenient way of identifying and thinking about those whom an organization may affect. All organizations must do this to ensure they are behaving in an ethical manner, just as all individuals must. Strictly speaking, it is not necessary for an organization to use the term "stakeholder" for it to appreciate the wide range of groups and individuals toward whom it has moral responsibilities by virtue of having an effect on them. However, "stakeholder" would appear to be a very useful collective noun in this regard. This line of reasoning provides a weak form of the argument for including moral stakeholders in the definition of a stakeholder being defended here.

A stronger reason is that, as discussed above, those who can be affected by an organization are also highly likely, perhaps bound, to be able to affect the company in some way and therefore qualify as strategic stakeholders—if not now, then in the future. Mitchell *et al.* (1997), citing Etzioni (1964), discussed three main types of power: coercive power, based on physical resources of force; utilitarian power, based on material or financial resources; and normative power, based on symbolic resources. In media-saturated contemporary society, even apparently quite powerless groups can wield considerable normative power if they succeed in attracting the attention of the media. For example, throughout the early-to-mid 1990s, one of Australia's largest companies—then known as BHP, now BHP Billiton—caused a major environmental problem in Papua New Guinea as a result of dumping millions of tonnes of mine tailings from its Ok Tedi copper mine directly into the Fly River system. Landowners downstream from the mine protested for a considerable period to no avail. However, when the landowners issued a multi-billion-dollar damages claim in an Australian court through a Melbourne legal firm, the issue suddenly garnered worldwide media attention. BHP endured a torrid public relations crisis and was ultimately forced to reach an accommodation with the affected landowners. Had BHP conducted adequate stakeholder analysis in the first instance, they would have identified the disenchanted landowners as a group affected by the company's operations. (Irrespective of stakeholder theory, this gives rise to clear ethical obligations. However, stakeholder analysis would have provided a timely reminder of those obligations to the company by helping management identify relevant groups.) It should then have been apparent that this landowner group also had the potential ultimately to affect the company (i.e., become a strategic stakeholder) through the exercise of normative power. In a candid "mea culpa" press interview at the conclusion of the crisis, then BHP CEO Jerry Ellis acknowledged precisely this point (Stevens, 1996).

Phillips (2003) argued that, from a normative-stakeholder theory perspective, attention should be paid to strategic stakeholders based on their derivative legitimacy, that is, their capacity to impact the firm's moral stakeholders. The argument advanced in this chapter, from an instrumental-stakeholder theory perspective, posits that moral stakeholders should be paid additional attention over and above that due to them simply as human beings because of the latent possession of normative power even by the apparently powerless. Moral stakeholders or claimants matter to instrumental-stakeholder theory because they can quickly transform into influencers. In addition, stakeholder analysis helps companies identify the basic moral responsibilities they owe to all human beings they affect.

3. Conclusion

This chapter proposes the adoption of stakeholder thinking in public relations, arguing for the integrated application of such obviously parallel concepts as the theory of stakeholder identification and salience (Mitchell *et al.*, 1997) and situation theory (J. Grunig & Hunt, 1984). We examined one of the most contentious problems in the field of stakeholder theory, namely, the vexed issue of who (or what) a stakeholder is. The lack of consensus in the literature on the definition of a stakeholder was discussed, as well as the pitfalls of very broad definitions that appear to include just about everyone. We noted the significance of the construct of legitimacy in this regard, and its inherent complexities. It was argued, in support of Phillips (2003), but contra Mitchell *et al.* (1997), that "non-legitimate stakeholder" is a contradiction in terms. A revised version of Freeman's (1984) broad definition of a stakeholder was proposed, incorporating a significant amendment with regard to the legitimacy of strategic stakeholders, that is, those who can affect the organization. Stakeholder responsibility (Windsor, 2002) was proposed as the basis for evaluating the legitimacy of potential stakeholders, thereby providing a framework for identifying who is *not* a stakeholder. The managerial significance of the chapter lies in this framework, which offers practical guidance for addressing a critical but often perplexing area of management decision-making.

References

Andriof, J., Waddock, S. A., Husted, B. W., & Sutherland, S. (Eds.) (2002). *Unfolding stakeholder thinking* (Vol. 1). Sheffield: Greenleaf Publishing.

Black, L. D., & Hartel, C. E. J. (2004). The five capabilities of socially responsible companies. *Journal of Public Affairs, 4*(2), 125–144.

Bowie, N. E. (1991). New directions in corporate social responsibility. *Business Horizons, 34*(4), 56–65.

Bronn, P. S., & Bronn, C. (2003). A reflective stakeholder approach: Co-orientation as a basis for communication learning. *Journal of Communication Management, 7*(4), 291–303.

Carroll, A. B. (1979). A three-dimensional conceptual model of corporate social performance. *Academy of Management Review, 4*(4), 497–505.

Clarkson Centre for Business Ethics (1999). *Principles of stakeholder management.* Toronto, ON: University of Toronto.

Clarkson, M. B. E. (1995). A stakeholder framework for analyzing and evaluating corporate social performance. *Academy of Management Review, 20*(1), 92–117.

de Bussy, N. M., & Ewing, M. T. (1998). The stakeholder concept and public relations: Tracking the parallel evolution of two literatures. *Journal of Communication Management, 2*(3), 222–229.

Donaldson, T. (2002). The stakeholder revolution and the Clarkson principles. *Business Ethics Quarterly, 12*(2), 107–111.

Donaldson, T., & Preston, L. E. (1995). The stakeholder theory of the corporation: Concepts, evidence, and implications. *Academy of Management Review, 20*(1), 65–91.

Freeman, R. E. (1984). *Strategic management: A stakeholder approach.* Boston: Pitman.

Freeman, R. E., & Phillips, R. A. (2002). Stakeholder theory: A libertarian defense. *Business Ethics Quarterly, 12*(3), 331–349.

Freeman, R. E., & Reed, D. L. (1983). Stockholders and stakeholders: A new perspective on corporate governance. *California Management Review, 25*(3), 88–106.

Frooman, J. (1999). Stakeholder influence strategies. *Academy of Management Review, 24*(2), 191–205.

Gibson, K. (2000). The moral basis of stakeholder theory. *Journal of Business Ethics, 26*(3), 245–257.

Grunig, J. E., & Hunt, T. (1984). *Managing public relations.* Orlando, FL: Holt, Rinehart & Winston.

Grunig, J. E., & Repper, F. C. (1992). Strategic management, publics, and issues. In J. E. Grunig (Ed.), *Excellence in public relations and communication management* (pp. 117–157). Hillsdale, NJ: Lawrence Erlbaum Associates.

Grunig, J. E., Grunig, L. A., & Ehling, W. P. (1992). What is an effective organization? In J. E. Grunig (Ed.), *Excellence in public relations and communication management* (pp. 65–90). Hillsdale, NJ: Lawrence Erlbaum Associates.

Guth, D. W., & Marsh, C. (2006). *Public relations: A values-driven approach* (3rd ed.). Boston: Pearson Allyn & Bacon.

Heugens, P., Van Den Bosch, F. A. J., & Van Riel, C. B. M. (2002). Stakeholder integration. *Business and Society, 41*(1), 36–60.

Hill, C. W. L., & Jones, T. M. (1992). Stakeholder-agency theory. *Journal of Management Studies, 29*(2), 131–154.

Humber, J. M. (2002). Beyond stockholders and stakeholders: A plea for corporate moral autonomy. *Journal of Business Ethics, 36*(3), 207–221.

Jawahar, I. M., & McLaughlin, G. L. (2001). Toward a descriptive-stakeholder theory: An organizational life cycle approach. *Academy of Management Review, 26*(3), 397–414.

Jensen, M. C. (2002). Value maximization, stakeholder theory, and the corporate objective function. *Business Ethics Quarterly, 12*(2), 235–256.

Kaler, J. (2002). Morality and strategy in stakeholder identification. *Journal of Business Ethics, 39*(1/2), 91–99.

Marcoux, A. M. (2003). A fiduciary argument against stakeholder theory. *Business Ethics Quarterly, 13*(1), 1–24.

Mitchell, R. K., Agle, B. R., & Wood, D. J. (1997). Toward a theory of stakeholder identification and salience: Defining the principle of who and what really counts. *Academy of Management Review, 22*(4), 853–886.

Phillips, R. A. (1997). Stakeholder theory and a principle of fairness. *Business Ethics Quarterly, 7*(1), 51–66.

Phillips, R. A. (2003). Stakeholder legitimacy. *Business Ethics Quarterly, 13*(1), 25–41.

Phillips, R. A., & Reichart, J. (2000). The environment as a stakeholder? A fairness-based approach. *Journal of Business Ethics, 23*(2), 185–197.

Ray, G. (2003). For the beasts of the field. *Newcastle Herald.* Newcastle (November 29).

Sheehan, P. (2003). *The electronic whorehouse.* Sydney: Macmillan.

Starik, M. (1995). Should trees have managerial standing? Toward stakeholder status for non-human nature. *Journal of Business Ethics, 14*(3), 207–217.

Sternberg, E. (1994). *Just business.* London: Little Brown.

Sternberg, E. (1999). *The stakeholder concept: A mistaken doctrine.* Issue Paper No. 4: Foundation for Business Responsibilities, London.

Stevens, M. (1996). BHP visits the school of hard knocks. *The Weekend Australian,* 54 (June 15).

Stoney, C., & Winstanley, D. (2001). Stakeholding: Confusion or utopia? Mapping the conceptual terrain. *Journal of Management Studies, 38*(5), 603–626.

Suchman, M. C. (1995). Managing legitimacy: Strategic and institutional approaches. *Academy of Management Review, 20*(3), 571–610.

Windsor, D. (2002). Stakeholder responsibilities: Lessons for managers. *Journal of Corporate Citizenship,* (6), 19–35.

16 Introducing the Institute for Public Relations

Dedicated to the Science Beneath the Art

Frank E. Ovaitt, Jr.

1. Introduction

This chapter introduces the Institute for Public Relations, an independent non-profit organization located at the University of Florida in the United States. The organization exists to build and document research-based knowledge in the field of public relations, and to channel such knowledge into practice and education. While the organization celebrates its fiftieth anniversary in 2006, it is not yet well known outside the United States. All Institute publications are available free on our website, www.instituteforpr.org. Many of the papers there have been authored by members of the Commission on Public Relations Measurement & Evaluation, formed under the Institute's auspices in 1998, and of the Commission on International Public Relations, formed in 2005.

2. About the Institute

No occupation attains the status of a profession without a substantial body of codified professional knowledge and educational systems to help create and disseminate that knowledge. This is as true of public relations as it is of medicine, law, accounting, or teaching. In each case, there is science underlying the art, and it is the working knowledge of that science combined with creativity that marks the best professionals.

The Institute for Public Relations (USA) was chartered in 1956 as the Foundation for Public Relations Research and Education. The name spoke to its role as custodian of the professional body of knowledge. Today, we still serve the profession by continuously expanding the frontiers of research-based knowledge and channeling this into public relations practice and education. That's what we mean when we say that the Institute is dedicated to *the science beneath the art of public relations*.

The purpose of this chapter is to introduce the Institute to those who don't know us and our work, and to renew friendships with those who have had dealings with us before. Thus, let me offer a few more facts about our organization before turning to some of the research that is available at no cost on our website.

We trace our history to 1956 when leaders of the Public Relations Society of America formed the organization. Thus, 2006 will represent our fiftieth anniversary. Yet, because we were focused within the United States for most of those years, we are only now achieving broad awareness in the rest of the world. In 1989, the organization became independent of PRSA and adopted a new name. And for more than ten years, the Institute for Public Relations has been located at the College of Journalism and Communications of the University of Florida. As an independent organization, we work freely with many universities and public relations associations in the US and around the world. Ours is not a membership-based model. The Institute supports itself by program revenues and generous contributions by many of the world's leading PR agencies, corporations, PR research companies, and educators. That is how we are able to provide all of our research and publications free at www.institute forpr.org.

3. Research Agenda

Much of the work available on our website has come from two organizations formed under the auspices of the Institute. The Commission on Public Relations Measurement & Evaluation was the first of these, established in 1998 with membership drawn from the four pillars of PR measurement: corporate, agencies, research providers, and academics. This body defined the model of combining personal expertise and *pro bono* service. The commission establishes standards and methods for public relations research and measurement, and produces authoritative best-practices white papers. Among recent initiatives of this group are these 2005 projects:

- *Putting PR Research and Evaluation into Historical Perspective* by Dr. Walter Lindenmann reviews sixty years of progress and draws lessons for today.
- *A New Model for Media Content Analysis* by Dr. David Michaelson (David Michaelson & Co.) and Toni Griffin (MetLife) suggests that commonly used analysis methods fail to address the fundamental information needs of practitioners. The authors propose a better approach based on four overlooked factors and support their argument with MetLife case histories.

In 2005, the Institute gave birth to the Commission on International Public Relations, to build and document research-based knowledge in this special field of practice. In particular, this group will seek to examine international practice in terms of its contribution to business and management, and to international relations. Among its first outputs were these two papers:

- To better understand what exists today—and where future research should focus—Dr. Juan-Carlos Molleda and Alexander Laskin of the University of Florida authored a paper entitled *Global, International, Comparative and Regional Public Relations Knowledge from 1990 to 2005*. This report is the first step in a long-term effort that will be expanded to include publications in many countries and languages.

- The Polish Public Relations Consultancies Association and the International Public Relations Association cooperated with the Institute on a study of media bribery in Poland. This study was a follow-up to our 2003 International Index of Bribery for News Coverage, and will provide a benchmark for subsequent surveys in other countries. The published paper was authored by Dr. Katerina Tsetsura of the University of Oklahoma.

Our research program also supports new works through conferences and a variety of awards. These include the Pathfinder Award for an original program of scholarly research, the Ketchum Excellence in PR Research Award (and related internship), and the Northwestern Mutual Best Master's Thesis Award.

One of our most important awards was created by the measurement commission. This is the Golden Ruler Award, unique for its singular focus on recognizing excellence in public relations research and measurement. The primary objective of this award is to identify superb examples of measurement integrated into PR practice, and then to publish these on our website.

3. Educational Agenda

The Institute for Public Relations Forums is a primary channel for disseminating research-based knowledge and encouraging its use. We seek to combine theory and practice, academic and professional faculty, to offer programs that truly stand apart.

The flagship program is our Public Relations Executive Forum for high-potential, mid-career corporate communications professionals. A related program, the Public Relations Leadership Forum, serves such individuals in the agency world (and corporate people whose primary responsibilities include managing the agency).

In 2005, the Institute took over management of the Summit on Measurement, which is presented annually on the University of New Hampshire campus. This event brings together the leading thinkers in PR measurement with working professionals seeking to improve their use of research. In 2006, we presented a brand new program, the Summit on Corporate Communications.

We also work with other organizations to cooperatively produce programs that fit our mission. An example is the Business School Seminar series with Henley Management College and *PR Week* in the United Kingdom, which in 2005 explored *The Value of Reputation: How to Build it and Avoid Risks*.

Finally, our Annual Distinguished Lecture is a tradition that dates back to the early 1960s. Every year for forty-five years, we have hosted a major figure in PR practice or education, or another related field, addressing a topic of vital importance to our profession. In 2004, we also held an International Distinguished Lecture outside of the US. The venerable Harold Burson, speaking in London, addressed the provocative topic, "Has Public Relations Become Too Important to Leave to the Public Relations Professionals?"

4. Education-Industry Affairs Agenda

The third major area of Institute programming seeks to enhance relationships between the academy and the profession, supporting undergraduate and graduate education, and helping to ensure a robust supply of new professionals who are well grounded in the science beneath the art of public relations. Current elements include:

- The International Public Relations Research Conference, which the Institute supports in conjunction with the University of Miami and a variety of other sponsors. This is a unique conference for PR academic research, both in format and its ability to attract top-level professionals to learn from the educators as well as to present research themselves.
- Working with other leading public relations organizations to amplify the profession's voice to influence the direction and standing of academic education for public relations: fighting for higher standing and teachers who meet rigorous standards for their knowledge of PR through academic accreditation processes and the updating of curricular guidelines.
- Launching a program to bring senior PR educators into major agencies and corporate public relations shops for a professor-in-residence internship.
- Establishing a viable certification program in measurement and evaluation for professionals who want to improve and document their credentials in this area.

Facing Facts: PR vs. Advertising Credibility[1]

I can't possibly review the total body of work by the Commission on Public Relations Measurement & Evaluation. Those resources are readily available and free on the Institute website, for you and the colleagues and students you may send there. So let me focus instead on one major project that is moving forward with two members of our measurement commission.

No matter how many times it has been said—nor how much professionals want to believe it—there is no known research to support the claim that PR-generated media coverage is worth two or three times advertising. The claim is usually attributed to supposedly greater credibility of news columns when compared to ads. Dr. David Michaelson, principal of David Michaelson & Company, LLC, and Dr. Don W. Stacks, a professor at the University of Miami, set out to establish some real knowledge on this subject. With funding from PRtrak, the two researchers compared the impact of editorial coverage, print advertising, web pages, and radio advertising on factors relating to purchase decisions. Specifically, they looked at consumer differences in message recall, credibility, product rating, and interest. The experimental study involved a hypothetical product and students whose media use had been determined to be no different than that of the general population. Overall, the researchers found no statistically significant differences between editorial and advertising on any variable. In particular, PR-generated coverage and print advertising enjoyed equal credibility, and both scored higher than web pages and radio advertising (see Figure 16.1).

Should PR professionals be disappointed with this news? Not at all, say the researchers. First, the results suggest there is an advantage to delivering product messages through a variety of channels. Furthermore, with PR-generated publicity being the clear equivalent of advertising, it bolsters the argument for shifting more resources to public relations, which has traditionally operated with much smaller budgets. Michaelson and Stacks acknowledge, however, that what they really have at this stage is a pre-test determining that the survey method would produce reliable data. They used minimal sample sizes for each cell and relied on a convenience sample that was biased in two ways. First, it was composed only of college students. Second, all data were collected in Miami. These factors significantly limit their ability to represent the data as conclusive. Consequently, the researchers are now extending the original study with minor modifications to the research design while increasing the reliability of the sample to include a full demographic range of the U.S. population. The Institute has obtained sponsors for this next stage, and the work should be completed and published in the first half of 2006.

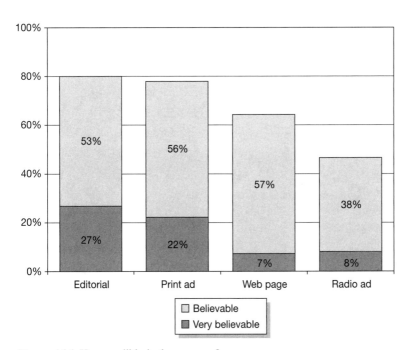

Figure 16.1 How credible is the message?

Conclusion

In any field experiencing such sharp growth as public relations, it sometimes seems to the Institute leadership that we must run as hard as we can just to stay in place—and harder still if we want to make progress. It's not just that the science beneath the art keeps evolving and expanding. The number of people entering this type of work also continues to expand rapidly, and the barriers to entry remain relatively low. Thus, there are always too many practitioners around who frankly have never mastered the knowledge foundations of the profession.

The Institute for Public Relations seeks to help fill this gap both by contributing to research-based knowledge in the field and mainstreaming this knowledge into practice and education. Further, we seek to build bridges to bring the profession and the academy closer together. As an independent non-profit organization, we are supported by our program revenues and generous contributions from corporations, agencies, research companies, and educators. In return, everything we publish is available free on our website. For more information, please see www.instituteforpr.org.

Note

1   Institute for Public Relations, Facing facts: PR vs. advertising credibility. *PR News*, 61 (June 13), 8; adapted and used with permission.

17 Introducing the Chartered Institute of Public Relations Initiative

Moving On from Talking About Evaluation to Incorporating It into Better Management of the Practice

Anne Gregory and Jon White

1. Introduction

At times, the debate about evaluation in public relations can seem like a car, stuck in mud or snow, trying to move forward. The engine revs, the wheels spin, exhaust fumes and friction smoke cloud the scene, but—in the end—the car remains stuck. So, too, the evaluation debate: a great deal of discussion, but no forward movement. A review of public relations literature at any time in the past twenty to thirty years will quickly find the same themes whenever evaluation is raised. The debate about evaluation goes on, but little if any progress is made.

In the United Kingdom, recent initiatives taken by the country's Chartered Institute of Public Relations (CIPR) have tried to move the debate on evaluation forward in the UK, from discussion to implementation. The CIPR has, in fact, gone further, to recognize that the problems of effective evaluation are problems of management of the practice itself.

2. Recent Commentary

McCoy (2005) suggested that the most common buzzwords in public relations in the last ten years have been evaluation and accountability (2005). She pointed to trade media and industry bodies' educational and promotional initiatives to support best practice in measurement and evaluation. She also commented on academic activity in developing evaluation models, citing examples such as Macnamara (1992), Cutlip, Center, and Broom (1994), Watson (1997), and Lindenmann (1998). After reviewing mass communication theory, she said that "PR practitioners must break away from reliance on domino models and first consider more conservative expectations of effects and, second, aim for alternative potential outcomes" (p. 8). In other words, the claims for the effectiveness of a public relations program and actions needed to be tempered by knowledge of research methods and current media effects theory.

The need for research knowledge has also been taken up by Watson and Noble (2005) who argue, "anyone managing public relations campaigns and activities . . . needs to be an effective commissioner and user of research" (p. 49). Xavier and her associates (2005) take a cautionary view of progress on the use of evaluation, "whereas Center and Jackson (2003) suggest there is an increasing emphasis on measuring outcomes in terms of impacts on publics, a number of studies have established that generally evaluation is restricted to program output (Gregory, 2001; Pohl & Vanderventer, 2001; Walker, 1997; Watson, 1997)" (p. 418). Australian research shows that despite the attention paid to evaluation by academia and industry, practitioners still focus on measuring outputs rather than outcomes to demonstrate performance. Australian practitioners continue to rely on media-based evaluation methods, as do practitioners in other countries, such as the United Kingdom.

The Benchpoint report, prepared for the 2004 annual Measurement Summit in the United States and undertaken online in September 2004 by Gaunt and Wright, found, from responses from 1,040 practitioners in twenty-five countries, that:

- Demand for measurement is driven by CEOs—"measurement is an integral part of PR".
- In external communication, more practitioners measure outputs than outcomes with media evaluation, internal reviews, and benchmarking being most used for measuring outcomes (44% of respondents see these as only "somewhat effective"). Opinion surveying is regarded as the most effective tool. Dashboards, league tables, and Advertising Value Equivalents (AVEs) were seen as least effective.
- In internal communication, there is greater use of feedback tools, but 23% use instinct alone. Employee surveys and focus groups are considered most effective, benchmarking and dashboards least effective. Only 18% regard meeting the budget as a success criterion.
- The main barriers to measurement are: cost (77%), time (59%), lack of expertise and questionable value of results (58% each).
- On Return on Investment (ROI), 65% of respondents think it possible to apply this to public relations, although only 13% think this strongly. Eighty-eight percent are interested in an ROI tool.
- Seventy percent of respondents will be doing more on measurement in the future.

3. Recent Work in the United Kingdom

Industry-wide work on evaluation in the UK has been led by the Chartered Institute of Public Relations and, in parallel, by the Public Relations Consultants Association (PRCA). Major contributions have also been made by the research and evaluation companies who have developed their own proprietary approaches, especially in the area of media and reputation research and evaluation.

The Institute, along with the PRCA, produced its first Evaluation Toolkit in 1999 (Fairchild, 1999), which laid down the principle of embedding research within the cycle of program planning. It stated clearly that research was needed prior to a program being devised in order to assist effective objective setting. In addition, on-going evaluation was integral to the progress of the program and summative evaluation was required to gauge its efficiency and effectiveness. Later editions of the toolkit provided more detailed metrics, particularly in the areas of media evaluation, and added to the range of metrics that could be used.

In 2003 (IPR/DTI, 2003), the Institute produced an important study on the status of the public relations industry in the UK with recommendations for action "to improve the competitiveness and overall performance of public relations within the UK economy" (p. 2). The co-sponsor of the study was the UK government's Department of Trade and Industry (DTI). Their co-sponsorship was important as a signal that they recognized that the public relations industry made a significant contribution to the wealth of the nation. This was the first study sponsored by government focused solely on public relations—previous government-funded studies had considered public relations alongside or as a part of marketing.

The research comprised an extensive literature review, 812 returned questionnaires followed up by four discussion groups, and seven one-to-one interviews. The sections on research and evaluation revealed that, in general terms, the public sector believed that audience research was more important than the private sector. The effectiveness of audience research was largely seen as poor and its frequency was, at best, sporadic. There was no consistent view on the best way to measure the effectiveness of public relations, although periodic surveys, individual feedback and use/sales of services/products were regarded as broadly effective. Not surprisingly, in the private sector share price was seen as a key indicator. There was general agreement that public relations performance can be measured separately from organizational performance. Five percent of consultancies stated that they measured the quality of relationships with stakeholders on behalf of their clients.

In terms of the specifics of measuring the effectiveness of programs or campaigns, content analysis was regarded as the most effective output measure, although consultants rated the volume of coverage especially highly. Respondents also listed the parameters they felt should be measured: audience awareness, understanding, attitude, and response. Broadly speaking, media key performance indicators (KPIs) were regarded as indicators and not an end in themselves, although some respondents cited quality, quantity, and key messages in the media as important performance parameters. Again, contribution to business objectives was seen to be an overall measure of performance, but how public relations activities contribution to these might be made was not specified.

The qualitative interviews with the discussion groups and individuals were more enlightening. There was a clear recognition that effective evaluation would be different depending on the type of organization—for example, the evaluation requirements for a consumer-goods company will be quite different than that for a public-sector organization. Outcomes and especially the impact on key individuals were regarded as more important than outputs or overall coverage. The complexity of measuring public relations effects was noted, as was the requirement for sophisticated research for longer-term program effects that demanded time and resources.

One of the study's principal recommendations was that more work should be done to "collate and promote resources on the return on investment (ROI) in public relations and identify best practices relating to how boards and management teams request, receive, consider and utilize public relations advice and support to help their organization better achieve their business objectives" (p. 5). Why ROI was identified as a priority is not clear. Another recommendation proposed that other metrics measuring the effectiveness of public relations activities should be used as alternatives to Advertising Value Equivalents (AVEs) and that metrics demonstrating attitudinal and behavioral change should be encouraged.

Following this study, the UK Institute, along with the Communication Directors' Forum (CDF), commissioned Metrica Research to undertake further research into "Best Practice in the Measurement and Reporting of Public Relations and ROI". Metrica reported in May 2004 (IPR/CDF, 2004). This two-part research study comprised one hundred telephone interviews with senior public relations practitioners, predominantly Group Heads of Communication and Public Relations Directors, but also included some CEOs. This was complemented by desk- and web-based research reviewing existing best practice and case studies supplemented by contributions from the Institute, PRCA, and the Association of Media Evaluation Companies (AMEC).

The main conclusions from this study are illuminating. There are major areas of public relations performance where numerous organizations "do not expect to make assessments in a quantifiable, tangible way" (p. 9). This is particularly where public relations is "performing longer-term functions such as influencing awareness, opinion, perception and attitude" (p. 9). A small but significant number of respondents did not feel that ROI is a suitable measure in these instances.

Some respondents showed an understanding of the need to demonstrate the value of public relations, but did not know how to go about it in an evidence-based way. Others were determined to pursue their own methods, either because they did not see the value of alternatives or did not wish to change.

Overall, the researchers detected defensiveness within the industry regarding the value of its work. Despite this, considerable effort is being expended in attempting to demonstrate value. Between 45% and 60% attempt to measure the tangible benefits and performance of public relations. Six in ten respondents said that an ROI measure would help and a small number, three or four, actually had an ROI-related measure in place.

There was confusion over the formal definition of ROI (a ratio of how much profit or cost saving is realized from an activity against its actual cost, often expressed as a percentage). However, there were examples where specific programs have yielded an ROI. For example, research commissioned by Shine Communications, Timberland's UK public relations consultancy, revealed that 18–24-year-olds were a new and ideal market for their products. As a result of the public relations-led campaign, an increase of 26% in UK store sales was recorded, with two specific editorial pieces each leading to stock sell-outs within one day. Another example was the launch of Volvo's 4×4 vehicle, the XC90, in the UK via a media-relations campaign. Sales achieved largely through public relations activities resulted in the cancellation of a £2.5 million advertising campaign (see also Watson & Noble, 2005: 144–147).

It is clear from this research, echoed in the earlier DTI/IPR research, that different types of program require different types of metrics. While ROI may be appropriate for marketing communications, it may not be for longer term, influencing, or crisis-management programs.

The overall conclusion from the Metrica research was that although there could not be a universal ROI metric linked to revenue and profit, there are many examples where public relations performance is being measured, for example in media evaluation, measures of audience reach and frequency, benchmark and tracking studies, direct response, KPIs, and trend analysis. Some of this performance information, but by no means all, could provide the base data for formulating a kind of ROI indicator. It was suggested that the term ROI was confusing and misleading and that a "better alternative therefore would be to speak of evidence-based PR" (p. 10). The key to demonstrating the contribution of public relations was seen to be in reinforcing the necessity for clear, research-based objectives that can be measured and evaluated. The range of metrics, which can be used for evaluation (indicated earlier), can then be deployed as appropriate.

Although this research sought to slay the myth that there could be one universal public relations measurement method (often referred to as the "silver bullet"), discussion in the industry continued. Research by Murray and White (2004) with chief executives into their attitudes toward public relations was highly illuminating. They interviewed fourteen chief executives and chairmen from major UK and international organizations and discovered that they "intuitively" valued public relations. They saw it as an essential cost of business, and essential to business and organizational performance. They also felt that public relations is "not amenable to precise measurement, being long-term and iterative in effect, or being an aid to avoiding surprises or mistakes. They do not feel a great need to demonstrate a return on investment in their PR" (p. 4).

The quest for definitive information on the performance of public relations appears to be a practitioner's obsession—a preoccupation, as one CEO put it, of the sellers of public relations services rather than buyers of the same services. CEOs are used to handling information that is not exhaustive: often it is simply not available, or would take too much time to obtain. Their decision-making is pragmatic and characterized as "satisficing", which results in decisions that will do and satisfy the situation, rather than being the best decisions that could possibly be made based on the best information (Simon, 1982).

CEOs feel there is under-investment in public relations and a better case more effectively made would help release resources, but they also identify a lack of talent and expertise among practitioners, "which—if addressed—would also answer questions about the value of public relations practice" (p. 4). Training and education was seen as critical to improving the caliber of practitioners.

Research by Gregory and Edwards (2004) into the practice of public relations by companies in the UK *Management Today* magazine's "Most Admired" company list and by Gregory, Morgan, and Kelly (2005) on "Most Admired" companies and public-sector organizations, found that a range of evaluation metrics were used (usually between four and eight), and the most frequently used metrics were informal and/or qualitative such as journalist feedback and discussions with stakeholders. It is as if the respondents were "just checking" that everything was on track and appears to follow the "satisficing" principle outlined above. It must be added, however, that these Most Admired companies researched and planned their public relations work meticulously and this gave them a sound basis upon which to "just check" the results of their activities. This approach supports the proposition in the Murray and White (2004) research that indicated that an intuitive sense of what is working reflects life in business generally. Intuition and a general sense of purpose and direction are regarded as vital to success alongside rigorous research. The one solidly consistent quantitative measure for private sector companies was the share price.

It was discovered that the status of the senior public relations practitioner was high in these Most Admired organizations with 43% on the Board or Executive Committee and many others reporting directly to the CEO. Asked why public relations was regarded so highly, it seemed that the handling of crises was critical. Either these organizations had recognized that good public relations had been essential to preserving their reputation in a crisis (reflected also by Murray & White, 2004) or that a lack of such a function had left them dangerously exposed.

4. Recent Developments

Recognizing that the evaluation debate was still developing and alert to the fact that the industry was still seeking the evaluation silver bullet, the Chartered Institute of Public Relations set up a small task force of Executive Board members in 2005 to produce a definitive policy statement on evaluation. It collaborated with Henley Management College, an international university level management development center located in the UK, to draw together the practitioner and academic literature on evaluation to examine best practice cases. The resultant policy statement (see www.cipr.co.uk/research) is supplemented by a web-based resource of literature and cases. The policy statement sets out underlying principles of public relations practice, which, taken together, remove many of the difficulties in the debate about evaluation:

- Public relations is part of the management task and is subject to the same disciplines such as the need to set direction, allocate and manage resources, and monitor progress.[1]
- Measurement and evaluation are problematic in *all* areas of management. Complexity is a key feature and in the dynamic interrelated business world it is difficult to separate out the effect of one area of management such as public relations.
- Despite this difficulty, the situation can be ameliorated by better planning and objective setting, particularly better project management where precise, measurable objectives allow for better judgments of progress.
- Public relations can be measured and evaluated in terms of:
  - contribution to social and economic development (for example, in Northern Ireland where reconciliation work has led to economic development and community building);
  - contribution to management, leadership, and organizational performance by aiding better decision-making and avoiding mistakes (for example work by Diageo's public affairs department has led to a more favorable tax regime for the company's products than might otherwise have been the case);
  - as a process and as part of program development and implementation (for instance, the Volvo example given earlier);
  - contribution and competence of individual practitioners (for example, "Evolve"—the UK government's capability framework for government communicators).
- Available methods, research-based, provide information that is good enough for decision-making for planning public relations programs. Time and availability of resources are practical obstacles to the use of available methods.
- Available research methods and approaches are adequate for measuring the contribution of public relations in the areas outlined above. The evidence from the case studies shows clearly that public relations is creating value. ROI may play a part in demonstrating public relations can build market share; social research can demonstrate value in other areas. Each method has its limitations; therefore, a raft of measures, appropriate to the particular situation, needs to be employed.

In parallel developments, the UK's Public Relations Consultants Association, PRCA, has established a web-based resource, PR-Value.com, which helps clients and consultancies plan and then evaluate the *business value* of public relations. It is intended to support the assessment of public relations' effectiveness well beyond the traditional coverage. The Association makes clear that, to demonstrate public relations' full value, evaluation has to get as close as possible to business level outcomes.

Like the CIPR's policy statement, the PRCA recognizes that evaluation of public relations activities must be based on most likely explanations of effectiveness—explanations that will do—rather than definitive explanations.

5. Conclusions

Recent UK experience, set out in meetings and in practitioner material (White, 2005, for example), suggests that it is time for the public relations industry worldwide to move on and adopt available evaluation and measurement methodologies while working on their refinement and extension. As indicated in the literature review and the discussion of UK initiatives, there is widespread understanding of the doubts about methodology and barriers to practitioners undertaking evaluation. The UK's CIPR has issued its challenge to the industry in its manifesto-style statement that defines the role of public relations and how planning, research, objective setting, and evaluation can progress practice. It is the authors' view that public relations professional and trade bodies, individual practitioners, and academics should study this policy urgently with the aim of early adoption. It could assist the metaphorical car to stop spinning its wheels in the mud and gain traction.

It also allows the debate to move on, to the application of standard and accepted management approaches such as project and program management to public relations practice—in short, to improving the capabilities of practitioners as managers. It also points to the next stage in establishing the value of public relations, which is to be found in its contribution to improved decision-making (which improves management practice), to organizational functioning, and ultimately organizational value. Judgments of organizational value—by investors or government funding agencies, for example—are based in large part on the sense that they have of management competence and organizational strength. Public relations has clear contributions to make to both, and it is time that practitioners and the professional associations that serve them moved to focus on the value of these contributions.

As the CIPR policy sets out and J. Grunig commented at BledCom 2005, evaluation falls into four areas: societal, organizational, program, and functional/individual performance. The monitoring and measurement of behavior in relationships is the way forward, especially if the paradigm of relationship management is accepted for public relations, as argued by Ledingham and Bruning (2000) and others. The search for the single evaluation measure (silver bullet) that keeps arising is—we believe—a futile distraction. Indeed, this quest fails to appreciate the complexity of the work that public relations practitioners do. Public relations, as L. Grunig pointed out at the BledCom 2005 meeting, is concerned with ill-defined problems. It cannot be evaluated simply because it does not deal with simple issues and the relationship-building process is not simple.

Business, too, recognizes now that a simple, single financial measure does not give an accurate reflection of the standing of a company. The introduction of techniques such as Kaplan and Norton's (1992) balanced scorecard and triple-bottom line reporting is evidence that major organizations worldwide understand the reality that a range of stakeholder relationships are defining their ability to operate and prosper. Share prices and profits are no longer the only measure to be considered. Stakeholders reinforce the legitimacy of organizations and maintain their license to operate and hence relationships with them have value and create value.

The use of available balanced scorecard (see Zerfass, 2005) and equivalent approaches that include non-financial aspects of company reporting will not only indicate the contribution of public relations activities to business activities, but demonstrate the complex and sophisticated nature of public relations work and the value that it creates.

One of the most troubling outcomes from recent work in the UK for the progress of public relations practice was the lack of confidence in practitioners found by Murray and White's research among CEOs. As noted by Murray and White, training and education, particularly in research methodology, was seen as important in improving the quality and perception of practitioners.

So how does the PR industry move forward? The authors' proposals are:

- Consider the CIPR policy statement for early adoption at organizational and personal practitioner level.
- Increase the range of properly researched case studies of effective public relations (not necessarily award entries) in order to provide evidence for effective planning, research, and evaluation. Create a worldwide database.
- Encourage practitioners to stop over-simplifying communication problems, or seeing public relations problems as primarily problems of communications. Communication is an important aspect of relationships, but needs to be understood in the context of complex operational environments and relationships.
- Encourage practitioners, through the availability of professional development courses, to improve their research and analytical skills. Support research methods training in undergraduate and postgraduate courses in public relations.
- Move the public relations research agenda away from a focus on program outputs to an emphasis on the measurement of relationships and reputation, and to understanding the nature of those relationships and the attendant perceptions, attitudes, and behavior.

The timescale for these changes is pressing. It was emphasized at BledCom 2005 that "successful practitioners are those who can handle complexity" (Watson, 2005). Public relations practitioners work in a complex world full of "ill-structured problems" where their input is in high demand. There is no reason for delay.

Note

1 There is a management cliché that suggests what cannot be measured, cannot be managed. This statement has sometimes been invoked to suggest that public relations, because it cannot be measured, cannot be managed. However, turning the statement around, what can be managed can be measured. Clearly, public

relations can be managed, and is therefore amenable to measurement—or, as amenable to measurement as any other management discipline.

References

Center, A., & Jackson, P. (2003). *Public relations practices* (6th ed.). Upper Saddle River, NJ: Prentice Hall.

Chartered Institute of Public Relations (2005). *Measurement and evaluation: Moving the debate forward.* London. Available online at www.cipr.co.uk/News/research/ evaluation_June05.pdf.

Cutlip, S. M., Center, A. H., & Broom, G. M. (1994). *Effective public relations* (7th ed.). London: Prentice Hall.

Fairchild, M. (1999). *The public relations research and evaluation toolkit: How to measure the effectiveness of PR.* London: Institute of Public Relations and Public Relations Consultants Association.

Gaunt, R., & Wright, D. (2004). *PR measurement.* London: Benchpoint.

Gregory, A. (2001). Public relations and evaluation: Does the reality match the rhetoric? *Journal of Marketing Communication, 7*(3), 171–189.

Gregory, A., & Edwards, L. (2004). *Pattern of PR in Britain's "Most Admired" companies.* Leeds: Leeds Business School for Eloqui Public Relations.

Gregory, A., Morgan, L., & Kelly, D. (2005). *Patterns of PR in Britain's "Most Admired" companies and public sector organizations.* Leeds: Leeds Business School for Eloqui Public Relations.

Institute of Public Relations (IPR) & Department of Trade and Industry (DTI) (2003). *Unlocking the potential of public relations.* Available online at www.cipr.co.uk/ unlockpr.

Institute of Public Relations (IPR) & Communication Directors' Forum (CDF) (2004). *Best practice in the measurement and reporting of public relations and ROI.* Available online at www.cipr.co.uk.

Kaplan, R. S., & Norton, D. P. (1992). The balanced scorecard—Measures that drive performance. *Harvard Business Review, 70,* 71–79.

Ledingham, J. A., & Bruning, S. D. (2000). *Relationship building: A relational approach to public relations.* Mahwah, NJ: Lawrence Erlbaum Associates.

Lindenmann, W. K. (1998). Only PR outcomes count—That is the real bottom line. *Journal of Communication Management, 3*(1), 66–73.

McCoy, M. (2005). *Evaluating public relations' effects: Implications from mass communication theory and research.* Paper presented at the Chartered Institute of Public Relations Academic Conference, University of Lincoln (March 21–22).

Macnamara, J. M. (1992). Evaluation of public relations: The Achilles heel of the PR profession. *International Public Relations Review, 15*(4), 17–31.

Murray, K., & White, J. (2004). *CEO Views on reputation management.* London: Chime Communications. Available online at www.chime.plc.uk/downloads/reputationkm. pdf).

Pohl, G., & Vandeventer, D. (2001). The workplace, undergraduate education and career preparation. In R. L. Heath (Ed.), *Handbook of public relations* (pp. 357–368). Thousand Oaks, CA: Sage.

Simon, H. (1982). New developments in the theory of the firm. In Herbert Simon, *Models of bounded rationality. Behavioral economics and business organization* (Vol. 2, pp. 56–70). Cambridge, MA: MIT Press.

Walker, G. (1997). Public relations practitioners' use of research, measurement and evaluation. *Australian Journal of Communication, 24*(2), 97–113.

Watson, T. (1997). Measuring the success rate: Evaluating the PR process and PR programs. In P. J. Kitchen (Ed.), *Public relations: Principles and practices* (pp. 283–299). Boston: International Thomson Business Press.

Watson, T. (2005). *Towards a common nomenclature for public relations evaluation— Does return on investment (ROI) have a central role?* Paper presented at the 12th International Public Relations Research Symposium, Bled, Slovenia (July 1–3).

Watson, T., & Noble, P. (2005). *Evaluating public relations: The best practice guide to public relations planning, research and evaluation.* London: Kogan Page.

White, J. (2005). The true worth of public relations campaigns. *Hollis Europe directory of European public relations and public relations networks.* Teddington: Hollis.

Xavier, R., Patel, A., Johnston, K., Watson, T., & Simmons, P. (2005). Using evaluation techniques and performance claims to demonstrate public relations impact: An Australian perspective. *Public Relations Review, 31*(3), 417–424.

Zerfass, A. (2005). *The corporate communication scorecard: A framework for managing and evaluating communication strategies.* Paper presented at the 12th International Public Relations Research Symposium, Bled, Slovenia (July 1–3).

Index

Page numbers in *italics* denote figures and tables.